Frommer's®

VIRGIN ISLANDS

2nd Edition

By Alexis Lipsitz Flippin

T0049050

FrommerMedia LLC

Frommer's Virgin Islands, 2nd Edition

Published by
Frommer Media LLC

ISBN 978-1-62887-555-3 (paper), 978-1-62887-556-0 (e-book)

Editorial Director: Pauline Frommer
Editor: Holly Hughes
Production Editor: Cheryl Lenser
Cartographer: Roberta Stockwell
Photo Editor: Meghan Lamb
Indexer: Cheryl Lenser
Cover Design: Dave Riedy

Front cover/title page: British Virgin Islands from the air.

For information on our other products or services, see www.frommers.com.

Frommer Media LLC also publishes its books in a variety of electronic formats. Some content that appears in print may not be available in electronic formats.

Manufactured in Malaysia

5 4 3 2 1

HOW TO CONTACT US

In researching this book, we discovered many wonderful places—hotels, restaurants, shops, and more. We're sure you'll find others. Please tell us about them, so we can share the information with your fellow travelers in upcoming editions. If you were disappointed with a recommendation, we'd love to know that, too. Please write to: Support@FrommerMedia.com

FROMMER'S STAR RATINGS SYSTEM

Every hotel, restaurant and attraction listed in this guide has been ranked for quality and value. Here's what the stars mean:

★ Recommended
★★ Highly Recommended
★★★ A must! Don't miss!

AN IMPORTANT NOTE

The world is a dynamic place. Hotels change ownership, restaurants hike their prices, museums alter their opening hours, and buses and trains change their routings. And all of this can occur in the several months after our authors have visited, inspected, and written about these hotels, restaurants, museums, and transportation services. Though we have made valiant efforts to keep all our information fresh and up-to-date, some few changes can inevitably occur in the periods before a revised edition of this guidebook is published. So please bear with us if a tiny number of the details in this book have changed. Please also note that we have no responsibility or liability for any inaccuracy or errors or omissions, or for inconvenience, loss, damage, or expenses suffered by anyone as a result of assertions in this guide.

THE BEST OF THE VIRGIN ISLANDS

B road-shouldered peaks of luminous green rising out of the sea, the Virgin Islands number about 100, a handful governed by the United States and the rest by Great Britain. These islands are the pinnacle of an enormous underwater mountain chain. Beneath the surface, in gin-clear seas, the topography is spectacular, a huge draw for snorkelers and divers. Above sea level, harborfronts bustle with commerce. Minutes away are peaceful mountain aeries and sugary-sand beaches. The former haunt of conquistadors, pirates, and missionaries, today the Virgins are invaded by thousands of visitors annually seeking the recreational pleasures of sun and sea.

Of the three U.S. territories, **St. Thomas** is the transportation and business hub, attracting the most visitors, many of them disembarking from big cruise ships. Bucolic **St. Croix** has a laidback bohemian heart—it feels like a small town in the tropics. The dizzying accordion-fold landscape of lush little **St. John** is blanketed in green, two-thirds of it lying within one of America's most beautiful national parks.

With its steep mountains and scalloped coastline of blue coves and powdery beaches, the B.V.I. is a retreat for visitors who want to escape the scrum of modern civilization. Steady trade winds and protected harbors make the B.V.I. one of the world's top sailing grounds. The largest island, **Tortola,** is a base for boaters and daytrippers; stunning **Virgin Gorda** is the place to go for stays in stylish, secluded resorts. Dotted about the main islands are private-island resorts and uninhabited islands perfect for castaway day-tripping.

THE best BEACHES

Perhaps the most celebrated of the Virgin Islands' natural resources are its beautiful beaches. Best of all, every beach is open to the public and, with a few exceptions, free. Even private resorts, which often command some of the prettiest stretches of sand, are required to offer public access to their beaches.

- **Magens Bay Beach** (St. Thomas): This long, half-mile stretch of powdery sand, boasting remarkably calm waters, is the most popular and picturesque beach on St. Thomas. Two peninsulas protect the shore from erosion and strong waves, making Magens an ideal spot for swimming. Expect crowds in the high season. See p. 94.
- **Lindquist Beach** (St. Thomas): A lovely, undeveloped beach on the East End, Lindquist is only reachable by a dirt road; it's a favorite of locals who make Sundays here a lively beach funday. See p. 96.
- **Cane Bay** (St. Croix): This breezy North Shore beach has chairs for rent and sea grape trees for shade. It's right off the road for easy access. See p. 160.
- **Sandy Point** (St. Croix): The biggest beach in the U.S. Virgin Islands, Sandy Point is a real beaut—the final, redemptive scene of *The Shawshank Redemption* was filmed on its dazzling white sands. Because the beach is a protected reserve and nesting spot for endangered sea turtles, it's open to the public only on Saturdays and Sundays from 10am to 4pm. See p. 161.
- **Francis Bay** (St. John): With bottle-green seas limning a sprawling beach, Francis Bay is a bit of a sleeper on St. John's vaunted North Shore (it's the farthest beach east), well worth seeking out. See p. 217.
- **Honeymoon Beach** (St. John): Formerly part of the Caneel Bay resort, this beach is only reachable by trail, but shade trees, crystalline seas, and excellent snorkeling make it so worth the extra effort. See p. 215.
- **Jumbie Beach** (St. John): This tiny treasure is rarely overpopulated—the parking lot has room for only four cars. A dreamy private cove looks out to Trunk Bay and its busy scrum of visitors. See p. 216.
- **Cane Garden Bay** (Tortola): A half-moon bay framed on three sides by rising green hills, Cane Garden Bay is Tortola's most popular beach, with

On St. Croix, the dazzling sands of Sandy Point played a role in *The Shawshank Redemption* as the ultimate beach paradise.

calm, translucent waters. It does attract crowds—especially when cruise ships drop off van-loads of beachgoers in the morning—but this spacious strand has room for all. See p. 261.

o **Long Bay Beach East** (Tortola): Not long ago this fairly isolated beach was rarely visited by anyone but locals. Now it's a favorite cruise-ship day trip, but on weekends this half-mile stretch on Trellis Bay sand is still a local chill spot. See p. 262.

o **Smugglers Cove** (Tortola): This fetching West End beach is reached by driving down a (largely) dirt road through a grove of mature palm trees. The waters can get rough in winter. See p. 260.

o **Prickly Pear** (Virgin Gorda): Only reachable by boat, this classic pearly-white beach on an uninhabited island in the North Sound has a dinghy dock and a perfect boat-up beach bar, the **Sand Box.** See p. 289.

o **Savannah Bay** (Virgin Gorda): Just around the corner from Little Dix Bay, this glorious, little-used gem is a sinuous stretch of sand with shallow, clear waters pocked by coral outcroppings (good for snorkeling). See p. 289.

o **White Bay** (Jost Van Dyke): This breathtaking half-mile crescent is edged in white sand and backed by plush green hills. See p. 294.

o **Sandy Spit** (Little Jost Van Dyke): They call it the "Corona" beach for its starring role in the beer commercial as the quintessential castaway isle, a tasty spit of blinding white sand encircled by sapphire seas. See p. 299.

o **Loblolly Bay and Cow Wreck Beach** (Anegada): Protected by the fourth-largest coral reef in the world, the North Shore of this most remote Virgin Island has calm bays and blinding white-sand beaches, including these two wondrous sites for swimming and snorkeling. See p. 300.

THE most authentic EXPERIENCES

o **Island-Hopping by Sea:** Whether you're cruising the liquid expanse of the local waterways by ferry, sailboat, or daylong excursion, seeing the Virgin Islands by sea feels like the way nature intended it. Most visitors take to the waters at some point in their trip, skimming big-shouldered islands or exploring uninhabited cays. Everyone shares the same splendid vistas, no matter the vessel.

o **Waking Up to Tropical Birdsong and Roosters Crowing:** No matter where you are on the islands, you'll hear the musical chatter of colorful songbirds and the cock-a-doodle-dooing of roadside roosters in splendid plumages of gold, green, and blue.

o **Swimming with Turtles and Stingrays:** The Virgins' beauteous undersea habitat makes for a stupendous place to sightsee beneath the waves. Look for hawksbill turtles grazing on seagrass, angelfish darting in and out of rocks, and massive winged rays cruising sandy sea bottoms.

o **Kicking Back with Serious Views:** The islands' curvaceous terrain is pure eye candy, and practically every island has restaurants, cafes, and bars

It's not just Mardi Gras: Carnival festivities are held all year round in the Virgin Islands. St. John celebrates in early summer.

positioned to take full advantage of the swooning panoramic views. Claim your viewing spot (and a cool drink) at places like the hillside **Mafolie Restaurant,** scanning the glittering harbor in Charlotte Amalie (St. Thomas; p. 85); the **Windmill Bar,** looking down on Hawksnest Bay from its Susannaberg perch in St. John (p. 232); **Bananakeet,** 400 feet above the North Shore beaches of Tortola (p. 255); or **Hog Heaven** on Virgin Gorda, a pork-palace aerie in the clouds above the North Sound (p. 288).

o **Hiking with Bush Doctors:** Take a trek into magical bamboo forests and pineapple fields in Tortola with the wonderful guides at **Hike BVI** (p. 266), who'll show you how the local flora fed, sheltered, and doctored the island population for centuries.

o **Sailing, Sailing:** Many people believe the Virgins are the best place to sail in the world. Modern-day sailors ride the same prevailing trade winds that propelled pirates and explorers of yore. Near-perfect sailing conditions—wind speeds averaging 15 and 25 knots, unfailingly balmy air and sea temperatures, calm seas sheltered by surrounding islands—have helped make both the B.V.I. and the U.S.V.I. legendary in the boating world. High sailing season in the Virgins is November through June, when **international regattas** draw sailors for fierce (and fiercely celebrated) competitions. See p. 48.

o **Celebrating Carnival:** After years of postponements from hurricanes and pandemics, Carnival is back big-time. Be there for the parades of glittery costumes, synchronized dance troupes, Carnival clowns and majorettes, and music, music, music—oh my! The **St. Thomas Carnival,** the biggest

Trying to decide which Virgin Island to visit? Consider the following basics:

o American citizens don't need a **passport** to enter the U.S. Virgins, but everyone needs a passport to enter the British Virgin Islands.

o Major carriers connect into St. Thomas's **international airport** from cities around the world. The main B.V.I. airport, in Tortola, is small and largely handles inter-island flights and private charters.

o The U.S. Virgin Islands have **more hotel and resort rooms** to choose from, in all sizes and price ranges, than the B.V.I.

o The **U.S. dollar** is the official currency for both island chains, and **English** is the official language.

Obvious issues aside, American and British cultures have left different imprints on the Virgin Islands. **St. Thomas** offers a somewhat Americanized hurly-burly, with easy access to familiar global brands and a wide range of goods and services. But this is no fast-paced megalopolis—tropical foliage blankets the landscape with a fetching unruliness. Along "step streets" that climb the hills of Charlotte Amalie are colonial neighborhoods drenched in historic charm. **St. Croix** has a handful of international chains like Home Depot and K-Mart, but it has a uniquely rich culture and an earthy sensuality, with stretches of rural countryside and organic farms. With much of its terrain protected national parkland, **St. John** is a haven of tranquility.

Still, the **British Virgin Islands** are noticeably sleepier and less developed than the U.S.V.I., recalling the Caribbean of yore before the regional influx of high-rise condos and sleek hotel chains—and being a little remote hasn't hurt. **Tortola** is where the B.V.I. action is, limited as its shopping and nightlife may be. To the east, pristine **Virgin Gorda** has just 4,000 full-time inhabitants but some of the Virgin Islands' most gorgeous scenery and priciest resorts. Crime is minimal here—it's said you can leave your keys in your car at the airport or ferry dock. You'll find an even more laid-back vibe on less-populated islands like **Jost Van Dyke** and **Anegada,** as well as uninhabited isles with hidden coves and beaches where you may be the only sunbather around.

In truth, the days of traveling to one versus the other are pretty much history. Most people who visit the Virgins touch down on both U.S. and British. The region's reliance on tourism has made it increasingly easier to hop between islands via ferry or day-tripping excursions—just be aware of the government fees to do so and plan your trip accordingly. For suggested itineraries between the islands, see chapter 3.

in the region, is celebrated after Easter; the **St. John Festival** is held mid-June through July 4th; St. Croix has a holiday **Crucian Christmas Carnival;** and the B.V.I. does it big with its Carnival-style **Emancipation Festival** from late July through early August.

THE best SNORKELING SPOTS

o **Coki Point Beach** (St. Thomas): On the North Shore of St. Thomas, Coki Point offers crystal-clear seas and year-round snorkeling. It's often busy with families visiting Coral World next door. Explore the coral ledges to the right. See p. 95.

5

o **Buck Island** (off St. Croix): This tiny island, whose land and offshore waters together are designated as a national monument, lies 2 miles off the north coast of St. Croix. More than 250 recorded species of fish swim through its reef system. A variety of sponges, corals, and crustaceans also inhabit the area. See p. 185.

o **Maho Bay** (St. John): This popular beach is plenty roomy, with shade under sea grape trees. Big sea turtles feed on Maho's seagrass beds, so swim out with snorkel and mask and you're practically guaranteed to see them. See p. 216.

o **Salt Pond Bay** (St. John): This lovely Coral Bay crescent has lots of shade from sea grape trees and good reef snorkeling. See p. 217.

o **Trunk Bay** (St. John): You pay a small day-pass fee ($5) to hang out at this celebrated National Park Service beach. What really distinguishes it from its equally beautiful North Shore sisters is the cool Coral Reef Underwater Snorkeling Trail. See p. 215.

o **Waterlemon Cay/Leinster Bay** (St. John): Easily accessible Leinster Bay, on St. John's northern shore, offers clear, uncrowded waters teeming with sea life. From here you can swim and snorkel your way from Leinster's sandy beach or the coral shoreline to Waterlemon Cay. See p. 222.

o **Honeymoon/Caneel Bay beaches** (St. John): The only way to reach these stellar beaches, the former jewels of the Caneel Bay resort, is via walking trail or by boat. See p. 214.

o **Norman Island & the Indians** (B.V.I.): Snorkel the calm waters of the Bight near Norman Island. Bring some bread to draw reef fish to the surface

Snorkelers on a day-sail excursion explore a sea cave on Norman Island.

IT'S IN THE air

Breathe in those minxy trade winds—it's good for you. The U.S. Virgin Islands is one of three places in the entire world that has met the latest World Health Organization air-quality standards. According to IQAir, a Swiss-based technology company that monitors real-time air-quality information around the globe, the territory leads the Top 5 countries or territories ranked by annual average of fine particulate concentration weighted by population. The U.S. Virgin Islands is followed by New Caledonia, Puerto Rico, Cape Verde, and Saba. The report also measured air quality in cities, finding that of all the cities globally tested, the cleanest air to breathe is in Charlotte Amalie, followed by San Juan, Puerto Rico; Canberra, Australia; and Saint George's, Grenada.

when you snorkel the deep waters around the Indians, four fingers of rock jutting out of the sea and only accessible by boat. See p. 266.

o **Brewers Bay** (Tortola): The snorkeling is some of the best on the island at this northern beach, with healthy coral reef studding teal-blue shallows. See p. 261.

o **The Baths/Spring Bay** (Virgin Gorda): It's often overrun with boats, but the Baths—and nearby beaches Spring Bay and Devil's Bay—are still mindblowingly beautiful. The shallow crystalline seas and caves are fun to explore. See p. 288.

o **Savannah Bay** (Virgin Gorda): You won't have crowds to contend with at this stunning beach, where the waters are shallow and the reef is vibrant with sea life. See p. 289.

THE best DIVE SITES

o **Cow and Calf Rocks** (St. Thomas): This site, off the southeast end of St. Thomas (about a 45-min. boat ride from Charlotte Amalie), is the island's best diving spot and a good bet for snorkeling. You'll discover a network of coral tunnels filled with caves, reefs, and ancient boulders encrusted with coral. See p. 101.

o **The Cane Bay Wall** (St. Croix): Walk right off the beach into one of the most awesome dives in the Virgins. It's just a 100-yard swim to a 3,000-foot vertical wall drop-off. Even at depths of 30 feet, you'll see coral gardens abloom with fantastical formations and colorful tropical life. See p. 164.

o **Frederiksted Pier** (St. Croix): The Fredriksted pier has become one of the best spots in the islands for an electric night dive, where you take the plunge right offshore into a world of exotic creatures, including sea horses, lobster, and octopuses. See p. 165.

o **The Wreck of the RMS Rhone** (off Salt Island, B.V.I.): Many people think the *Rhone* wreck is the premier dive site not only in the Virgin Islands, but in the entire Caribbean. This royal mail steamer, which went down in 1867, was featured in the film *The Deep*. See p. 265.

- **Chikuzen** (off Tortola): This 246-foot Korean steel-hulled refrigerator ship, which sank far off the island's east end in 1981, is one of the British Virgin Islands' most fascinating dive sites. The hull—still intact under about 24m (79 ft.) of water—is now home to a vast array of tropical fish, including rays, barracuda, black-tip sharks, octopus, and drum fish. See p. 265.

- **Alice in Wonderland** (Ginger Island, off Tortola): This brilliant coral wall, off the shore of tiny Ginger Island, slopes from 12m (39 ft.) to a sandy bottom at 30m (98 ft.). It's a fantastic site because of the monstrous overhangs, vibrant colors, gigantic mushroom-shaped corals, and wide variety of sea creatures—everything from conch and garden eels to long-nose butterfly fish. See p. 265.

Exploring a coral-encrusted wreck with the St. Thomas Dive Center.

- **The "Art Reefs"** (the B.V.I.): The nonprofit **Beyond the Reef** (p. 265) repurposes hurricane detritus like sunken boats and planes in delightful ways and sinks them to become "art reefs." They include the former floating pirate bar known as **Willy T; Sharkplaneo,** three wrecked airplanes remade as sharks; and the **Kodiak Queen,** a decorated WWII Navy fuel barge, now enveloped in the arms of a sea monster and lying in a bay just outside Virgin Gorda. See p. 265.

THE best NATURE WALKS

- **The Rain Forest Hike** (St. Croix): At the northwestern end of St. Croix lies a 15-acre "rain forest," dense with magnificent tropical foliage. Little-traveled four-wheel-drive roads through the area make great hiking paths. See p. 167.

- **The Annaberg Historic Trail** (St. John): This quarter-mile paved walk is a highlight of the 10,000-acre U.S. Virgin Islands National Park. The trail traverses the ruins of what was once St. John's most important sugar-cane plantation. Slaves' quarters, a windmill tower, and ballast-brick buildings are remnants of a long-vanished era. Stunning views look across the Sir Francis Drake Passage toward Tortola and Jost Van Dyke. See p. 225.

- **Reef Bay Trail** (St. John): It's a hike, literally, but this 6-mile backcountry trek reveals Danish plantation ruins, the island's tallest trees, and petroglyphs carved by Amerindians into the rock walls of a waterfall pool. See p. 225.

- **Hike BVI Eco-Treks** (Tortola): Hike BVI offers some of the region's most interesting eco-tours and treks, from hikes along a trail lined with mahogany trees to snorkeling the blue waters of a secret lagoon. See p. 266.

- **The Sage Mountain National Park Hike** (Tortola): This dramatic 3- to 4-hour hike goes from Brewer's Bay to the top of Mount Sage, the highest peak in the Virgin Islands, at 523m (1,716 ft.). Along the way, you'll see ruins of old homes in addition to the beautiful flora and fauna of the park's primeval forest. See p. 266.

- **Virgin Gorda Peak** (Virgin Gorda): Trek to the top of the island's highest peak, Virgin Gorda (414m/1,359 ft.), on this 50-minute round-trip

Climbing Sage Mountain, the Virgin Islands' highest peak, on Tortola.

hike through tropical forest. The views from the top are utterly breathtaking—you'll have views of both the Caribbean and Atlantic oceans. See p. 290.

THE best LUXURY RESORTS

- **The Ritz-Carlton** (St. Thomas): This remains the top-tier place to stay on St. Thomas—and it should be; it's triple the price of the rest. Presided over by a grand Italianate palazzo and fronted by a soft-sand beach, it's a big, full-service resort with luxurious (if somewhat generic) manicured comfort; rooms and suites are spacious and outfitted with sumptuous bathrooms and balconies overlooking the pool and sea. See p. 78.

- **Lovango Resort and Beach Club** (Lovango Island): An instant classic from veteran Nantucket innkeepers, Lovango is just flat-out dreamy. Showcasing tropical hardwoods, alfresco pebble showers, and slatted doors open to the breezes, Lovango's treehouses and glamping tents epitomize stripped-down luxury in a wondrous setting—and you're just a short boat ride away from the bustle of St. Thomas. Dining along the docks is utterly memorable. See p. 80.

- **The Buccaneer** (St. Croix): Built around the ruins of an old sugar plantation, the family-owned Buccaneer is a class act, stretching over many rolling acres with an 18-hole golf course, eight championship tennis courts, two freshwater pools, a spa, a 2-mile jogging trail, and three scenic beaches. It's a great family choice, too. See p. 138.

Set on its own cay, the eco-conscious Lovango Resort and Beach Club strikes a note of unfussy luxury.

o **Rosewood Little Dix Bay** (Virgin Gorda): In 2024, Little Dix will celebrate 60 years of understated elegance, the kind of gracious old-school hospitality that has made this 494-acre resort a treasure for generations. Gutted by the 2017 hurricanes and reopened in 2020, the property feels refreshed but still familiar, with a half-mile crescent strand of sand (and excellent snorkeling right off the beach), the best spa in the Virgins, and, in the wooden Pavilion—which survived the storm, barely—the resort's beating heart. See p. 280.

o **Guana Island** (Guana Island): Of all the very fine resorts in the B.V.I., this private island eco-retreat may be tops in terms of sheer romantic seclusion. It's a throwback to the days before technological intrusions ruled daily life. Expect elegant rusticity, an ode to the good life of honor bars and afternoon tea. The sea breezes are the best A/C you'll ever need. See p. 307.

THE best SMALL HOTELS, INNS & BED & BREAKFASTS

o **At Home in the Tropics** (St. Thomas): Everything you want in a B&B and more, including killer breakfasts, a couple of cute dogs, and million-dollar views of the Charlotte Amalie harbor. See p. 74.

o **Olga's Fancy** (St. Thomas): You're in good hands with innkeeper pros at this sly sleeper in Frenchtown—and a stay here may be the best bargain in town. Climb the steps to a treehouse of a lobby for liquid bonhomie with other guests, or take a dip in the pool. Rooms are simple and simply furnished, but those views! See p. 76.

o **Feather Leaf Inn** (St. Croix): The old Estate Butler's Bay sugar plantation has been handsomely repurposed as an intimate resort and lush eco-retreat on the island's west coast. Rooms in the main house have sweeping Butler's Bay views. See p. 146.

o **The Fred** (St. Croix): For boutique chic, you can't beat the Fred, which brings pop color and a cheeky good nature to the Fredricksted seafront. See p. 145.

o **King Christian** (St. Croix): The expansive revamp of the King Christian hotel and surrounding properties has been nothing less than transformative for the Christiansted harborfront. Renovated rooms have smart boutique stylings, and new first-floor cafes and shops would look right at home in the most chic neighborhoods. See p. 144.

o **The Waves Cane Bay** (St. Croix): Another style overhaul (same designer as King Christian's, above) has made these 11 Cane Bay rooms fashionable in a textural, organic sort of way. See p. 142.

o **Estate Lindholm** (St. John): St. John's top B&B, Lindholm combines vintage island charm with serious comfort. See p. 203.

o **Saba Rock** (Virgin Gorda): Saba Rock 2.0 tries to be all things to all people—and handsomely succeeds. We saw sunburnt children happily eating snacks in the restaurant as rowdy sailors from neighboring Necker Island plunged off the decks. It's been rebuilt to last, with a gorgeous new restaurant and upstairs Sunset Bar. Smartly designed rooms have sea views and superb soundproofing for when the bar gets pumping. See p. 281.

Smartly rebuilt after the hurricanes, Virgin Gorda's Saba Rock resort ticks off all the boxes.

o **The Hideout** (Jost Van Dyke): Bringing luxury stylings to barefoot-casual Jost, each of the Hideout's seven villas has its own private plunge pool. See p. 295.

o **Anegada Beach Club** (Anegada): The post-hurricane reboot of this already stylish glamping retreat is stunning, and the beachside palapas (one with sea-facing his-and-hers tubs) capture Anegada as its breezy best. See p. 303.

THE best AFFORDABLE LODGINGS

o **Bluebeards Castle** (St. Thomas): This sprawling, centrally located complex works on so many levels it's easy to dismiss the somewhat generic rooms; but even there, your comforts are attended to, including reliably good beds. The views from the resort restaurants are smashing. See p. 74.

o **Cinnamon Bay Campground** (St. John): It's gone glamping, but it's still a bargain stay on beautiful Cinnamon Bay. See p. 204.

o **Wyndham Tortola BVI Lambert Beach Resort** (Tortola): This is a real find, on a beautiful beach, with one of the biggest pools in the B.V.I. and a lovely restaurant/bar. See p. 252.

o **Cooper Island Beach Club** (Cooper Island): This escapist's retreat on Cooper Island is smartly designed and very comfortable, with eight rooms in simple cottages built of reclaimed timber. It's "fan-ventilated"—that is, no A/C—and don't expect TV either. Do expect yachties and divers dropping in at the lively bar and restaurant. See p. 248.

o **Anegada Reef Hotel** (Anegada): This congenial 20-room hotel has been in the hospitality business for nearly 50 years. Rooms have been nicely refreshed, and you can blast the air-conditioning if you prefer it to ceiling fans. But it's still the kind of place where, if the bartender isn't around, you make your own cocktails and write down what you had. See p. 304.

Smartly updated rooms with a top beach and pool make Tortola's Wyndham Lambert Beach resort a great value.

THE best FAMILY RESORTS

- **The Ritz-Carlton** (St. Thomas): This tony resort teems with kids snorkeling and standup paddleboarding, sliding down the water slide at the family pool, and playing in the sand at the beach. See p. 78.
- **The Buccaneer** (St. Croix): This longtime family favorite resort has three beaches with gentle seas and facilities for just about every sport you can think of—tennis, golf, swimming, jogging, sailing, scuba diving, and snorkeling. Mermaid Beach is packed with toys, including an oversize chess set. See p. 138.
- **Westin St. John Resort & Villas** (St. John): This contemporary megaresort, set on 34 acres of neatly landscaped grounds and fronting a nice beach with gentle seas, embraces families with the Westin Family Kids Club (ages 3–12), a massive pool, and tons of watersports. See p. 197.
- **The Palms at Pelican Cove** (St. Croix): This small resort has a lot to offer families—all kids 17 and under stay for free in their parent's room, and kids 10 and over are treated to complimentary scuba lessons. The resident iguana and pelican don't hurt either. See p. 141.
- **Rosewood Little Dix Bay** (Virgin Gorda): A half-mile beach lined with clear, gentle seas and stocked with water toys galore; a dedicated Rosewood Explorers children's center; a range of half- and full-day activities like sandcastle building and treasure hunts; and all the baby paraphernalia you need (baby bathtub, monitor, diaper pail, . . .) make this one of the region's best choices for families. See p. 280.

St. Croix's Buccaneer Resort lays on an impressive roster of activities for families.

THE best RESTAURANTS

- **Blue 11** (St. Thomas): One of the island's most innovative chefs does multi-course tasting menus with depth and precision in this minimalist-chic Yacht Haven Grande restaurant. See p. 82.
- **Gladys' Cafe** (St. Thomas): We don't care that it's smack-dab in tourist central in downtown Charlotte Amalie: This is a local treasure. A bigger location in Royal Dane Mall (after a devastating fire) gives Gladys' more walls of native stone on which to hang splashy works of local art. Expect deftly prepared island specialties and fresh fruit juices (passionfruit, guava, sorrel), miraculous thirst quenchers on a hot day. See p. 86.
- **Oceana** (St. Thomas): You're in the hands of a pro, Executive Chef Patricia LaCorte, in this gorgeous and secluded Frenchtown restaurant overlooking the Baye de GriGri. See p. 88.
- **Sunset Grille** (St. Thomas): Nazareth Bay in a buttery sunset glow makes this beachside resto in the Secret Harbour Resort a quintessentially swoony spot for dinner. Food is very well-prepared, too. See p. 92.
- **The Galleon** (St. Croix): One of the island's most accomplished chefs has landed here, happily, after peripatetic stops at tip-top restaurants in the States. The result is delicious, inventive food and drinks. See p. 156.
- **La Reine Chicken Shack** (St. Croix): Get in line for great roast chicken and barbeque ribs in hungry-man portions. See p. 155.
- **Savant** (St. Croix): This sexy Christiansted spot sets the stage for what is no less than the best food on St. Croix. See p. 153.

Savant on St. Croix offers a beguiling mix of Caribbean, Thai, and Mexican flavors.

- **Too Chez** (St. Croix): Dustin Kendrick is a master at creating flavorful, unfussy dishes like baked shrimp scampi. Too Chez is now in the historic Quin House, former home of his family's fabled restaurant, Kendricks. See p. 153.
- **Miss Lucy's** (St. John): It's a legend, yes, because it serves some of the best island food on St. John, on tables set along the comely shoreline of Friis Bay. See p. 212.
- **Brandywine Estate Restaurant** (Tortola): The newly rebuilt Brandywine still overlooks Brandywine Bay and still serves refined Mediterranean fare, and it's just as romantic and special-occasion as it ever was. See p. 259.
- **The Dove** (Tortola): Set in a handsomely restored historic West Indian cottage, this longtime favorite in Road Town serves contemporary classics. See p. 254.
- **Sugarcane** (Virgin Gorda): Resurrected from the wreckage of Hurricane Irma, this restaurant is back in a sumptuous poolside setting. Take a dip or just admire the amazing Nail Bay views and balmy breezes. The excellent food sends it to another level. See p. 286.
- **Saba Rock** (Virgin Gorda): Get a front-row seat to the glittering maritime ruckus that is the North Sound at night and dine well while you're at it. What an evening you will have! See p. 286.
- **The Restaurant at Leverick Bay** (Virgin Gorda): The old-school house restaurant at the Leverick Bay Resort is where you go for a proper steak and a two-fisted cocktail. It's beloved by young and old alike. See p. 284.

THE best LOCAL BUYS

The U.S. Virgin Islands are rightfully known as the shopping mecca of the Caribbean. It's tempting indeed to comb the historic streets of St. Thomas's capital, Charlotte Amalie, in search of bargains amid the outposts of duty-free "luxury" goods, those international brands of china and crystal, jewelry, and cosmetics that blanket every cruise port. But for those seeking original, artisanal gifts made by people who actually live here, here's a sampling of our favorite Virgin Islands mementos.

- **Hot sauce:** Virgin Islanders love their hot sauce (aka "pepper" sauce), and many island cooks prepare and bottle their own. Look for local favorites like **Miss Anna's** (St. John), **Blind Betty's** (St. Croix), **Jerome's** (St. Thomas), and **ValleyDoll** (St. John), sold in gift shops and food stores around the islands, such as **St. John Spice** on St. John (p. 230).
- **Zora's leather sandals:** Ninety-year-old Zora Galvin has been making great-looking, indestructible leather sandals for 60 years. Her charming Charlotte Amalie shop also has other fabulous things for sale, including handmade "Monster" bags (made by another resident nonagenarian), glass artworks, prints, collages, rugs, and kirtas. See p. 122.

Crucian market baskets, found at select stores throughout the U.S.V.I.

o **Crucian hook bracelets:** Designer Sonya Hough created the original St. Croix C-clasp hook bracelet back in 1964, and it's been a must-buy on the island ever since. Hough is retired now, but you can still buy her classic hook bracelet (or hook ring, necklace, or charm) at **Sonya's** (p. 182). Other island artisans have their own versions: Whealan Massicott at **ib Designs** (p. 182), for example, makes his St. Croix hook bracelets with wave, petroglyph, anchor, and other island designs.

o **Moko Jumbie artwork:** A traditional presence at Carnival in St. Croix, Moko Jumbies are costumed stilt dancers with a ghostly presence ("moko" is a West African term for healer and "jumbie" is a West Indian expression for spirit). Look for custom-made baby onesies, totes, and tea towels with Moko Jumbie designs at **Franklin's on the Waterfront** in Frederiksted (p. 183).

o **Local art:** Head to **Bajo El Sol Gallery & Art Bar** (p. 228) in St. John for work by the best island artisans, including St. Thomas painter Shansi Miller and woodworker Avelino Samuel. In St. Thomas, the top galleries for local artworks are **Mango Tango** (p. 121) and the new **81C gallery** (p. 121) in downtown Charlotte Amalie. In Christiansted, St. Croix, the 40-year-old

Many Hands gallery continues to feature original work by local artists and craftspeople (p. 180).

o **Woven market baskets:** The St. John market basket—traditionally carried by slaves on market days—is a beloved island icon. The Henry family of **Crucian Bayside Creations** handcrafts beautiful woven baskets inspired by these traditional baskets (p. 228).

THE VIRGIN ISLANDS IN CONTEXT

S ugary-sand beaches shaded by palm trees and crystal-line waters teeming with sea life: That's the CliffsNotes version of the U.S. and British Virgin Islands. Sure, most visitors will likely spend days on end hanging out on some impossibly beautiful beach, playing in cerulean seas, and savoring fresh-caught fish. But outside the tourist bubble lies a fascinating history that particularly encapsulates the age of colonialism. Like so many other islands in the Caribbean, the Virgin Islands were inextricably intertwined with the empire-expanding ambitions of Western Europe and the use of slave labor to get it done. This chapter offers a look at the cultural influences coursing just beneath the surface of any modern-day escape to the Virgin Islands. It also includes tips on the best times to visit and the islands' top festivals and days of celebration.

THE ISLANDS IN BRIEF

The islands described in detail below are the main inhabited islands and the most frequently visited in both the U.S. and British Virgin Islands. Use the information to help guide you to your own idea of paradise. No matter where you're based, you will definitely want to go **island-hopping** to visit lesser-known islands, and certain popular spots, like the Baths (Virgin Gorda), that are B.V.I. must-sees.

The U.S. Virgin Islands

The U.S. Virgin Islands consist of three main islands: St. Thomas, St. John, and St. Croix, plus several smaller islets. The 2020 census reported a total population of some 87,000 people.

ST. THOMAS

The most developed of the U.S. Virgin Islands may be the most "unvirgin" of them all, but few can deny its physical beauty. St. Thomas is sprawling and mountainous, with breathtaking vistas and palm-fringed beaches. It's the commercial heart of the Virgin

Islands, but it offers something for everyone, from duty-free shopping to sizzling nightlife to laidback aeries far from the hustling scrum. The harbor at **Charlotte Amalie,** the capital, bustles with the energy of a small city. It's one of the largest cruise-ship ports in the Caribbean, and in the mornings crowds of cruise-ship passengers disembark and are spirited into big vans and open-air "safari" buses to excursions around the island. The cruise-ship herds also head to the city's shopping bazaars and malls, chasing down duty-free shopping bargains. Much of the retail action lies in a labyrinth of cobblestoned streets in the city's historic section (built by the Danish), where picturesque alleyways are packed with touts inviting shoppers in for a look. It's a beehive of activity during cruise-ship hours (roughly around 8am–4pm) in high season, but every afternoon before dark the big ships slip back out to sea, and the city belongs once more to locals and non-cruise visitors.

> ### Mapping the Virgins
>
> The U.S. Virgin Islands are located some 90 miles (145km) east of Puerto Rico, with a combined landmass roughly twice the size of Washington, D.C. The British Virgin Islands lie east of the U.S.V.I., some 97km (60 miles) east of Puerto Rico, and comprise a total landmass of 153 sq. km (59 sq. miles), a little smaller than Washington, D.C.

St. Thomas may have a cosmopolitan sheen, but it's got a distinctively Caribbean pulse. Even here, where everyone seems to be breathlessly chasing the almighty dollar, island time rules. Yes, **Magens Bay Beach,** with its tranquil waves and long sweep of sugar-white sand, is likely to be packed on

St. Thomas's bustling capital, Charlotte Amalie, is a magnet for Caribbean cruise ships.

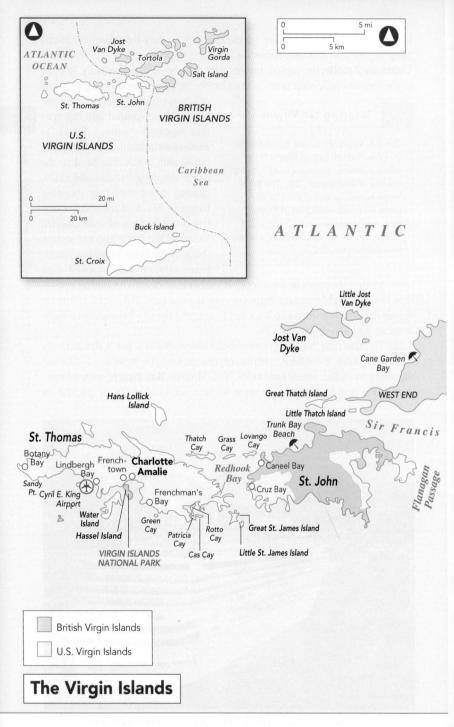

The Virgin Islands

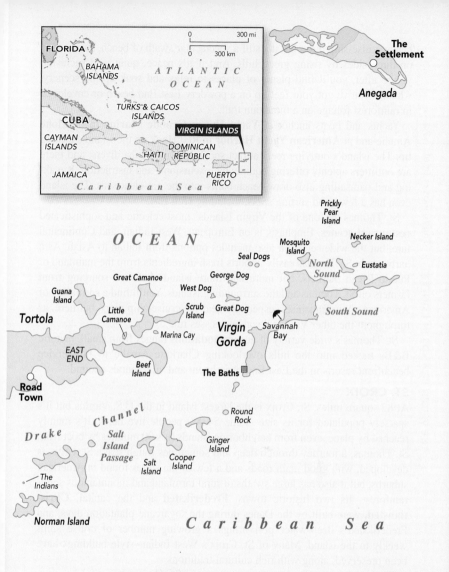

The Settlement

Anegada

FLORIDA

ATLANTIC OCEAN

BAHAMA ISLANDS

TURKS & CAICOS ISLANDS

CUBA

CAYMAN ISLANDS

HAITI

DOMINICAN REPUBLIC

JAMAICA

PUERTO RICO

VIRGIN ISLANDS

Caribbean Sea

0   300 mi
0   300 km

OCEAN

Prickly Pear Island

Necker Island

Mosquito Island

Seal Dogs

North Sound

Eustatia

Great Camanoe

George Dog

West Dog

Guana Island

Scrub Island

Great Dog

Little Camanoe

Marina Cay

Virgin Gorda

Savannah Bay

South Sound

Tortola

EAST END

Beef Island

The Baths

Road Town

Channel

Round Rock

Drake

Salt Island Passage

Ginger Island

Salt Island

Cooper Island

The Indians

Norman Island

Caribbean Sea

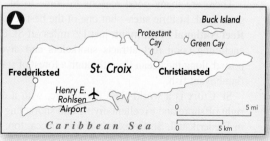

Buck Island

Protestant Cay

Green Cay

St. Croix

Frederiksted

Christiansted

Henry E. Rohlsen Airport

0   5 mi
0   5 km

Caribbean Sea

heavy cruise-ship days, but it's still a spectacular swath of beach, surrounded on three sides by rising green hills. And if it's peace, quiet, and seclusion you're after, you'll find plenty of places to relax and soak up the scenery, whether you've got your feet up on a powdery East End beach or enveloped in rainforest foliage on a mountain trail.

Yachts and boats anchor at **Yacht Haven Grande Marina** in Charlotte Amalie and at **American Yacht Harbor** in Red Hook on the island's eastern tip. The island's outlying reefs attract snorkelers and scuba divers, and there are outfitters aplenty offering equipment, excursions, and instruction. Kayaking and parasailing also draw beach bums into the gin-clear seas. The island even has a few good surfing spots, including Hull Bay.

St. Thomas has one of the Virgin Islands' most eclectic and sophisticated **restaurant scenes.** Emphasis is on European, West Indian, and Continental fare, but the wide selection also includes options from Italian to Asian. As a harbor hub, St. Thomas easily imports fresh ingredients from the mainland or Puerto Rican markets, but more and more island chefs are sourcing from farmers on St. Thomas and the surrounding islands. You'll find a sprinkling of American chain franchises, especially near the cruise-ship piers, but here, as throughout the other Virgins, local businesses rule.

St. Thomas's wide variety of **accommodations** ranges from small, historic B&Bs tucked into the hills overlooking Charlotte Amalie to full-service beachfront resorts in the East End. Apartment and villa rentals abound.

ST. CROIX

At 82 square miles, St. Croix is the largest island in the U.S. Virgins but it's sparsely populated for its size (some 54,000 people live here). It's mainly reached by plane, even from neighboring islands (it's 90 minutes by boat from St. Thomas, a journey through deep and sometimes rough seas). St. Croix is developed, with good main roads and a few of the stores found in American suburbs, but it also has large swaths of rural farmland and mountainous semi-rainforest. Its two historic towns, **Frederiksted** and the capital, **Christiansted,** were built by the Danes during the sugarcane-plantation days, and Frederiksted's deep-water port brings a growing number of cruise ships weekly to the island. Many of St. Croix's West Indian–style buildings have been preserved, along with rich cultural traditions.

There are many good reasons to come to St. Croix—beautiful beaches, great food, historic sites—but one of the best reasons is to visit **Buck Island Reef National Monument,** just 1½ miles off St. Croix's northeast coast. The encircling coral reef attracts snorkelers and divers, who can follow signs posted along the ocean floor through a forest of staghorn coral swarming with flamboyant fish.

St. Croix is a world-class diving site, with a deep trench for wall-diving right offshore and excellent diving and snorkeling around the cruise-ship pier in Frederiksted. St. Croix is a tennis mecca, too: The **Buccaneer Hotel** has some of the best courts in the Virgin Islands and hosts several annual tournaments. Other sports for active vacationers include horseback riding,

Relics of St. Croix's plantation past, like this former sugar mill on the grounds of the Buccaneer Resort (p. 138), are woven into a vibrant island culture.

parasailing, sport fishing, and water-skiing; kayakers can explore one of the world's few healthy bioluminescent bays. St. Croix is also gaining traction as a health-and-wellness destination, and practices what it preaches, with a growing presence in solar and wind energy and a boom in sustainable and organic farming.

Restaurants on St. Croix reflect the island's intriguing multicultural mix—the citizenry comprises a large Latino population (many Puerto Ricans and Dominicans migrated here in the mid–20th century), the descendants of black slaves (Afro-Caribbean), *mestivos,* and expats from around the world. (It has a thriving gay population as well.) You will find plenty of small, creative local eateries serving up dishes and snacks ranging from West Indian curries to French croissants. St. Croix has few ultra-luxury **hotels,** but it does have attractive inns and B&Bs, and many visitors opt to rent villas and condos at often-reasonable weekly rates.

ST. JOHN

St. John is one breathtakingly beautiful island, with some of the most pristine beaches in the entire Caribbean. And it will likely stay that way: Two-thirds of the island is protected parkland, the **U.S. Virgin Islands National Park.** Guided walks and safari bus tours are available to help you navigate the park, which is full of secret coves, hiking trails, and the ghostly remains of sugar-cane plantations. A third of the park is underwater. **Trunk Bay,** which boasts one of the island's finest beaches, has an amazing underwater snorkeling trail. As you can imagine, scuba diving is a major attraction on St. John.

The island is a very popular day-trip destination for sail-snorkel outings and cruise-ship excursions, although cruise ships don't dock here (the port can't accommodate big ships). Day-trippers largely arrive by passenger ferry from St. Thomas. Since fewer visitors stay overnight, St. John's **dining** and **lodging** options are modest. St. John has both upscale restaurants and colorful West Indian eateries, many located on the charming little harbor of the island's main town, **Cruz Bay,** and several serve fresh seafood. Nightlife usually consists of sipping rum drinks in a bar in Cruz Bay, and maybe listening to a local calypso band. St. John has one big resort (the Westin) and a sprinkling of charming inns, as well as a glamping campground and an eco-resort, but most people who visit the island rent villas, houses, or condos.

The British Virgin Islands

The British Virgin Islands comprise some 60 islands, 15 of which are inhabited. The total population of the B.V.I. is around 30,000 people.

TORTOLA

The main island of the British Virgins, Tortola is a beautiful place to stay and use as your base to day-trip to outlying islands. Virgin Gorda (see below) is less developed and has much better (and pricier) resorts, but Tortola has alluring charms and scenery that just doesn't quit. **Road Town** is the island's sailing hub and capital, and an increasingly popular port of entry for cruise ships. Though it was hard-hit by Hurricane Irma in 2017, beautification efforts and road expansions have since turned Road Town from fairly charmless to fresh and colorful. Head west or east out of town, and you'll find a dramatic topography of such cinematic beauty it nearly stops you in your tracks.

The island's best and most unspoiled beaches, including **Smugglers Cove** (with its secluded collection of snorkeling reefs), lie at the island's western tip and along the northern shoreline. Tortola's premier beach is **Cane Garden Bay,** a 2.4km (1½-mile) stretch of white sand bookended by rising green hills. Clean, gentle surf and a smooth sand bottom make it one of the safest places for families with small children—and there's plenty of ocean for everyone, even on the busiest cruise-ship days. Hikers on Tortola can explore **Sage Mountain National Park,** where trails lead to a 543m (1,781-ft.) peak that offers panoramic views. The park is rich in flora and fauna, from mammee trees to cooing mountain doves.

But what really makes Tortola exceptional is boating. It is *the* boating center of the British Virgin Islands, which are among the most cherished sailing territories on the planet. Tortola offers some 100 charter yachts and 300 bareboats, and its marinas and shore facilities are the most extensive in the Caribbean Basin. It's a big reason why Tortola makes a great base from which to go island-hopping.

Food in Tortola is simple and straightforward, with menu staples of local fish, conch fritters, and fresh fruit juices (laced with rum, island-style). The nightlife is laidback, with **full-moon parties** on the beach and a roster of local musicians playing at beach bars on Cane Garden Bay. Tortola, however,

Tortola makes a good base for excursions to the other British Virgin Islands, like this outing with Kuralu Daysail Charters (p. 263).

currently has a dearth of **lodgings** and a few very basic hotels; many people who stay awhile choose to rent villas, houses, or condos.

VIRGIN GORDA

Virgin Gorda is the third-largest member of the B.V.I. archipelago, with a permanent population of about 4,000 people. Virgin Gorda is uncrowded and incredibly scenic, with swooping roads that lace the tops of emerald peaks and some of the cleanest and clearest water on the planet. In fact, being on the water, whether under sail or with snorkel and mask, is the default mode on Virgin Gorda. It's a sun-and-sea worshiper's dream come true.

Many visitors come over for a day to check out the **Baths,** an astounding collection of gigantic boulders and crystalline tide pools on the southern tip. Crafted by volcanic pressures millions of years ago, the rocks have eroded into rounded, sculptural shapes—and you can snorkel among the big boulders in fetching turquoise seas.

It may be small and its population sparse, but Virgin Gorda is home to some of the best **hotels** and most exclusive villas in the world, including **Rosewood Little Dix Bay.** You will pay dearly for the privilege of staying here. Community is strong here, and in Spanish Town, the island's main village, you'll find upscale **restaurants** side by side with modest local joints serving West Indian cuisine.

ANEGADA, JOST VAN DYKE & OTHER ISLANDS

For those who *really* crave a secluded getaway, the most remote British Virgin Island, **Anegada** (p. 300), has a small population and limited commercial activity but wonderful beaches and beachside restaurants. Rugged little **Jost**

Van Dyke (p. 292) is known for its lively beach bars, diving, and sportfishing. For those with deep pockets, a number of **private islands** (p. 307), owned by some of the world's wealthiest people, offer limited guest accommodations.

THE VIRGIN ISLANDS TODAY

The American way of life prevails today in the U.S. Virgin Islands, and it has swept across to the British Virgin Islands, as well. When islanders need something, they have it shipped from Miami. In clothes, cars, food, and entertainment, America, not Great Britain, rules the seas around both archipelagos. The British Virgins even use the U.S. dollar as their official currency, instead of British pounds. Modernity has creeped in—Wi-Fi and cellphones are ubiquitous—but there is an increased awareness of the need for more self-sufficiency, especially in the wake of the 2017 hurricanes. Small farms are thriving, traditional recipes are embraced and reimagined by clever island chefs, and even old-school "bush doctor" remedies are gaining attention from a younger, DIY-trending generation of islanders.

THE MONSTER THAT WAS irmaria

Five years later, talk of the twin terrors the locals call "Irmaria" still brings shudders to people who lived through the back-to-back Category 5 hurricanes of September 2017.

When **Hurricane Irma** hit the Virgin Islands on September 6, its 185mph sustained winds raged for 8 straight hours, broken only by a 20-minute respite when the eye of the hurricane passed over. The sun came out and winds stopped, giving many residents a brief chance to dash to sturdier shelter. At day's end, as one survivor said: "Not a leaf was left on a tree." On St. John, the famed Caneel Bay resort was demolished. St. Croix deployed boats to send food, batteries, and other supplies to its battered sister islands.

Two weeks later, another, even more powerful Category 5 hurricane, **Maria,** trained its sights on St. Croix. Many of the island's rugged mahogany trees lining main roads, some of them up to 200 years old, were upended, their roots already waterlogged by Irma's pounding rains. Workers at St. George Botanical Gardens reported a 20-foot-high wall of vegetation debris in the courtyard. On

St. Thomas, the Marriott hotel at Frenchman's Reef bore the brunt of Irma (it took 5 years to re-open).

On Tortola, Irma's 40-foot waves sent boats and massive shipping containers onto land, and the normally crystalline waters of Cane Garden Bay turned brown from debris raining down the mountains. Trellis Bay was littered with yachts. Metal signage from the island of St. Martin washed up in Virgin Gorda's North Sound. Homes were cleaned out right down to the slabs, furnishings hoovered out of busted windows.

Even old-timers who had ridden out many a storm were still bearing witness to Irma's ferocity years later. It was "an ugly grey monster, the first hurricane I could see coming with my eyes," said one Tortola taxi driver. B.V.I. resident Chuck Krallman, in a viral Facebook post, reported that Road Town looked like a "scene from a Zombie Apocalypse." Amazingly, only seven people lost their lives in the storms, but 90% of the buildings in the Virgin Islands were damaged, and many remain in a state of disrepair today.

The islands were still reeling from the worldwide global recession—and its attendant falloff in tourism revenues—when two of the most destructive hurricanes in history struck: Irma and Maria, Category 5 storms that ripped through the islands 2 weeks apart in September 2017. In the B.V.I., Tortola and Virgin Gorda bore the brunt of the storms. In the U.S.V.I., St. Thomas and St. John were the most hard-hit by Hurricane Irma, and Hurricane Maria did its worst on St. Croix. Two years later, as the battered islands struggled to rebound, the Covid-19 pandemic virtually shut the door on business.

Today, with Covid-19 restrictions gone and protocols relaxed, the Virgin Islands are roaring back after 5 years of disaster. Through it all, the islands, like the rest of the Caribbean, have come to realize that conservation of the natural environment—both land and sea—is paramount. Awareness of the perils of overdevelopment (and fast and shoddy development) has seeped into the collective consciousness. The B.V.I., in particular, is committed to adding green spaces to its existing national park system, which includes Gorda Peak National Park and Devil's Bay National Park on Virgin Gorda and Sage Mountain National Park on Tortola. St. John, the smallest of the U.S. Virgin Islands, is the most protected landmass in the Caribbean, with more than 60% of its acreage directly controlled by the U.S. National Park Service (and more parcels added on an ongoing basis).

LOOKING BACK: VIRGIN ISLANDS HISTORY

A Brief History

Christopher Columbus is credited with "discovering" the Virgin Islands in 1493, but, in fact, they had already been inhabited for 3,000 years. It is believed that the original settlers were the nomadic Ciboney Indians, who

DATELINE

1493 Columbus sails by the Virgin Islands, lands on St. Croix, and is attacked by Carib Indians.

1625 Dutch and English establish frontier outposts on St. Croix.

1650 Spanish forces from Puerto Rico overrun English garrison on St. Croix.

1653 St. Croix taken over by the Knights of Malta.

1671 Danes begin settlement of St. Thomas.

1672 England adds the British Virgin Islands to its empire.

1674 King Louis XIV of France makes St. Croix part of his empire.

1717 Danish planters from St. Thomas cultivate plantations on St. John.

1733 Danish West India Company purchases St. Croix from France; slaves revolt on St. John.

1820s Sugar plantations on the Virgin Islands begin to see a loss in profits.

continues

A 51ST state?

The U.S. Virgin Islands are an unincorporated territory administered by the U.S. Department of the Interior. Politically speaking, the Virgin Islands, like Puerto Rico, remain outside the family of the United States. They are only permitted to send a nonvoting delegate to the U.S. House of Representatives. U.S. Virgin Islanders are not allowed to vote in national elections, a sore spot for some local residents. Many hope to see another star added to the American flag in the near future—feeling that only full statehood will provide the respect, power, and influence needed to turn the islands into more than just a "colony." Progress in this direction moves sluggishly, if at all.

When the 1936 Organic Act of the Virgin Islands was passed under the Roosevelt administration, residents ages 21 and over were granted suffrage and could elect two municipal councils and a legislative assembly for the islands. In 1946, the first black governor of the islands, William Hastie, was appointed; by 1970, U.S. Virgin Islanders had been given the right to elect their own governor and lieutenant governor.

migrated from the South American mainland between 300 and 400 B.C. In St. John, petroglyphs carved into rocks bordering freshwater pools are evidence of the presence of the **Taino** tribe, an Arawak people who lived here from A.D. 700 into the 1490s. Another ancient site, a Taino ball court, was uncovered by archaeologists in 2004 in the Belmont neighborhood of Tortola; one of the large stones had been carved with a petroglyph of the sun. Peaceful agriculturists, the Taino were the first real homesteaders on the islands, arriving here from Venezuela, presumably in dugout canoes with sails. Their legacy lives on today in the use of hammocks (they slept in hammocks of cotton and reeds), canoes, and native foods like corn and sweet potatoes. In the 15th century,

1834	England frees 5,133 slaves living in the British Virgin Islands.
1848	Under pressure, the Danish governor of St. Croix grants slaves emancipation.
1867	First attempt by the United States to purchase the Virgin Islands from the Danish.
1916	Denmark signs treaty with the U.S. and sells St. Thomas, St. Croix, and St. John for $25 million.
1927	United States grants citizenship to U.S.V.I. residents.
1936	U.S. Virgin Islanders granted rights to vote in local elections.
1940	U.S. Virgin Islands used as a port during World War II, leading to population growth.
1946	First black governor of the U.S.V.I., William Hastie, is appointed.
1954	The U.S.V.I. falls under jurisdiction of Department of the Interior.
1966	Queen Elizabeth II visits the British Virgin Islands.
1967	B.V.I. get a new constitution.
1989	Hurricane Hugo rips through the islands, hitting St. Croix especially hard.
1995	Hurricane Marilyn causes millions of dollars of damage and leaves thousands homeless.

they clashed with warlike Carib Indians, who worked them to death as slaves or ate them. But it was ultimately the harsh treatment and disease brought by European explorers that sounded the death knell for the native populations, which were wiped out in less than 20 years after the advent of European colonists.

The Age of Colonization

In November 1493, on his second voyage to the New World, **Christopher Columbus** spotted the Virgin Islands, naming them *Las Once Mil Virgenes,* after the Christian St. Ursula and her martyred maidens. Short of drinking water, he decided to anchor at what is now Salt River on St. Croix's North Shore. His men were greeted by a rainfall of arrows. Embittered, Columbus called that part of the island *Cabo de Flechas,* or "Cape of the Arrows," and sailed toward Puerto Rico.

As the sponsor of Columbus's voyage, Spain claimed the Virgin Islands; however, with more interest in the Greater Antilles, wealth-seeking Spain chose not to colonize the Virgins. The Virgins had no gold or silver; St. Thomas in particular was very hilly and lacked prime agricultural land. The Virgins did, however, have one valuable commodity: Their central location. Powerful east-to-west ocean currents and maritime trade routes flowed right to its door, meaning European ships (and pirates) could reach the islands more quickly. As one historian said, "Anything you drop off the African coast lands here." Other European colonizers soon moved in.

In 1625, both the English and the Dutch established opposing frontier outposts on **St. Croix.** Struggles between the two nations for control of the island continued for about 20 years, until the English prevailed—for a time. Then the struggle for St. Croix widened: In 1650, Spanish forces from Puerto Rico overran the British garrison on St. Croix, and soon after, the Dutch invaded.

1996 Water Island, off the coast of St. Thomas, is officially declared the fourth U.S. Virgin Island.

2000 St. Croix becomes the first "casino island" in the Virgin Islands.

2008 B.V.I. become one of the world's leading offshore financial centers.

2009 Islands experience drop-off in tourism as U.S. economy goes into recession.

2017 The Virgin Islands are devastated by two Category 5 hurricanes, Irma and Maria.

2019 Covid-19 pandemic shuts down businesses throughout the Virgins.

Pandemic protocols instituted by U.S. and B.V.I.

2021 The St. Croix oil refinery, under the management of Limetree Bay Refining, has a breakdown and spills crude oil, gases, and petrochemicals on downwind neighborhoods.

2021 The B.V.I. Prime Minister is arrested in a sting operation in Miami on drug smuggling charges.

2022 Most Covid-19 pandemic restrictions finally lifted for entry into U.S. and B.V.I.

2

The Name Game

St. Croix's indigenous name was Ay Ay, Taino for "the river." In early Danish times, **Charlotte Amalie** was called "Taphus," for its many taverns. When the United States purchased the Virgin Islands in 1917, **St. John** was still known by its Danish name, "St. Jan." On the B.V.I., it's theorized that **Cooper Island** was named for its barrel-making history (coopers prized the white cedar that grew there for making rum barrels). **Salt Island** was clearly named for its saltwater ponds: Every spring, B.V.I. residents raked up sea salt on Salt Island when the ponds evaporated.

In 1653, the island fell into the hands of the Knights of Malta, who gave St. Croix its French name. However, these aristocratic French cavaliers weren't exactly prepared for West Indian plantation life, and their debts quickly mounted. By 1674, King Louis XIV of France took control of St. Croix and made it part of his kingdom.

The English continued to fight Dutch settlers in **Tortola,** considered the most important of the British Virgin Islands. Finally, in 1672 England was able to add the entire archipelago to its growing empire.

Colonial powers once battled for control of these islands, as the cannons at Fort Christianvaern in Christiansted, St. Croix, attest. See walking tour on p. 170.

Meanwhile, in March 1671, the Danish West India Company attempted to settle **St. Thomas.** Two ships were sent; only one, the *Pharaoh,* completed the voyage, with about a third of its crew surviving. Eventually, however, reinforcements arrived, and by 1679, at least 156 Europeans were reported to be living on St. Thomas, along with their slaves. As noted by historian Isaac Dookin in his book *A History of the Virgin Islands of the United States,* with the native population decimated, the Europeans had turned to alternative sources for laborers to work the plantations, leading to the "institution of Negro slavery in the Virgin Islands." Over the next century and a half, St. Thomas's harbor became famous (or infamous) for its slave market—some

historians estimate that nearly 250,000 slaves were sold on the auction blocks at Charlotte Amalie before being sent elsewhere, often to America's South. St. Thomas also gained infamy over the years as a West Indies base for maritime raids by such legendary **pirates** as Sir Francis Drake, Captain Kidd, Blackbeard, and others.

In 1717, planters from St. Thomas sailed to **St. John** to begin cultivating plantations. The plantation system drastically altered the physical landscape of the island. Thousands of acres of virgin forest were razed, with slaves doing the hard labor. By 1733, an estimated 100 plantations (mainly sugar cane) were operating on the island. That year, the **slaves rebelled** against their colonial masters, taking control of the island for about 6 months and killing many Europeans.

A walking tour guide in Charlotte Amalie recounts St. Thomas's nefarious past as a haven for Caribbean pirates.

It took hundreds of French troops from Martinique to quell the rebellion; many of the rebellion leaders shot themselves before the French could reach them.

That same year, 1733, France sold St. Croix to the **Danish West India Company,** which divided the island into plantations. The already flourishing slave trade boomed. During the Napoleonic Wars, Great Britain occupied the Danish islands for two short periods—from 1801 to 1802, and again from 1807 to 1815—but handed them back after peace treaties were signed.

As early as 1792, Denmark had announced that it planned to **end the slave trade,** but it did not actually do so until 1848, well after the British had freed the 5,133 slaves on their islands in 1834. (Much of the B.V.I.'s plantation land was bought by these former slaves.) Emancipation was perhaps inevitable, however, as the great economic boom that had sustained the Virgin Islands' plantations had already begun to wilt by the 1820s. The introduction of the sugar beet drastically reduced demand for cane sugar, which virtually bankrupted plantation owners. Cuba eventually took over the sugar market in the Caribbean. By 1872, in fact, the British had so little interest in the British Virgins that they placed them in the loosely conceived and administered Federation of the Leeward Islands.

With so many nationalities and ethnicities involved over the centuries, the Virgin Islands developed an atmosphere of religious tolerance (which happened to be good for global trade, too). Religious denominations in St. Thomas included Lutheran, Moravian, Episcopalian, and Reformed Dutch, and seven churches often shared services and ministers. A Jewish congregation founded the St. Thomas Synagogue in 1796. "We shook hands with the world every day," said one historian.

Enter the United States

In 1867, the United States attempted to purchase the Danish West Indies (St. Thomas, St. Croix, and St. John), but the treaty was rejected by the U.S. Senate in 1870; the asking price was $7.5 million. After it acquired Puerto Rico in 1902, following the Spanish-American War, the United States expressed renewed interest in buying the Danish islands. This time, the United States offered only $5 million; the Danish parliament spurned the offer.

On the eve of its entry into World War I, the U.S. Navy began to fear a German takeover of the islands, which would give the Kaiser's navy a base to prey on shipping through the Panama Canal. Once again, the United States offered to purchase the islands—and 1916 Denmark agreed to sell them, for $25 million, a staggering sum to pay for island real estate in those days. By 1917, the U.S. was in full control, and Denmark retreated from the Caribbean after a legacy of nearly 2½ centuries.

During the Prohibition era, some islanders profited from the U.S. connection by making rum and shipping it illegally to the United States, often through Freeport, in the Bahamas. But it wasn't until 1927 that the United States granted citizenship to the island residents, and not until 1936, under Franklin Roosevelt, that the first Organic Act gave the islanders voting rights in local elections. This act was revised in 1954, when the U.S.V.I came under the sovereignty of the U.S. Department of the Interior, granting islanders a greater degree of self-government.

Jobs generated by World War II finally woke the islands from their long economic slumber. The U.S.V.I. were used as a port during the war, and visitors first started to appear on the islands. In the postwar U.S. economic boom, the Virgin Islands at long last found a replacement for sugar cane: tourism. In the years since, the economy of both the British and the U.S. Virgins became one of the most stable and prosperous in the Caribbean.

The British Virgin Islands Develop

The British Virgin Islands were finally freed from the Leeward Islands Federation in 1956, and in 1966, Queen Elizabeth II visited this remote colonial

READ THE ISLANDS' HISTORY IN THEIR
architecture

Some of the architectural legacy left by the colonizing Danes still remains in the islands, especially in Christiansted and Frederiksted on St. Croix, and in Charlotte Amalie on St. Thomas.

Many of the commercial buildings constructed in downtown Charlotte Amalie are restrained in ornamentation. You'll see a lot of pilasters and classical cornices on buildings, and door arches and windows framed in brick. Such flourishes were often added in the final stages to "dress up" a building. Cast-iron grillwork on some of the second-floor overhanging balconies also adds a certain architectural flair. Also notice how many buildings in St. Thomas have courtyards, which added to the living space on the second floor. These courtyards originally held kitchens and, almost more vital, cisterns to capture precious rainwater.

In recent decades, as the original plaster and stucco have been stripped from the old buildings' walls, restorers have discovered underneath the rubble well-designed shapes and patterns of old brick and "blue bitch"—a native stone made of volcanic tuff. See if you can spot any of these.

Similar building techniques were used on St. Croix. Christiansted remains one

of the most historically authentic towns in the West Indies, true to its original Danish colonial flavor. The basic style was a revival of the European classic look of the 18th century, but with variations to accommodate the tropical climate. As early as 1747, the Danes adopted a strict building code, which spared Christiansted from some of the violent fires that occasionally wiped out Charlotte Amalie. Frederiksted, the other major town of St. Croix, has a well-designed waterfront, with blocks of arcaded sidewalks. The quarter is protected by the government as part of Frederiksted's National Historic District.

Great architecture was never the forte of the British Virgin Islands. During a time when major buildings might have been created, the B.V.I.s were too economically depressed to finance major structures of lasting significance. Therefore, for much of its history, its people have lived in typical West Indies shanties, with an occasional public building constructed in a vague imitation of 18th-century European style. Yet the B.V.I.s left the world one lasting architectural heritage: native son William Thornton, whose designs were used for the U.S. Capitol building in Washington.

outpost. By 1967, the British Virgin Islands had received a new constitution. As a British Overseas Territory, the B.V.I. government today is largely autonomous, and its duly elected premier is the head of government (working under a governor appointed by the king of England).

Tourism was slower to come to the British Virgins than to the U.S. Virgin Islands, but it is now a mainstay of the economy, as is financial services. Today the B.V.I. is one of the world's leading offshore financial centers and tax havens; some 40% of the world's offshore companies are formed in the British Virgin Islands. In 2011, the local population boasted one of the highest incomes per capita in the Caribbean—around $40,000 per family. Islanders mourned the death of the longtime British monarch Queen Elizabeth II in

2022, but as Prince William said in his visit to the region in 2022, the "future is for the people to decide upon."

Tourism & the Economy Today

Let's face it: It's been a rough few years for the Virgin Islands, particularly in a region where tourism accounts for 60% of the government GDP. Writing this book has been as much about rediscovery as it is about the excitement of excavating the new. It's veering between those jubilatory *Yes!* moments when you discover a favorite spot *is still there* and having your heart break a little for those places that have turned to dust.

Today the Virgins are clearly on the upswing. After 2 lean years of pandemic shutdowns, the World Travel and Tourism Council says that the region's recovery is outpacing the rest of the world. In the U.S.V.I, first-quarter visitor arrivals surged 153% compared to the same period in 2021, and the entire region is experiencing some of the biggest new airlift growth in the Caribbean.

Caribbean Journal named St. Thomas the 2022 Innovative Destination of the Year for its nimble response to the pandemic and forward-thinking reimagining (to the tune of $146 million) of downtown Charlotte Amalie and its waterfront promenade, after years of decline. The Biden-Harris

A British phone box at Virgin Gorda's Saba Rock resort (p. 281).

Administration Infrastructure Act has allocated $25 million to the islands to expand roads—including a tree-lined highway on St. Thomas's Veterans Drive and a new promenade—and modernize bridges and transit.

In the B.V.I., classic resorts like Little Dix Bay, the Bitter End Yacht Club, and Saba Rock have made stunning comebacks after near-annihilation, and the territory is doubling down on its eco-retreat/organic farm/herb doctor heritage. Environmental groups like Beyond the Reef are busy repurposing hurricane wreckage (like sunken boats and planes) into cheeky interactive "art reefs" for divers. And for the first time since 2006, travelers will be able to fly direct into the B.V.I. via daily American Airline flights between Miami and Tortola.

Rosewood Little Dix Bay Resort (p. 280) was completely rebuilt after the 2017 hurricanes.

And say what you will about cruise ships, but the cruise business has been a lifeline to taxi drivers, excursion operators, and small business owners in the last few lean years. In St. Thomas in 2022, first-quarter cruise-ship arrivals were up 153% over 2021. In 2023, the U.S. Virgin Islands should expect to receive an additional 440,000 cruise-ship visitors through an agreement with the Royal Caribbean cruise line. Cruises to the Frederiksted Pier in St. Croix will triple in 2023. It's a particular boon for St. Croix, where the government is investing some $247 million in rebuilding Frederiksted—and at the same time working to balance that growth against what U.S.V.I. Governor Albert Bryan calls the unique "culture and spirit" of the island. To that end, a good portion of government funds are local-directed, included a new $27-million stadium and the rebuilding of the Frederiksted pool and its recreation center, a beloved community hub where island children learned to swim and elders played dominos.

And after years of the B.V.I. getting all the bareboat cruising attention, St. Thomas's Yacht Haven Grande was named the 2022 Yacht Marina of the Year. All the big boys are cruising through Charlotte Amalie during the high holiday season (including David Geffen), and even the Moorings has set up shop here.

Finally, it's looking as if the customary off-seasons are no longer the islands' downtime. "I am advised," B.V.I. Premier Natalio Wheatley said drily, "that the tourism off-season is changing." High tourist season traditionally kicks off in late November or December and winds down in April, but the islands' hot summer events—including poker runs, Christmas in July, and the August

THE SARGASSUM blues

Sargassum seaweed is elemental to the marine ecosystem, an essential nursery for fish and food source for crabs, turtles, and birds. While landfall is a periodic natural occurrence that takes place during the hottest months of the year, an unusually high level of sargassum buildup has become an annoyingly regular late-summer occurrence on Caribbean beaches, and in 2022 U.S. Virgin Islands Governor Albert Bryan declared a state of emergency. (Scientists lay the blame on global warming and fertilizer run-off from farms along Brazil's deforested Amazon River.)

A sargassum landfall is generally more smelly nuisance than public health threat. When the orange-tinted seaweed washes up on beaches, it turns the seawater brown and outright stinks (rotting eggs is a frequent comparison) as it decomposes on the beach. At its worst, sargassum buildup clogs boat engines, propellers, and water desalination plants and chokes coral reef life.

In the B.V.I., public officials are using drones to track sargassum deposits. In true island fashion, entrepreneurs are being encouraged to find ways to convert seaweed into something useful, like biofuel or fertilizer—but to do so, the sargassum has to be fresh; ergo the value of tracking drones. In the Virgins, beachside hotels and resorts under threat do daily rakings, but many have already established alternative plans for guests if the seaweed proliferation can't simply be raked away.

Emancipation Festival—are stretching the season into September, when peak hurricane season shuts it all down once again.

THE VIRGIN ISLANDS IN POPULAR CULTURE

Books

FICTION

Don't Stop the Carnival (Little Brown & Co., 1992) by Herman Wouk is "the Caribbean classic"; all readers contemplating a visit to the Virgin Islands might want to pick it up. Wouk lived in St. Thomas in the 1950s, and his novel is based on actual people he met during that time. Bob Shacochis's *Easy in the Islands* (Grove, 2004) giddily re-creates the flavor of the West Indies with short stories. *Tales of St. John & the Caribbean,* by Gerald Singer (Sombrero Publishing Co., 2001), is an easy read: a collection of amusing and insightful stories, and the best volume if you'd like a behind-the-scenes look at St. John after the tourists have taken the ferry back to St. Thomas for the night. *How to Escape from a Leper Colony* (Graywolf Press, 2019) is a novella and stories by Tiphanie Yanique, who has written for the *New York Times* and the *Wall Street Journal*. Yanique grew up in the Hospital Ground neighborhood in St. Thomas. The title novella refers to Hassel Island, which was once a leper colony.

Robert Louis Stevenson is said to have used Norman Island, in the B.V.I., as a fictional setting for his 1883 classic *Treasure Island* (multiple publishers). This swashbuckling adventure has intrigued readers for years with such characters as the immortal Long John Silver. The book, which gave rise to such memorable lines as "shiver me timbers," continues to find new generations of readers.

My Name Is Not Angelica (Yearling Books, 1990) by Scott O'Dell is a young-adult historical novel based in the Virgin Islands in the early 18th century. It tells the saga of a slave girl, Raisha, who escapes bondage; the grim realities of slavery are depicted.

COOKBOOKS

The Sugar Mill Caribbean Cookbook (Harvard Common Press, 1996) is an iconic book by Jinx Morgan and her late husband, Jefferson, the former owners of the Sugar Mill in Tortola. Its recipes include such signature Sugar Mill dishes as Rasta Pasta, rum-glazed chicken wings, and lobster and christophine curry. *Food & Folklore of the Virgin Islands* (Romik, 1990) by Arona Petersen, a well-known St. Thomas writer and folklorist born in 1908, captures the regional flavor of Virgin Islands fare, with idiomatic dialogues of island people perfectly re-created as she spins old island tales and wisdom. In her story, "What Does Tomorrow Mean? In Any Language, Wait," appears this passage: "Wat I trying to say is dat waitin is wat life is about. Everybody waitin fo something or udder, mannin or nite. Tain get wan purson wat, livin ain waitin-fo a bus, fo a taxi, fo a airplane, fo a steamer, fo a letter to come back. Some doan even know wat dey waiting for but dey still waitin." Her books are sold in local shops.

HISTORY BOOKS

A History of the Virgin Islands (University Press of the West Indies, 1994) by Isaac Dookhanhas has a scholarly bent, but it's concise and entertaining and is the best-researched survey of what was going on long before your arrival. *Cruz Bay from Conquest to Exploitation, a Forgotten History* (Little Nordside Press, 2017) is by author and historian David Knight, Sr., who was selected by the V.I. State Historic Preservation Office to conduct a study to determine if the capital of St. John, Cruz Bay, met the qualifications to be designated as a historic district; he did, and it has.

Author, shipwreck diver, and St. Croix sailing guide Stanford Joines traveled the world for 8 years studying historical archives (British National Archives and The Hague among them) and the sailing logbooks of buccaneers. With the help of archivists, historians, and retired amateur sleuths, he wrote *The Eighth Flag* (independently published, 2018), a pirate history from a sailor's point of view. The title comes from the fact that some seven flags flew over the Virgins at one time or another; the eighth flag was the pirate flag. St. Croix was a pirate bastion and sold their loot through the Danish, back when the governor of St. Thomas liked to impale escaped slaves and other horrors. Joines' ancestor, the famous pirate Henry Morgan, was 19 at the time.

Valerie Sims grew up in the Virgin Islands, and her memoir *Vintage St. John* (Vintage World Media, 2020) is a collection of stories through seven generations of St. John's history.

A good read for preteen travelers, *Caribbean Pirates* (Macmillan-Caribbean, 1986) by Warren Alleyne attempts to separate fact from fiction in the sagas of the most notorious pirates in history. Some of the material is based on published letters and documents.

OUTDOOR ADVENTURE BOOKS

Sailing enthusiasts say you shouldn't set out to explore the islets, cays, coral reefs, and islands of the B.V.I. without *The Sailing Lifestyle* (Fireside, 1988), John Rousmanière's well-researched guide. *Exploring St. Croix* (Travelers Information Press, 1987) by Shirley Imsand and Richard Philobosian is a very detailed activity guide of this island. The authors take you to 49 beaches, 34 snorkeling and scuba-diving sites, and 22 bird-watching areas, and lead you on 20 different hikes. *A Guide to the Natural History of St. John* (Virgin Islands Conservation Society, 1971) by Doris Jadan is a thoroughly charming (and sweetly illustrated) guide to the flora and fauna of the island. *A Guide to the Birds of Puerto Rico & the Virgin Islands* (Princeton University Press, 1989) by Herbert A. Raffaele, Cindy J. House, and John Wiessinger is worth getting for the illustrations alone, with 273 depictions of the 284 documented species on the islands.

Film

Film production reached its heyday on St. Thomas in the '70s and '80s, when major TV shows such as *Charlie's Angels, The Love Boat,* and *All My Children* were shot here. Many movies have been shot in the Virgin Islands, including *Open Water* (2003), the hair-raising adventure story of a couple stranded in shark-infested waters (based on a true story) and *The Deep* (1977), shot around the wreck of the RMS *Rhone* near Salt Island, the B.V.I. The final scene of *The Shawshank Redemption* (1994), when Andy Dufresne escapes the harsh Shawshank Prison for an idyllic tropical island, was filmed on Sandy Point, in St. Croix. The final island scene in *Trading Places* (1983), starring Eddie Murphy and Jamie Lee Curtis, was also shot in St. Croix. A

Essential Guide to Sailing the Virgin Islands

For more than half a century, the *Yachtsman's Guide to the Virgin Islands* has been the classic cruising guide to this area (it's now in its 13th edition). The detailed, 288-page text is supplemented by 27 hand-drawn sketch charts, aerial photographs, and numerous landfall sketches showing harbors, channels, landmarks, and such. Subjects covered include piloting, anchoring, communication, weather, fishing, and more. The guide also covers the eastern end of Puerto Rico, Vieques, and Culebra. Copies are available at major marine outlets and online bookstores.

Don't Let the Jumbies Get Ya!

"Don't let the Jumbies get ya!" is an often-heard phrase in the Virgin Islands, particularly when people are leaving their hosts and heading home in the dark. Jumbies, capable of good or evil, are supernatural beings that are believed to live around households. It is said that new settlers from the mainland of the United States never see these Jumbies and therefore need not fear them. But many islanders believe in their existence and, if queried, may enthrall you with tales of sightings. No one seems to agree on exactly what a Jumbie is. Some claim it's the spirit of a dead person that didn't go where it belonged. Others disagree. "They're the souls of live people," one islander told us, "but they live in the body of the dead." The most prominent Jumbies are "Moko Jumbies," colorful stilt walkers seen at all Carnival parades.

1980s film classic, *The Four Seasons* (1981), a tender-sweet melodrama starring Carol Burnett and Alan Alda, was filmed in part in the Virgin Islands.

The 1990 television remake of Ernest Hemingway's *The Old Man and the Sea,* starring Anthony Quinn, was filmed on the half-moon bay at Smuggler's Cove, on Tortola in the B.V.I. The ruins of the movie set still remain.

The true classic of the archipelago is *Virgin Island* (1958), starring John Cassavetes and Sidney Poitier. Filmed on Guana Island, in the B.V.I., it is a fairy-tale type of story about a young man and woman who buy a small, uninhabited island and go there to find their dream. The film was based on the actual experiences of novelist Robb White, who with his wife bought Marina Cay in 1937 for $60 and decided to pursue a Robinson Crusoe existence on the islands. He wrote about it in three memoirs: *In Privateers Bay*, *Our Virgin Island*, and *Two on the Isle*.

Music

As the Caribbean rhythms go, the Virgin Islands encompass it all, from reggae to classical to steel drums to spiritual hymns, but soca, reggae, calypso, and steel-pan beats seem to dominate the night.

Though it originated in Trinidad, **calypso** has its unique sounds in the Virgins. It is famously known for expressing political commentary through satire. If you add a little soul music to calypso, you get **soca,** a music form that also made its way north to the Virgin Islands from Trinidad. **Reggae** originated on Jamaica but is alive and well in the Virgins. Virgin Islanders have put a unique stamp on reggae, making it their own.

Scratch bands are popular in the British Virgins, in the musical form known as **fungi. Merengue** is also heard in the Virgins, having "floated over" from Puerto Rico and the Dominican Republic. **Zouk** is dance music from Martinique.

Throughout the year in various bars, clubs, and concerts, you can hear the music of the islands. Find out what's happening by reading the local newspapers. Of course, the leading musicians of the islands make recordings,

A steel-pan musician on the streets of Cruz Bay on St. John.

including the hypnotic and tantalizing roots-reggae stylings of St. Croix native **Dezarie,** whose albums, including *Gracious Mama Africa* and *Fourth Book,* have earned her the title of St. Croix's Roots Empress. Another St. Croix–born singer is **Mada Nile,** known for her poignant lyrics. **Sistah Joyce,** a reggae and calypso artist from Virgin Gorda, is acclaimed for her hard-hitting lyrics as evoked by her recordings "Remembah" and "60 Years Strong." She scored a hit with her debut album *H.Y.P.O.C.R.I.C.Y* and has been Calypso Queen four times in the Calypso Competitions at the August Emancipation Festival in the B.V.I.

Island-bred reggae bands such as **Midnite** (from St. Croix) and **Inner Visions** (from St. John), were popular in the '80s and '90s. *Midnite Intense Pressure,* Midnite's debut album, firmly established them as a force in roots music; the group was known for its fiery lyrics. Inner Visions was made up of first- and second-generation members of the Pickering family, with names like Grasshopper and Jupiter.

"All Hail Our Virgin Islands"

Caribbean composer and celebrated U.S. Virgin Islander Alton Augustus Adams was a self-taught musician. He put together a juvenile orchestra at the age of 14 and was the first Black bandmaster in the U.S. Navy. He even wrote a book, *The Memoirs of Alton Augustus Adams, Sr.* Adams is beloved as the composer of the stirring regional anthem of the U.S. Virgin Islands, "The Virgin Islands March." It is, in the words of St. Thomas historian Felipe Ayala, "a poem set to music."

EATING & DRINKING

Overall, you will eat very well in the Virgin Islands. Many fine talents, both local and imported, are ensconced in kitchens throughout the region, and competition breeds excellence. In addition, traditional Caribbean cuisine is alive and well in the Virgin Islands, with classic island dishes prominent on restaurant menus, and not just the laidback local spots. Even upscale resorts serving an international clientele favor menus with an island spin, encouraging a Caribbean/Continental fusion.

Dining in the Virgin Islands is generally more expensive than it is in North America because much of the food must be imported. Whenever possible, take advantage of fresh regional foods, like **locally caught fish,** especially mahi-mahi, wahoo, yellowtail, grouper, and red snapper. The sweet **Caribbean lobster** is another local specialty. More and more, **farm-fresh produce** is making a reappearance, and you'll find locally grown foods sold in the island's grocery stores—fresh fruit, bananas, sweet potatoes, cassava, even microgreens. See "Groceries, Markets & More" boxes in chapters 4, 5, 6, and 7.

Tips on Dining

TIPPING   Tipping is generally expected (in the range of 15%–20%), except in those restaurants where a service charge (generally 15%) has been automatically added to the bill.

WHAT TO WEAR   Used to be that in some of the posher resorts it was customary for men to wear a jacket, but these days, virtually no establishment requires it. If in doubt, ask the restaurant beforehand. Even at the better places, women's evening attire is casual-chic. During the day, always wear something over your bathing suit if you're in a restaurant—in fact, in St. John and the B.V.I. in particular, you should cover up in all public places (men have to wear shirts).

RESERVATIONS   Most places require reservations, especially in high season. But even in the slower seasons (or shoulder seasons), many smaller restaurants need to know how many people to expect for the evening's meal, so reservations may be required there as well. On Anegada, reservations (and requests for lobster) must be made at most restaurants before 4 or 5pm.

The Cuisine

You may want to start your meal with a bowl of *kallaloo,* or **callaloo,** a West Indian–style gumbo made in an infinite number of ways with a leafy green vegetable similar to spinach. It may come flavored with hot peppers, a ham bone, fresh seafood, okra, onions, and spices. We've also eaten a wonderful breakfast dish of steamed callaloo with sauteed mushrooms, onions, and halved cherry tomatoes.

The classic vegetable dish, which some families eat every night, is **peas and rice.** It usually consists of pigeon peas flavored with ham or salt meat, onion, tomatoes, herbs, and sometimes slices of pumpkin. Pigeon peas, one of the most common vegetables in the islands, are sometimes called congo peas or *gunga.* **Fungi** (pronounced with a hard *g*) is a simple cornmeal dish not unlike grits or polenta, made more interesting with the addition of okra and other ingredients. Sweet fungi is served as a dessert, with sugar, milk, cinnamon, and raisins. More adventurous diners might try **curried goat,** the longtime classic West Indian dinner prepared with herbs, cardamom pods, and onions. The famous **johnnycakes** that accompany many fish and meat dishes are made with flour, baking powder, shortening, and salt, then fried or baked. Similar to a johnnycake but more like an empanada is **pattie/pate**

Flavorful West Indian cooking at St. Thomas's Petite Pump Room (p. 87).

(pronounced *pah-tay*). Fillings include saltfish, ham, and cheese. You can find good ones at **Ashley's** near the airport (p. 93).

Way back when, locals gave colorful names to the various fish brought home for dinner, everything from "ole wife" to "doctors," both of which are whitefish. "Porgies and grunts," along with yellowtail, kingfish, and bonito, also show up on many Caribbean dinner tables. Fish is often boiled in a lime-flavored brew seasoned with hot peppers and herbs, and is commonly served with a Creole sauce of peppers, tomatoes, and onions, among other ingredients. **Conch** shows up on the menu in all sorts of interesting manifestations; every restaurant has its own version of **conch fritters. Saltfish and rice** is an excellent low-cost dish; the fish is flavored with onion, tomatoes, shortening, garlic, and green peppers. **Saltfish salad,** traditionally served on Maundy Thursday or Good Friday, consists of boneless salt fish, potatoes, onions, boiled eggs, and an oil-and-vinegar dressing. **Herring gundy,** another old-time island favorite, is a salad made with salt herring, potatoes, onions, green sweet and hot peppers, olives, diced beets, raw carrots, herbs, and boiled eggs.

Ground provisions is the name for starchy vegetables introduced by the British that have sustained islanders during lean times. These include **breadfruit, cassava, dasheene, and sweet potatoes. Okra** (often spelled *ochroe* in the islands) is a mainstay vegetable, usually accompanying beef, fish, or chicken. It's often fried and flavored with hot peppers, tomatoes, onions, garlic, and bacon fat or butter. **Accra,** a popular dish, is made with okra, black-eyed peas, salt, and pepper, all fried until they're golden brown. **Sweet potato**

pie is a Virgin Islands classic, made with sugar, eggs, butter, milk, salt, cinnamon, raisins, and chopped raw almonds.

The deliciously exotic **fruits** of the islands are fabulous alone or as fresh-squeezed juices. Many are seasonal. Summertime is the best time for **mango** and **genip** (pronounced *kenip*), an almost candy-like little fruit. In the spring, enjoy **sugar apples** and **passionfruit.** In the fall, look for **papaya** and **soursop.** Other island fruits include **guava, prickly pear,** and **tamarind** (has a chocolatey flavor). Sometimes dumplings made with **guava, peach, plum, gooseberry, cherry, or apple** are served for dessert.

The B.V.I. in particular has a number of inexpensive **roti** joints, serving up East Indian–style wholewheat flatbreads stuffed with curried chicken, fish, or potatoes and peas. Try **Naturally Tasty by RotiMan** near the Road Town ferry terminal (p. 255).

Virgin Islanders like their **hot sauce** (aka "pepper" sauce), and many island cooks prepare and bottle their own, a number of which are available for sale in stores around the islands. Foodies and bloggers have a field day defending their favorites, including **Miss Anna's** (St. John), **Blind Betty's** (St. Croix), **Jerome's** (St. Thomas), and **ValleyDoll** (St. John). Even Miss Gladys, proprietor of **Gladys' Café** in St. Thomas (p. 86), makes and bottles her own hot-sauce concoctions in such flavors as mango, mustard, and tomato and sells them in her restaurant. **St. John Spice** (stjohnspice.com), on the harbor in Cruz Bay, has a good selection of bottled hot sauces, which make great gifts to take home.

Drinks

The islands' true poison is **rum.** To help stimulate the local economy, U.S. Customs allows you to bring home an extra bottle of local rum, in addition to your usual 5-liter liquor allowance.

Long before the arrival of Coca-Cola and Pepsi, many islanders concocted their own fruit drinks using whatever fruit was in season. Fresh fruit concoctions are ubiquitous on menus today. American sodas and beer are sold in both the U.S. Virgin Islands and the British Virgin Islands. Beer, wine, and liquor are sold in grocery stores.

Water is generally safe to drink on the islands. Much of the water is stored in cisterns and filtered before it's served. Still, delicate stomachs should stick to bottled water or club soda. Some resorts have their own desalination plants, providing water that is delicious and highly drinkable.

RESPONSIBLE TRAVEL

Many of the islands were clear-cut in the 1700s to make way for sugar plantations, destroying much of the natural landscape. All through the 1900s, while real estate developments on St. Thomas continued to mushroom, little concern was given to preserving and sustaining the natural resources of the U.S.V.I. Today, particularly in the massive rebuild after the 2017 hurricanes, local governments and private industry are taking sustainable development and preservation of the island ecosystem more seriously than ever before.

MARINE PROTECTIONS   The sparkling marine waters of the Virgin Islands require special stewardship. On St. John, the National Parks Service is particularly protective of its marine assets. The B.V.I. is a leader in environment regulations regarding the islands' pristine seas. The use of **jet skis** is not allowed in the marine parkland around St. John and was until recently banned in the B.V.I., where they can now only be operated in controlled environments. Boaters are asked to anchor using mooring balls, or, if you must anchor, look for a sandy bottom that's clear of coral or seagrass meadows where sea turtles feed. Do not anchor or tie your boat to mangroves. Don't drag dinghies onto the beach; look for dinghy moorings or docks. Never throw trash, particularly plastic, overboard (turtles choke on plastic bags). Divers and snorkelers should take care not to touch or accidentally brush up against delicate coral.

ECO-ADVENTURES   Low-impact activities like **hiking, snorkeling,** and **kayaking** are hugely popular in the Virgin Islands. The St. Thomas–based **Virgin Islands Ecotours** (viecotours.com; © **877/845-2925**) offers tours with professional naturalists of the protected mangrove lagoon Cas Cay on St. Thomas, and kayaking, snorkeling, and hiking tours on St. John's North Shore and East End. On Tortola, **Hike BVI** offers eco-treks into bamboo meadows, up Sage Mountain, and around Shark Bay. Based in Jost Van Dyke, **Jost Van Dyke Scuba** (jostvandykescuba.com; © **284/443-2222**), in partnership with BVI Eco-Tours, has a variety of guided tours, including snorkeling, bird-watching, sightseeing, snorkeling and diving.

ECO-LODGINGS   A number of truly eco-friendly lodgings are found on the islands. On St. John, you can stay in eco-tents and campsites on the beach at **Cinnamon Bay** (p. 204) or in rustic ridge-line tents and environmentally friendly villas at **Concordia Eco Resort** (p. 199). On St. Croix, **Mount Victory Camp Eco-Lodge** (p. 148) relies on renewable energy to power its cottages.

The British Virgin Islands are less developed than their American cousins, and lodgings there have long touted their eco-friendly bona fides. The **Cooper Island Beach Club** (p. 248) meets the middle ground between luxury and roughing it. All of **Guana Island** (p. 307), a private resort, is a wildlife sanctuary watched over by attentive owners (it even has its own organic orchard and a smattering of flamingoes in the salt pond). **Lovango Cay** (p. 210) is off the grid and makes its own highly potable water.

VOLUNTEER VIRGIN ISLANDS   A number of Virgin Islands environmental nonprofits and organizations offer volunteer opportunities. The B.V.I. in particular has a number of very active eco-nonprofits that promote local conservation and sustainability practices. They include:

- **Association of Reef Keepers (ARK)** (www.bviark.org; ⓒ **284/546-0164**): For 25 years, ARK has been focused on protecting the sustainability of the islands' marine environment and coral reef conservation. Its active programs include coral restoration, protecting sea turtle nesting sites, and maintaining sustainable cruising and yachting practices.

- **Beyond the Reef** (https://1beyond thereef.com; ⓒ **284/346-1444**): Beyond the Reef is involved in ocean clean-up and coral restoration and creates groundbreaking Art Reefs (artificial underwater reefs)—like the *Kodiak Queen,* a WWII-warship-turned-undersea-art-gallery off Virgin Gorda, and the *Willy T,* a wooden schooner festooned with sculptures and sunk near Peter Island in 2019—to create what they call "an interactive experience for scuba divers." It's also a money-raiser—a $5 admission fee to dive these Art Reef sites goes straight to B.V.I. kids' swim programs. Beyond the Reef has

Eco-conscious "art reefs" around the B.V.I. have been created by Beyond the Reef.

pulled together such events as an Anegada Beach Cleanup in 2022, which attracted nearly 300 volunteers. And, in a partnership with Commercial Dive Services, it's clearing B.V.I. waters of abandoned fishing gear—which comprises half the ocean trash and ensnares marine wildlife.

- **Green VI** (greenvi.org; ⓒ **284/346-4040**): Green VI is involved in waste projects like the much-loved **Glass Studio** (scheduled to reopen 2025), in which glass blowers turn waste bottles into beautiful works of art. It promotes energy renewables (like biofuels and the solar tree on display in the Noel Lloyd Action Park on Tortola) and the reduction of water pollution.

- **Friends of the Virgin Islands National Park** (friendsvinp.org; ⓒ **340/779-4940**): This nonprofit partners with the U.S. Virgin Islands NPS in actively seeking volunteers to help in trail maintenance, its sea turtle program, and beach cleanups. It also has an Artist-in-Residence program on St. John that works with young Virgin Islanders.

- **The Nature Conservancy: Virgin Islands** (www.nature.org/en-us/about-us/where-we-work/caribbean/virgin-islands/; ⓒ **305/445-8352**): A 1730s-era Danish plantation on St. Croix is the preserve of this worldwide nonprofit. **Estate Little Princess** is home to the Coral Innovation Hub, a ground-breaking "coral laboratory" for undersea coral conservation. The

Sustainable Eating

It takes a whole lot of fossil fuels to import food onto these remote islands. That's why it's heartening to see the rebirth of small farms and sustainable farming throughout the Virgins, a movement that is catching fire in particular on St. Croix, with its farmers markets, farm co-ops, and **Virgin Islands Sustainable Farm Institute** (vi.locallygrown.net). On St. Thomas, West End farms in Estate Bordeaux are using government grants to increase capacity in the loamy volcanic soil. You can do your part in saving energy by eating local whenever you can: dining on seafood caught in and around the waters of Virgin Islands and buying produce and fruit from the weekly farmers markets and produce stands.

plantation ruins are also a lab for masonry apprentices hard at work restoring 18th-century walls of coral and limestone.

o **Ridge to Reef Farm** (www.ridge2reef.org; ℂ **340/473-1557**): Growing organic fruits and vegetables and raising livestock, these St. Croix farmers are passionate community activists for eating sustainable, organic, and local, with regular "slow down" farm dinners starring local chefs and live music. Day volunteers are welcome, and farm and agritourism internships are offered.

o **St. Croix Environmental Association** (SEA; www.stxenvironmental.org; ℂ **340/773-1989**): This nonprofit conservation- and education-minded group does a lot of work with island schoolchildren, hosting sea turtle projects, eco-fairs, snorkel clinics, and kayak excursions.

WHEN TO GO
Weather

Sunshine and warm temperatures are practically an everyday affair in the Virgin Islands. Temperatures climb into the 80s (high 20s Celsius) during the day and drop into the more comfortable 70s (low 20s Celsius) at night. Winter is generally the dry season in the islands, but rainfall can occur at any time of the year. You don't have to worry too much, though—tropical showers usually come and go so quickly you won't even really notice. November is traditionally the wettest month—if you're out exploring for the day, you may want to bring an umbrella or rain hat just in case.

HURRICANES The hurricane season, the dark side of the Caribbean's beautiful weather, officially lasts from June to November. It peaks in September and October. The Virgin Islands chain lies in the main pathway of many a hurricane raging through the Caribbean, and the islands are often hit. If you're planning a vacation in hurricane season, stay abreast of weather conditions and consider investing in trip-cancellation insurance.

Islanders certainly don't stand around waiting for a hurricane to strike. Satellite forecasts generally give adequate warning to both residents and visitors. And of course, there's always prayer: Islanders have a legal holiday in the third week of July called Supplication Day, when they ask to be spared from devastating storms. In late October, locals celebrate the end of the season on Hurricane Thanksgiving Day.

Average Temperatures & Rainfall (in.) for St. Thomas

	JAN	FEB	MAR	APR	MAY	JUNE	JULY	AUG	SEPT	OCT	NOV	DEC
TEMP (°F)	77	77	77	79	79	82	82	83	82	83	81	77
TEMP (°C)	25	25	25	26	26	28	28	28	28	28	27	25
RAINFALL (IN.)	1.86	.95	.97	8.32	9.25	1.62	2.25	3.6	2.04	4.43	7.77	2.46

The High Season & the Off Season

High season (or winter season) in the Virgin Islands, when hotel rates are at their peak, runs roughly from late November to May. Package and resort rates are at their highest during the Christmas holidays. February is the busiest month. If you're planning on visiting during the winter months, make reservations as far in advance as possible.

Off season traditionally begins when North America starts to warm up, and vacationers, assuming that temperatures in the Virgin Islands are soaring into the 100s (upper 30s Celsius), head for less tropical local beaches. However, the Virgin Islands are actually quite balmy year-round, thanks to the fabled trade winds—with temperatures varying little more than 5° between winter and summer. There are many advantages to off-season travel in the Virgin Islands. First, from mid-April to mid-December, hotel rates are slashed—often in half. Second, you're less likely to encounter crowds at beaches, resorts, restaurants, and shops. A slower pace prevails in the off season, especially in St. Croix and St. Thomas, and you'll have a better chance to appreciate the local culture and cuisine. These advantages, plus a raft of exciting summer festivals, is making **summer in the Virgins increasingly more popular,** bumping right up into high hurricane season, when **most island businesses shut down for a couple of months** (around mid-August into mid-October), many using this time for construction and/or restoration or just heading out into the world for some R&R.

The social scene in both the B.V.I. and the U.S.V.I. is intense from mid-December to mid-April. After that, it slumbers a bit. If you seek escape from the world and its masses, summer is still the way to go.

Holidays

In addition to the standard legal holidays observed in the United States, **U.S. Virgin Islanders** also observe the following holidays: Three Kings' Day (January 6); Transfer Day, commemorating the transfer of the Danish Virgin Islands to the Americans (March 31); Organic Act Day, honoring the legislation that granted voting rights to the islanders (June 20); Emancipation Day, celebrating the freeing of the slaves by the Danish in 1848 (July 3); Hurricane Supplication Day (July 25); Hurricane Thanksgiving Day (October 17); Liberty Day (November 1); and Christmas Second Day (December 26). The

Virgin Islanders celebrate Carnival several times a year. St. Croix's "Mardi Croix" takes to the streets in February.

islands also celebrate 2 Carnival days on the last Friday and Saturday in April: Children's Carnival Parade and the Grand Carnival Parade.

In the **British Virgin Islands,** public holidays include the following: New Year's Day, Commonwealth Day (March 12), Good Friday, Easter Monday, Birthday of the Heir to the Throne (June 21), Whitmonday (sometime in July), Territory Day Sunday (usually July 1), Festival Monday and Tuesday (during the first week of August), St. Ursula's Day (October 21), Christmas Day, and Boxing Day (December 26).

The Virgin Islands Calendar of Events

FEBRUARY

Mardi Croix, St. Croix. This colorful Mardi Gras–style parade starts in La Vallee and ends at Cane Bay Beach on the North Shore. Go to www.gotostcroix.com/events/mardi-croix. First Saturday before Fat Tuesday and Ash Wednesday.

BVI Wreck Week, B.V.I. It's a dive party in the B.V.I. with divers descending on the islands to celebrate famed local wrecks and the local maritime history. Expect curated

dives, scuba/resort packages, a Pirate Party at Hendo's Hideout (Jost), a closing barbeque at Nanny Cay (Tortola), and events at celebrated spots like Cooper Island and Bitter End Yacht Club (Virgin Gorda). See bvi-wreckweek.com. Mid-February.

MARCH

St. Thomas International Regatta (STIR), St. Thomas. This is one of three regattas in the Caribbean Ocean Racing Triangle (CORT) series. Top-ranked international racers come to St. Thomas to compete in front of the world's yachting press. The St. Thomas Yacht Club has hosted the 5-day event for nearly 50 years. Visit stthomasinternationalregatta.com. Late March.

Transfer Day, U.S.V.I. This holiday commemorates the day the U.S. Virgins were transferred from Denmark to the United States. On this day, vendors sell Danish products, and visits to the remains of Danish ruins and forts are arranged. Visit www.stcroixlandmarks.org. March 31.

B.V.I. Spring Regatta & Sailing Festival, Tortola. This is the third of the CORT events (see St. Thomas International Regatta, above). A range of talents, from the most dedicated racers to bareboat crews out for "rum and reggae," participate in the 7-day race. Contact the B.V.I. Spring Regatta Committee in Tortola at ℂ **284/541-6732,** or sail over to bvispringregatta.org for information. 7 days in late March/early April.

Virgin Gorda Easter Festival, Virgin Gorda. Easter weekend is a big event on Virgin Gorda, featuring a Cultural Food Fair, street parades, entertainment, and nonstop partying. Arrive on Good Friday, Holy Saturday, or Easter Sunday, and you should have no trouble finding the party. Easter weekend.

Virgin Islands Carnival, St. Thomas. This annual celebration on St. Thomas, with origins in Africa, is the most spectacular and fun carnival in the Virgin Islands. "Moko Jumbies," people dressed as spirits atop stilts nearly 20 feet high, parade through the streets. Steel and fungi bands, "jump-ups," and parades are part of the festivities. Events take place islandwide, but most action is on the streets of Charlotte Amalie. For a schedule of events, visit www.facebook.com/USVI-Festivals. After Easter.

St. Croix International Regatta, St. Croix. Celebrating its 30th anniversary in 2023, this 3-day regatta is held at the St. Croix Yacht Club on Teague Bay. It draws serious yachties from the B.V.I., the U.S.V.I., and Florida. Visit www.stcroixyc.com for details. Mid-April.

Agrifest: St. Croix Agricultural Fair, St. Croix. Celebrating its 50th year, this 3-day festival is one of the island's highlights, a family-friendly event featuring music, crafts, and lots of locally made food and island-grown produce. Go to www.viagrifest.org for details. Memorial Day weekend.

St John Festival (Carnival), St. John. This month-long cultural event takes place on St. John, with steel-pan concerts, calypso shows, parades, beauty pageants, and fireworks displays. For more information, call ℂ **800/372-USVI** [8784]. The carnival begins the first week of June and lasts until July 4.

King of the Wing, St. Thomas. Magen's Bay is the site of the battle for the island's tastiest chicken wings, a 1-day annual charity event that in 2022 drew a crowd of 8,000 people. The winner that year was Barefoot Buddha's guava sweet 'n' sour barbecue wings. It's held from noon to 5pm. For details, go to www.kowvi.com. Second Saturday in June.

Mango Melee and Tropical Fruit Festival, St. Croix. Mango aficionados and devotees of other tropical fruit converge here for tastings, cooking demonstrations, and contests at the St. George Village Botanical Gardens. For more information, call ℂ **340/692-2874.** Early July.

Independence Day, St. John. The elements of Carnival are combined with emancipation and independence celebrations in this festive event, which culminates on July 4 with a big parade. Thousands of St. Thomas residents flock to St. John for parades, calypso bands, colorful costumes, and events leading up to the selection of Ms. St. John and the King of the Carnival. Call the St. John tourist office at ℂ **340/776-6201** for details. July 4.

One Virgin Islands Poker Run, B.V.I. "Poker runs" are charitable competitions where participants travel from one checkpoint to another collecting playing cards, competing for the best winning hand. The mode of transportation: boats, the faster and sleeker the better. Competitors make stops at beach bars in Tortola, Jost, Virgin Gorda, and Trellis Bay. This 3-day-weekend festival, with music, fashion shows, and cash prizes, raises monies for local schools. The 2022 race drew 150 boats. Go to www.onevipokerrun.com for more details. Mid-July.

AUGUST

B.V.I. Emancipation Festival Celebrations, Tortola and around the islands. This glittery 10-day Carnival-style party celebrates the 1834 Emancipation Act that abolished slavery in the British Virgin Islands. Join locals as they dance to soca and reggae bands, and take part in the pageantry, from the Emancipation Day Parade to boat races, torchlight processions, donkey races, and other festivities. Go to www.bvitourism.com or caribbeanevents.com/event/bvi-emancipation-festival. Late July and early August.

SEPTEMBER

Love City Car Show, St. John. This fun car show at the Coral Bay Ballfield features some 200 vintage cars, from dune buggies to Volkswagen bugs. Food, drink, and DJ'd music, plus awards—including a "Best Junker" prize. Admission $7 adults, $3 kids (includes a free Matchbox car). For more, go to www.lovecitycarshow.com. Labor Day Monday.

Scrub Island Billfish Invitational, B.V.I. These two 3-day fishing tournaments leave from the Scrub Island Marina and head to the vaunted North Drop for peak marlin action. Go to www.scrubislandinvitational.com. Late August or early September.

NOVEMBER

Paradise Jam College Basketball Tournament, St. Thomas. Big-time college hoops action is the draw at this men's and women's basketball tournament held at the University of the Virgin Islands Sports & Fitness Center. Past teams have included Kansas, Duke, Providence, and Maryland. For information, go to www.facebook.com/ParadiseJam1. Mid- to late November.

Cane Bay Music Festival, St. Croix. This North Shore festival has a full lineup of musicians on multiple stages. Go to www.visitusvi.com. Last week in November.

Anegada Lobster Fest, B.V.I. It's a 2-day beach party and scavenger hunt on the white sands of Anegada to celebrate the island's famously sweet Caribbean lobster. Go to www.bvitourism.com/events. Last weekend in November.

DECEMBER

Crucian Christmas Festival (Carnival), U.S.V.I. This major event launches the beginning of a 12-day celebration that includes the **Christmas Boat Parade** (Dec. 10; Christiansted harbor) and the **Crucian Christmas Festival** (Dec 31–Jan 7; Frederiksted Carnival Village and around the island), with calypso music, parades, horse races, food fairs, and fireworks. It finishes with the Feast of the Three Kings (Jan. 6), a parade of flamboyantly attired merrymakers. For info, go to www.facebook.com/USVIFestivals.

Foxy's Old Year's Night, Jost Van Dyke, B.V.I. It's a mega-party on Jost's Great Harbour as Foxy rings in the New Year with weekend-long events, from a Caribbean barbecue to DJ music on the beach to a 2013 headliner concert that showcased Bunny Wailer. For information, go to foxysbar.com. December 31.

SUGGESTED ITINERARIES

Sprinkled scattershot between the Caribbean and Atlantic oceans, the Virgin Islands mark the easternmost point of the Lesser Antilles, part of a necklace of islands that stretches southeast from Cuba and curls back west again at Trinidad and Tobago. Despite being the progeny of two different nations, the U.S. and British Virgin Islands have a brotherly closeness—not only are the islands a breezy ferry ride or plane hop away from one another, but you're almost always eyeballing another Virgin Island no matter where you are. From Jost Van Dyke you can watch the glittering lights of cars weave along the coastal road of St. Thomas; from Tortola's West End the broad-shouldered hills of St. John are a comforting constant.

The two island chains share the same sparkling waterways, the same marine playgrounds, the same balmy trade winds. You'll find the same classic island dishes on restaurant menus and hear the same lilting rhythms in ramshackle beach bars. And the islands all share the same somber history of colonization, the sugar trade, and slavery—vestiges of centuries-old plantations crop up everywhere you go.

It's easy to visit both on the same trip: Ferries connecting St. Thomas, St. John, Tortola, and Virgin Gorda run regular routes and even link up to some of the smaller islands, such as Anegada and Jost Van Dyke, albeit on a limited, seasonal basis. Still, don't expect things here to run with the efficiency of a Swiss clock. During the pandemic, many routes were cancelled or severely limited, though at press time ferry schedules were slowly returning to business as usual; please **check updated ferry schedules closely and plan your itinerary accordingly.**

THE U.S. VIRGIN ISLANDS FOR FAMILIES

You could easily spend a week or more in each of the U.S. Virgins—St. Thomas, St. Croix, and St. John—and still have plenty more to do and see. It is, however, possible to sample all three islands with this 10-day itinerary. Ferries between St. Thomas and St. John run regularly all day long (it's just a 20-minute trip from Red Hook on

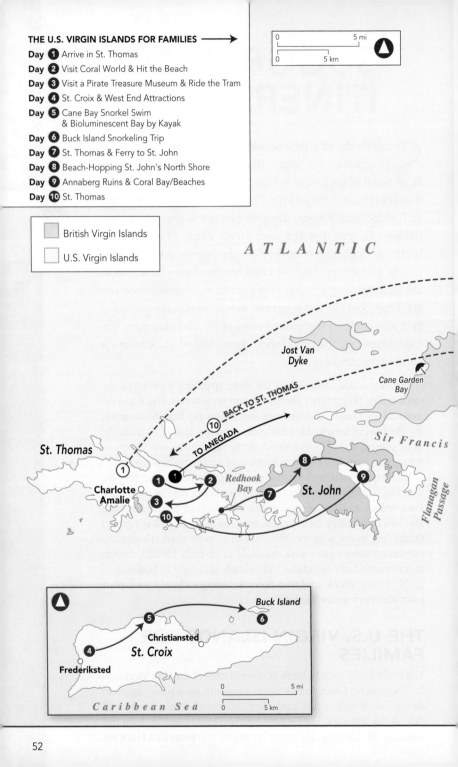

THE U.S. VIRGIN ISLANDS FOR FAMILIES ➔

Day **1** Arrive in St. Thomas
Day **2** Visit Coral World & Hit the Beach
Day **3** Visit a Pirate Treasure Museum & Ride the Tram
Day **4** St. Croix & West End Attractions
Day **5** Cane Bay Snorkel Swim
      & Bioluminescent Bay by Kayak
Day **6** Buck Island Snorkeling Trip
Day **7** St. Thomas & Ferry to St. John
Day **8** Beach-Hopping St. John's North Shore
Day **9** Annaberg Ruins & Coral Bay/Beaches
Day **10** St. Thomas

British Virgin Islands
U.S. Virgin Islands

0   5 mi
0   5 km

ATLANTIC

Jost Van Dyke

Cane Garden Bay

St. Thomas

BACK TO ST. THOMAS

10

TO ANEGADA

Sir Francis

Charlotte Amalie

1   **1**   **1**   **2**   *Redhook Bay*

8

3

7   **St. John**   **9**

10

Flanagan Passage

Buck Island

5

6

Christiansted

4   **St. Croix**

Frederiksted

0   5 mi
0   5 km

Caribbean Sea

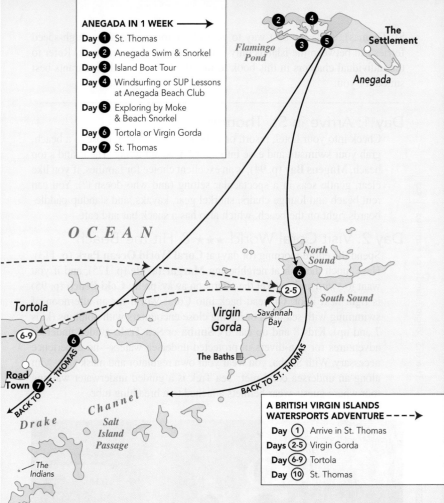

ANEGADA IN 1 WEEK ⟶
Day **1** St. Thomas
Day **2** Anegada Swim & Snorkel
Day **3** Island Boat Tour
Day **4** Windsurfing or SUP Lessons at Anegada Beach Club
Day **5** Exploring by Moke & Beach Snorkel
Day **6** Tortola or Virgin Gorda
Day **7** St. Thomas

The Settlement

Flamingo Pond

Anegada

O C E A N

North Sound

South Sound

Tortola

Virgin Gorda

Savannah Bay

The Baths

Road Town

BACK TO ST. THOMAS

BACK TO ST. THOMAS

Drake   Channel

Salt Island Passage

The Indians

Norman Island

Caribbean   Sea

A BRITISH VIRGIN ISLANDS WATERSPORTS ADVENTURE - - - - ⟶
Day ① Arrive in St. Thomas
Days ②-⑤ Virgin Gorda
Day ⑥-⑨ Tortola
Day ⑩ St. Thomas

Suggested Itineraries: The Virgin Islands

St. Thomas), while the best way to get to St. Croix is via plane; high-speed ferries run between the islands only once a day 2 or 3 days a week. Refer to the individual chapters in this book to find the lodgings and restaurants best suited for you.

Day 1: Arrive in St. Thomas

Check into your hotel, resort, or villa. If you're staying close to a beach, grab your swimsuit and ease into laidback island living. The island's top beach, **Magens Bay** (p. 94), is an excellent choice for families, if you like clear, gentle seas in a spectacular setting (and who doesn't?). You can rent beach and lounge chairs, snorkel gear, kayaks, and standup paddle-boards right on the beach, which also has a snack bar and cafe.

Day 2: Visit Coral World ★★★ & Hit the Beach

Spend the entire morning (or day) at **Coral World Ocean Park** (p. 113). Have lunch there or at neighboring **Margaritaville** (p. 125), and if you want to swim and snorkel the afternoon away, pretty **Coki Beach** (p. 95) is right next door. Or head back into Coral World for an afternoon of swimming with sea lions or having close encounters with dolphins (kids 7 and up). Kids 8 and up can try **Snuba** or **Sea Trek,** guided undersea adventures for non-divers in protected undersea waters—no experience necessary. With Snuba, you wear your own regulator and mask and swim along an undersea coral reef; Sea Trek is a guided underwater walking tour where guests wear helmets attached to a breathing tube.

Coral World's Sea Trek adventures let non-divers explore the sea floor.

Day 3: Visit a Pirate Treasure Museum ★★ & Ride the Tram ★★

Head to **Bluebeards Castle** resort and climb the stone stairs of one of the oldest structures on the island, a lookout keep that dates from 1685. Upstairs is the very cool **Bluebeard's Tower Museum** (p. 111), where a collection of undersea treasures brought up from the seas around St. Thomas include pieces of eight. Hit the pool or beach at your resort for a leisurely afternoon of swimming. Before sunset, take the tram ride on the **Paradise Point Skyride** (p. 112) and stay for dinner with a view.

Day 4: St. Croix ★★★ & West End Attractions

Take a morning flight from St. Thomas to St. Croix; airtime: 25 minutes. If you're traveling by seaplane (from the St. Thomas seaport), you'll land right on the Christiansted waterfront—and you should explore the island's East End from here (see "Day 5," below). If you fly on a regular air shuttle into the St. Croix airport, you'll be closer to West End attractions like the **St. George Village Botanical Garden** (p. 178) or the **Ridge to Reef** rainforest farm (p. 148). If you're staying on the West End, hit the beach, either at your lodging or at **Rainbow Beach** (p. 161) for snorkeling, kayaking, and swimming (you can rent water toys on the beach). If it's a Saturday or Sunday, take a dip at the beautiful beach at **Sandy Point** (p. 161; the wildlife refuge is closed during turtle nesting season April–September).

Day 5: Cane Bay Snorkel Swim ★★ & Bioluminescent Bay by Kayak ★★

Spend the morning at **Cane Bay Beach** (p. 160), on the island's North Shore, where you can snorkel right off the beach. Have lunch at the family-friendly open-air **Landing Beach Bar** (p. 152). If the moon cycle is right, schedule a see-through-kayak tour of the **bioluminescent bay** in the **Salt River National Historical Park and Ecological Reserve** (p. 163).

Day 6: Buck Island Snorkeling Trip ★★★

The only marine national park in the United States is well worth a day trip of fine snorkeling, swimming, and hiking. A number of excursion companies, including **Big Beard's Adventure Tours** (p. 186), offer full- and half-day sails to Buck Island National Reef Monument that often include beach barbecues.

Day 7: St. Thomas & Ferry to St. John ★★★

The seaplane out of St. Croix conveniently arrives at the seaplane terminal in Charlotte Amalie, located next door to the Charlotte Amalie ferry terminal. Ferries to St. John from here run far less frequently than ferries from Red Hook, at St. Thomas's East End, and take longer (45 min. as opposed to a pleasant 20-min. ride from Red Hook). It may be worth taking the Charlotte Amalie ferry, however, to avoid the sometimes

Gorgeous Trunk Bay is one of St. John's most visited beaches.

traffic-ridden taxi ride to Red Hook. Both ferries land at the dock at **Cruz Bay** (p. 191), St. John's main town.

If you're hungry, dine at one of the Cruz Bay waterfront eateries, like **High Tide Bar & Grill** (p. 209); your kids can play in the sand and sea while they're waiting for their meals. Pick up your rental Jeep here in Cruz Bay. St. John is a great place to rent a car for a few days, so you can fully explore its wonderful beaches and national parkland.

Then check in at your villa or resort—St. John's has a wide-ranging stock of rental villas, which can be an excellent option for families.

Day 8: Beach-Hopping St. John's North Shore ★★★

This is the day to **beach it,** and St. John has an abundance of excellent strands of sand for swimming, snorkeling, and exploring. The island's most famous beach, **Trunk Bay** (p. 215), has an underwater snorkeling trail, but you'll be happy with any of the great North Shore beaches, including Maho Bay, which has an abundance of turtles. Go to chapter 6 for more great beaches on St. John.

Day 9: Annaberg Ruins ★★★ & Coral Bay/Beaches ★★

It's just a 20-minute drive from Cruz Bay to Coral Bay, but you'll be busy in between. In the morning, stroll the **Annaberg sugar plantation ruins** (p. 226). Close to the ruins is **Leinster Bay/Waterlemon Cay** (p. 222), with great snorkeling and turtles.

Have lunch in the historic little settlement of **Coral Bay,** whether state-of-the-art conch fritters at the seaside at **Miss Lucy's** (p. 212) or juicy burgers at **Skinny Legs** (p. 213). Then head to the half-moon beach at

Salt Pond Bay (p. 217) for a leisurely afternoon of sunning and snorkeling.

Day 10: St. Thomas

Plan your ferry trip back to St. Thomas around your departure itinerary. Take the Red Hook ferry if you're staying overnight at an East End resort before flying home; ferry into Charlotte Amalie if you're going directly from there to the airport.

A BRITISH VIRGIN ISLANDS WATERSPORTS ADVENTURE

We guarantee that an 8-day week exploring the British Virgin Islands should erase all the stresses of modern civilization. Ten days to 2 weeks: Even better. This is a watersports paradise, with fantastic conditions for sailing, snorkeling, diving, kitesurfing, kayaking, standup paddleboarding, swimming—you name it.

Day 1: Arrive in St. Thomas

Currently the only direct flight into Tortola, the B.V.I.'s main island, is from Miami. For most people, St. Thomas (or San Juan) is the gateway to the British Virgin Islands. Remember to build time into your schedule to make the ferry or plane connections to your B.V.I. destination. Depending on your arrival into St. Thomas (or San Juan), that may include a night's stay-over.

Giant boulders create a stunning, intriguing seascape at the Baths, on Virgin Gorda.

Days 2–5: Virgin Gorda ★★★

We suggest starting your B.V.I. trip in Virgin Gorda, if the ferries (or plane connections) comply. If you're relying on ferries, you may have to take a ferry first to Tortola and then catch a second ferry to Virgin Gorda. The entire trip can take an hour or two, but cruising along on the beautiful Virgin Islands waterways is a wonderful way to ease into island time—and the scenery is unbeatable.

Break up your Virgin Gorda stay into two parts: the Valley and the North Sound. We recommend first exploring the watery attractions in and around the Valley—the **Baths and Spring Bay** (p. 288), **Savannah Bay** (p. 289), and **Mahoe Bay** (p. 289). Then spend 2 days exploring the island's other end—where you can sail or kitesurf the North Sound, snorkel around Prickly Pear Island, dive or snorkel Eustachia Reef, or take a **See It Clear glass-bottom-boat tour** with Gumption (p. 289). At some point, head up to **Hog Heaven** (p. 288) for a casual lunch with breathtaking views.

Days 6–9: Tortola ★★★

The British Virgin Islands' largest and most populous island, Tortola has a leisurely sensibility and uncrowded beaches. Base yourself in a villa or resort on the North Shore, like the **Wyndham Lambert Bay** (p. 252), or closer to the West End at the boutique **Sugar Mill Hotel** (p. 251) or the **Long Bay Beach Resort** (p. 250). Spend time swimming **Cane Garden Bay** (p. 261) or snorkeling **Smugglers Cove** (p. 260) or **Brewers Bay** (p. 261). Take a kayak snorkeling excursion in a secret lagoon with **Hike

Divers find fascinating reefs and wrecks to explore all around the B.V.I.

BVI (p. 266). From Tortola a number of boat outfitters do fabulous **snorkel-sail or scuba day trips** to the territory's beautiful cays and coves, including **Norman Island and the Indians** (p. 262), as well as to the fanciful new **"art reefs"** (p. 265) repurposed from hurricane wreckage.

It's also easy to do a half- or full-day trip from Tortola's West End to the nearby island of **Jost Van Dyke** (p. 292), where your day might be spent beaching it at White Bay, snorkeling tiny Sandy Spit, or hiking the 20-minute trail to the island's "bubbly pool," where waves splashing through a split in beachside cliffs create a natural jacuzzi effect.

Day 10: St. Thomas

Fly or take a short (45- to 60-min.) ferry ride from Tortola back to St. Thomas. Plan your return ferry trip around your departure itinerary. Keep in mind that the Charlotte Amalie ferry terminal is much closer to the airport than the Red Hook terminal, and traffic gridlock between the island's East End and West End (where the St. Thomas airport is located) is not uncommon.

ANEGADA IN 1 WEEK

Anegada is the kind of spellbinding place you'll want to really settle into and explore. If you're arriving by ferry, it's a little bit of a schlep to reach (if you fly into St. Thomas, you'll have to ferry to Tortola first and then take a second ferry from there). If money is no object, you can fly or helicopter directly into Anegada from St. Thomas or San Juan. Many people visit the island via boat charters, popping over just for the day or lingering for several days.

Day 1: St. Thomas/Tortola

If you're landing on St. Thomas in the afternoon, spend the night in St. Thomas and take the first ferry the next morning out to Road Town, Tortola, then catch the seasonal ferry from there to Anegada. If you're flying in later, you can probably still catch a ferry to Tortola, but you'll have to overnight there (see p. 246 for Tortola lodging options).

Day 2: Anegada Swim & Snorkel

Arrive in Anegada and settle into your lodging. Take a swim or snorkel on the beach at **Loblolly Bay** or **Cow Wreck Beach** (p. 300). Be sure to make reservations for dinner by 4pm, so you can dine out on Anegada lobster at any one of the island's many beachside bar/restaurants, whether **Big Bamboo, the Lobster Trap, Cow Wreck Beach Bar, Potter's,** or **Sid's Pomato Point** (p. 305).

Day 3: Island Boat Tour

Sign up for an **island boat tour** ★★ with either **Sherwin Walcott's Sea Adventures** (p. 306) or **Kelly's Land & Sea Tours** (p. 306). These half- and full-day powerboat sightseeing/snorkeling excursions might include "float snorkeling" **Horseshoe Reef** (p. 300), a visit to **Cow Wreck Beach** (p. 300), and seeing the **conch shell islands** (p. 304). Reserve your spot at dinner once more.

Day 4: Windsurfing or SUP Lessons at Anegada Beach Club

Anegada has some of the best conditions in the B.V.I. for kite and board sports ★★★. **Tommy Gaunt Kitesurfing** (p. 307) operates a full-service kitesurfing school at the **Anegada Beach Club** (p. 303), offering all levels of kiting and standup paddleboarding (SUP) lessons. You could spend an entire day here

Anegada's famous conch shell islands.

and have lunch at the resort's poolside restaurant. If it's 4pm, reserve dinner!

Day 5: Explore by Moke & Beach Snorkel a Beach

Most people rent **mokes or scooters** (p. 302) to fully explore Anegada, seeking out flamingoes and other big birds in the protected salt ponds of the island's interior. Spend the morning on your moke and have lunch at **Big Bamboo** or **Cow Wreck Beach Bar & Grill** (p. 305). Hit the beach in the afternoon at **Flash of Beauty** (p. 300) and explore the reef with snorkel gear.

Day 6: Tortola or Virgin Gorda

Take the ferry back to Road Town and spend the afternoon on a **taxi tour** (p. 245) of Tortola, or spend a last leisurely day swimming and snorkeling at **Smugglers Cove, Cane Garden Bay,** or **Brewers Bay** (p. 260).

Day 7: St. Thomas

Plan your return ferry trip back around your airport departure itinerary. Your best bet is likely taking the short (45- to 60-min.) ferry ride from Road Town, Tortola, to Charlotte Amalie, St. Thomas.

ST. THOMAS

St. Thomas may be the market hub and transportation gateway of the Virgin Islands, but it is much more than harbor bustle and commercial hustle. Rimmed in sparkling turquoise seas, the island offers plenty of diversions that leave the hubbub far behind. Yes, the 32-square-mile island is home to the busiest cruise-ship harbor in the West Indies. It's the business center and government seat of the U.S. Virgins. But more than any other Virgin Island, St. Thomas has something for everyone, from stunning beaches to mountain aeries.

An ambitious $146-million revitalization of the historic waterfront in the capital city, Charlotte Amalie, promises a smartly reinvigorated downtown and a world-class oceanside promenade, which *Caribbean Journal* has called "the next great Caribbean waterfront." By expanding the curving harborside roadway and seafront promenade, the Charlotte Amalie revamp is turning the attention back to the harbor, the true lifeblood of the island. It's an elegant facelift designed to "set the stage" for visitors, as one local historian puts it. It started with Main Street—longtime home to duty-free shops hawking jewelry and watches—which in 2021 was handsomely repaved with Eurocobble and native blue bitch stone. The redo is already attracting more commercial activity than downtown has seen in years. The harbor is certainly a vision at night, when the inky blue seas are ablaze with twinkling lights.

The island is also roaring back from 5 years of natural disasters and a global pandemic. *Caribbean Journal* named it the 2022 Innovative Destination of the Year for its "nimble and creative" response to the pandemic and its reimagining of downtown Charlotte Amalie. The island's main event, Carnival, is back in full, celebrating its 70th year in 2022. Already one of the Caribbean's most popular cruise destinations, in 2023 St. Thomas is expected to increase its volume of cruise passengers by 70%.

ESSENTIALS

Arriving

BY PLANE

If you're flying to St. Thomas, you will land at the **Cyril E. King Airport** (STT; www.viport.com/cekastt; ☎ **340/774-1629**), 3 miles

St. Thomas: Gateway to the Other Virgins

Most people who visit the other Virgin Islands—both U.S. and British—travel through St. Thomas to get there. Even if you plan to stay in St. Thomas your entire trip, day trips to one or several other islands should be high on your vacation agenda. St. Thomas has two ferry terminals: **Marine Terminal,** in Charlotte Amalie, and **Red Hook,** on the island's east end. A robust ferry system delivers passengers between the islands; see p. 314 for a list of ferries, their contact info, and where they go. To stay updated on ferry departure times, check the recent issue of the free weekly publication *This Week.* Keep in mind that everyone—including U.K. citizens—traveling to the British Virgin Islands needs a passport and must pay a $20-per-person passenger tax at departure.

(about a 15-min. drive) west of Charlotte Amalie's central business district on Route 30. From here, you can easily grab a taxi to your hotel or villa. Chances are you will be staying east of Charlotte Amalie, so keep in mind that getting through town often involves long delays and rush-hour traffic jams.

Many people flying from North American mainland cities and from overseas connect through Miami or San Juan, Puerto Rico. Flight time from Miami is about 2½ hours, from Puerto Rico (just 68 miles from St. Thomas) approximately 30 minutes.

Direct flights to the U.S. Virgin Islands are available on **American Airlines** (www.aa.com; © **800/433-7300** in the U.S.) from New York City, Boston, Miami, and San Juan. **Delta** (www.delta.com; © **800/221-1212** in the U.S.) offers direct flights from Atlanta and New York City. **JetBlue** (www.jetblue. com; © **800/538-2583**) has direct flights from Boston and San Juan. **United Airlines** (www.united.com; © **800/864-8331** in the U.S.) has direct flights from Chicago, Dulles (Washington, D.C.), Houston, and Newark. **Spirit Airlines** (www.spirit.com; © **855/728-3555**) has direct flights from Fort Lauderdale and Orlando. **Sun Country Airlines** (www.suncountry.com; © **651/905-2737**) has direct flights from Minneapolis/St. Paul.

Cape Air (www.capeair.com; © **800/227-3247** in the U.S. and U.S.V.I.) offers daily service between St. Thomas and San Juan, Puerto Rico, and has expanded its service to include flights between St. Thomas and both St. Croix and Tortola.

Seaborne Airlines/Silver Airways (www.seaborneairlines.com; © **801/401-9100**), now operating out of San Juan, is currently the major carrier between St. Thomas and St. Croix, offering regularly scheduled daily 20–25-minute flights on 34-seat turboprop planes and seaplanes carrying 15–17 passengers. Regular planes fly between Cyril E. King airport in St. Thomas and the Henry E. Rahlsen airport in St. Croix; seaplanes fly between the St. Thomas seaplane base (next to the Charlotte Amalie ferry terminal) and the St. Croix seaplane seaport in the Christiansted waterfront. Seaborne also flies between St. Thomas and Tortola (Beef Island), Anguilla, Dominica, San Juan, and St. Kitts.

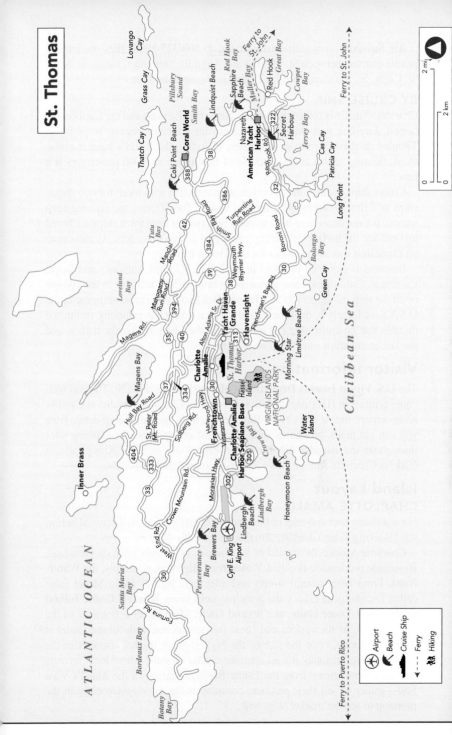

St. Thomas

Air Sunshine (www.airsunshine.com; ℂ **800/327-8900**) flies on-demand private charters between St. Thomas and Anguilla, Dominica, Nevis, St. Kitts, St. Croix, St. Maarten, Tortola, Virgin Gorda, and San Juan.

BY CRUISE SHIP

Charlotte Amalie is one of the world's busiest cruise ports and the Caribbean's largest duty-free port. Most major cruise lines include regular stops in St. Thomas on their Caribbean itineraries, including the world's biggest cruise ships, floating "cities at sea" capable of holding up to 6,000 passengers at a time.

Cruise ships dock at one of two major piers, each with room for two mega-ships at a time: **Havensight Pier** and **Crown Bay.** During the cruising high season, it's not unusual to have another one, two, or even three ships anchored just outside the harbor, delivering passengers ashore in tenders. At press time an expansion was in the works for the Crown Bay pier.

Business is expected to boom in 2023. The V.I. Port Authority and Royal Caribbean Cruise Line have partnered to bring a 70% increase in the volume of cruise ship passengers to St. Thomas. But know that cruise-shipping in the U.S.V.I. is largely a daytime activity: An island-wide gambling ordinance dictates that no cruise ship can overnight in the Charlotte Amalie harbor, and the last cruise ships must be gone by 10pm.

Visitor Information

The **U.S. Virgin Islands Department of Tourism** has three St. Thomas welcome centers: in Havensight Mall, in downtown Charlotte Amalie; at Cyril E. King airport; and at the Crown Bay Center, near the cruise ship dock. Here you can get maps, brochures, and even a list of legal shoreline fishing sites throughout the islands. Administrative offices are at 2318 Kronprindsens Gade in Charlotte Amalie (www.visitusvi.com; ℂ **340/774-8784**).

Island Layout

CHARLOTTE AMALIE

For a walking tour and map of the landmarks and attractions discussed below, see "Walking Tour: Charlotte Amalie," on p. 105.

Charlotte Amalie, the capital of St. Thomas, is the only town on the island. Its seaside promenade is called **Waterfront Highway,** or simply, the **Waterfront.** From here, several streets and alleyways lead to **Main Street** (also called Dronningens Gade), the principal links being **Raadets Gade, Tolbod Gade, Store Tvaer Gade,** and **Strand Gade.** Main Street is home to all the major shops. At its western end (near the intersection with Strand Gade) is **Market Square,** once the site of the biggest slave market auctions in the Caribbean Basin; today it's an open-air cluster of stalls where local farmers and gardeners—many from the Estate Bordeaux farms on the island's West End—gather to sell their produce. Saturday is the big day. Go early in the morning to see the market at its best.

From the Paradise Point Skyride (p. 112), passengers get sweeping views of Charlotte Amalie and its busy cruise port.

Running parallel to and north of Main Street is **Back Street** (also known as Vimmelskaft Gade), which is lined with a few stores and cafes. *Note:* It can be dangerous to walk along Back Street at night, but it's reasonably safe for daytime shopping.

In the eastern part of town, between Tolbod Gade and Fort Pladsen (northwest of Fort Christian), lies **Emancipation Park,** commemorating the liberation of the slaves in 1848. Most of the major historic buildings lie within a short walk of this park. Southeast of the park looms **Fort Christian.** Crowned by a clock tower and painted rusty red, it was constructed by the Danes in 1671. The **Legislative Building,** seat of the elected government of the U.S. Virgin Islands, lies on the harbor side of the fort. **Kongens Gade** (or King's Street) leads to **Government Hill,** which overlooks the town and St. Thomas Harbor. Here you'll find **Government House,** a white-brick building dating from 1867; **Hotel 1829** (a mansion built that year by a French sea captain); and a stone staircase known as the **Street of 99 Steps** that climbs to the summit of Government Hill.

WEST OF CHARLOTTE AMALIE

The most important of the outlying neighborhoods to the west of Charlotte Amalie is **Frenchtown,** which has a number of good restaurants and interesting bars. Some older islanders here still speak a distinctive Norman-French dialect. To reach Frenchtown, take Veterans Drive west along the waterfront, turning left (shortly after passing the Windward Passage Hotel on your right) at the sign pointing to Olga's Fancy.

Several mid-grade hotels lie to the immediate west of Charlotte Amalie, attracting visitors with more moderate hotel rates than those charged at the mega-resorts that dot the South Coast. The disadvantage in staying here is that you may have to depend on public transportation to reach the beach. The biggest attraction is that you'll be on the very doorstep of Charlotte Amalie, filled with restaurants, bars, shopping, and historic charm.

EAST OF CHARLOTTE AMALIE

Traveling east from Charlotte Amalie, along a sometimes traffic-clogged highway, you'll see St. Thomas Harbor on your right. If you stay in this area, you'll be in a tranquil setting just a short car or taxi ride from the bustle of Charlotte Amalie. The major disadvantage is that you must reach the sands by some form of transportation; if you want to run out of your hotel-room door onto the beach, look elsewhere.

THE SOUTH COAST

This fabled strip offers good, soft-sand beaches and full-service resorts, away from the bustle of Charlotte Amalie. If you feel the need for a shopping binge, cars, hotel shuttles, and taxis can quickly deliver you to Charlotte Amalie.

THE EAST END

The East End is reached by traversing a twisting road east of Charlotte Amalie. Once you're here, you can enjoy sea, sand, and sun with little to disturb you (the East End offers even more isolation than the South Coast). This section of bays and golden sands is the site of such lovely beaches as Sapphire Beach and Lindquist Beach. Here you'll find the luxe Ritz-Carlton resort as well as a smattering of smaller, less-expensive (and somewhat cookie-cutter) resorts and condos. The settlement at **Red Hook** is a bustling community with raffish charm and lots of seaside bars and affordable eateries. It is the departure point for ferries to St. John and Lovango Cay.

THE NORTH COAST

The renowned beach at **Magens Bay** lies on the lush North Coast. Be aware that the beach is often overrun with visitors, especially when cruise-ship arrivals are heavy. The North Coast has few buildings and not much traffic, but what it does have are scenic vistas, among the most panoramic on the island. Note that traveling the roads can be like riding a rollercoaster—the roads have no shoulders and can be especially scary for those not familiar with driving on the left. A lot of the northwest coast, especially at Botany Bay, Bordeaux Bay, and Santa Maria Bay, isn't linked to any roads. Estate Bordeaux has some beautiful, rural stretches of lush mountain farmland, where farmers raise produce and livestock in the loamy green hills.

Getting Around

Renting a car is a great way to see the island and save money on taxi fares. On average, a taxi costs $8 to $25 per person per trip, which can add up if you plan a couple of outings from your resort every day. On the other hand, roads on the island can be steep, narrow, poorly lit, and twisting (and often not in the best of shape), so driving St. Thomas can be a challenge even for experienced drivers—particularly at night. Plus, driving on the left can take a little adjustment for those used to driving on the right. The local driving adage is: "shoulder to shoulder"—your left shoulder should be to the shoulder of the road.

Also keep in mind that normal traffic congestion at rush hours in Charlotte Amalie is compounded by the morning arrival of sometimes thousands of cruise-ship passengers and the taxis and safari vans waiting to deliver them to their day's excursions. The good news is that the harborfront road has been expanded from two to four lanes, which has greatly diminished waterfront traffic.

BY CAR

Several leading North American **car-rental firms** have offices at the airport: **Avis** (www.avis.com; ✆ **800/331-1212** or 340/774-1468), **Budget** (www.budgetstt.com; ✆ **800/626-4516** or 340/776-5774), and **Hertz** (www.hertzstt.com; ✆ **340/774-1879**). **Thrifty** (www.thriftystt.com; ✆ **340/776-1500**) and **Dollar** (www.dollarstt.com; ✆ **340/774-0011**) are airport-adjacent (with free

Downtown Charlotte Amalie's bustling shopping streets thrive on the cruise-ship trade. See p. 117 for recommendations of shops that stand out from the crowd.

regular shuttles to the rental lot), meaning you may find better rates there. A recommended local car-rental firm is **Discount Car Rental,** 14 Harwood Hwy., located just outside the airport on the main highway (www.discountcar. vi; © **877/478-2412** or 340/776-4858), which offers a 12% discount when you book online. Its stable of cars includes SUVs and jeeps. *Note:* You need to be 25 years of age and older to rent a car in St. Thomas. U.S.-government-issued driver's licenses are valid for stays of up to 90 days.

DRIVING RULES   *Always drive on the left.* The speed limit is 20 mph in town, 35 mph outside town. Seat belts are required by law, and it's illegal to talk on cellphones while driving.

PARKING   Downtown Charlotte Amalie is a labyrinth of one-way streets, so driving in town can be slow going. If you can't find a place to park along the Waterfront (free), go to the sprawling lot to the east of Fort Christian, across from the Legislature Building. Parking fees are nominal here, and you can park your car and walk northwest toward Emancipation Park, or along the Waterfront, until you reach the shops and attractions.

BY TAXI

Taxi rates are set by the island's Taxi Association and fares are widely posted, even in taxis; check out the official fares in the free magazine *This Week* offered in most businesses. Look for officially licensed taxis only: You can spot them by their dome lights and the letters TP on the license plate. Still, be sure to confirm the rate with the driver before you get into the taxi. A typical fare from the airport to the Ritz-Carlton on the East End is $27 for one passenger and $18 each for two or more; from the airport to the ferry dock in Red Hook it's $23 per person ($17 each for two or more). Surcharges are added after midnight. Add on $2 per bag for luggage.

   Taxi vans and **open-air safaris** (converted truck beds with open-air seating) are ubiquitous around the island. Taxi vans are equipped to transport approximately 8 to 12 passengers to multiple destinations on the island, while safaris can often fit up to 26 people. It's cheaper to hop on a van or safari than ride a taxi on your own if you're going between your hotel and the airport, but keep in mind you will be making stops along the way—an exhausting proposition if you have arrived on a late flight. The cost for luggage ranges from $1 to $2 per bag. Call © **340/774-7457** to order a taxi van.

   It's easy to find taxi drivers. Just have your hotel or restaurant call a taxi for you, no matter where you are. Even better: Get the card of a favorite taxi driver and let him or her know your itinerary—or call the drivers we recommend below. Taxi drivers also make wonderful **sightseeing guides.** Prices for private tours depend on the number of passengers, the price of gas, and hours. A 2-hour sightseeing tour for one passenger is $55; for two or more it's $25 per person. A half-day tour that might include shopping, eating, and beach stops would start around $300.

   If you're looking for a taxi driver/tour guide, we recommend **Llewelyn Powell** (© **340/771-1568** or 776-3887) or **Tony Renal** (© **340/514-9083**).

You can also contact **Big Love Taxis** (✆ 340/201-7299). For 24-hour radio-dispatch taxi service with **V.I. Taxi Dispatch,** call ✆ 340/774-7457.

BY WATER TAXI

Getting around by **water taxi** is another way to travel. Longtime operator **Dohm's Water Taxi** unfortunately closed after the 2017 hurricane. **Dolphin Water Taxi** (www.dolphinshuttle.com; ✆ 340/774-2628) is a recommended private taxi service that offers land-water taxi services between the airport in St. Thomas and St. John and the B.V.I. A one-way water taxi from the airport to Cruz Bay, St. John, is $78 per person (airport taxi transfer $19, plus $59 for Red Hook water taxi to Cruz Bay). **SeaHorse Water Taxis** (seahorsevi.com; ✆ 833/340-0340 or 340/474-4905) also offers personalized land-water taxi services in the U.S.V.I. and B.V.I.

BY BUS

VITRAN public buses (www.vitranvi.com; ✆ 340/774-5678) run in the city and the country between 6:30am and 8:35pm daily, but waits can be long. Ride fares are $1.

ON FOOT

Walking is the best way to explore the historic section of Charlotte Amalie during the day—and the expansion of the waterfront promenade has created more harborside to stroll. You will need a car or taxi to reach many other island attractions, including Coral World and Magens Bay.

[FastFACTS] ST. THOMAS

Banks FirstBank Virgin Islands (www.1firstbank.com/vi/en; ✆ 866/695-2511) has two full-service locations on the island (with 24-hr. ATMs) at FirstBank Plaza and Port of Sale. FirstBank also has ATMs at Cyril E. King Airport, Schneider Hospital, and the Government Employees Retirement System (GERS) building. **Oriental** (formerly Scotiabank) (orientalbank.com/en/vi; ✆ 800/981-5554 or 340/774-0037) has several locations on St. Thomas, including a full-service branch at Altona and ATMs on the Charlotte Amalie waterfront and in the Havensight shopping mall, the

Ron de Lugo Federal Building, Red Hook Harbor, Nisky Shopping Center, and Tutu Park Mall. **Banco Popular** (www.popular.com/vi; ✆ 800/724-3655) has five full-service branches (including ATMs) at Hibiscus Alley, VI Popular Center, Sugar Estate, Fort Mylner, and Red Hook, plus additional ATMs at UVI Brewers Bay and Walgreens St. Thomas. Most island banks are open Monday to Thursday 8:30am to 3pm and Friday 8:30am to 4pm. Some banks have Saturday hours (9am–noon).

Business Hours
Increasingly, business and store hours are daily 9am to 5pm. Some shops close on

Saturdays at 1pm and others only open on Sunday for cruise-ship arrivals. Bars are usually open daily 11am to midnight, although since the pandemic many have been closing earlier than usual.

Dentists VI Dental Center, Foothills Professional Building, 9151 Estate Thomas, Ste. 203 (www.videntalcenter.com; ✆ 340/776-6056), has a team of dentists that are members of the American Dental Association. Call for information or an appointment.

Doctors Schneider Regional Medical Center, 9048 Sugar Estate, Charlotte Amalie (www.srmedicalcenter.org; ✆ 340/776-8311),

69

provides services for locals and visitors. For 24-hour medical care, call the **Red Hook Family Practice** (✆ 340/775-2303) or **Doctors on Duty** (✆ 340/776-7966).

Drugstores In business for more than 40 years, **Drug Farm Pharmacy** (www.drugfarmpharmacyinc.com; ✆ 340/7767098), at the Lockhart Gardens Shopping Center (4406 Weymouth Rhymer Hwy., Charlotte Amalie), is open Monday to Saturday 9am to 5:30pm and Sunday 9:30am to 2:30pm. **Walgreens** (4030 Annas Retreat; ✆ 340/777-9255) is open 7 days a week from 8am to 10pm.

Emergencies For the police, call ✆ **911;** ambulance, ✆ **911;** fire, ✆ **921.** To report a boating mishap, call the **U.S. Coast Guard Rescue** (✆ **787/729-2381;** after hours 787/510-7923), which operates out of San Juan, Puerto Rico. Scuba divers should note the number of a **decompression chamber** (✆ 340/776-8311) at the **Schneider Regional Medical Center** on St. Thomas.

Hospitals The **Schneider Regional Medical Center,** 9048 Sugar Estate,

Charlotte Amalie (www.srmedicalcenter.org; ✆ **340/776-8311**), is a 169-bed acute-care facility.

Newspapers & Magazines Copies of U.S. mainland newspapers, such as The New York Times, USA Today, and The Miami Herald, arrive daily in St. Thomas and are sold at newsstands. The Virgin Island Daily News (www.virginislandsdailynews.com) covers local, national, and international events. St. Thomas This Week, a magazine packed with visitor information, is distributed free on the island. A local online news site is The St Thomas Source (stthomassource.com).

Post Office The main post office is at 9846 Estate Thomas, Charlotte Amalie (✆ 340/774-1950) and is open Monday to Friday 7:30am to 5pm and Saturday 7:30am to noon. A second post office location, near the Emancipation Garden on 5046 Norre Gade, is book-ended by two wonderful WPA-era murals.

Safety The Virgin Islands are a relatively safe destination, but there has been an uptick in crime, including robberies and muggings, in Charlotte Amalie both during

and post-pandemic. Wandering the town at night, particularly on Back Street, is not recommended. Avoid frequenting Charlotte Amalie's bars alone at night. Store your valuables in hotel safes if possible, and keep doors and windows shut at night.

Taxes The only local tax is a 12.5% hotel tax.

Telephone All island phone numbers have seven digits. It is not necessary to use the 340 area code when dialing within St. Thomas. Numbers for all three islands, including St. John and St. Croix, are found in the U.S. Virgin Islands phone book.

Toilets You'll find public toilets at beaches and at the airport, but they are limited in town. Most visitors use the facilities of a bar or restaurant.

Transit Info Call ✆ 340/774-5100 for airport information and ✆ 340/776-6282 for information about ferry departures for St. John.

Weather For emergency (hurricane and disaster) weather reports, contact the **Virgin Islands Territorial Emergency Management Agency (VITEMA),** go to www.vitema.vi.gov, or call ✆ **340/774-2244.**

WHERE TO STAY

It's an exciting time for St. Thomas. The ambitious revitalization of Charlotte Amalie's waterfront is inducing hotel developers to invest in some of Charlotte Amalie's most interesting properties, including the International Plaza building. Also up for sale at press time was the historic Hotel 1829. Historically, Charlotte Amalie has been home to small inns and B&Bs, while the East

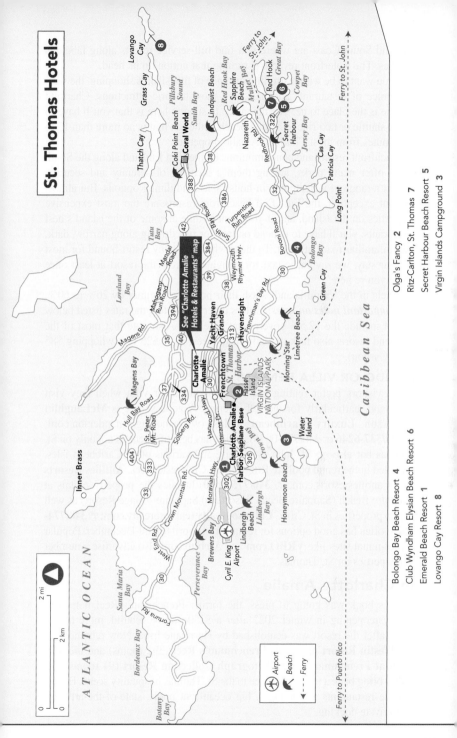

St. Thomas Hotels

Bolongo Bay Beach Resort 4

Club Wyndham Elysian Beach Resort 6

Emerald Beach Resort 1

Lovango Cay Resort 8

Olga's Fancy 2

Ritz-Carlton, St. Thomas 7

Secret Harbour Beach Resort 5

Virgin Islands Campground 3

See "Charlotte Amalie Hotels & Restaurants" map

End and South Coast are where you find full-service resorts along fabulous beaches. The waterfront revamp is turning that notion on its head.

If you want to be within strolling distance of the island's shopping, the widest choice of restaurants and bars, and most historic attractions, Charlotte Amalie is the place to be. The downside to staying here is that you'll have to take a shuttle or taxi ride to a good beach, although that is no more than 15 to 20 minutes from most Charlotte Amalie properties.

Beachfront resorts and condominiums on the East End and along the South Coast offer many perks, among them a measure of serenity and security. Expect a range of watersports, in-house spas, and dining options. But almost without exception, the East End beachfront resorts are the most expensive properties on the island, and if you want to dine at some of the island's best restaurants, you'll have to depend on taxis or risk driving along narrow, dark, and unfamiliar roads at night. To those who opt to stay resort-bound for most of their stay, we say call a taxi for a night out from the resort at least once while you're here.

Hotels in the Virgin Islands slash their prices in summer by 20% to 60%. *Two important notes on rates:* Unless otherwise noted, the rates listed below do not include the 12.5% government hotel tax. Also note that most of the high-end resorts also tack on daily resort fees, from $25 to a whopping $85 (Ritz-Carlton).

CONDO OR VILLA RENTALS

Many visitors prefer renting a condo, apartment, or villa when they visit the island, particularly for the self-catering. A good source is **McLaughlin Anderson Luxury Caribbean Villas** (www.mclaughlinanderson.com; ✆ **800/537-6246** or 340/776-0635), which has beautiful rentals not only on St. Thomas but also on St. John, St. Croix, and various other Caribbean isles. Included in the rental pool are Ritz-Carlton Club residences. **Antilles Resorts** (www.antillesresorts.com; ✆ **340/775-2600**) handles the property rentals at Sapphire Beach (Sapphire Beach Resort and Sapphire Village Resort) as well as two properties in St. Croix. **Calypso Realty** (calypsorealty.com; ✆ **340/774-1620**) often has good options for rentals from April to mid-December. Popular owner-rental sites like **VRBO.com** and **Airbnb.com** also advertise a number of properties on St. Thomas.

In Charlotte Amalie

As this book was going to press, the former Frenchman's Reef hotel was finally reopening in winter 2022 after a $250-million rebuild, more than 5 years after the resort was demolished by Hurricane Irma. Now rebranded as the **Westin Resort & Spa at Frenchman's Reef** (392 rooms) and the **Seaborn at Frenchman's Reef/Autograph Collection Resort** (94 rooms), the hotels bring back a major presence to the St. Thomas hospitality scene. Expect seaside restaurants and lounges, big oceanfront pools, state-of-the-art spas, and private docking.

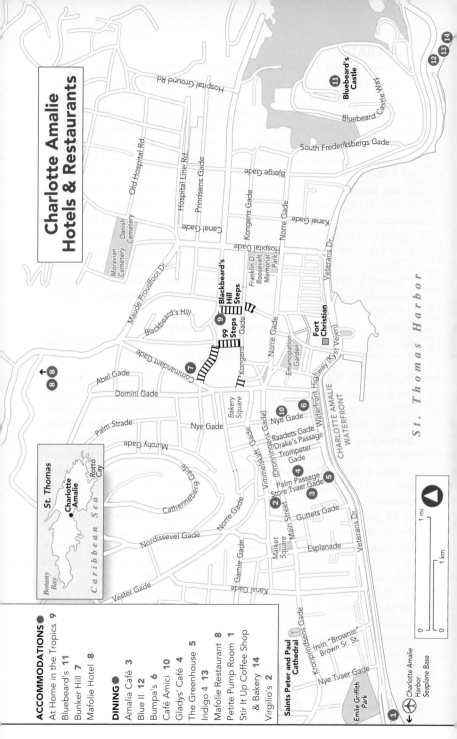

Charlotte Amalie
Hotels & Restaurants

St. Thomas

Botany Bay

Caribbean Sea

Charlotte Amalie

Rotto Cay

St. Thomas Harbor

73

MODERATE

At Home in the Tropics ★★   This award-winning guesthouse is one of the top B&Bs in the entire Virgin Islands, and with only four rooms, it can be a tough booking any time of year. It's set in a traditional West Indian house, with original lattice work and brick ballast and splendid views of Charlotte Amalie harbor. Dating from 1803 (it was originally the barracks for a Danish governor's private guard), the inn feels exclusive and private, with a small harborside pool and lovely rooms with tile floors and breeze-filled windows— the balmy trade winds are a constant, welcome presence. Breakfasts are legendary here, with treats such as breadfruit ginger muffins, broccoli cheese fritters, and banana pancakes, and the owners grow their own passionfruit, mangos, bananas, soursop, cherries, and gooseberries. The B&B is also largely off the grid, using recycled water and powered by solar panels. It's located right off a flower-filled step street up in the historic Blackbeard's Hill neighborhood, close to the shops and eateries of downtown Charlotte Amalie. The location along the step street might be challenging for those with mobility issues. The B&B is accessible by car or taxi, but the parking area/taxi drop-off is 18 steps up.

Blackbeard's Hill, 1680 Dronningens Gade. ✆ **877/7881803.** www.athomeinthetropics. com. 4 units. $245–$409 double. Rates include breakfast. Well-behaved children 15 and up only. **Amenities:** Outdoor swimming pool; free Wi-Fi.

Bluebeards Castle ★   There's a whole lot to like about Bluebeards, which is transforming its image from stodgy old timeshare to percolating destination resort. It's got an incredible location up on the Charlotte Amalie hillsides. Enjoying those fine views are two restaurants and a **Frenchtown Brewery** taproom. Bluebeards has historical bona fides: The property dates to the 1600s and is centered around one of the oldest castle towers in town, now a museum of undersea treasures. And a major renovation has turned studios and suites (many still individually owned) into surprisingly well-outfitted and comfortable lodgings, with excellent beds and private balconies for soaking up the dazzling views of the Charlotte Amalie harbor and hillsides. Our favorites are the spacious hilltop villas, with their west-facing vistas, but the building access is via a walkway and stairs that might challenge those with mobility issues. Bottom line, don't expect cutting-edge style or luxurious bathrooms and you'll be just fine. This is a buzzy beehive of a place, with a constant shuttle of visitors, locals, and taxi vans—and those views! It's within walking distance (down some steep hills) of the newly renovated waterfront and (a little farther down) the shops in downtown Charlotte Amalie, and the front-desk team stays on top of it all. This is good value in St. Thomas.

1331 Estate Taarneberg. www.bluebeards.com/st-thomas. ✆ **340/774-1600.** 166 units. Studios and suites $271–$479. **Amenities:** 2 restaurants; 2 bars; taproom; sundries store; concierge; fitness center; outdoor pool; free Wi-Fi.

Mafolie Hotel ★   This good-value gem sits high in the hills above Charlotte Amalie and its sparkling harbor—the views are splendid during the day

A traditional West Indian house makes a charming setting for the guesthouse At Home in the Tropics.

but off-the-charts gorgeous at night. The excellent **Mafolie Restaurant** (p. 85) is a big proponent of the island's farm-to-table movement with a menu featuring fresh local produce and just-off-the-boat seafood. The hotel is under new management, and room upgrades are in the works (including good Serta king and queen mattresses), but don't expect swank; in fact, some units are a little dark, "standard" rooms are just 250 square feet, and a handful must be entered on the road side of the resort. (They even tout "the island's tiniest room"—at 120 square feet, it's a bargain, with a full bed and those killer views.) Another concession: You're so high up you'll likely need a taxi or car to get down into Charlotte Amalie. Of the 22 rooms, 10 have outdoor balconies (ask for one), with those glittering harbor views at your feet; five are suites. The Mafolie pool and pool bar enjoy the same panoramic vista, so have a toast to life at the top.

7091 Estate Mafolie. www.mafolie.com. © **340/774-2790.** 22 units. $139–$239 double. Rates include breakfast. **Amenities:** Restaurant; 2 bars; concierge; pool; free Wi-Fi.

INEXPENSIVE

Bunker Hill ★   One of Charlotte Amalie's little hillside hotels, this economical, owner-operated hotel has its issues. If mobility is a challenge, know that the hotel is only accessible via a series of stairs (no elevator) and is laid out on different levels. Yet some people embrace the realities of a vintage, slightly outdated, perhaps maintenance-challenged hotel, especially when the location is prime and the price is right—and at Bunker Hill the rates are economical enough to live with the imperfections. Let's just say that Bunker Hill is one of those places that operates best when the owner is in the house, and yes, the economy rooms are cramped and the A/C units often rattle and hum. On the plus side, there's a sun-splashed deck with a little pool for cooling off, and the staff is very helpful and hospitable. The in-house restaurant, **The Green House,** serves a good island dinner 6 nights a week, the big family suites are bright and spacious, and four rooms have balconies. Among several outdoor sitting areas is a very pleasant dining terrace (full breakfast is included) with an old-fashioned awning and city vistas. One thing that never gets old are those Charlotte Amalie views of red-tile rooftops and robin's-egg skies.

2307 Commandant Gade. No website. ✆ **340/774-8056.** 27 units. $120–$150 double; $230 suite. Rates include breakfast. **Amenities:** Restaurant/bar; concierge; outdoor pool; free Wi-Fi.

Frenchtown
INEXPENSIVE

Olga's Fancy ★★ Owner Candy Giovans was raised at the top of the 99 Steps on Blackbeard's Hill; her father, a Greek immigrant, built the pool at Blackbeards. She is a brain trust for all things St. Thomas. Olga's Fancy—once part of the Danish governor's estate and later the Russian consulate, presided over by the ambassador's wife, Olga—literally rests upon layers of history: Beneath the lobby is a 300,000-gallon cistern from the early 19th century, and a number of native stone walls and outbuildings also date from that era. Part of the Hassel Island coal ship industry was here, where island women were tasked with moving buckets of coal atop their heads during WWII provisioning. Most of the hotel rooms are in two sections on the hillsides, reached via a series of outdoor stairs from the lobby and pool deck. The Pool View Rooms overlook downtown Charlotte Amalie and the seaplane terminal; the Ocean View Rooms on the inn's backside face the Caribbean sea and Water Island—these we love for their gorgeous patio views. For those with mobility issues, two Seaside King rooms across the road have minimal stairs and a private feel. Olga's is nothing, well, fancy—decor is basic but pleasant (comfy

Tropical breezes waft through the patios of Olga's Fancy.

beds) and bathrooms are small. The tropical-hued open-air lobby is the hotel's plant-filled beating heart, and the pool is mighty fine on a hot day. Candy and her husband, Eddie, will sell you a couple of cold Caribe beers for sipping around the pool, and you'll get to know the neighbors in no time. This is a great little find that's within walking distance of Frenchtown restaurants and bars (**Oceana,** p. 88, is practically in the inn's backyard), the seaplane pad, and the Charlotte Amalie ferries; it's close to the airport and a very doable stroll to Charlotte Amalie's historic downtown. A peach of a place and extra points for excellent value.

#8 Honduras, Frenchtown. www.olgasfancy.com. ✆ **340/643-4247.** 17 units. $119–$195 double. **Amenities:** Pool; free Wi-Fi.

West of Charlotte Amalie
MODERATE

Emerald Beach Resort ★   Yes, it's located just across from the airport, but for many visitors that's a big part of its draw—take a dip in the ocean, towel off, hop on a plane. This nicely landscaped 90-room resort also happens to front a very pretty white-sand beach, Lindbergh Bay, and its 90 rooms are "100% oceanfront"—meaning you get a private balcony facing the beach no matter which room you book. Rooms are sunny and comfortable, with tile floors and tropical accents. A complimentary shuttle service runs hourly into downtown Charlotte Amalie, 2 miles to the east. The pool looks out onto Lindbergh Bay. It has a casual beachfront seafood restaurant (**Caribbean Fusion**), a cafe serving coffee, breakfast, and smoothies, and a beach bar offering pizza, burgers, and other pub-style food. All in all, good value and good vibes.

8070 Lindbergh Bay. www.emeraldbeach.com. ✆ **340/777-8800.** 90 units. $160–$292 double. Children 11 and under stay free in parent's room. **Amenities:** Restaurant; 2 bars; fitness center; pool; tennis court; watersports; free Wi-Fi.

The South Coast
EXPENSIVE

Bolongo Bay Beach Resort ★   Bolongo Bay is a casual, barefoot kind of place. A complex of pink two-story buildings, it's built around a crescent-shaped beach on the sands of Bolongo Bay. That means plenty of watersports activities (even scuba-diving lessons). It's now the only all-inclusive in the Virgins, and that includes all meals and unlimited cocktails, beer, and wine—but you can also go the simple room-rate route and skip all-inclusive altogether. Both include complimentary access to the resort's watersports equipment, including snorkel gear, kayaks, windsurfers, Hobie Cats, and SUP. Bolongo Bay has some nice reef snorkeling. Of the resort's 74 rooms, 64 units face the beach, with king or queen beds and an oceanfront balcony or terrace opening onto the beach. Ten "value" rooms with double beds face the garden courtyard. All are simply furnished in summery rattan and have a fridge. On-site is the poolside restaurant and swim-up pool bar **Iggie's Oasis,** which features live music nightly from 6 to 9pm. Iggie's Beach Bar & Grill has remained closed since the 2017 hurricanes.

7150 Bolongo. www.bolongobay.com. © **800/524-4746** or 340/775-1800. 74 units. $435–$580 double European Plan; $550–$730 all-inclusive. **Amenities:** 2 restaurants; 2 bars; babysitting; children's programs (ages 4–12); exercise room; 2 outdoor pools; 2 tennis courts; watersports equipment/rentals; free Wi-Fi.

The East End
EXPENSIVE

The Ritz-Carlton, St. Thomas ★★★   For now, this is the island's one true luxury resort. Fronted by white-sand beaches and the protected turquoise waters of Great Bay, the Ritz covers a sprawling 30 acres of oceanfront on the southeastern tip of St. Thomas, 4 miles (a 30-min. drive) from Charlotte Amalie. Its centerpiece is a Venetian-style palazzo, surrounded by terraced gardens. Pathways lead down to the remodeled infinity pool and a beach with canopied chairs and bustling food and beverage services. All day long, the resort's aquatic toys see plenty of use on Great Bay, from stand-up paddleboards to Hobie Cats to kayaks to snorkel equipment—it's a veritable kids' playground, with a full-service dive shop, **Patagon Dive Center,** right on property. Lots of day-sail excursions leave right from the Ritz beach, including the property's own private 65-foot luxury catamaran, *Lady Lynsey*. The Ritz staff throughout is unparalleled. The resort offers daily fitness classes, from yoga to Pilates, and property walks.

Among the many luxuries at the Ritz-Carlton is an extensive spa with open-air cabanas.

The elegantly appointed main lobby has a chilly, generic feel, but the Ritz rooms are the island's best by far, supremely comfortable and spacious, with great big bathrooms (tubs and rain showers) and Frette linens. All rooms have bay views and private terraces. An extensive spa has luxurious treatment rooms and open-air cabanas. Of the restaurants, **Alloro** is an elegant space for fine Sicilian dining—its pastas are very good and reasonably priced—and **Sails** is a beautiful, lively seaside spot beneath a sweeping canopy of white sail. Lots of families love the **Ritz Club Level lodgings** for round-the-clock food and drink. But can I grouse a little about the (very wonderful) Ritz breakfast buffet in the **Bleuwater** restaurant? At these prices you'd think *something* would be complimentary, but no, the buffet costs a whopping $38 per person—tack that onto the daily $85 resort fee, and you're in deep. In addition to the 180 hotel rooms, the resort also has a number of Ritz-Carlton Destination Club timeshare villas.

6900 Great Bay. www.ritzcarlton.com/en/hotels/caribbean/st-thomas. ℭ **340/775-3333.** 180 units. $724–$1,039 double; $1,116–$1,539 Club Level double; $1,704 suite; $1,900–$4,639 Club Level suite. Daily resort fee $85. **Amenities:** 4 restaurants; 3 bars; market & sundries shop; ATM; babysitting; boutique; concierge; full-service health club and spa; 2 outdoor pools; room service; 2 tennis courts; watersports equipment/rentals; free Wi-Fi.

Secret Harbour Beach Resort ★

This boutique all-suites condo resort sits on the white-sand beach at Nazareth Bay, near Red Hook Marina, with excellent snorkeling just outside your door. The four low-rise buildings have

Aqua Action Dive Center offers diving, snorkeling, and stand-up paddleboarding on Nazareth Bay at the Secret Harbour Beach Resort.

southwestern exposure (great sunsets), and each room is beachfront or ocean view, mere steps from the sand (some bottom-floor suites even have outdoor showers on their patios). Each room and suite comes with a private deck or patio and a fully equipped kitchen. The resort rooms are individually owned, so it's impossible to say what the decor will be like, though most have attractive furnishings. There are four types of accommodations: studio suites, one-bedroom suites, two-bedroom suites, and three-bedroom suites. Each one- and two-bedroom suite has a pullout couch. Secret Harbour is also home to one of the best restaurants on the island, the **Sunset Grille** (p. 92). The resort has a full-service dive site on the premises, **Aqua Action Dive Center** (www. aadivers.com; ⓒ **340/775-6285**), which offers PADI courses, snorkeling equipment, and snorkeling outings.

6280 Estate Nazareth. www.secretharbourvi.com. ⓒ **800/524-2250** or 340/775-6550. 60 units. $358–$473 double; $469–$600 1-bedroom suite; $762–$860 2-bedroom suite; $964–$1,071 three-bedroom suite. Children 12 and under stay free in parent's room. Extra person $35/day. **Amenities:** Restaurant; bar; dive shop; fitness center; pool (outdoor); 3 tennis courts (lit); watersports center and equipment/rentals; free Wi-Fi.

MODERATE

Club Wyndham Elysian Beach Resort ★ This condominium complex overlooks its own secluded cove bobbing with boats and white-sand beach on Cowpet Bay, a 30-minute drive from Charlotte Amalie. It's not luxurious like the Ritz next door, but it's tranquil and secluded, and the exquisite white-sand beach and free-form swimming pool sweeten the deal. The one-bedroom condos (which can hold up to four people) contain kitchenettes and balconies, and 14 offer sleeping lofts that are reached by a spiral staircase. Look for standard-issue tropical decor, with rattan and bamboo furnishings, ceiling fans, and natural-wood ceilings. Some units have loft bedrooms with large balconies. Rooms in buildings V to Z are some distance from the beach, so try to avoid them when booking. Because the Elysian once operated as a hotel, the complex has resort amenities, including two good restaurants. The **Caribbean Fish Market** (p. 91), a fun spot with tables right on the beach, serves creative West Indian cuisine, and **Sangria's** (p. 93) is the place to come for beachside breakfasts, lunch, and early dinners.

6800 Estate Nazareth. clubwyndham.wyndhamdestinations.com. ⓒ **340/775-1000.** 180 units. $215–$260 double; $399 suite. **Amenities:** 2 restaurants; 2 bars; exercise room; outdoor pool; small spa; tennis court; watersports equipment/rentals; free Wi-Fi.

Lovango Cay

EXPENSIVE

Lovango Resort & Beach Club ★★★ It was long the dream of Nantucket innkeepers Mark and Gwenn Snider to support a year-round work force, despite operating in a seasonal destination. So, they went searching for a southern locale to guarantee their staff year-round employment. Buying an island in the Caribbean wasn't really on their radar, but when the opportunity came up, they jumped and in 2019 became the owners of 44 acres of the

A private treehouse room at the eco-conscious Lovango Resort & Beach Club.

100-acre Lovango Cay, a private island 10 to 15 minutes by boat from St. John (20 min. from St. Thomas). The island was home to just a handful of residents and the remains of a pre–WWI schoolhouse. But it had a summit with gorgeous Congo Cay views and three largely untouched beaches protected by a pristine necklace of coral reef. What the Sniders have built since is nothing short of miraculous. A stay here is truly a memorable experience, and yes, you will pay dearly to do so. You'll sleep in private treehouses or luxury glamping tents high up along the ridge (a villa has its own private pool and sleeps six), with breathtaking views of the sea and surrounding islands. Treehouses and tents have slatted wooden doors and windows open to the breezes, with Brazilian teak walls and beautiful cedar flooring oiled with chemical-free Heritage oil. Wooden beds are draped in gauzy white netting (and cooling fans inside the netting), and outdoor pebble showers have rain-shower heads. Day beds on the spacious decks and patios let you lounge and soak up the views. It's a short stroll down the hill to an uninhabited stretch of beach, where you can snorkel with angelfish. Hiking trails ramble through thickets of woods to shimmering beaches. Little wonder the resort has become a big-time day-trip destination for dinner or lunch at the dreamy waterfront restaurant (the Lovango Ferry does pick-up and drop-off at both Cruz Bay and Red Hook; $25/person round-trip) or to shop **Lovango Village,** little rows of whitewashed West Indian cottages selling high-end goods, including HIHO clothing, made in the B.V.I. It's the kind of thoughtful support for local initiatives that the Sniders have strived for—including a partnership with St. Croix's Sion Farm Distillery to create Lovango's line of breadfruit booze, Little Gem Spirits. The resort is off the grid and makes its own water. And the Lovango name? African slaves imported by the colonial Danish reportedly came from an African empire known as Lovango.

Lovango Cay. www.lovangovi.com. ℂ **340/625-0400.** 20 units. $995–$1,225 glamping tent; $1,350–$1,635 treehouse; $2,800–$3,300 villa. Rates include breakfast (delivered to your room) and boat transfers. **Amenities:** 2 restaurants; 2 bars; beach club; concierge; hiking trails; outdoor pool; shops; free Wi-Fi.

Camping Out on Water Island

St. Thomas has its own bucolic pocket of rusticity—and it's just off the hustle and bustle of the Charlotte Amalie harbor: **Water Island.** At the **Virgin Islands Campground** on **Water Island** (www.virginislandscampground.com; ℭ **340/776-5488**), guests stay in the most eco-sensitive lodgings on St. Thomas. They're hardly roughing it: The digs are wood-frame-and-canvas cottages with wind-drawn electricity, nice beds, and crisp linens. Each opens onto private, ocean view terraces. The campground has no restaurant, but you can grill your own meals in the common area known as the **Pavilion;** you can also store your

food in a refrigerator or freezer. Or just take the 5-minute walk from the campground to the island's idyllic **Honeymoon Beach ★★**, where you can take a swim, snorkel, or dine at one of two **beach bars** (p. 115), open daily from 10:30am to 8:30pm.

A 3-night minimum stay is required; cabins cost $239 to $269 per night; Seaview Cottage sleeps five, while the Coral House and Seaview Cottage sleep four. Water Island is very small; to get around, simply hike along the island's pristine trails. For information on getting to and visiting Water Island, see p. 115.

WHERE TO EAT

The dining scene in St. Thomas these days is among the best in the West Indies, but it has its drawbacks: Fine dining—and even not-so-fine dining—tends to be expensive, and you may have to travel by taxi or car to reach some of the best spots.

You'll find an eclectic mix of global cuisines here, including Italian, Mexican, Asian, and French. American fast-food franchises, pizza joints, and East Indian roti shacks are also part of the scene. But some of the best food on St. Thomas is island-bred: West Indian–style cuisine and interesting fusions thereof. We particularly like those places that take advantage of the island's natural bounty with menus featuring fresh-caught seafood, fresh fruit, and locally grown produce. Finally, go where the locals go: They know the best spots and are happy to recommend their favorites.

EXPENSIVE

Amalia Café ★ SPANISH   Set on an alfresco terrace on Palm Passage in the center of Charlotte Amalie, this long-established spot serves up some of the most savory Spanish cuisine in town. You can order one of the hearty entrees (paella Valenciana, say, or *zarzuela de mariscos,* seafood casserole) or make a meal out of tapas, flavorful small plates that might include garlic shrimp, chorizo sautéed in cider, or clams in a green sauce. Wash it all down with the Amalia's signature sangria.

24 Palm Passage. www.amaliacafe.com. ℭ **340/714-7373.** Reservations recommended. Entrees lunch $15–$23, dinner $28–$49. Mon–Sat 11am–9:45pm; closed Sun.

Blue 11 ★★★ CARIBBEAN   Chef David "Benji" Benjamin is one of St. Thomas's culinary stars and has been cooking on the island since he was 16

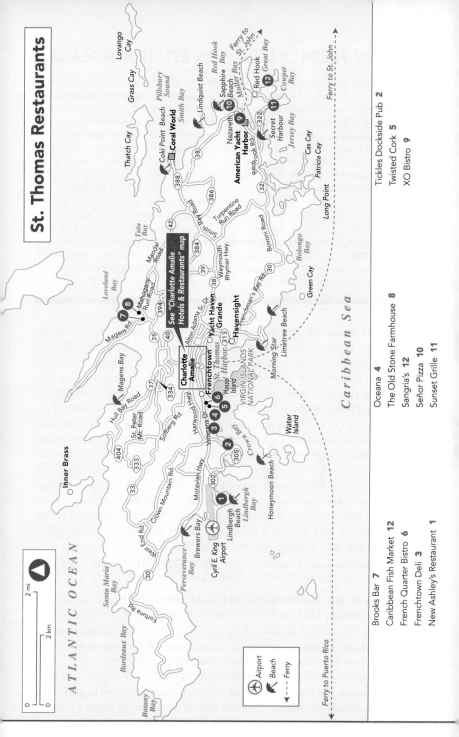

St. Thomas Restaurants

Brooks Bar **7**
Caribbean Fish Market **12**
French Quarter Bistro **6**
Frenchtown Deli **3**
New Ashley's Restaurant **1**

Oceana **4**
The Old Stone Farmhouse **8**
Sangria's **12**
Señor Pizza **10**
Sunset Grille **11**

Tickles Dockside Pub **2**
Twisted Cork **5**
XO Bistro **9**

FARM-FRESH produce ON ESTATE BORDEAUX

In 1984 the late Myron ("Buddy") Henneman planted a chemical-free garden in a serene spot high up in the green hills of the island's western end, with vistas of blue seas and robin's-egg skies. The loamy volcanic soil here was once tended by French farmers who immigrated from St. Barts. Pretty soon the government was offering Henneman agricultural land leases. Today, the Green Ridge Guavaberry Farm is thriving, part of the island's burgeoning agrarian renaissance. Some 20 **Estate Bordeaux farms** now grow crops of astonishing diversity in these quiet green hills, an edenic haven from the scrum of civilization far down below. The land will grow just about anything, including peas, Asian dragonfruit, okra, cashews, even the healing "tree of life," the meranga bush (said to be good for the liver). You can buy produce from this and other Estate Bordeaux farms, as well as fresh-baked bread, eggs, honey, and exotic island juices, in the **Saturday morning market** at Market Square, in Charlotte Amalie, and on the second and last Sunday of every month at the **Bordeaux farmers market** (10am–4pm), in an open-air pavilion near the entrance to the Preserve at Botany Bay.

years old at vaunted spots like Agave and the Ritz-Carlton. Benjamin opened this sleek, compact spot in the middle of a global pandemic in June 2020. In lieu of glittering ocean views or mountain scenery, there's a hushed reverence for what's on the plate. Blue 11 plays by Benjamin's rules, serving dinner only and your choice of 7-, 9-, or 11-course tasting menus. Dietary restrictions do apply and substitutions are allowed, but give it all a chance if possible. Benjamin is both technician and alchemist. This is exquisitely refined Caribbean soul food, locally sourced, island-centric, and cleverly reconfigured in braises, foams, and reductions. Steamed mussels, a seared scallop and grouper, and breadfruit are set in a pea-green necklace of reconstructed callaloo soup. Jerk chicken comes with plantain gnocchi; braised short ribs nestle in a sweet potato puree and cinnamon port reduction. For dessert, homemade donuts are drizzled with chocolate and caramel sauce over banana caramel ice cream. The topnotch staff delivers a tightly run service with smiles and warmth—they seem to love working here and touting this food.

Yacht Haven Grande. www.blue11vi.com. ℂ **340/777-2511.** 7-course menu $104, 9-course $121, 11-course $132. Tues–Sun 6–10pm.

Indigo 4 ★★ CARIBBEAN/INTERNATIONAL   This marina-side spot gives celebrated local chef David "Benji" Benjamin a second space at The Shops at Yacht Haven Grande (along with Blue 11, see above), here showcasing Benjamin's creative, seasonally focused takes on Continental and Caribbean dishes. The menu appears straightforward enough—steaks, pork chops, fish of the day—but here that steak may come with a horseradish and green banana mash, and that pork chop set in stewed black beans and topped with a homemade mango chutney. Outdoor seating with marina breezes makes a sunny spot for breakfast. Inside, patterned chairs in blue and gunmetal play off wooden walls of burnt orange; it's a sophisticated look for savvy palates.

Yacht Haven Grande. indigo4vi.com. ✆ **340/714-4447.** Entrees $35–$65; tomahawk steak $125. Tues–Sun 5:30–10pm; Sun brunch 10am–2pm.

Mafolie Restaurant ★★ CARIBBEAN/INTERNATIONAL   Here's a chance to appreciate the magnificence of the Charlotte Amalie harbor from 900 feet up when you dine in the open-air dining room of the Mafolie Hotel. Start with the seafood kallaloo soup, the mango avocado salad with carambola (star fruit), or sweet potato crabcakes. Entrees include a sizzling-hot jerk salmon or a buttery grilled Caribbean lobster. Could the decor use a little pick-me-up? Sure, I guess. Is it still working out the post-pandemic kinks when it comes to service standards? Well, who isn't?

7091 Estate Mafolie. www.mafolie.com. ✆ **340/774-2790.** Entrees $30–$50. Tues–Sun 5–9pm.

Virgilio's ★★ ITALIAN   Many people think this is the best Italian restaurant on the island, tucked away in an alley right off Main Street. Now in its 35th year, Virgilio's serves up Sicilian classics and homemade pastas and risottos, including a hearty "Lasagna de Maria," from a Virgilio family recipe. You can also get traditional veal and chicken dishes, as well as a sprinkling of fresh-made pizzas, including a terrific *pizza del mare*, with shrimp and calamari, and an array of antipasti, salads, and soups. The restaurant's old-world charm is enhanced by wood beams and vaulted brick. Paintings in ornate frames line buttery-yellow walls.

5150 Dronningens Gade (entrance on Storetvaer Gade, a narrow alley running btw. Main and Back sts.). www.virgiliosvi.com. ✆ **340/776-4920.** Reservations recommended. Entrees lunch $24–$44, dinner $28–$48. Mon–Sat 11:30am–10pm; closed Sun.

MODERATE

Café Amici ★★ ITALIAN/CARIBBEAN   New chef-owner Karrl Foster (former chef of Blue Orchid at St. Peter Greenhouse) took the reins of this long-time reliable lunch spot in 2021—a good sign for the continued revitalization of Charlotte Amalie's downtown historic district. An expanded menu was introduced in late 2022, with pastas including a penne primavera and two lasagnes. The cocktail list has gotten longer and sexier, now with 18 wines by the glass and local Frenchtown Brewery beer on tap. But Café Amici is best known for its brick-oven pizzas, and these remain delicious and satisfying. Choices range from a simple Margherita to a Pesto di Pollo (chicken) and the Agnello, with ground lamb, sun-dried-tomato pesto, artichoke, red onions, and arugula. Flatbreads and sandwiches are also in the mix. Appetizers include lots of interesting salads, such as a Catania beet salad and a tuna salad made with fresh ahi, farro, spinach, and an Italian salsa verde.

A.H. Riise's Alley. cafeamicistthomas.com. ✆ **340/779-9000.** Pasta $23–$25; pizza $15–$24. Mon–Sat 11am–3pm or later (hours expected to expand; call ahead).

4

ST. THOMAS | Where to Eat

PROVISIONING RESOURCES ON ST. THOMAS

More than any other Virgin Island, St. Thomas has no lack of stores to find what you need to eat and drink and stock your pantry. That's because it's a prime provisioning stop for boaters, and many people who visit the island stay in rented houses, villas, and condos (even resorts) with full kitchens. Here's a sampling of resources:

o **The Works:** Many people who are renting villas stock up on money-saving bulk grocery items, produce, fresh meats, and liquor and wine at **Cost U Less** (www.shopcostuless. com/stores/st-thomas-cost-u-less; *(C)* **340/777-3588**), a Costco-type warehouse at 4400 Weymouth Rhymer Highway in St. Thomas. It's open Monday to Saturday 8am to 9pm and Sunday 8am to 7pm.

o **Groceries:** Open daily, the chain grocery **Pueblo** (wfmpueblo.com) has two locations on St. Thomas: in the Subbase area near Crown Bay harbor and one block from Long Bay harbor. Also open daily is the local favorite **The Market STT** (formerly Plaza Extra) in Tutu Park Mall (www.themarketstt.com; *(C)* **340/775-5646**). In Red Hook, the **Food Center** (*(C)* **340/777-8806**) is the largest grocery on the East End; it's open

daily 7am to 10pm. Also in Red Hook, **Moe's Fresh Market** (www. moesvi.com; *(C)* **340/693-0254**), on 6205 Smith Bay Rd., is known for its gourmet selection of fresh and prepared foods—including Black Angus beef, seafood, and temperature-controlled wine cellar—and free provisioning services for yacht, villa, and hotel guests.

o **Fresh Seafood:** You can buy fresh-off-the-boat fish at the **Gustave Quetel Fish House** docks in Frenchtown any morning or at the Saturday market in **Market Square** in Charlotte Amalie. **S&P Seafoods**, 3801 Crown Bay (*(C)* **340/774-5280**), is a full-service fishmonger.

o **Fresh Produce/Fruit:** St. Thomas has a number of farmers markets, including the **Saturday market** (6–11am or noon) at Market Square in Charlotte Amalie, and the **Bordeaux farmers market** on the second and last Sunday of each month in Estate Bordeaux, on the island's West End.

o **Liquor:** Liquor stores abound along Main Street in Charlotte Amalie, and liquor, wine, and beer are sold in most grocery stores throughout the island.

Gladys' Café ★★ CARIBBEAN/AMERICAN   It's smack-dab in tourist central in Charlotte Amalie's historic downtown, but we don't care—we love the food at Gladys'. The cafe relocated to a bigger Royal Dane Mall location after its longtime space was devastated by a fire in late 2019. The new spot is sunny and bright, with high ceilings, a handsome wood bar, and native stone walls hung with colorful local art. Quench your heat fever with a fresh fruit juice of the day, like sorrel, passionfruit, or ginger beer with lemonade. West Indian specialties are done deftly and cleanly. Sample conch fritters or a fresh Caribbean lobster salad in a scooped-out avocado. "Ole Wife Fish," triggerfish in a just-right Creole sauce, is a favorite. Daily specials might be curry chicken with peas and rice and plantains or curry goat. If you like polenta or grits, its island counterpart is fungi, here topped with that tasty Creole sauce. Don't leave without taking home a bottle of Gladys's homemade hot sauce.

Royal Dane Mall. gladyscafe.com. ℭ **340/774-6604.** Reservations required for groups of 6 or more. Entrees $13–$25; sandwiches and burgers $10–$15. Daily 11am–5pm.

Petite Pump Room ★★ WEST INDIAN/INTERNATIONAL   Join the locals for a reliably tasty St. Thomas breakfast and lunch at this second-floor harborside spot in the ferryboat terminal in Charlotte Amalie. An old-timer, Petite Pump Room has been overlooking the harbor since 1970 and is still a reliable purveyor of flavorful West Indian cooking, with a daily menu of

conch fritters (a house specialty), grilled or blackened mahi, and conch in garlic butter sauce. Daily specials range from a Tuesday kallaloo to a Friday curried chicken. A veggie platter comes with what the islanders call "ground provisions" (starchy vegetables). Sides include rice, fungi, and fried plantains. If you want to start your day the true island way, ask for the local saltfish breakfast ($18): stewed saltfish, boiled egg, steamed okra and spinach, and butter bread, served with coffee or bush tea. The dark interior is the place to tuck into your feelings (and a shot glass of rum); head outside to the sunny seaside deck instead and watch ships cruise into the harbor. It's a very convenient spot for a bite if you're waiting for a ferry or seaplane.

Conch and other island classics star on the menu at the Petite Pump Room.

In the Edward Wilmoth Blyden Building, Veterans Dr. www.petitepumproom.com. ℭ **340/776-2976.** Entrees $10–$20 breakfast, $14–$32 lunch. Daily 7am–4:30pm.

INEXPENSIVE

Bumpa's ★ AMERICAN   A deli-style sandwich and breakfast joint, Bumpa's is perfect when you want something simple but well-made. Many people, locals and visitors alike, stop in early in the morning to breakfast on terrific French toast, omelets, and lemonade. Lunch features burgers and sandwiches like a mahi mahi reuben and a steak-and-plantain wrap. Bumpa's is located on the second floor of a building that faces the busy highway along the waterfront, but by all means, sit yourself outside for harbor views and breezes.

38-A Waterfront Hwy. ℭ **340/776-5674.** Entrees $7–$14 breakfast, $14–$28 lunch. Mon–Fri 7am–4:30pm.

Stir It Up Coffee Shop & Bakery ★★ COFFEE SHOP/BAKERY   This locally owned coffee and pastry shop opened in late 2018, and it's been in morning bustle mode ever since. Croissant sandwiches are the specialty—the bacon, egg, and cheese croissants practically fly out the door. But Stir It Up also has excellent pastries (strawberry and cream scones, cinnamon rolls), bread pudding, white-chocolate dragon-fruit latte, honey-vanilla matcha, and mango smoothies. Coffee is topnotch; they use Counter Culture, organic fairtrade coffee roasted in Durham, NC.

9100 Port of Sale Mall. www.facebook.com/stiritupvi. ℂ **340/642-9972.** Pastries and croissants $4–$6. Mon–Thurs 6am–3pm; Sat 7am–2pm; Sun 8am–noon.

Frenchtown
EXPENSIVE

Oceana Restaurant & Bistro ★★★ GLOBAL/ISLAND   This is the best fine-dining experience in all of St. Thomas, and hallelujah, it's back after having its roof blown away and furnishings scattered to the seven seas by the 2017 hurricanes. Oceana has a breathtaking seaside setting on a grassy lawn along the wonderfully named Baye de Gri-Gri. It's an open-air, breeze-filled stage set inside a beautifully restored West Indian great house on the estate grounds of the first Danish Customs House and in the 1890s a Russian Consulate known as Villa Olga. (Olga's Fancy, p. 76, is on the same property.) It's helmed by Executive Chef Patricia LaCorte, a French-trained chef who helped pioneer the foodie movement on St. Thomas back in the 1980s and still has

Locavore gourmet dining, an open-air seaside setting—the Oceana Restaurant & Bistro hits all the St. Thomas high notes.

things to prove. LaCorte opened Oceana in 2002, and the inviting open kitchen (her creation) lets you see LaCorte and her able staff at work. Pan-seared scallops come with a pumpkin puree and Calabaza ratatouille—a Caribbean-style version of the French classic, made with green plantains, peppers, and squash. A coriander-dusted *mahi a la plancha* is accompanied by toasted farro with sweet potato and fresh pineapple chutney. The Oceana bouillabaisse arrives brimming with market fish fresh off the docks at French-town. LaCorte buys locally whenever possible, including "eight or nine" greens from local farms and tomatoes, herbs, and fruit. A compote is made out of local gooseberries, and Oceana cocktails are cleverly infused with local herbs, like a Lavender Lemonade with smoked rosemary. In the bistro bar, walls are blanketed with fabulous local and global art, and nosh-style food includes flatbreads, a Mediterranean platter, charcuterie, mushroom toast, and a handful of hearty entrees. Post-hurricane, Oceana now has a newly rein-forced ceiling and roof, a strong and sturdy carapace for the finely wrought alchemy within.

#8 Honduras, Frenchtown. www.oceanavi.com. © **340/774-4262.** Reservations required. Entrees $3–$56. Tues–Sat 5–9:30pm.

MODERATE

French Quarter Bistro ★★ CAJUN/AMERICAN   This place does its namesake proud when it comes to a rollicking atmosphere—as soon as you walk in the door, you know you've come to the right place for *Cheers*-level bonhomie. The decor is casual, shall we say, and the lighting abysmal. What it lacks in ambience it makes up for in excellent-value dining, a seasoned, relentlessly good-natured service crew, and a Big Easy vibe. We all know New Orleans takes its food as seriously as its celebrations, and in this sense French Quarter Bistro gets an A for effort. The kitchen stews up a very respectable gumbo, thick and tasty, and an étouffée of shrimp and crawfish is rich and flavorful. They also do a solid job with standard bistro fare like strip steak and roast chicken; salads are fresh and generous. The good times roll on in St. Thomas.

Rue de Bethamny, Frenchtown. www.frenchquarterbistrovi.com. © **340/776-9708.** Entrees $21–$34. Mon–Fri 11am–10pm; Sat 5–9:30pm; Sun 10am–2:30pm and 5–9:30pm.

Twisted Cork ★★ AMERICAN   Wine's the focal point here, but the excellent bistro-style food is another big draw. A real chef is in the house: The Twisted burger is made from succulent braised brisket, which makes us hun-gry just writing about it, and the cheesy shrimp and grits comes in a classic Southern bacon gravy. If you rail against the scourge of invasive lionfish, then dine on Twisted Cork's sprightly fish-and-chips version and rid the seas of one less. The herbs infusing your craft cocktail and fresh salads come plucked right from the restaurant garden. Thursday night is jazz night.

3525 Honduras. twistedcorkvi.com. © **340/775-2675.** Entrees $24–$32; burgers and sandwiches $18–$24. Mon–Fri 11:30am–3pm and 5–8pm.

Frenchtown Deli ★★ DELI   The Frenchtown Deli has some of the island's most delicious deli-style sandwiches, along with homemade soups and salads. It's also a coffee shop with a full breakfast menu. This is a great takeout spot if you're looking for picnic fare for beach or boat excursions.

24-A Honduras, Frenchtown Mall. ⓒ **340/776-7211.** Sandwiches $9–$16; salads $4–$15. Mon–Fri 7am–8pm; Sat 7am–5pm; Sun 7am–4pm.

North of Charlotte Amalie

EXPENSIVE

Old Stone Farmhouse ★★★ INTERNATIONAL   Many a vaunted chef has shuffled through the kitchen line at this atmospheric restaurant, set in the stone field house and former stable of a 200-year-old Danish sugar plantation. The current occupant of the kitchen, Justin Werle, has some impressive cooking cred, having formerly worked with Dan Barber at Blue Hill in New York City and at Fearrington House in Chapel Hill, NC. Werle's Old Stone Farmhouse continues to be a special-occasion kind of place. You'll want to linger no matter where you dine, whether outside in the courtyard overlooking the plantation grounds or inside, where flickering candlelight casts shadows on native stone walls. Culinarily, Chef Werle takes a classic, French-influenced approach, with an emphasis on local sourcing. He gives fresh island seafood an elegant turn; here yellowfin tuna is poached in a velvety black pepper velouté. The creamy Caribbean conch chowder is built from a white mirepoix

Chef Justin Werle turns out classical fine dining in an atmospheric old plantation stable at the Old Stone Farmhouse.

base, and a piquant veggie ceviche stars king trumpet mushrooms. The restaurant wine cellar is one of the best in the Virgins.

Mahogany Run. www.oldstonefarmhouse.net. © **340/777-6277.** Reservations recommended. Entrees $34–$56. Wed–Sat 5:30–9pm; Sunday brunch 10am–2pm.

MODERATE/INEXPENSIVE

Brooks Bar ★★ CARIBBEAN   Local food doesn't get any better (or more local) than this. This open-air bar and restaurant along the road to Magens Bay is not, as one patron put it, a "sanitized presentation of the islands." In other words, if you're looking for design inspiration (high or low), this roadside joint offers neither. It's a few tables on a concrete patio and a porch out back. But it's clean and safe—and oh yeah, the food is great, a murderer's row of Caribbean goodness served in Styrofoam takeout containers. You don't have to gulp down one of the bar's famous glasses of Mamajuana to believe it. (Mamajuana is a Dominican spiced rum that is an instant belly heater and actually quite delicious, if your taste buds get a whiff before it sails down the gullet.) Main dishes include conch in butter sauce, "Ole Wife" fish, stewed oxtails, shrimp in a buttery garlic sauce, and barbeque ribs, and the cooks put as much care into the sides as they do the entrees, such as rice and peas, caramelized plantains, fungi, and fresh-made slaw and salads. It's open daily. "Sunday too?" "Yeah baby" as the waitress confirms. The night we visited, the spirited crowd was a legit melting pot: taxi drivers, retirees just off the plane, local families, sleek young hotel staff—all raising glasses of Mamajuana, and down the hatch.

6200 Magens Bay Rd. © **340/777-6871.** Entrees $18–$35. Daily 10:30am–9pm.

East End/Red Hook

EXPENSIVE

Caribbean Fish Market ★★ SEAFOOD/ASIAN Breezy and bright, this indoor/outdoor seafood eatery sits right on the beach at the Elysian Beach Resort, looking out onto the sapphire seas of Cowpet Bay. It's also right next door to the Ritz-Carlton, making it a very convenient place for Ritz guests to enjoy a solid seafood dinner done well—albeit at Ritz prices. The fresh catch of the day might be a crab-crusted local grouper served in a saffron-cream sauce. Here Caribbean lobster is butter-broiled or stuffed with shrimp and grilled; an Asian-inspired seafood hot pot comes in a lemongrass-ginger-coconut-curry broth. You can even start your meal

Seafood stars at the Caribbean Fish Market.

with seafood, from sweet-and-spicy Bang-Bang shrimp tacos to ahi tuna nachos. But there's plenty for carnivores (filet mignon in a fig demi-glace, bacon-stuffed pork chop) and vegetarians (eggplant frites, spicy Brussels sprouts, General Tso's cauliflower) as well.

Club Wyndham Elysian Beach Resort (p. 80), 6800 Estate Nazareth. www.caribbeanfish marketvi.com. ℂ **340/714-7874.** Reservations recommended. Entrees $31–$54. Daily 5–10pm; Sun brunch 10am–2pm.

Sunset Grille ★★ AMERICAN/INTERNATIONAL   This is one of the island's best-loved restaurants, on a low-rise waterside deck facing Secret Harbour, dotted with sailboats. The menu has plenty of flavorful turns, but Sunset Grille is basically a surf-and-turf kind of place. It's the seductive setting, however, that turns what is often a very good meal into a truly magical one. The last time we dined here, the protected cove was lit up in blazing orange from the setting sun, and as night crawled in, lights snaking beneath the inky black seas revealed a posse of night snorkelers. You'll want to experience the entire light extravaganza, so be there before sunset. Of the two main dining areas, the casual deck covered by a canvas top is more open to the elements. Some of the preparations we found unnecessarily fussy (and service not fussy enough), but all in all the dishes are fresh and well-prepared. We loved the *ropa vieja* spring rolls, and the tamarind salmon was cooked just right.

Secret Harbour Beach Resort (p. 79), 6280 Estate Nazareth. www.sunsetgrillevi.com. ℂ **340/714-7874.** Reservations required. Entrees $28–$58. Daily 5–10pm.

An island classic, Secret Harbour's Sunset Grille offers fine food and romantic water views.

MODERATE

Sangria's ★ PIZZA/COFFEE SHOP   This "beachside bistro" is the island hot spot for breakfast, lunch, and early pizza dinners (ideal for families with young kids). Breakfasts (Mon–Sat 6:30am–11pm) range from classic two-eggs-and-meat to plump omelets, Benedicts, pancakes, and breakfast burritos and quesadillas. Lunch (daily 11am–6pm) swings into sandwiches, salads, pizzas, and fun appetizers like Korean wings, tuna nachos, and conch fritters. Pizzas rule for the early evening menu (6–8pm). It's a wonderful, breezy place to dine on a sunny St. Thomas afternoon and watch the boats ply Cowpet Bay.

Club Wyndham Elysian Beach Resort (p. 80), 6800 Estate Nazareth. www.sangriasvi. com. ℂ **340/714-7874.** Entrees $15–$30. Daily 6:30am–8pm.

XO Bistro ★★ AMERICAN   This Red Hook restaurant hits the sweet spot when it comes to good, well-made food at not-off-the-charts prices. They've got a thing for American comfort food, and that's a niche you won't find much of around the Caribbean. (It's also, for a restaurant owner, an economical way to maneuver the shoals of inflated food costs, island-style.) So, a nightly XO home-cooking special might be a ground-meat casserole, chicken pot-pie soup, or a chicken-and-white-bean chili—rib-sticking and good. Prime rib arrives in classic fashion: over a big fluffy mound of mashed potatoes. But XO goes beyond, with elegant fish preparations (almond-encrusted salmon) and creative first courses, including street-corn guacamole and tuna tostadas. It's a great spot for dinner if you're a late arrival to the island—food is served until midnight. Look for fun events like Martini Mondays and Wine and Wig parties.

6501 Red Hook Plaza (across from the ferry dock). www.xobistro.net. ℂ **340/779-2069.** Reservations required. Entrees $26–$36. Daily 11am–2am (dinner served until midnight).

INEXPENSIVE

Señor Pizza ★ PIZZA   If you're burned out on conch (and even if you're not), you'll be quite satisfied with the big, cheesy pizza pies served at Señor Pizza. Slices are oversized, so one might be all you need for a tasty, filling lunch. They also deliver.

6501 Red Hook Plaza (across from the ferry dock). senorpizzausvi.com. ℂ **340/775-3030.** Whole pizza $14–$25. No credit cards. Mon–Fri 10am–10pm; Sat–Sun 9am–11pm.

Near the Airport

Whether you're flying out of St. Thomas or just arriving, do as the locals do and grab a **pate** (prounounced *pah tay* and sometimes spelled *patty*) to go at **New Ashley's Restaurant** (ℂ **340/775-1533**) on Airport Road. The Caribbean version of empanadas (and descended from slave cuisine), Caribbean pates are fried-dough meat patties filled with seasoned saltfish, beef, chicken, and conch. Ashley's pates ($4) are deservedly "world-famous." With a full menu of West Indian classics like stew chicken and curry goat, you can even eat in and sip a cold beer or a painkiller to blunt the pain of leaving.

If you get off the plane and are feeling peckish (no matter what time of day), head to **Tickles Dockside Pub** ★ (www.ticklesdocksidepub.com; ✆ **340/776-1595**) in Crown Bay Marina, a 5-minute drive from the airport. This open-air spot serves breakfast, lunch, and dinner and is open from 7am to 9:30pm. Tickles has sea and marina views (it's near the ferry dock to Water Island) and serves up good, reliable food, from burgers to island specialties like conch chowder—and it's a consistent winner in the *Virgin Island Daily News'* annual "Best of the VI" awards for coldest beer and best family restaurant.

EXPLORING ST. THOMAS
Beaches

St. Thomas's beaches are renowned for their powdery white sand and clear azure waters, including the very best of them all, Magens Bay. Chances are that your hotel is right on the beach, or very close to one. Keep in mind that all the beaches in the Virgin Islands are public—even the resort beaches—and most St. Thomas beaches lie anywhere from 2 to 5 miles from Charlotte Amalie.

THE NORTH COAST

The gorgeous white sands of **Magens Bay** ★★—the family favorite of St. Thomas—lie between two mountains 3 miles north of the capital. The turquoise waters here are calm and ideal for swimming, though the snorkeling isn't that good. The beach is no secret, and it's usually overcrowded, though it gets better in the midafternoon. There is no public transportation to get here (although some hotels provide shuttle buses). A taxi from Charlotte Amalie costs about $8.50 per person. If you've rented a car, from Charlotte Amalie take Route 35 north all the way. The gates to the beach are open daily from 6am to 6pm. After 4pm, you'll need insect repellent. Admission is $5 per person (free for children 12 and under) and $2 for parking. You can rent beach and lounge chairs ($5–$7) and snorkel gear ($15) or bring your own. The Yak Shak rents kayaks ($28–$30/hr.) and SUP boards ($30/hr.) right on the beach. Don't bring valuables, and don't leave anything of value in your parked car. Beach concessions include a **beach bar, snack bar,** and **cafe** serving breakfast,

---

HOT surfing SPOTS

Surfers come from miles around to test the swells at **Hull Bay,** on the North Shore, just west of Magens Bay, particularly the waves along the western tip. It's also where local fishermen anchor in the more tranquil areas. Don't expect much in the way of watersports outfitters. If you're relying on taxis, it costs about $15 per person to reach the bay. Two other beaches have good surfing, **Perseverance Bay** and **Caret Bay,** but these are the unofficial territory of French locals, who as one surfer said, "let you know if they don't like you."

lunch, and island specialties (including barbecue chicken or ribs, Caribbean jerk chicken, johnnycakes, and rice and peas); it's open daily 9:30am to 5pm.

A marked trail leads from Magens Bay to **Little Magens Bay,** a separate, clothing-optional beach that's especially popular with gay and lesbian visitors.

Coki Point Beach ★, next door to Coral World, is clean and sparkling and a favorite of families. It's noted for its fine snorkeling; look for rainbow-hued fish swimming among the rocks leading to the Coral World Observatory Tower. From the beach, there's a panoramic view of offshore Thatch Cay. Beachside concessions include lockers and lounge chairs ($5).

THE EAST END

Small and calm, **Secret Harbour ★** fronts the Secret Harbour Beach Resort and a collection of condos. With its white sand and coconut palms, it's a lovely little spot. The snorkeling near the rocks is not bad—and night snorkeling is also available. You can rent equipment or sign up for a 60-minute "Discover Snorkeling" course (all ages welcome) on-site at the Secret Harbour Beach Resort with **Aqua Action Dive Center** (© **340/775-6285**). It's an easy taxi ride east of Charlotte Amalie heading toward Red Hook.

Like Magens Bay Beach, **Sapphire Beach ★** is wide and safe and frequented by families. You'll have good views of St. John, Tortola, Jost Van

Calm waters make Secret Harbour a good bet for families.

IT'S THE LAW: reef-safe SUNSCREEN

Please use only mineral sunscreen—it's the law in the U.S. Virgin Islands!

To help preserve the glorious beaches and stunning underwater world that lure visitors to the Virgin Islands, avoid sunscreens that contain the "Toxic 3 Os" of oxybenzone, octinoxate, and octocrylene—they are prohibited in the United States Virgin Islands. Wear hats and rash guards (UV protective swimwear) and use only non-nano mineral sunscreen containing zinc oxide and titanium dioxide, the only sunscreen ingredients deemed safe and effective by the FDA. Always read the ingredient label to avoid sunscreen containing oxybenzone, octinoxate, and octocrylene.

Dyke, and offshore cays, and a large reef is close to the shore. Windsurfers like this beach a lot.

White-sand **Lindquist Beach** ★★ isn't a long strip, but it's hands-down one of the island's prettiest beaches. Part of the protected 21-acre Smith Bay Park, off Smith Bay Road, this photogenic beach has served as the backdrop in many films and TV commercials. It's got picnic tables and restroom facilities, but it's fairly remote and only fills up on weekends, especially Sunday Fundays. Admission fee is $5, and parking is $2. Bring snorkel and mask to see the bay's sea turtles.

THE SOUTH COAST

Frenchman's Bay Beach, fronting the old Marriott resort, was hit hard by the 2017 hurricanes. The resort reopened in late 2022, and it's still a lovely spot, with gentle swells. You can reach the beach by walking the cliffside walk down to the beach.

WEST OF CHARLOTTE AMALIE

Near the University of the Virgin Islands (and the airport), in the southwest, **Brewers Bay** ★ is one of the island's most popular beaches for locals, with a strip of white coral sand that's almost as long as the beach at Magens Bay. Bring your snorkeling gear: There is healthy coral reef about 15 feet down and beds of seagrass where green sea turtles feed. Vendors here sell light meals and drinks, but bring your own chairs. From Charlotte Amalie, take the Fortuna bus heading west; get off at the edge of Brewers Bay, across from the Reichhold Center.

Lindbergh Beach, with a lifeguard, restrooms, and a bathhouse, is fronted by **Lindbergh Bay Hotel and Villas** (www.lindberghbayhotelandvillas.com) and used extensively by locals, who stage events from political rallies to Carnival parties here. Beach-loving couples are also attracted to this beach. Drinks are served on the beach.

Watersports & Outdoor Adventures

St. Thomas's marine facilities are indubitably world-class, but the island has always been somewhat in the shadow of its vaunted B.V.I. neighbors. That shifted in 2022, when the island was named Yachting Destination of the Year by *Caribbean Journal* magazine, which particularly cited mega-yacht-central **Yacht Haven Grande,** in the Charlotte Amalie harbor (www.igymarinas.com/marinas/marina-yacht-haven-grande; ✆ **340/774-9500;** VHF channel 16 and 10), as a "white-hot yachting destination, reminding maritime travelers just how easy and convenient it is to set sail from American waters in the U.S. Virgin Islands." A four-time SuperYacht Marina of the Year winner, Yacht Haven welcomes the big boys (like David Geffen's *The Rising Sun*) with its 46 mega-yacht berths and a sterling range of dining, entertainment, and recreational options like lighted tennis courts and a lagoon pool.

With 123 berths, the full-service **American Yacht Harbor**, in Red Hook (www.igymarinas.com/marinas/american-yacht-harbor; ✆ **340/775-6454;** VHF channel 6454), is no slouch either. Lying on the east end of St. Thomas in Vessup Bay, the harbor is home to numerous boat companies, including day-trippers, fishing boats, and sailing charters.

BOAT CHARTERING/BAREBOATING Both marinas can refer both bareboat and fully crewed charters. Be sure to check out the classic *Yachtsman's Guide to the Virgin Islands,* available at major marine outlets, at bookstores, through catalog merchandisers, or directly from **Tropical Publishers** (www.yachtsmansguide.com; ✆ **877/923-9653**). St. Thomas's yacht scene is so hot that Tortola-based **Moorings** (www.moorings.com; ✆ **800/416-0247**), the big daddy of charter-yacht companies, has set up shop at Yacht Haven Grande. Moorings can arrange sailing, powered, and crewed charters. It's just one of several B.V.I. yacht chartering companies that have joined the post-pandemic market in St. Thomas, attracted by the relative ease of travel onto the U.S. island.

DAY SAILING/BOAT EXCURSIONS Island-hopping boat excursions ★★★ via captained sailboats or powerboats/yachts are the bread and butter of Virgin Island outfitting. Many are snorkel sails that include lunch and snorkeling in protected cays. In November 2022, the B.V.I. and U.S.V.I. governments agreed to a reciprocal regulatory program for the charter boat industry, loosening the complicated regulatory hoops that "foreign charter vessels" had been forced to undergo to operate commercially in the B.V.I. since the Covid-19 pandemic. What that means is that U.S.V.I. and B.V.I. charter vessels will once again be able to move more freely between the two territories.

Cruz Bay Watersports ★★ (cruzbaywatersports.com; ✆ **844/668-8753** or 340/776-6234), with a location at the Ritz-Carlton Resort, has a fleet of 50-passenger luxury catamarans that operate some of the best and most professional snorkel sails in the Virgins. The 65-foot *Lady Lynsey II* can carry up to 80 passengers. All come with swim platforms, waterslides, easy boarding ladders, and all snorkel gear and flotation devices. Snorkel sails to St. John often offer two snorkels to places like Maho Bay (sea turtles) and Caneel Bay, followed by a delicious picnic lunch either aboard the boat or at places like Pizza Pi and Lime Out. Five-hour snorkel sails to St. John range in price from $129 to $149 ($89–$99 children ages 3–12).

Cruz Bay Watersports (p. 97) offers a great range of snorkel sails.

Sonic Charters ★★ (soniccharterstthomas.com; ✆ **340/244-5096**) offers some of the best captained charters in the Virgins, with a fleet of 32- to 37-foot center consoles, as well as the 50-foot *New Magic,* a Sea Ray Sundancer sport cruiser, and the *Enchantment,* a 58-foot Viking Princess power yacht. Note that Sonic is one of the few U.S.V.I. charter operators that's fully licensed to operate in the B.V.I.—which means that they offer not only St. Thomas excursions (like a trip to the island's best surf spots) but full- and half-day excursions to Jost Van Dyke, Tortola, Norman Island, Cooper Island, and Peter Island. A 7-hour day trip to Jost might take in a visit to the Great Harbour, lunch at Sidney's Peace & Love Bar, and a snorkel around Sandy Spot, the "Corona" island (of beer commercial fame); depending on the boat, costs would run $700 (nine people max) to $1,600 (12 people max). Keep in mind that all passengers traveling into B.V.I. waters must pay a $65 cash customs fee, collected upon boarding the boat.

Sail with Captain Pat Stoeken on the *Independence* ★★ (www.independence 44.us; ✆ **340/512-2897**), a beautiful 44-foot clipper-bowed ketch. Captain Pat customizes half- and full-day snorkel-sails to St. John for small groups (up to six passengers). Some favorite stops include Whistling Cay, Mary's Point, Francis Bay, Hawksnest, and Scot Beach on St. John, as well as Lovango and Congo cays. Wind and seas permitting, Captain Pat loves to head up the south side of St. John to Rendezvous Bay, Little Lameshure Bay, and Tektite. Half-day rates are $110 per person and include snacks, an open bar, and all snorkel gear; full-day rates are $175 per person and includes a full pasta lunch, open bar, and all snorkel gear.

Seas the Day ★ (seasthedayusvi.com; ✆ **340/642-3895**) offers a wide range of sailing excursions, including customized half- and full-day sails aboard the 50-foot luxury catamaran S/Y *Sirena* or the 47-foot leopard catamaran S/Y *Pisces* for up to 12 people ($1,095 and up). SUPs, floats, and snorkel equipment (and trampolines!) are on board. You can take a full-day private charter to the beach bars of your dreams aboard the 45-foot double-decker power catamaran M/V *Sea Wolf* ($1,595 for up to 12 people).

Fury Charters ★ (usvisailing.com; ✆ **340/643-7733**) offers day and sunset sails with Captain Mike and crew aboard the *Fury,* a 46-foot Morgan ketch (circa 1981) that can accommodate up to 25 passengers. *Fury* has all the bells and whistles: snorkel equipment, floats, snacks, and an open bar. You can take a half-day Snorkeling with Turtles excursion ($120/person) in the National Wildlife Marine Refuge at Buck Island's Turtle Cove, home to a large population of green sea turtles. Sunset sails for up to 10 people include appetizers and open bar ($1,200 flat rate).

Although the 50-foot *Yacht Nightwind* did not survive the 2017 hurricanes, the ***Yacht Nightwind 2*** (✆ **904/347-9319**), sailing out of Sapphire Marina, has ably taken its place, offering full-day snorkel sails for up to 15 guests ($125/person) to St. John and the outer islands with Captain Wes, the son, appropriately enough, of *Nightwind*'s longtime captain Rick O'Dell. The cost includes lunch and free snorkeling instruction.

Sailing on Fury Charters' namesake ketch.

FISHING The Virgin Islands sit on the edge of the Puerto Rico Trench, which drops precipitously 6 miles down—it's the deepest trench in the Atlantic Ocean and the Caribbean and the official boundary between the two. The most celebrated fishing spots are the **North Drop,** about 20 miles north of St. Thomas, and the **South Drop,** 8 miles south of St. Thomas—trolling these waters is known as "working the Drop." Both areas draw vast schools of migrating bait fish and the big pelagics that are chasing them. The sportfishing is excellent in these waters—some 19 world records (eight for blue marlin) have been set here.

With 25 years of experience in the sportfishing industry, **Double Header ★★** (doubleheadersportfishing.net; ✆ **340/777-7317**) does both offshore fishing for tuna, mahi, wahoo, and marlin, and inshore angling for fish like yellowtail snapper, tarpon, and kingfish. Half-day charters are $700 to $800 (six persons max); full-day charters are $1,150 to $1,300 (six persons max). A designated 10-hour marlin hunt is $1,400 to $1,550, depending on the boat (all billfish are released). Double Header has a fleet that includes a 40-foot sportfishing boat and two 37-foot open fishing boats with large T-tops. Double Header operates out of Oasis Cove Marina, on the island's southern shore near Secret Harbour. All rods, reels, and tackle included.

Another company with nearly three decades of sportfishing experience, **Offshore Adventures ★★** (sportfishingstjohn.com; ✆ **340/513-0389** or 340776-6730) and its *Mixed Bag* lineup of boats departs from both St. Thomas (American Yacht Harbor in Red Hook) and St. John (the Westin resort and the NPS Cruz Bay dock). They offer customized inshore and offshore fishing expeditions. Inshore trips on the 40-foot *Mixed Bag III* (up to six persons) angle for snapper, kingfish, even shark and barracuda. Offshore trips troll the deep waters of the legendary North and South Drops for the big boys: yellowfin tuna, wahoo, mahi, and marlin. Half-day charters are $650 to $700, full-day charters $1,200 to $1,250 (depending on the boat). A 10-hour marlin trip is $1,300 to $1,400.

Ocean Surfari ★ (oceansurfari.com; ✆ **340/202-0444**), operating out of Red Hook Harbor, takes U.S.V.I. fishing charters out in 37-foot Calypso boats. Ocean Surfari's offshore sportfishing charters (six passengers max) cost $699 for 4-hour trips; $999 for 6-hour trips; and $1,299 for 8-hour trips. They also offer inshore bottom-fishing trips along deep-water reefs for $175 per person. They also offer complimentary pickups on St. John at the Cruz Bay Visitor Center.

You can line-fish from the rocky shore along **Mandahl Beach** on the north coast. The tourist office in Charlotte Amalie should have a listing of legal spots for line-fishing around the island.

GOLF Sadly, St. Thomas's lone golf course, **Mahogany Run,** on the North Shore at Mahogany Run Road, has remained idle since it was devastated by Hurricane Irma in 2017. The once-beautiful 130-acre 18-hole, par-70 course traversing sea cliffs and mossy peaks has been up for sale since 2018.

Virgin Islands Ecotours offers naturalist-led tours of St. Thomas's mangrove lagoons.

KAYAK TOURS **Virgin Islands Ecotours** (viecotours.com; ✆ **340/779-2155**) offers several kayak trips through the **Cas Cay mangrove lagoon** on the southern coastline. A 3-hour kayak, hike, and snorkel tour is $109 for adults, $79 for children ages 7 to 12. The tour is led by professional naturalists who allow for 30 to 40 minutes of snorkeling. It also offers sunset and night kayak tours.

SCUBA DIVING/SNUBA For novices, the best scuba-diving site off St. Thomas is **Cow and Calf Rocks,** off the southeast end (45 min. from Charlotte Amalie by boat); here, you'll discover a network of coral tunnels filled with caves, reefs, and ancient boulders encrusted with coral. The *Cartanser Senior,* a sunken World War II steel-hulled freighter that lies in about 50 feet of water, is beautifully covered with coral and home to myriad colorful resident fish. **Flat Cay,** a small island about 3 miles southwest from St. Thomas, has a spectacular reef alive with hard corals, sponges, and colorful fish. Some of the best dive sites off St. Thomas's northeastern coast include **Carval Rock,** just northeast of Lovango Cay, with rock formations, swim-throughs, and a multitude of corals and fish at depths of 15 to 80 feet; and **Congo Cay,** with rock formations and larger fish like eagle rays and reef sharks.

Experienced divers may want to dive at exposed sheer rock pinnacles like **French Cap Pinnacle,** 6 miles offshore, which are encrusted with hard and soft corals and frequented by lobsters and green and hawksbill turtles. Because it's exposed to open-ocean currents, these can be very challenging dives, but from January through May you can hear the undersea songs of migrating humpback whales.

One of the best places to learn to dive is the **St. Thomas Dive Center** ★ (formerly the St. Thomas Diving Club), at the Bolongo Bay Beach Resort (www.stthomasdivecenter.com; © **340/776-2381**). This full-service, PADI five-star IDC center offers open-water certification courses for $325 to $600. A two-tank dive morning or afternoon dive is $130; a night dive is $100.

Red Hook Dive Center ★, American Yacht Harbor, Red Hook (www.redhookdivecenter.com; © **340/777-3483**), is another well-respected full-service diving center offering professional instruction (beginner to advanced), daily beach and boat dives, and custom dive packages. An introductory resort course costs $90, with

Exploring coral-encrusted rocks with the St. Thomas Dive Center.

two-tank morning and afternoon dives for $119. Night dives are $109. They'll also take a snorkel straggler or two while others in the same group are diving.

Coki Dive Center ★, Coki Beach (cokidive.com; © **340/775-4220**), right next door to Coral World, is a full-service PADI dive center offering scuba-diving courses and guided boat, beach, and night-dive tours for beginners and certified divers alike. You can also rent diving gear here. A 2- to 3-day PADI Scuba Diver Course is $375. A two-tank morning boat dive is $125; a one-tank beach dive off Coki Beach is $80. Night dives are $90.

The PADI 5-star **Aqua Action Dive Center** (www.aadivers.com; © **340/775-6285**), on-site at the Secret Harbour Beach Resort, offers an introductory Discover Scuba course ($95/person, 10 years and older) as well as shore diving ($95/person) off the beach at Secret Harbour and two-tank boat dives ($135/person) for experienced divers.

Non-divers and beginning swimmers can still have a diving experience with **Virgin Islands Snuba Excursions** (www.visnuba.com; © **340/693-8063**). These unique excursions are offered both at **Coral World Ocean Park** (p. 113) on St. Thomas and at Trunk Bay on St. John. With Snuba's equipment—an air line that attaches to a tank floating on the surface—even novices can breathe easily underwater without the use of heavy and restrictive dive gear. The Snuba operations begin in waist-deep water and make a gradual descent to a depth of 20 feet. Kids ages 8 and up can participate, and no snorkeling or scuba experience is needed. Guided underwater tours take 1½ to 2 hours, cost $89 per person, and include a complimentary pass to Coral World. Reservations are required.

SNORKELING The island's best snorkeling spots include the rocks around **Coki Beach;** you can rent snorkeling gear for the day from the Coki Dive

Center (see above) for $10; locker rentals are $5. Another good spot to snorkel is **Secret Harbour;** you can rent full snorkel gear at Aqua Action Dive Center (see above) at the Secret Harbour Beach Resort; Aqua also offers half- and full-day snorkel-sail excursions. Snorkel gear is $20 a day and $80 a week. Green sea turtles and critically endangered hawksbill turtles snack on seagrass at **Brewers Bay,** on the island's southwest coast, close to the artificial reef created by the 1976 airport expansion; it's now home to a healthy population of hawksbill turtles. It's also close to the University of the Virgin Islands' **Center for Marine and Environmental Studies** and the **Sea Turtle Research and Conservation project** (www.uviseaturtleresearch.com), a research group dedicated to tracking and protecting the island's sea turtle populations. Another good beach for spotting sea turtles is pretty **Lindquist Beach,** in the 21-acre Smith Bay Park on the island's east coast.

Seeing the Sights

In 1733, the Danish government acquired the Virgin Islands from the Danish West India Company. While the Danes did not find the land suitable for agriculture, St. Thomas instead became a bustling port—and a center for transporting slaves. The Virgin Islands remained under Danish rule until 1917, when the U.S., fearing German infiltration in the Caribbean during World War I, purchased the islands from Denmark. For more detailed history, see p. 27 in Chapter 2.

Today the U.S. Virgin Islands claims the highest per-capita income in the Caribbean, with some 50,000 settlers of varying ethnicity making their home in St. Thomas alone. The port is also the busiest cruise-ship harbor in the West Indies, outranking Puerto Rico.

Today you can see many vestiges of the island's history in the capital, **Charlotte Amalie,** whose architecture reflects the island's culturally diverse

Day Tripping to St. John

Most visitors to St. Thomas include a day trip to beautiful sister island St. John for swimming, snorkeling, hiking, or just hanging out on one of the island beaches. Ferries to St. John leave every hour on the hour from Red Hook ($6/person) and last only 15 to 20 minutes; you can also catch less frequent ferries from the Charlotte Amalie ferry terminal. It's easy to make a day of it: The last ferry returning from Cruz Bay, St. John, is at 11pm. Car ferries also run between Red Hook and Cruz Bay, traveling every half-hour from 7am to 7pm daily; book ahead on one of three carriers: **Boyson** (☏ **340/776-6294**); **Love City** (☏ **340/779-4000**); or **Global Marine** (☏ **340/779-1739**). Car-ferry rates run from $42 to $50 round-trip; arrive at least 15 minutes before departure. If you don't have a car, have taxi driver **Kenneth Lewis** (☏ **340/776-6865**) or one of his cohorts meet you at the ferry terminal in St. John for transportation to and from the beach, the park, or wherever you decide to spend the day. At the end of your day, return to Cruz Bay for shopping and dinner and catch the ferry home right there on the harborfront.

In 1917 the U.S.V.I. was officially transferred from Denmark to the United States at Legislature House, a former military barracks on King's Wharf in Charlotte Amalie.

past: You'll pass Dutch doors, Danish red-tile roofs, French iron grillwork, and Spanish-style patios. The town is filled with historic sights, like **Fort Christian,** an intriguing 17th-century building constructed by the Danes. With its white houses and bright red roofs glistening in the sun, the city is terraced along green hills that rise sharply from the harbor. For dramatic views of Charlotte Amalie's harbor, take a ride on the Paradise Point Skyride (p. 112). Farther west, Harwood Highway (Rte. 308) will lead you to **Crown Mountain Road,** a scenic drive opening onto the best views of the hills, beaches, and crystal-clear waters around St. Thomas.

Most people see the sights around the island on an **island taxi tour.** Expect to pay about $50 for a single-passenger tour or $25 per person for two or more passengers for 2 hours of sightseeing in a shared car. Most taxi drivers offer them, so they can vary in quality. We recommend **Llewelyn Powell** (✆ **340/771-1568** or 340/776-3887) and his associates.

HISTORIC WALKING TOURS

Well worth your time is a **historic walking tour ★★★** of downtown Charlotte Amalie with the engaging and informative guides of the **St. Thomas Historical Trust** (www.stthomashistoricaltrust.org; ✆ **340/774-5541**). The tours take in the breadth and depth of 400 years of St. Thomas history; highlights include Fort Christian, the 99 Steps, and Hotel 1829. The 3-hour rambles start around 9am at the Emancipation Park Center and cost $54.67 per person. The Trust was established in 1966 and has been a leader in historic preservation and restoration initiatives around the island.

The walking tour below should whet your appetite for an on-the-ground tour of the historic district of Charlotte Amalie.

WALKING TOUR: **CHARLOTTE AMALIE**

START:	**King's Wharf**
FINISH:	**Waterfront**
TIME:	**2½ hours**
BEST TIME:	**Before 10am and after 3pm to avoid cruise-ship hordes**
WORST TIME:	**Around midday to 4pm, when traffic and pedestrians are at their most plentiful**

It is easy to see how the natural colors and charm of the Caribbean come to life in the waterfront town of Charlotte Amalie. The capital of St. Thomas once attracted seafarers from all over the globe. At one time, it was even the biggest slave market in the world. Today, the handsome old warehouses that line the cobbled downtown streets have been converted into shops and restaurants. In fact, the main streets, called "gade" (a reflection of their Danish heritage), now coalesce into a virtual shopping mall packed with duty-free shops. On their eastern flank is Kongens (King's) Quarter, the oldest section of town. Most of its historic sites can be seen on foot in about 2 hours. Start your walking tour along the eastern harborfront at King's Wharf.

As you're walking the historic district, look for **ashlar stone,** larger rectangular stones that arrived as ship ballast and were placed in front of important buildings or to note the beginning or end of a block. The streets are dotted with **"blue bitch" stone,** a strong native stone in a slate-blue hue that's hard to cleave—traditionally you have to burn it for days to cut. Even the stone gutters are made of blue bitch.

1 King's Wharf

This is the site of the Virgin Islands Legislature. The two-story structure was first built in 1824 as a military barracks for the Danish Police. The current building dates from 1874. In a ceremony on this site in 1917, ownership of the Virgin Islands was officially transferred from the Danish West Indies to the U.S.—bought for a then-pretty price of $25 million.

From here, walk away from the harbor up Fort Pladsen to:

2 Fort Christian

Dating from 1680 and named after the Danish king Christian V, this handsome salmon-red structure is the oldest standing building in the entire U.S. Virgin Islands. It has been a fort (with 3- to 6-foot-thick walls), a governor's residence, a prison (with a downstairs dungeon), a police station, and a court. It was named a National Historic Landmark in 1977. The fort and museum were reopened to the public on Transfer Day 2017 after a meticulous restoration effort, closely hewing to historical accuracy, dragged on for 13 long years—only to shutter 5 months later after the September 2017 hurricanes. It reopened once more in 2018.

4

ST. THOMAS

Walking Tour: Charlotte Amalie

Built in 1680, the landmark Fort Christian (p. 105) has over the years been a fort, a governor's manor, a prison, a police station, and a court.

Continue walking up Fort Pladsen to:

3 Emancipation Garden

This is where a proclamation freeing African slaves and indentured European servants was read on July 4, 1848. The *Freedom Statue* of a conch blower memorializes the blowing of the conch that let other islanders know about the "Fireburn" labor revolt by enslaved peoples in St. Croix. The park is now mostly a picnic area for local workers and visitors.

Southwest of the park is the:

4 Grand Hotel

When it opened as a hotel in 1837, it was a grand address, with the island's first spiral staircase built out of stone. But it later fell into decay and closed in 1975. At press time, the Grand Hotel was being revitalized once more as a multi-purpose complex of shops and cafes—a boon for the downtown waterfront.

Northwest of the park, at Main Street and Tolbod Gade, stands the:

5 Central Post Office

Pop in to see the two remarkable WPA murals by American artist Stevan Dohanos, who gained fame as an illustrator for *The Saturday Evening Post*.

From the post office, walk east along Norre Gade to the:

6 Frederik Lutheran Church

This, the island's oldest church building, was built between 1780 and 1793. The original Georgian-style building, financed by a free black parishioner, Jean Reeneaus, was refurbished in 1826 and again in 1870 with Gothic and gabled flourishes. It has a "welcoming arms" entrance stairway and is recognizable by its distinctive yellow-gold hue. (It also has one of the biggest ovens on the island.)

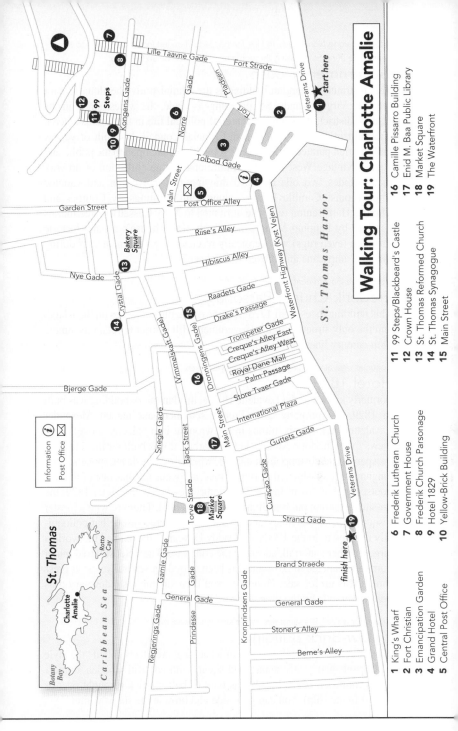

Walking Tour: Charlotte Amalie

St. Thomas Harbor

Information ⓘ
Post Office ✉

St. Thomas

Botany Bay
Caribbean Sea
Charlotte Amalie
Rotto Cay

1 King's Wharf
2 Fort Christian
3 Emancipation Garden
4 Grand Hotel
5 Central Post Office

6 Frederik Lutheran Church
7 Government House
8 Frederik Church Parsonage
9 Hotel 1829
10 Yellow-Brick Building

11 99 Steps/Blackbeard's Castle
12 Crown House
13 St. Thomas Reformed Church
14 St. Thomas Synagogue
15 Main Street

16 Camille Pissarro Building
17 Enid M. Baa Public Library
18 Market Square
19 The Waterfront

Walk east along Norre Gade to Lille Taarne Gade. Turn left (north) and climb to Kongens Gade (King St.), passing through a neighborhood of law firms, to:

7 Government House

This restrained Georgian building is the administrative headquarters for the U.S. Virgin Islands. Set on Kongens Gade, the widest street in the historic district, it's been the center of political life in the islands since it was built in 1850 for the Danish Colonial Council. It's built of yellow ballast brick painted white. The first two floors are open to the public and contain vintage West Indian furniture and a state collection of artwork that includes two oils and two drawings by native son and vaunted Impressionist Camille Pisarro, along with paintings by Courbet and Thomas Hart Benton (and one attributed to Mary Cassatt). Three murals here are by Peppino Mangravite. Much of the house's art and historic furniture (even rugs) was heroically rescued by government staff during the 2017 hurricane and moved to safekeeping.

Next to the Government House is:

8 Frederik Church Parsonage

This building dates from 1725. It's one of the oldest houses on the island, and the only structure in the Government Hill district to retain its simple 18th-century lines.

Continue west along Kongens Gade until you reach:

9 Hotel 1829

Formerly known as the Lavalette House, this landmark building was built in 1829, the property of a French sea merchant named Alexander Lavalette (look for his initials in the wrought-iron balcony above). With views over Charlotte Amalie and the harbor, it was built during a time of prosperity and cosmopolitan culture, when even the slaves spoke several languages. It's fashioned of rubble masonry walls and has one of the few bootscrapers in town. In its 20th-century heyday as the Hotel 1829, the on-site restaurant put fine dining on the map in St. Thomas, with a lobster bisque that was legendary and a famous Hemingwayesque bar colloquially referred to in the 1960s as "Daddy Daycare." It even had the world's largest amber waterfall, adorning the courtyard. The hotel suffered major hurricane damage in 2017 and has been closed for several years; at press time it was up for sale. Hopefully you'll be sipping a sundowner on its perfect veranda by the time you read this.

Next door (still on the same side of the street), observe the:

10 Yellow-Brick Building

This structure was built in 1854 in what local architects called "the style of Copenhagen"—it's square and squat, with colorful wooden shutters and a roof tiled of marble. It was built of ballast brick (brought over as ballast in the ship). You can go inside and browse the shops within.

At this point, you might want to double back slightly on Kongens Gade to climb the famous:

11 99 Steps/Blackbeard's Castle

These steps (actually 103 in total) were erected in the early 1700s and take you to the summit of Government Hill. You will find yourself near the foot of more stairs leading to Blackbeard's Castle, a watch tower built in 1679 by the Danes and originally known as Skytsborg. It's not open to the public.

From the top of the hill, immediately to your right on the south side of the street, you'll see:

12 Crown House

This stately 18th-century private house was the home of Peter von Schol-ten, the Danish ruler who famously freed the slaves in 1848 without the permission of the Danish king and issued the proclamation of emancipa-tion in 1848 (see Emancipation Garden, p. 106). Von Scholten also reportedly had a "free-colored" consort for 20 years, the daughter of a freed mulatto woman and a Danish bureaucrat. The house has pitch-pine flooring and 18-foot ceilings; like other historic homes in the area, its "trade ceilings" were built to capture the prevailing winds blowing east to west across town.

Walk back down the steps and continue right (west) along Kongens Gade, then down a pair of old brick steps until you reach Garden Street. Go right (north) on Garden Street and take a left onto Crystal Gade. On your left, at the corner of Nye Gade and Crystal Gade, you'll see:

13 St. Thomas Reformed Church

This Classical Revival building is from 1844, but it holds one of the old-est congregations in the Virgin Islands, established by Dutch traders

Step Streets & the Three Queens

Back in the 1700s when the Danes were laying out the grid for Charlotte Amalie, the town's vertical topography required a different kind of infrastructure: the construction of *frigangs*, aka stone "step streets," that climb the steep hill-sides rising from the Charlotte Amalie harbor. Charming and picturesque, the streets were built from the ballast in the hulls of Danish ships. Today the Char-lotte Amalie Historic District has more step streets than anywhere else in the world. Maintenance of these centuries-old streets and beautification efforts are ongoing. Of the town's 47 step streets, the most famous is the **99 Steps** (103, to be exact), which has been planted with aromatic flowers like jasmine, to attract birds, and yellow cedar, the national flower. On the step street known as **Blackbeard's Hill** (which turns into Dronningens Gade), just below Blackbeard's Castle, the statue *The Three Queens of the Virgin Islands* hon-ors the three former slave women who in 1878 led a labor revolt in St. Croix, known as Fireburn for its destruction by fire of much of Frederiksted. These three "queens"—Mary, Agnes, and Matilda—were not noble by birth but are so honored for their impact on the country. The proliferation of flaming orange ixora planted here symbolizes the fires of the insurrection.

around 1660. The church has been buffeted by fire and natural disasters: Fire destroyed two early-19th-century iterations (and a 1995 hurricane, Marilyn, damaged the sanctuary), but much of the 1844 structure, designed like a Greek temple, has been beautifully restored.

Continue up Crystal Gade. On your right (north side), you'll come to:

14 St. Thomas Synagogue

This is the oldest synagogue in continuous use under the American flag, and the second oldest in the Western Hemisphere. Nine Sephardic Jewish families founded the congregation in 1796; the current building was erected in 1833. It still maintains the tradition of having sand on the floor, said to have muffled the sounds of worshippers' footsteps during the persecution of Jews during the Spanish Inquisition (many communities of Sephardic Jews flourished in the Caribbean after being driven out of Spain in 1492). The structure is made of local stone, ballast brick from Denmark, and mortar made of molasses and sand; the pews are made of local mahogany. It's open for **tours** ★★ (appt. only; synagogue.vi; ✆ **340/774-4312**) Monday to Thursday 9:30, 10:30, and 11:30am, and 1:30, 2:30, and 3:30pm; Friday 9:30, 10:30, and 11:30am, and 1:30 to 3pm. A gift shop is located just outside the sanctuary.

Retrace your steps (east) to Raadets Gade and turn south toward the water, crossing the famous Vimmelskaft Gade or "Back Street" (it can get a bit seedy at night, so be aware if you are walking after dark). Continue along Raadets Gade until you reach:

15 Main Street

This is Charlotte Amalie's major artery and most famous shopping street.

Turn right (west) and walk along Main Street until you come to:

16 Camille Pissarro Building

Camille Pissarro, a Spanish Jew who became one of the founders of French Impressionism, was born in 14 Main Street as Jacob Pizarro in 1830. Before moving to Paris, he worked for his father in a store on Main Street. On the second floor is **Gallery Camille Pissarro,** with a few Pissarro paintings on display and prints by local artists for sale.

Continuing west along Main Street, you will pass on your right the:

17 Enid M. Baa Public Library

This building, formerly the von Bretton House, dates from 1818.

Keep heading west until you reach:

18 Market Square

This was the center of a large slave-trading market before the 1848 emancipation and is officially called Rothschild Francis Square. Today it's an open-air fruit and vegetable market, selling, among other items, *genips* (grape-type fruit; to eat one, break open the skin and suck the pulp off the pit) and seafood on Saturdays. The wrought-iron roof covered a railway station at the turn of the 20th century. The market is open Monday to Saturday, but Saturday is its busiest day; hours vary, but generally 9am to 3pm.

If the *genip* doesn't satisfy you, take Strand Gade down (south) to:

19 The Waterfront

Also known as Kyst Vejen, this is where you'll have an up-close view of one of the most scenic harbors in the West Indies.

OTHER CHARLOTTE AMALIE ATTRACTIONS

Bluebeard's Tower Museum ★★ MUSEUM Built in 1685, this was one of the lookout keeps built to watch over and protect the Charlotte Amalie harbor; the original brick in the ceiling was brought over as ship ballast. Over the years, it's been a prison and a governor's mansion and was even at one time the Bluebeard resort's honeymoon suite—and it was built to last, with walls that are at least a foot thick. Museum curator, diver, and treasurehunter Sean Loughman calls his collection of historic flotsam and jetsam brought up from the sea a "poor man's museum," a motley assemblage of artifacts that includes a captain's dinner plate from a ship that went down in the harbor in October 1867, during a hurricane that killed 500 people ("not a leaf left on the tree"), followed by a tsunami and earthquake 2 weeks later. It's a cool little place, with wooden nails, muskets from the 1860s, cannon-

Random artifacts from the sea intrigue visitors to Bluebeard's Tower Museum.

balls, swords, an early-19th-century left-handed dagger, pieces of eight (the phrase "hand over fist" comes from the process of striking silver coins), RMST clock hands, and a jumble of dinner plates wrapped in metal from a supply ship that went down in 1816—as the wreck oxidized, the plates fused with the metal. Sean starred with Philippe Cousteau in the Travel Channel's *Caribbean Pirate Treasure* and also sells a few treasures (including shipwreck pirate coins) at his shop on the first floor of Bluebeards Castle resort. Hours for the museum can be iffy, but try to schedule one of Sean's guided tours ($10) of the Tower. And keep in mind, as Sean reminds you: Blackbeard was real; Bluebeard is fiction.

Bluebeards Castle Resort. Museum Tower tour ($10) by appointment only; call ✆ **340/998-3819**. $5 self-guided tour (open hours change regularly).

Mountain Top ★ VIEW You come not for the massive warehouse of tourist gewgaws or the frozen banana daiquiris in foot-tall glasses in rainbow hues. No, you come for what is still one of the most **breathtaking views** ★★★ in all the Caribbean, overlooking the shimmering sapphire seas of Magens Bay, at what is St. Thomas's highest point. (You can get similar great views without all the tourist trinkets at **Drake's Seat,** where Sir Francis Drake is said to have had a lookout point, as any good pirate plunderer did back in the day.) A

MEMORIES OF A carnival CHILDHOOD

In the 1970s and early '80's, my childhood revelry days, plans for the **St. Thomas Carnival** went into full swing at the first of the year, after the holiday celebrations were over. They actually started at the end of the previous Carnival as troupes began thinking of ways to add more excitement, glamour, and fun to the coming year's events. My father helped design and build floats with Hecter Roebuck, affectionally known as Grandfather Roebuck, of the Elskoe Roebuck Carnival troupe. I was part of the "glitter brigade," when all of Hecter's "grandchildren" gathered after school to sprinkle glitter on costumes and float details. We were rewarded for our efforts in candy. At the end of the day, we went home happily full of M&Ms and Skittles, our school uniforms and gym clothes spangled with gold and silver glitter.

There were 2 weeks of daily Carnival activities, but leading up to that magical parade weekend in April were several other equally exciting events. Schools competed heavily against one another for top prizes in the **Children's Parade,** while top local troupes like the Gypsies, Jesters, Gathering of the Eagles, Easter Parade, and Elskoe Roebuck battled in an array of spots for the adults' parade. The entries brought that year's Carnival theme to life with costumes and floats. Individual entries poked fun at political satire and events of the day, while majorettes, pageant queens, Moko Jumbies, Indians, and clowns brought up the rear of the parade.

My fondest memories of Carnival include getting brand-new jeans and that year's Carnival T-shirts to wear to the parade and lacing up my sneakers with bells like a V.I. Carnival clown. We are not talking circus clown, mind you—a Carnival clown costume is velvet trimmed in sparkling sequin, with a hooded cape (emblazoned with initials or a decal) and bells, all topped off with a hat, a mask, and a whip. The Carnival clowns did precisely choreographed dance routines as they marched. In spring, every troupe practiced their own dance routines after school and on Saturdays. The big performance was judged at the Post Office Square downtown and at the stadium where the parade ended. Carnival Road March competitions celebrated that year's most popular musical composition.

number of tour companies can deliver you to the top, as will any good taxi driver. Contact Big Moe at **Paradise Taxi & Tours USVI** (paradisetaxiusvi. weebly.com; ✆ **404/713-8430**) for its Tropical Island Scenic Tour, which also includes stops at Drake's Seat, Fort Christian, and the Skyline Drive Lookout ($34/person).

St. Peter Mountain Rd. www.mountaintopvi.com. ✆ **340/774-2400.** Free admission. Daily 9am–5pm.

Paradise Point Skyride ★ VIEW This aerial tramway takes riders to a 700-foot peak above Charlotte Amalie and the St. Thomas harbor—a great vantage point for seeing the giant cruise ships from above. The tram, similar to those used at ski resorts, operates six cars, each with an eight-person capacity, for the 7-minute round-trip ride. It transports customers from the Havensight area to Paradise Point, where you can disembark to visit shops, take photos from the Skywalk, or sip a cocktail (including the famed Bailey's

St. Thomas's Carnival parade takes over Charlotte Amalie every April.

the bands begin to play, we'd run out of our homes in our pajamas to the Waterfront to tramp behind our favorite band. Exhausted at the end, we headed to the **Carnival Village** in the Fort Christian parking lot for hot bush tea, pates and johnnycakes, a fried chicken leg, or a bowl of hot soup.

The **Carnival Food Fair** brought out the best in local culinary skills. Delicacies prepared by the island's best cooks filled the fair tables: candies, pastries, preserves, and stews. Vendors sold an array of local fruit trees and plants and native crafts. All the things you normally couldn't find year-round were available at the fair.

Nick "Daddy" Friday, the lead singer of the Jam Band, the most popular Carnival local band, captured the essence of Carnival in a Road March–winning song **"Show Time"**—and that's what Carnival is in the Virgin Islands. At Daddy Friday's funeral in 2005, an attendee noted: "If Jam Band was passing by a cemetery on a good day, a parade day, I believe dead people would get up and start to dance."

—*St. Thomas historian Felipe Ayala*

I was not always allowed to go to **J'ouvert,** the early-morning tramp before the parade, but that is still one of the most exciting and best-attended events of Carnival. The minute we heard

Bushwacker drink). It's even got a fine-dining restaurant: **PRIME at Paradise Point** ★ (www.facebook.com/PRIMEatParadisePoint; ✆ **340/690-2191**) gets raves for its prime steaks and prime Charlotte Amalie views.

Havensight Mall. www.paradisepointvi.com. ✆ **340/774-9809.** Reservations required. $25 adults, $17 ages 6–12, free for children 5 and under. Daily 9am–5pm.

ATTRACTIONS AROUND THE ISLAND

Coral World Ocean Park ★★ AQUARIUM   This fabulous little ocean park has a small footprint but packs an outsize conservation message. It's a labor of love, owned and largely supported by a philanthropist passionate about animals. It's not just an aquarium; it's a technical research facility doing target training with sharks, turtles, and stingrays as well as a rebab for turtles injured in shark and human encounters. When we visited, tire-size loggerhead turtles were being hand-fed lettuces by staff, and small children were agog at a roomful of rainbow lorikeets. A three-story **Undersea Observatory** 100 feet offshore lets you see aquatic reef life without getting wet. The biggest new attraction is the state-of-the-art **Dolphin Sea Sanctuary**—at nearly 2 acres, it's one of the largest ocean dolphin sanctuaries in the world. It holds six Atlantic bottlenose dolphins, all born and raised in captivity and four of whom were living in a pool in the desert (Arizona's Dolphinarius) before being relinquished to Coral World in 2019. Seeing them interact in their new environment has been a thrill for all involved. "They now live in an in-ocean environment, not a stagnant lagoon, like at many other dolphin facilities," says Coral World's Valerie Peters. "They have moon, tides, currents, even 3-foot waves." Although breeding was not part of the strategic plan, a 23-year-old named Ping had a successful pregnancy in 2022, a clear indication that the animals have acclimated to the natural ocean waters. The **Dolphin Splash & Swim** ($182.50/person, ages 7 and up) gives visitors the chance to gently interact with the dolphins in the water; other dolphin encounters are also available.

Coral World is also one of three facilities in the world where you can swim with sea lions. The South American sea lions here are 500 pounds of pure mush. "They're like big lab dogs, with no concept of personal space," says Peters. The **Sea Lion Swim** ($182.50 all visitors; includes Coral World admission; children 7 and older only) lets you swim with the sea lions; the **Sea Lion Encounter** ($119 adults, $71.40 accompanied children 9 and under; includes Coral World admission) lets you interact with sea lions without getting wet. For the **Shark Encounter** ($64 all visitors; includes Coral World admission), you enter a shallow pool with juvenile sharks. Age and/or height and weight restrictions apply to all activities.

Non-divers can get some of the thrill long known to scuba aficionados by participating in **Sea Trek,** which is slightly different from **Snuba,** also offered here (p. 101). For $86 per person, you are fully immersed undersea with a helmet and a breathing tube attached to an air source at the observatory tower. You then enjoy a 20-minute stroll in water that's 18 feet deep, observing rainbow-hued tropical fish and coral reefs as you stroll along the seafloor. No experience necessary.

Note: Reservations for all are required, so log on to the park's website.

The marine park also has duty-free shops and a nature trail. The on-site cafe, damaged in the 2017 hurricanes, will be replaced by a **fine-dining restaurant** in 2023. Coral World's guests can take advantage of adjacent **Coki Beach** for swimming and snorkeling. You can rent lockers, lounge chairs, and watersports equipment at the **Coki Dive Center** (p. 102) or right on the beach.

6450 Estates Smith Bay, a 20-min. drive from Charlotte Amalie off Rte. 38. coralworldvi. com. ℭ **340/775-1555.** Admission $19 adults, $10 children ages 3–12. Daily 9am–4pm.

FRENCHTOWN

Route 30 (Veterans Dr.) will take you west of Charlotte Amalie to the 19th-century fishing settlement of **Frenchtown.** Early French-speaking settlers arrived on St. Thomas from St. Barts after they were uprooted by the Swedes. Many of today's island residents are the direct descendants of those long-ago immigrants, who were known for speaking a distinctive French patois. The narrow, winding streets of this colorful neighborhood trace the harbor where

"Frenchies" worked largely as fishermen but also as boat-builders, farmers, craftspeople, and stone masons. Back in the day, Frenchtown was known as "Cha-Cha Town" for the little fish Frenchtown fishermen sold in the streets, calling out "Cha-cha for sale." Today the area has a number of excellent restaurants and taverns, including **Oceana** (p. 88). Fisherman still dock and sell their catches at the **Gustave Quetel Fish House** in the mornings; holding pride of place here is a large David Francke 2006 mural of fishermen fixing their nets. The mustard-hued **St. Anne Chapel** (cathedralvi.org/chapel-of-saint-anne), on Gallows Hill, is over a century old, one of the oldest active churches in St. Thomas still in its original structure.

French Heritage Museum ★ MUSEUM Overseen with care by Henry Richardson, this quaint little museum opened in 2004 in two traditional Frenchtown cottages. The museum is basically one big room of stuff that the 75-year-old Frenchtown Civic Organization has collected over the years: woven baskets and jaunty straw hats; a gleaming mahogany bed in a coverlet of handwoven lace; plus coal pots, vintage sewing machines, and early electric toasters, the household detritus of a distinctive society that emigrated from Normandy and Brittany via St. Barts. A second historic structure, the **Louis Phillipe Greaux House,** was donated to the museum by the Greaux family and moved here in 2007.

14-15 Rue de Ste. Barthelemy, Frenchtown. ℭ **340/714-2583.** Donations welcome. Mon–Fri 10am–1pm.

Excursions from St. Thomas
WATER ISLAND
Water Island, ¾ mile off the coast from the harbor at Charlotte Amalie, is the fourth-largest island in the U.S. Virgins, with nearly 500 acres of land. Irregular in shape, 2½-mile-long Water Island is fringed with many bays and peninsulas, and studded with several good, sandy beaches along with secluded coves and rocky headlands. Established as the fourth U.S. Virgin Island in 1996, Water Island was once a part of a peninsula jutting out from St. Thomas, but a channel was cut through, allowing U.S. submarines to reach their base in a bay to the west. This residential island of some 200 people has a rich history that includes freed slaves, novelist Herman Wouk, and singer-songwriter Jimmy Buffett (see "Water Island Lore & History," p. 116).

At palm-shaded **Honeymoon Beach,** you can swim, snorkel, sail, water-ski, or sunbathe. The beach has been significantly improved in the past few years, as loads of rocks and gravel were hauled off and trees and brush removed. The sand was sifted to get rid of debris, and a dredge removed the seaweed and deposited white sand on the shore. Today it looks quite beautiful.

Ten years ago, there was no commerce on the island—no restaurants, shops, or hotels (although you can rent houses or villas). But that's no longer the case. Honeymoon Beach is where the action is, with **Dinghy's Beach Bar** (dinghysbeachbar.com; ℭ **340/227-5525**) and **Heidi's Honeymoon Grill** (ℭ **340/690-0325**), Providence Hill, offering food and drink. Dinghy's rents lounge chairs ($10/day) and kayaks, snorkel gear, and SUPs (rented by the hour). Dinghy's is open daily from 10:30am to 8:30pm. Heidi's is open for breakfast and lunch (daily 8:30am–3pm). You can stay overnight on Water Island in eco-tent cottages in the **Virgin Islands Campground** (p. 82). At press time, a proposal to build a 14-room hotel, **Flamingo Bay Eco Resort,** on the southern end of Water Island in an abandoned 1950s fort complex, was under consideration.

You can get to the island by ferry, private boat, or even on cycleboat excursions. The **Water Island Ferry** (waterislandferry.com; ✆ 340/690-4159) travels between the island's Philips Landing and Crown Bay Marina several times a day for $10 one-way, $15 round-trip ($3/$5 children). A free shuttle operated by Dinghy's Beach Bar (see above) takes ferry passengers to Honeymoon Beach. Pedal your way to Water Island on an excursion with **St. Thomas Cycleboats** (stthomascycleboats.com; ✆ 340/643-9401; 16 passengers max), basically a motorized floating bar/bike with "interactive cycle stations"—you may or not feel like pedaling as you sip a rum punch. A 3-hour trip to Water Island from the Crown Bay Marina is $85 per person.

WATER ISLAND lore & history

To the native residents of St. Thomas, Water Island remains a land of legend and lore, having been settled by the Arawak Indians in the early 15th century. In the days of Caribbean piracy, as evoked by Disney's *Pirates of the Caribbean* movies, the island was used for anchorage and fresh water, as pirates found numerous freshwater ponds here. Islanders on St. Thomas claim that millions of dollars in pirate treasure remain buried on Water Island, but so far no one has dug it up. An old leather trunk was once discovered, but it was empty except for one gold doubloon.

When European colonization arrived in the late 17th century, many Danes tried to use the island for raising cows and goats, but its land proved too arid. White plantation owners and colonists shunned the island, so unlike the rest of the Caribbean, Water Island was farmed by nonwhite plantation owners, freed men of color like Jean Renaud, a free mulatto who owned the entire island in 1769, working it with 18 slaves.

In 1944, the United States bought the island for $10,000. The military began planning Fort Segarra here, but World War II ended before it could be built. Traces of "the fort that never was" can still be seen today.

In 1950, the Department of the Interior leased the island to Water Phillips, a developer, for $3,000 annually. He built homes and a 100-room hotel. Popular in the 1950s, the hotel became the setting for Herman Wouk's 1965 novel, *Don't Stop the Carnival*, which Jimmy Buffet turned into a short-lived musical in 1997. (Incidentally, native residents of St. Croix claim that the novel was based on a hotel being built in the harbor of Christiansted.) In 1989, Hurricane Hugo severely damaged the hotel, and it was shut down; it lies dormant today. Phillips' lease ran out, and in 1996, Water Island was transferred to the federal government, in whose hands it remains today. At present (and likely to remain so for a long time to come), no foundations have been poured on Water Island. Nothing has been inaugurated. The cost of developing roads, irrigation, and sewage lines in this eco-sensitive environment is a daunting challenge and a dream that, for the immediate future, remains too expensive an undertaking.

HASSEL ISLAND

In the same bay as Water Island, and even closer to shore, is 136-acre **Hassel Island** (www.hasselisland.org). Like Water Island, Hassel Island was once connected to the mainland of St. Thomas, until a channel was dug in 1865 for easier passage of ships. Today this island is almost completely deserted and protected as part of the Virgin Islands National Park, which prohibits most forms of development. There are no hotels or services of any kind here.

Hassel Island was once used by the Danes to defend the port of Charlotte Amalie; **Prince Frederik's Battery,** built in the late 1700s, still hugs the shoreline. During the early 19th century's Napoleonic Wars, the British occupied the island, and the ruins of two forts that the troops constructed here, Willoughby and Shipley, can be explored today. In 1840, the Danes built a marine railway operation for boat and sail repairs, one of the earliest steam-powered marine railways in the Western Hemisphere. As late as the 1960s, the **Creque Marine Railway** was still in operation, the oldest surviving example of a steam-powered marine railway in the world. You can see the ruins from the Frenchtown shoreline. During the latter part of the 19th century, Hassel Island was also a coal depot, and "coal women"—who famously carried heavy loads of coal in baskets on their heads—were able to fuel a ship in 6 to 7 hours. At night, the coal carriers drank a drink called "mauby" to "cleanse" themselves. This fermented drink, made from the roots and bark of trees, is set outside to ferment, and when the foam rises, locals say "Mauby Wukin' Hard!"

In 1978, some 90% of Hassel Island was sold to the U.S. National Park Service by its then owners, the Paiewonski family. For almost 30 years, the island sat untouched and deteriorating until it was discovered by MTV location scouts as the ideal setting for the 27th season of the network's popular *Real World* franchise. *Real World: St. Thomas* debuted in 2012, with the participants living in an old estate. Today, the MTV crew is long gone, but you can visit Hassel through **St. Thomas Historical Trust** (www.stthomashistorical trust.org/hassel-island-tour), which offers 2½-hour **self-guided walking tours** of the island ($75; maximum 8 people). Participants meet at the Historical Trust Museum and ride on boats leaving from the Charlotte Amalie harborfront to the island. Trails take you across gentle hills with dry woods, lots of plants, and plenty of cacti—you'll think you're in the Arizona desert. The western shore has white sands shaded by sea grapes. The island has little shade, so bring along hats and plenty of sunscreen.

SHOPPING

For centuries, St. Thomas has been the marketplace of the Caribbean and the hub of the supply chain. Discounted, duty-free shopping in the Virgin Islands makes it possible to find well-known brand names here at good savings off mainland prices. And each U.S. resident is given a $1,600 duty-free allowance—even kids. Even better: St. Thomas has no sales tax. But be warned—savings are not always guaranteed, so make sure you know the price of the

THE NOTORIOUS LAIR OF epstein island

The late Jeffrey Epstein, secretive financier and convicted sex offender, owned two small private islands located off the East End of St. Thomas, Little and Great St. James. He lived on 78-acre Little St. James, better known by the locals as Epstein Island; visitors included luminaries like former President Bill Clinton and Britain's Prince Andrew. Epstein flouted local laws, barreling through unauthorized construction activity despite stop-work orders and making environmentally questionable moves like blocking the beach with rocks so no one could anchor.

The V.I. Department of Planning and Natural Resources responded by charging him with hefty fines, penalties that ultimately totaled some $3 million. The fines were paid, but the rocks remained and construction proceeded apace. Security guards roamed the island and, as the *Virgin Island Daily News* reported, would walk to the water's edge whenever guides led scuba divers to spots around it.

When news of Epstein's arrest for pedophilia hit, it became, as one local put it, "our dark corner." Epstein bought Little St. James for $8 million in 1998 and neighboring 160-acre Great St. James for $18 million in 2016. In December 2022, Epstein's estate agreed to "wind down its business operations in the U.S. Virgin Islands" and pay the V.I. government $105 million to settle claims that his legal team fraudulently obtained massive tax benefits to buy Little St. James. Sadly, it was also revealed that Epstein had bulldozed the remains of historic slave structures on Great St. James to make room for a large development—a compound that was never completed. The settlements will be funded by the sale of the islands, at a current price tag of $55 million each—and part of the 2022 settlement is that the government pockets half of the proceeds of the sale of Little St. James.

item back home to determine if you are truly getting a good deal. For more help, the local publications *This Week in St. Thomas* and *Places to Explore* have updates on sales and shop openings.

Most shops are open Monday to Saturday 9am to 5pm. Some stores are open Sunday and holidays if a cruise ship is in port.

The Best Buys & Where to Find Them

The best buys on St. Thomas have traditionally included china, crystal, perfumes, jewelry (especially emeralds), Haitian art, clothing, watches, and items made of wood. St. Thomas is also the best place in the Caribbean for discounts in porcelain, but remember that U.S. brands are often 25% off the retail price on the mainland. Look for imported patterns for the biggest savings. Cameras and electronic items, based on our experience, are not the good buys they're reputed to be.

The major shopping in St. Thomas has traditionally been along the historic harborfront of Charlotte Amalie. It's an active shopping scene in an atmospheric historic setting (some shops occupy former pirate warehouses), and the principal shopping street, **Main Street,** has been beautifully repaved with Eurocobble and native blue bitch stone. Alas, most of the duty-free shops tout the same stuff: high-end jewelry, watches, electronics, perfumes, china, and souvenir tchotchkes made in China. Shops selling locally made arts and crafts and unique artisanal wares are few and far between.

Downtown Charlotte Amalie streets still have their old Danish names, so Main Street is called **Dronningens Gade.** To the north is **Back Street,** or Vimmelskaft. Many shops are also spread along the **Waterfront Highway** (also called Kyst Vejen). Between these major streets lies a series of side streets, passageways, and stone alleys—Tolbod Gade, Raadets Gade, Royal Dane Mall, Palm Passage, Storetvaer Gade, and Strand Gade—each one packed with duty-free shops and the occasional cafe, like Gladys' (p. 86) and Amalia (p. 82).

The duty-free scene continues at **Havensight Mall** (www.wico-ltd.com/ havensight-mall), right on the Havensight cruise-ship dock at the eastern edge of Charlotte Amalie, but you'll see little here you won't find at most other Caribbean duty-free ports—other than shops selling watersports apparel: Caribbean Surf (www.facebook.com/caribbeansurf; ✆ **340/776-4540**), a surf shop selling men's and women's rash guards, swimsuits, surfboards, paddle-boards, and gifts; and Ocean Surfari (shop.oceansurfari.com; ✆ **340/779-7833**), offering casual wear from swimsuits to dresses, hoodies, coverups, shirts, shorts, plus hats and flipflops.

The mega-yacht marina next door, **Yacht Haven Grande** (www.igymarinas. com/marinas/marina-yacht-haven-grande), has a sprinkling of boutique shops interspersed among a number of waterside restaurants. At the other big cruise dock and marina in Charlotte Amalie, Crown Bay, **Crown Bay Center** has jewelry, clothing, and gift stores/kiosks and a good bookstore.

Fish Face (p. 121), on Charlotte Amalie's Palm Passage, curates local art, crafts, and clothing.

Note that it is illegal for most street vendors (food vendors being the only exception) to ply their trades outside of the designated area called **Vendors Plaza,** at the corner of Veterans Drive and Tolbod Gade facing the St. Thomas waterfront. Vendors selling souvenirs and food converge here Monday through Saturday at 7:30am, usually packing up around 5:30pm. Some hawk their wares on Sundays when cruise ships are in. As of late 2022, Vendors Plaza vendors will be ensconced in colorful **new kiosks** instead of tents.

When you tire of hunting for French perfumes and Swiss watches along Main Street, head for **Market Square,** as it's called locally, or more formally, Rothschild Francis Square. It's between Main and Back streets, off Strand Gade. This former slave market has a Victorian tin roof and comes alive for the **Saturday farmers market ★**, where vendors sell fresh produce, fruit, and seafood.

All the major stores in St. Thomas are located by number on an excellent map in the center of the publication *St. Thomas This Week*, distributed free to all arriving plane and boat passengers, and available at the visitor center. A lot of the stores on the island don't have street numbers or don't display them, so look for their signs instead.

Shopping A to Z

In the 300-year-old historic district of Charlotte Amalie and in the areas around the cruise-ship piers, you will find many of the same shops you see in other duty-free Caribbean ports and cruise-ship centers—as one visitor noted, the street is paved with "jewels and booze." When the cruise ships are in, shop owners ratchet up the hard sell along Main Street (Dronningens Gade in Danish). If you poke around the cobblestoned alleyways between Main Street and the harbor, you may find a gem that's a little off the standard tourist radar.

For **jewelry and watches,** the choices are practically endless, with an emphasis on high-end rocks. **Diamonds International ★**, 5184 Dronningens Gade, has the island's largest selection of diamonds (www.diamondsinternational. com; ✆ 349/774-2184); it also has locations in Havensight Mall and Crown Bay Center. **Cardow Jewelers,** 1 Main St. (www.cardow.com; ✆ 340/776-1140), is often called the Tiffany's of the Caribbean, with one of the largest selections of fine jewelry in the world; its two other locations are at Crown Bay Center and the St. Thomas airport. A **Rolex Boutique** (www.rolex.com/rolex-dealers/ usvirginislands.html; ✆ 340/777-6789) is in a historic building at 37 Main St.

For **electronics,** reliable dealers include **Boolchand's,** Havensight Mall (boolchand.com; ✆ 340/776-0794), and **Royal Caribbean,** 5178 Dronningens Gade (www.royalcaribbeanvi.com; ✆ 340/776-4110; second location at Crown Bay Center).

For **porcelain and china,** the **Lladró Boutique,** AH Riise, 37 Main St. (www.lladro.com, ✆ 340/776-3503), represents a Spanish company famed for its high-end porcelain figurines. Ubiquitous in the Caribbean, **Little Switzerland,** 5182 Dronningens Gade (www.littleswitzerland.com; ✆ 284/809-5560), offers some of the finest crystal sold on the island, as well as fine jewelry and watches; it has two more locations, in Havensight Mall and Crown Bay Center.

ART & ANTIQUES

Creative Native ★★   Ama Dennis, photographer, framer, electrical engineer, and sixth-generation Virgin Islander, opened this gallery and studio in February 2022 in a historic (1841) downtown building, formerly part of the old Grand Hotel. She trains her camera on the history and culture of the Virgin Islands through a fine-arts perspective: a chiaroscuro rendering of her great-grandmother's demi-johns holding guavaberry wine; the outdoor fermentation of a local drink known as mauby ("Mauby Wukin' Hard"); and a moody nighttime diptych of Charlotte Amalie's historic Main Street, newly restored with native blue bitch rock replacing modern concrete. Local symbols abound, including the conch, which represents freedom—slaves blew it during the 19th-century island revolts. It's open Monday to Friday 10am to 5pm and Saturday 10am to 2pm. 9160 Estate St. Thomas, Charlotte Amalie. thecreativenative.art. 🕾 **340/626-0226.**

81C ★★★   This downtown art gallery and studio opened with a bang in 2020 with an exhibition of works by top St. Thomas artist Shansi Miller. The two-story building on Kronprindsens Gade was built in 1819 as a rum warehouse. The curators also collaborated on an art hotel–style collection of local artworks for display inside a **luxury nine-bedroom rental villa** on Magens Bay (www.oneperfectdayvilla.com). 81C Kronprindsens Gade, Charlotte Amalie. 81cvi.com. 🕾 **917/327-1561.** Call for hours.

Fish Face ★★   The owners, artists themselves, are thoughtful curators of local arts and crafts and other good stuff, including comfy HIHO clothing (started by a B.V.I. windsurfer), affordable Caribbean sea jewelry, beautiful market baskets handmade in St. Croix, and the owner's own undersea fish photography. Palm Passage, Charlotte Amalie. fishfacevi.com. 🕾 **340/775-5129.**

Gallery Camille Pissarro ★
Impressionist artist Camille Pissarro was born in 1830 in this circa-1811 building and lived here until he was 26. Inside are prints and originals by local artists in three high-ceilinged rooms. It's just opposite the Royal Dane Mall at the top of a flight of uneven steps. *Note:* The gallery was closed at press time, but plans were underway to open. 14 Main St. www.pissarro.vi. 🕾 **340/774-4621.**

Mango Tango Art Gallery ★★
One of the island's leading galleries, a longtime presence on St. Thomas, was opened in 1988 by Jane Coombes and her late husband, Smokey Pratt. It sells both original artwork and less-expensive art prints,

Island artists display their works at Mango Tango Art Gallery.

posters, and decorative maps. Al Cohen Plaza, Raphune Hill, Rte. 38. www.mango
tangoart.com. ✆ **340/777-3060.**

S.O.S. Antiques ★ This gallery is packed with antique maritime col-
lectibles, including maps and charts, prints, sextants, and barometers. It also
stocks a number of weapons, including antique and reproduction cannons,
swords, pistols, and daggers. The highlight: genuine shipwreck salvage, such
as actual pieces of eight mounted in 14-karat and 18-karat gold (you can also
buy them unset). 5132 Dronningens Gade 1. ✆ **340/774-2074.**

CLOTHING

Lovango Cay Shops ★★ Whether you're actually staying at the fabulous resort at Lovango Cay, the little island between St. Thomas and St. John,
or you've boated there for lunch, dinner, or a beach club day, check out the
shops in the Lovango "Village." Each shop is its own mini-West Indian cottage. This is where you'll find the local B.V.I. clothing brand HIHO. **Lovango
Style** features chic resort wear and accessories; **SEEH** is a one-of-kind shop
featuring luxury sustainable fashion and clean beauty items; **Beach Read
Nook** offers page turners of all kinds; and **The Resort Shop** has all things
Lovango. The **Lovango General Store** stocks sundries and snacks, including
the resort's own collection of breadfruit booze, Little Gem, made by the
breadfruit-distilling folks at the Sion Farms Distillery in St. Croix. Lovango Cay
Resort. www.lovangovi.com. ✆ **340/625-0400.**

Zora of St. Thomas ★★★ Nonagenarian Zora Galvin has been making
hand-crafted leather sandals in Charlotte Amalie for 60 years. In addition to her
classic-looking, full-grain, "practically indestructible" (says one fan) sandals
custom-fit to your feet, Zora also offers a line of solidly practical, toe-enclosed
footwear that the islanders call "limin' shoes." The leather comes straight
from the cattle yards of Chicago, and ladies and gents in the know make this
their first stop on arrival in the islands (the shoes take 4 to 6 days to complete)
to have Zora draw a rough pattern of their feet on butcher paper ("I still can't
draw a foot," Zora says). Her circa-1860s shop, a former U.S. consulate, carries the delightful canvas "monster" bags and backpacks of another crafty
nonagenarian—Zora's good friend, collagist, and children's book author
Diane Redfield Massie—who works on her whimsical creations upstairs in
the airy loft. Also in the mix are good hand-knotted Oriental rugs and dhurries
and ethereal printed kirtas for sipping guavaberry wine on breezy patios. You
might spot something from Zora's equally talented daughters, painter Shansi
Miller and artisan Timisa Miller, who creates handmade jewelry and lumines-
cent works of dichroic glass. (Zora also for years conducted the Community
Band at the Carnival parades and other events with a bougainvillea-draped
baton.) If you swoon for all things hand-crafted, top-quality, and made-
with-love, this is the mother lode. 5040 Norre Gade, Ste. 2, Charlotte Amalie. www.
facebook.com/people/Zora-of-St-Thomas/100057586744267/. ✆ **340/774-2559.**

FOOD

The Belgian Chocolate Factory ★ Get your handmade Belgian chocolates—some made with local fruits like mango and papaya—at this bustling factory/store in the Charlotte Amalie historic district. 5093 Dronningens Gade, Ste. 3, Charlotte Amalie. ✆ **340/777-5247.**

Gladys' Café ★ Enjoy local favorites like conch chowder and "Ole Wife" fish in this 40-year-old restaurant, but you don't have to dine to purchase a bottle of Gladys' homemade hot sauce, in flavors from mango to mustard to tomato. Royal Dane Mall, Charlotte Amalie. gladyscafe.com. ✆ **340/774-6604.**

Gustave Quetel Fish House ★★ Show up at this Frenchtown fish house any morning to buy (and have cleaned) fresh seafood. Look for lobster, red snapper, alewife (triggerfish), and strawberry grouper (hein). Frenchtown docks.

> ### Diamonds Are Forever
>
> **Jewelry** is the most common item for sale in St. Thomas. Look carefully over the selections of gold and gemstones (emeralds are traditionally considered the finest savings). Gold that is marked 24-karat in the United States and Canada is marked 999 (or 99.9% pure gold) on European items. Gold marked 18-karat in the United States and Canada has a European marking of 750 (or 75% pure), and 14-karat gold is marked 585 (or 58.5% pure).

Market Square ★★ This former slave-trading market in downtown Charlotte Amalie has a Saturday morning fresh fruit and vegetable market that's worth a visit. In addition to fresh fruit juices (mango, passionfruit, and more), it sells fruits (soursop, coconuts, sugar apples), vegetables (spinach, kale, cukes, peppers), what the locals call "ground provisions" (root vegetables, cassava, sweet potatoes), herbs (lemongrass, sage, cilantro, bay leaves), and fresh fish and lobster. Flea market stuff is of varying quality. Dronningens Gade, Charlotte Amalie. Saturday 6–11am to noon.

LINENS

Mr. Tablecloth ★ This Charlotte Amalie shop has a voluminous selection of tablecloths and accessories, plus doilies. In addition to fine-linen tablecloths, the shop sells microfiber stain-resistant tablecloths. 6 Main St. mrtablecloth-vi.com. ✆ **340/774-4343.**

ST. THOMAS AFTER DARK

St. Thomas's party vibe is on simmer all the time, and even the lowliest beach shack has its own master mixologist and often live music on tap. The three main neighborhoods for nightlife are **Red Hook,** on the island's east end, where a number of bars and casual seaside eateries feature live music, including Tap & Still and Duffy's Love Shack (p. 125); the charming streets of **Frenchtown,** with lively restaurants and bars like the French Quarter Bistro; and **Havensight,** where Yacht Haven Grande is a hot destination with waterfront restaurant/bars like Navy Beach, Isla, and Blue 11. Alas, downtown

The poolside Iggie's Oasis, at the south coast's Bolongo Bay Beach Resort (p. 77), offers live music nightly.

Charlotte Amalie is no longer the swinging neighborhood it used to be back in the 1960s and '70s, when steel bands played the clubs and Back Street was the place to go dancing. These days, downtown is slightly seedy after dark. But with the revitalization of the waterfront, things are improving fast.

Sipping a cocktail while overlooking the glittering harbor high up in the Charlotte Amalie hills is pretty fabulous and ultra-romantic. It's hard to beat the **harbor views ★★★** at **Mafolie Restaurant** (www.mafolie.com/mafolie-restaurant) or Bluebeards Castle's **Castle Gastropub** (www.facebook.com/deckwithaviewVI; ✆ 340/643-8366).

The island has a thriving **Sunday Funday brunch culture** where you can eat and drink and bounce to live bands or DJs while sitting pretty by the seaside. But islanders love listening to **live music most any day of the week.** Head to the following recommended venues for live music and good times:

o **West ZanziBar ★** (www.westzanzibar.com; ✆ 340/779-9269), a sizzling lounge and grill inside a sugar windmill at Crown Bay Center, serves up West Indian "comfort food" (like steaming pots of kallaloo and garlic shrimp) with a steady diet of live music and DJ stylings: Reggae Mondays, Tuesday live calypso bands, Wednesday old-school DJs, Thursday contemporary DJs, Friday live music, and a powerhouse Saturday-night DJ series, featuring top DJs from around the islands, from Avalanche to Joker. Sunday is sports day—the bar has eight TVs for your sports-viewing pleasure.

o **Virgin's Haven Bar & Grill** (www.facebook.com/virginshaven; ✆ 340/227-9933), at the Havensight dock, features bands and DJs on Whine Down Sundays along with a traditional West Indian menu of saltfish, johnnycakes, "fry" chicken, and conch soup from **Gigi's** (✆ 340/690-9449).

o **Hook'd USVI** (hookdusvi.com; ✆ 340/714-4665), in the American Yacht Harbor in Red Hook, has live music on Fabulous Fridays on its alfresco deck.

The Performing Arts

The beautiful 1,100-seat outdoor amphitheater known as the Reichhold Center for the Arts (www.uvi.edu/reichhold), for nearly 50 years one of the premier performing arts venues in the Caribbean, suffered serious damage from the 2017 hurricanes. Restoration efforts were still ongoing at press time. The center was the site of big-time performances over the years by the likes of Ray Charles, Count Basie, and Alvin Ailey.

Margaritaville Vacation Club by Wyndham (☏ **340/775-8300**), at Smith Bay, has a **Carnival show** with music on Sunday evenings (6–8pm), with live music and fire dancers. It's open to the public; the stage is in between the lobby and the Margaritaville restaurant and beachfront. Locals say it's fun and "not cheesy."

Bars & Clubs

Duffy's Love Shack ★   Advertised as "the world's coolest parking-lot bar," this local institution is pretty casual, which means you will probably be dancing with brand-new best friends by evening's end. The waterside joint has tiki-bar tchotchkes, an indoor thatched-roof bar, and really good bar food (including Polynesian pu-pu platters and mahi-mahi tacos), which also makes it instantly family-friendly. It's open daily 11:30am till late; the kitchen closes at 10pm. 6500 Red Hook Plaza, Rte. 38. www.duffysloveshack.com. ☏ **340/779-2080.**

The Greenhouse ★   This St. Thomas old-timer is an open-air waterfront bar and restaurant enjoying a prime spot in downtown Charlotte Amalie. It's a cruise-ship hangout during the day, but after the ships slip away before dusk, the Greenhouse regroups with a **happy hour** (4:30–7pm) that offers two-for-one drinks and discounted appetizers, every single day. The Greenhouse is open daily 11am until the last customer leaves. Veterans Dr. www.thegreenhouse restaurant.com. ☏ **340/774-7998.**

Taphus Beer House ★   If you like your bars tucked into historic buildings and your drinking atmosphere speakeasy-dark, this downtown beer house has a barstool just waiting for you. It feels worlds away from the barking touts selling watches on Main Street. The authentic 18th-century atmosphere doesn't

---

Carnival: The Biggest Party of Them All

In its 70th year, the annual celebration on St. Thomas was back in business in late April 2022, after 2 years of cancelled (or virtual) events during the Covid-19 pandemic. The St. Thomas Carnival is the most spectacular and fun carnival in the Virgin Islands, where "Moko Jumbies," people dressed as spirits atop stilts nearly 20 feet high, parade through the streets. It's a glitter-fest of costumed paraders (including the Gypsies in tie-dye and Shaka Zula traditional Indians in fierce tribal makeup), dancing troupes and majorettes, boat shows, reggae, soca, and calypso bands, and "jump-ups." **J'Ouvert** (French for "day open"), the opening fest, kicks off the big week-long celebrations on the Monday before Ash Wednesday. A Food Fair showcases West Indian local and cultural delicacies. For a personal look at growing up with Carnival, go to "Memories of a Carnival Childhood," on p. 112. For more on the St. Thomas Carnival, go to www.facebook.com/USVI-Festivals.

quit, and the drinks are fine. Charlotte Amalie was originally known as "Taphus" for the city's abundance of tap rooms. Some things never change. 5120 Dronningens Gade, Charlotte Amalie. ☎ **340/774-4010.**

Bowling

Chicken 'n Bowling ★   Do what the locals do on a rainy day and head to this fun and funky bowling alley/bar/rotisserie chicken joint in Havensight. It's got only six bowling lanes, but the succulent roast chicken should keep you occupied, or the sliders, or mains like chicken fried rice and veggie bowls. And bowling's not the only game in the house—how about a couple of Ping-Pong tables, a smattering of arcade games, billiards, foosball, darts? Book bowling lanes in advance on the website. Open Monday through Friday 4pm until midnight, Saturday and Sunday 1pm until midnight. Havensight. www. bowlingvi.com. ☎ **340/715-2442.** Bowling $50/hr. up to 6 people. Rotisserie chicken $26; sliders $10; Entrees $8–$15.

Breweries

Frenchtown Brewery & Tap Room ★★   St. Thomas's first craft brewery opened in 2015, making delicious small-batch, tap-only brews, including a West Coast–style IPA and a Farmhouse Saison. Crowlers (32-oz cans) can be made on the spot. Call about open hours, but the brewery is generally open Fridays from 4 to 7pm, with tasting tours on Wednesday 4:30 to 7:30pm and Saturday from 3 to 5pm. Frenchtown Brewery also has a second location in **Bluebeards Castle** resort, with four beers on tap and stunning views over the Charlotte Amalie harbor. You can find Frenchtown brews on tap in bars throughout St. Thomas. 24A Honduras, Frenchtown, on 2nd fl. above Sea La Vie. frenchtown brewing.com. ☎ **340/690-2104.**

St. Thomas's first craft brewery, Frenchtown Brewery, has two locations.

Leatherback Brewing Co. ★   This St. Croix–based craft brewery has a St. Thomas beer garden and tasting room, where you can sample its range of beers, from IPAs to cream ales to sours. The tasting room is open Tuesday and Wednesday noon to 7pm and Thursday to Saturday from noon to 10pm. 9718 Estate Thomas, Charlotte Amalie. leatherbackbrewing.com. ☎ **340/725-4577.**

Gaming Center

The island has no casinos per se, but a handful of "gaming centers" offer slots known as video lottery terminals (VLTs), notably near the cruise-ship piers. **Bushwackers Gaming Center** (www.bushwackersvi.com), at Crown Bay Marina, has two bars and live music along with a wide selection of slot machines. **Winner's Circle** (www.winnerscirclevi.com), at the Havensight Cruise Ship dock, has a slot and video-poker room along with a bar/restaurant, the Rum Hut, across the road. VLTs are part of the V.I. Lottery.

Gay & Lesbian Nightlife

St. Thomas might be the most cosmopolitan of the Virgin Islands, but it is no longer the "gay paradise" it was in the 1960s and '70s. The major gay scene in the U.S. Virgins is now on St. Croix (see chapter 5). That doesn't mean that gay men and lesbians aren't drawn to St. Thomas. They are, but many attend predominantly straight establishments, such as the **Greenhouse** (see "Bars & Clubs," above).

ST. CROIX

At 84 square miles, the "plantation island" is certainly the largest U.S. Virgin Island, but its small-town lifestyle has a languid cadence. St. Croix is a place of bucolic pleasures, with the main towns on east and west coasts sandwiched by rural farms, semi-rainforest, and pockmarked roads shaded by mahogany trees. High-rises? No building can be over three stories tall. As one shopkeeper put it, the island isn't necessarily packaged for tourists—with St. Croix, "you get what you get."

But what you get is pretty wonderful. A natural necklace of coral reef encircles and protects gentle bays and golden-sand beaches. The lack of light pollution brings the galaxies alive, especially at sites like Point Udall. The Crucian populace is all over the multicultural map—from Latin to Caribbean Creole to statesider—a diverse population that's been called a "cultural callaloo." But the community vibe is always warm and embracing, especially on Sundays, when just about everyone on island is beachside. No wonder many people think St. Croix is the best-kept secret in the Caribbean.

At the same time, St. Croix has an earthy sophistication, with one of the Virgins' most vibrant arts scenes. It's a bubbling cauldron of working artisans. Inventive chefs were doing cutting-edge farm-to-table practices here before it became ubiquitous, infusing dishes with locally grown foods and flavors and drinks with local herbs and juices. Today St. Croix has one of the region's most sophisticated restaurant scenes—just check out our "Best Restaurants" selection in Chapter 1 if you don't believe us. In St. Croix, living well the nice and easy way is the best revenge.

In St. Croix you also have a living museum of the region's tangled past. Much of the architecture from the 18th-century Danish occupancy remains enshrined in picturesque Christiansted, the capital city on the island's East End. Its sleepy little West End twin, Frederiksted, reflects a past that encompasses the ground-shattering "Fireburn" slave revolts of 1878. Colonial structures lining the waterfront were scorched and refashioned with Victorian facades—what remains is a style mash-up, a fetching welcome mat for the cruise-ship crowds strolling the waterfront. The impressive 1,526-foot Frederiksted Pier was rebuilt in 1994 to handle deep-water ships, and its massive pilings have become a magnet for both marine life and scuba divers. When the big ships are in dock, Frederiksted's harborfront feels practically Lilliputian.

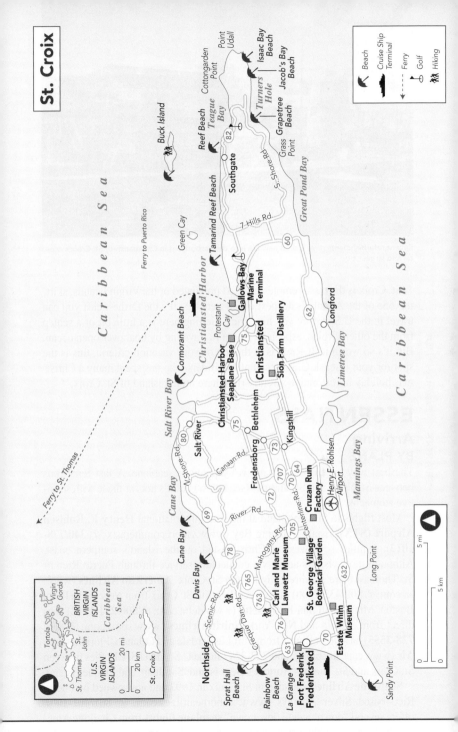

St. Croix

Caribbean Sea

Buck Island

Point Udall

Cottongarden Point

Isaac Bay Beach

Jacob's Bay Beach

Reef Beach

Teague Bay

Turners Hole

Grapetree Beach

Grass Point

82

Great Pond Bay

Southgate

Tamarind Reef Beach

Green Cay

Ferry to Puerto Rico

7-Hills Rd.

60

S. Shore Rd.

Cormorant Beach

Christiansted Harbor

Protestant Cay

Gallows Bay

Marine Terminal

Longford

62

Limetree Bay

Christiansted Harbor Seaplane Base

Christiansted

75

Sion Farm Distillery

Salt River Bay

N. Shore Rd.

80

Salt River

Bethlehem

75

Kingshill

73

Mannings Bay

Cane Bay

Canaan Rd.

Fredensborg

707

70

64

Henry E. Rohlsen Airport

River Rd.

72

Cruzan Rum Factory

Centerline Rd.

69

78

Cane Bay

Mahogany Rd.

Davis Bay

765

Carl and Marie Lawaetz Museum

St. George Village Botanical Garden

632

Long Point

763

Scenic Rd.

Creque Dam Rd.

76

Estate Whim Museum

Northside

Sprat Hall Beach

Rainbow Beach

La Grange

631

Fort Frederik

Frederiksted

70

Sandy Point

Caribbean Sea

Ferry to St. Thomas

Caribbean Sea

5 mi

5 km

0

0

Inset (top left)

BRITISH VIRGIN ISLANDS

Tortola

Virgin Gorda

St. John

U.S. VIRGIN ISLANDS

St. Thomas

Caribbean Sea

St. Croix

20 mi

20 km

0

Legend

Beach

Cruise Ship Terminal

Ferry

Golf

Hiking

Recent refurbishments have kicked new life into the harborfront in Christiansted, St. Croix's capital and largest city.

St. Croix is the most remote and least populated of the Virgin Islands, skirting one of the Atlantic's deepest ocean trenches. It's the farthest east you can travel in the U.S. before you hit Africa. Getting here is a little bit of a schlep from the other Virgins, especially if you're traveling by boat over open ocean. But it's so worth it. If R&R is at the top of your vacation criteria, this is the spot for you; just ask U.S. President Joe Biden, who has spent many a Christmas holiday in restorative serenity right here on the island of St. Croix.

ESSENTIALS

Arriving
BY PLANE

The best way to reach the island is by plane or seaplane. A fast ferry runs between St. Croix and St. Thomas (see below) but it's not for those with sensitive stomachs.

Most flights to St. Croix land at the small international **Henry E. Rohlsen Airport (STX),** Estate Manning Bay (www.viport.com/herastx; ⓒ **340/778-1012**), 6 miles southwest of Christiansted on the island's southern coast. Although most visitors arrive via connecting service through Puerto Rico or St. Thomas, there are direct flights into St. Croix. **American Airlines** (www.aa.com; ⓒ **800/433-7300**) runs direct flights to St. Croix from New York (JFK), Boston, Miami, and San Juan. **Delta** (www.delta.com; ⓒ **800/221-1212**) flies direct from Atlanta and New York. **Spirit Airlines** (www.spirit.com; ⓒ **855/728-3555**) has direct flights from Fort Lauderdale and Orlando, Florida. **Cape Air** (www.capeair.com; ⓒ **800/227-3247** in the U.S. and U.S.V.I.) flies between St. Croix and St. Thomas, Tortola's Beef Island, San Juan, and Vieques Island.

Seaborne Airlines, founded in St. Croix in 1992 and now owned by Puerto Rico–based Silver Airways (www.seaborneairlines.com; ⓒ **801/401-100**), offers several "downtown to downtown" **seaplane flights** from Charlotte Amalie, St. Thomas, landing right at the seaport on the Christiansted waterfront.

A number of major car-rental firms maintain kiosks at the airport, including **Avis** (www.avis.com; ℭ **340/778-9355**), **Budget** (budgetstcroix.com; ℭ **340/778-9636**), and **Hertz** (www.hertz.com; ℭ **340/778-9744**). The oldest independent car agency in St. Croix, **Olympic Rent-A-Car** (www.olympicstcroix.com; ℭ **340/718-3000**), offers free airport drop-off and pick-up. Otherwise, taxis are on call at the airport and in downtown Christiansted to transfer you to your destination.

Flight time to St. Croix from St. Thomas is 25 minutes; between St. Croix and San Juan 50 minutes; and between St. Croix and Vieques 25 minutes. There are no direct flights to St. Croix from Canada or the United Kingdom; connections are made via Miami.

BY BOAT

Ferries are a boon for those instances when flights are suddenly cancelled (like everywhere else, the Caribbean is suffering through a pilot shortage) and you have to make a connecting flight out of St. Thomas. Know that the 90-minute trip traverses open ocean, and when seas are up, it can be rough passage for those who suffer from motion sickness. We highly recommend taking Dramamine or some sort of remedy before the trip. Crews have expandable barf bags on hand. Know that in the islands, ferry schedules are always subject to change or cancellations, especially in the event of inclement weather.

Native Son Ferry (www.nativesonferry.com; ℭ **340/774-8685**) runs a 200-passenger high-speed ferry between St. Thomas and St. Croix once a day on Wednesday, Friday, and Saturday ($90–$120 round-trip), leaving at 8am from the Edward Blyden Marine Terminal in downtown Charlotte Amalie (St. Thomas) and returning at 4pm from Gallows Bay Marine Terminal in Christiansted (St. Croix).

QE IV Ferry (www.qe4ferry.com; ℭ **340/473-1322**) offers service between St. Croix and St. Thomas once daily Wednesday through Monday, leaving the Gallows Bay terminal at 8am and returning from the Blyden Terminal (Charlotte Amalie) at 3pm. Fares are $70 one-way ($120 round-trip).

BY CRUISE SHIP

While ferry boats arrive in Christiansted, the island's main cruise ship pier, the **Ann E. Abramson Pier,** sits on the Fredricksted waterfront, a natural deepwater port. The upgraded pier has the capacity to accommodate two mega-ships at a time. Dock enhancements have already upped cruise-ship visitation from one ship every 3 weeks to one or two ships making port stops weekly. Those numbers are only expected to rise in the coming years. A 2022 agreement between the V.I. Port Authority and Royal Caribbean Cruise Line promised by 2023 to triple the volume of cruise-ship passengers (to 140,000 passengers yearly) arriving at the Frederiksted Pier in St. Croix—and for the first time cruise ships will have to pay a per-passenger fee ($7), a boon to local coffers. For its part, the V.I. government has agreed to implement improvements to the St. Croix cruising experience, including trolleys for easier commutes downtown, a new mini-golf course, the reopening of Whim Museum (after 5 years of languishing from hurricane damage), and the addition of local food tours.

While planes and ferries arrive in Christiansted, cruise ships dock in the deep-water port of Frederiksted, St. Croix's other main town.

As in St. Thomas, a territorial gambling ordinance prevents any cruise ship from overnighting at the Frederiksted Pier.

Visitor Information

A **U.S. Virgin Islands Department of Tourism** visitor center (www.visit usvi.com) is located in Christiansted on King Street. The St. Croix administrative office for the tourism department is at 321 King St. (© **340/772-0357**), in Frederiksted. Tourist offices provide free maps to the island. *St. Croix This Week*, distributed free around the island, has detailed maps of Christiansted, Frederiksted, and the entire island, pinpointing individual attractions, hotels, shops, and restaurants and listing the week's events and happenings. A local independent website, **Go to St. Croix** (www.gotostcroix.com), is a fabulous wealth of detailed information.

Island Layout

St. Croix has only two sizable towns, 15 miles apart: **Christiansted** on the north-central shore and **Frederiksted** along the southwest (leeward) coast. Both have the same street names and are known as the "twin cities." Despite Frederiksted's natural deep-water port, Christiansted is bigger and more populous. The Henry E. Rohlsen Airport is on the south coast. Directly west are the towers of the former Hovensea oil refinery, once the island's largest industry; its future remains up in the air (see "Battle over Big Oil," p. 134).

Route 82 (also called East End Rd.) leads east from Christiansted, while Route 75 runs west from Christiansted through the central heartland. Melvin H. Evans Highway, Route 66, runs along the southern part of the island. You can connect with this route in Christiansted and head west all the way to Frederiksted. No roads circle St. Croix's coast.

CHRISTIANSTED

Founded in 1733 by a Danish governor-general of St. Thomas, Christiansted is the former capital of the Danish West Indies, with a population of around 3,000 people. Built by African slaves, the town has a historic district comprising four main streets leading toward the water: Strand Street, King Street, Company Street, and Queen Street. It's compact and easily explored on foot—so park your car and start strolling. You will find open-air parking on both sides of Fort Christiansvaern. All streets start at the harbor and go up slightly sloped hillsides, and each street heads back down the hill to the port so you can't get lost. Be sure to check out the sights and restaurants on the **newly renovated harborfront.** See the "Walking Tour: Christiansted" map, on p. 170, to orient yourself.

THE NORTH SHORE

This coastal strip that stretches from Cottongarden Point, the eastern tip of the island, all the way west past Christiansted and up and around Salt River Bay, comes to an end as it reaches the settlement of Northside in the far west. It is the most touristy region of St. Croix, site of the best beaches, the most hotels, and the densest shopping. It is also the takeoff point (at Christiansted Harbor) for excursions to Buck Island, St. Croix's most popular attraction. Many visitors confine their stay in St. Croix entirely to the north coast. The northern coastline is not only long but also diverse, going from a lush tropical forest that envelops most of the northwest to the eastern sector, which is dry with palm-lined beaches.

THE EAST END

The East End begins immediately east of Christiansted, the capital, taking in Tamarind Reef Beach and Reef Beach before it reaches Teague Bay, coming to an end at Cottongarden Point, the far eastern tip of St. Croix. This section of St. Croix is linked by Route 82 (East End Rd.). The Buccaneer, St. Croix's premier resort, is found here, along with the Tamarind Reef Hotel. The area is far less congested than the section immediately west of Christiansted, and many visitors prefer the relative isolation and tranquility of the East End. This section of St. Croix is somewhat dry, the landscape a bit arid, but its

---

Centerline Road: Linking Christiansted and Frederiksted

Centerline Road runs through the heart of the island, connecting the East End with the West End and the island's main towns of Christiansted and Frederiksted. As local historian Felipe Ayala noted, when the road was first laid out—like many others on the island—it was planted "with so much forethought": Majestic mahogany trees, the island's traditional roadside tree, were interspersed with fruit trees, so that people walking the route in the hot sun would have shade and sustenance. The road was finally paved in the 1930s during New Deal times by Civilian Conservation Corps crews. The work was a big leap in the development of the island's highway infrastructure. A number of the old mahogany trees that lined the route were felled during the hurricanes of 2017.

BATTLE OVER big oil

The former HOVENSA oil refinery, refining crude from Venezuela, was up until 2012 St. Croix's main employer, forming a sprawling industrial village on its idyllic south shore. The refinery has remained closed since then—except for one calamitous reopening in 2021—in the wake of relentless EPA violations (corroded pipelines, pollution of the island aquifer by petrochemicals). For some, like former V.I. Governor Kenneth Mapp, the refinery has been an "economic lifeline" for the U.S. territory, providing a not insignificant source of revenue for the U.S. Virgin Island government ($25 million a year) and employing more than 400 area workers. For others the refinery is not just a blight on the landscape but environmentally unsafe—especially in the aftermath of a horrific 2021 refinery breakdown that spewed crude oil, gases, and petrochemicals into neighborhoods downwind of the refinery. (The *Washington Post* headline read "The Island Where It Rains Oil.") In summer 2022, a pile of petroleum coke fuel smoldered uncontrollably for 23 days. A coalition of scientists, nonprofits, and students have opposed the refinery reopening, and in late 2022 the EPA weighed in with a status report that basically said the troubled facility needed a new Clean Air Act permit to come into compliance before reopening—a timeline that may kick the can down the road for a couple more years. It's an interesting conundrum for the Biden Administration, which has made renewable energy a big part of its agenda—and whose leader has enjoyed St. Croix as a favored family vacation spot over the years.

compensating factor is a lineup of palm-lined beaches. The best place for a beach picnic is Cramer Park at the far eastern tip, a U.S.V.I. territorial beach popular with islanders.

FREDERIKSTED

Sleepy little Frederiksted, population 1,000, has a tumultuous past. This oceanfront town was established in 1751 as a West End twin to Christiansted and in 1848 was the site of an uprising that led to the jubilant emancipation of the island's enslaved people. Its colonial architecture was heavily damaged by an earthquake and tsunami in 1867 and by fire from the legendary "Fireburn" labor revolt in 1878. Much of the town was rebuilt in the Victorian style. A colorful row of arcaded buildings lines the street along the waterfront park, greeting the big cruise ships that arrive at the town's deep-water pier weekly in high season. The two major streets, both of which run parallel to the water, are Strand Street and King Street. Nearby are some of the best beaches on the island, including Rainbow Beach and Sandy Point National Wildlife Refuge.

Getting Around

If you plan to do some serious sightseeing on the island, you'll need to rent a car, as getting around by public transportation is a slow, uneven process.

BY CAR

Remember to *drive on the left.* In most rural areas, where roads are often winding and pockmarked, the speed limit is 35 mph; certain parts of the major artery, Route 66, are 55 mph. In towns and urban areas, the speed limit is 20 mph. Keep in mind that if you're going into "bush country," you'll find the roads very difficult. Two rough-driving roads are "The Beast" (so nicknamed by North Shore Ironman competitors), a steep switchback hill off North Shore Road between Cane Bay and the Carambola resort; and Mahogany Road, which leads along winding, potholed roads from the West End up into the "Rain Forest." Sometimes the government smooths the roads out before the rainy season begins (often in October or November), but they rapidly deteriorate. As they say on St. Croix, the way to spot a drunk driver stateside is somebody weaving all over the road. The way to spot a drunk driver on STX is somebody *not* weaving all over the road.

St. Croix offers moderately priced car rentals, even on cars with automatic transmissions and air-conditioning. However, because of the island's higher-than-normal accident rate (which is partly the result of visitors who forget about driving on the left-hand side of the road), insurance costs are a bit higher than elsewhere. **Budget** (www.budget.com; ✆ 800/472-3325 or 340/778-9636) and **Avis** (www.avis.com; ✆ **340/778-9355**) maintain locations at the airport; look for their kiosks near the baggage-claim areas. Local agencies also located at the airport include **Centerline Car Rentals** (stxrentalcar.com; ✆ **888/288-8755**) and **Olympic Rent-A-Car** (www.olympicstcroix.com; ✆ **340/718-3000**), which offers free airport drop-off and pick-up. Another locally owned agency, **JohnHope Automotive** (johnhopeauto.com; ✆ **340/489-0409**), specializes in luxury SUV rentals (Audis, BMWs, Mercedes) and will deliver anywhere on the island. Resorts like the Buccaneer can also arrange to have rental cars delivered directly to the hotel. Some credit card companies grant you collision-damage protection. If yours doesn't, it may be wise to invest in some from the car-rental agency.

BY TAXI

Taxi rates are standardized throughout the Virgin Islands, and most drivers carry a sheet with the latest government-set fares. Official taxi rates are also posted at Henry E. Rohlsen International Airport. Even though rates are standardized, cabs are unmetered, so agree on the rate before you get in. Keep in mind that rates are listed for one to two persons, with the cost of additional riders in parentheses. From the airport, expect to pay about $25 ($15/additional rider) to Christiansted and about $20 ($10/additional rider) to Frederiksted. Traveling from the airport to the Buccaneer Resort is $30, plus $15 for each additional person; to Divi Carina Bay it's $50, plus $25 for each additional rider. A luggage fee is also charged, a flat rate of $2 per bag.

As in the rest of the Virgin Islands, most drivers use vans or open-air safari buses (converted truck beds with open-air seating). Note that you can often flag a ride with vans and safari vehicles along the road.

We highly recommend the following taxi drivers (who double as wonderful tour guides): **Ames Joseph** (✆ **340/277-6133**), **Steve Nesbitt** (✆ **340/473-1039**), and **Warren Brooks** at Native Son (✆ **340/626-2767**). **Sweeney's Tours** (p. 136) are always reliable. If none are available, contact the **St. Croix Taxicab Association** (✆ **340/778-1088**).

GUIDED TAXI TOURS Most taxis also specialize in guided island tours and group sightseeing excursions, with standardized hourly rates dependent on the vehicle (sedan/minivan/van) and number of passengers. So a 1-hour tour in a sedan or minivan for one to four people will be $40; a van tour for up to 14 people will be $55; and a safari vehicle carrying up to 25 people will be $80 (plus fees for any additional passengers). Tipping is absolutely appreciated (and likely expected).

Sweeney's Tours (📞 **340/773-6700**) and its local guides do a comprehensive 5-hour historic island tour ($71/person) that takes in 18th-century sugar plantations, the Botanical Gardens, and other heritage sites. Another good option is **Prince Taxi and Safari Tours** (www.princetaxisafaritours.com; 📞 **340/642-3811**) for its history- and culture-inflected island tours.

BY BUS

Air-conditioned **VITRAN (Virgin Islands Transportation)** buses (www.vitranvi.com; 📞 **340/773-1664**) run between Christiansted and Frederiksted every 2½ hours Monday through Friday between 5:30am and 8:10pm. Other routes run from La Reine Terminal to Tide Village; and from Sunshine Mall to La Reine Terminal. The fare is $1 (free for adults 60 and older and anyone with disabilities).

[FastFACTS] ST. CROIX

Banks FirstBank Virgin Islands (www.firstbankvi.com; 📞 **340/773-0440**) has full-service locations in Christiansted (12–13 King St. and Orange Grove); in Frederiksted (6A Strand St.); and at Sunny Isle Shopping Center. **Oriental** (formerly Scotiabank; orientalbank.com/en/vi; 📞 **800/981-5554** or 340/774-0037) has a full-service location in Sunny Isle Shopping Center and ATMs in both Christiansted (1156 King St.) and Frederiksted (11-12 Strand St.). **Banco Popular** (www.popular.com/vi; 📞 **800/724-3655**) has full-service locations in Christiansted (Orange Grove) and Sunny Isle. Most are open Monday-Thursday 9am-3pm and Friday 9am-4pm; both Oriental and FirstBank have Saturday morning hours.

Business Hours Typical business hours are daily 9am to 5pm (some businesses close or open late on Sun).

Dentists The V.I. Dental Center, 4006 Estate Diamond, Ste. 101 (www.videntalcenter.com; 📞 **340/772-6000**), has a team of dentists that are members of the American Dental Association. The nonprofit primary healthcare center **Frederiksted Health Care,** 516 Strand St., Frederiksted fhc-inc.net; 📞 **340/772-0260**), offers outpatient dentistry services in several locations around St. Croix.

Doctors For a referral, contact **Plessen Healthcare** (plessenhealthcare.com; 📞 **340/249-1065**). The nonprofit primary healthcare center **Frederiksted Health Care** (fhc-inc.net; (ℂ) **340/ 772-0260**) offers outpatient health services in several locations around St. Croix. Its main location is the **Inge-borg-Nesbitt Clinic,** 516 Strand St., Frederiksted. Its other locations are the Mid-Island Health Center (4100 Sion Farm), North Shore Health Center (6c La Grande Princesse), Dental East (1-E Estate Orange Grove), and the Lena Schulterbrandt Health Offices in Frederiksted's Sunshine Mall; check the website for specific hours.

Drugstores Mt. Welcome Pharmacy, East End Rd, Gallows Bay (www.mt welcomerx.com; (ℂ) **340/ 719-7283-7666**), open Monday-Friday 8:30am-6pm, Saturday 9am-4pm, and Sunday 9am-2pm. A second location is at the North Shore Health Center in La Grand Princesse, Northshore Rd. ((ℂ) **340/ 719-7979**).

Emergencies To reach the police, fire department, or an ambulance, call (ℂ) **911.**

Hospitals The main facility is **Governor Juan F.**

Luis Hospital & Medical Center, 4007 Estate Diamond Ruby (www.jflusvi.org; (ℂ) **340/778-6311**).

Newspapers & Magazines St. Croix has its own online newspaper, **St. Croix Source** (stcroixsource. com). **The Virgin Island Daily News** (www.virgin islandsdailynews.com) covers all the Virgin Islands. A good source of local information is **St. Croix This Week,** distributed free by the tourist offices to hotels, restaurants, and most businesses. A helpful website is **Go to St Croix** (www. gotostcroix.com).

Police Police headquarters is on Market Street in Christiansted. In case of emergency, dial (ℂ) **911;** for nonemergency assistance, call (ℂ) **340/778-2211.**

Post Office The post office is on Company Street at 2119 Market Sq. ((ℂ) **340/ 773-3586**), in Christiansted. Hours of operation are Monday-Friday 8:30am-4:30pm.

Safety St. Croix is generally safer than St. Thomas, but at press time, crime was on the upswing. Most crime is petty theft, usually of

possessions left unguarded at the beach while vacationers go into the water for a swim, or muggings of visitors wandering the dark streets and back alleys of Frederiksted and Christiansted at night. Exercise caution at night by sticking to the heart of Christiansted and not wandering around the back streets in Frederiksted. Avoid night strolls along beaches. Night driving in remote parts of the island can also be risky.

Taxes The only local tax is a 12.5% surcharge added to all hotel rates.

Telephone You can dial direct to St. Croix from the mainland by using the 340 area code. Omit the 340 for local calls. Make long-distance, international, and collect calls as you would on the U.S. mainland by dialing 0 or your long-distance provider.

Toilets There are few public restrooms, except at the major beaches and the airport. In Christiansted, the National Park Service maintains some restrooms within the public park beside Fort Christiansvaern.

WHERE TO STAY

St. Croix's lodgings are uniquely Crucian—international chain brands are practically nonexistent. The big resorts lie along the North Shore and a drive away from Christiansted or Frederiksted and their restaurants, shopping, and nightlife. The main lodgings in Christiansted (and to a lesser extent, Frederiksted) are smaller hotels and inns, close to restaurants, shops, and nightlife. Villas and condos are popular choices, offering privacy and the chance to save money by preparing your own meals.

In general, rates are steep, but in summer, hotels slash prices by as much as 50%; some close altogether in late summer and early fall. All rooms are subject to a 12.5% hotel tax, not included in the rates given below.

North Shore & East End

At press time, Carambola Beach Resort & Spa was still working out the kinks of its reopening in 2022 after extensive damage from the 2017 hurricanes. The third in the triumvirate of RockResorts built in the U.S. Virgin Islands by the Rockefellers, this 28-acre resort lies 30 minutes west of Christiansted on the island's north shore. Unfortunately, the island's outstanding golf course, the Carambola Golf & Country Club, had not reopened at press time. Check the Carambola website (www.marriott.com/en-us/hotels/stxbr-carambola-beach-resort-st-croix-us-virgin-islands) for updates.

EXPENSIVE

The Buccaneer ★★★ Family-run since 1947, this ultra-gracious resort is a St. Croix legend and the island's premier lodging. It's now part of Wyndham's vaunted Trademark Collection, which opens the resort to Wyndham's vast reservations network. The pros at the Buccaneer have been in the hospitality game a long time, and it shows—the resort has a warm, easygoing vibe; all is copacetic here. But these sprawling 340 acres also bear witness to the island's plantation heritage. A large sugar-cane factory worked by hundreds of enslaved peoples once stood on these landscaped grounds, and remnants of that occupation include the large sugar mill (ca. 1733) occupying a prime spot on the property. On the modern side of the equation, the resort is big enough to encompass a par-70 18-hole golf course, a 2-mile jogging path, and two freshwater pools. The Buccaneer has one of the top tennis facilities in the Virgin Islands, with six Plexipave tennis courts, two grass courts, and a pro shop. In the baronial-arched, pink-tinged Great House, the open-air **Terrace** restaurant offers fabulous views of Christiansted and the sea; and you can arrange beachfront massages through the full-service **Hideaway Spa & Salon.** Water toys galore, gentle bays for swimming, and all that grassy acreage makes this a no-brainer

St. Croix's premier resort, the sprawling Buccaneer, offers golf, two pools, two beaches, a spa, and an impressive tennis facility.

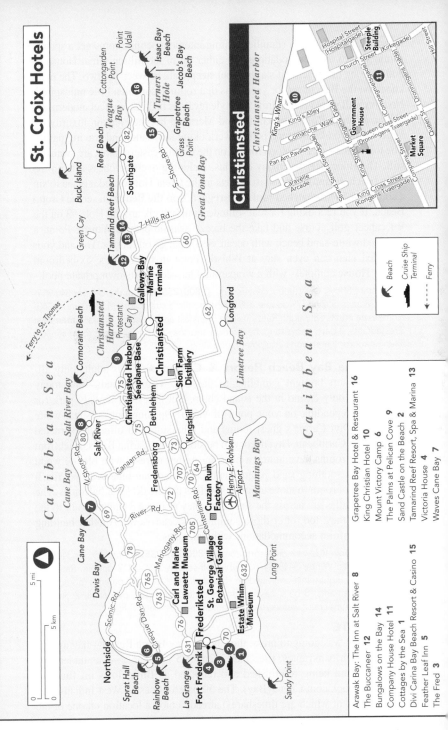

St. Croix Hotels

Arawak Bay: The Inn at Salt River **8**
The Buccaneer **12**
Bungalows on the Bay **14**
Company House Hotel **11**
Cottages by the Sea **1**
Divi Carina Bay Beach Resort & Casino **15**
Feather Leaf Inn **5**
The Fred **3**
Grapetree Bay Hotel & Restaurant **16**
King Christian Hotel **10**
Mount Victory Camp **6**
The Palms at Pelican Cove **9**
Sand Castle on the Beach **2**
Tamarind Reef Resort, Spa & Marina **13**
Victoria House **4**
Waves Cane Bay **7**

Christiansted

Beach
Cruise Ship Terminal / Ferry
- - - - Ferry

139

for vacationing families (families renting interconnecting rooms get a special summer rate). Accommodations are either up in the hilltop Great House or dotted along the beach—it's a short but steep walk between the two. The main knock on the Buccaneer for years was that room decor felt a little uninspired. No more: All were given significant style revamps in 2022 and feel modern and classic at once. Rooms on Grotto and Mermaid beaches remain luxuriously large, with wonderful stone patios overlooking sea, sand, and waving palms. The top-of-the-line Doubloon rooms, on the resort's eastern flank, are swankier still. The Buccaneer has many delights, including oversize chess sets on the main beach, bountiful breakfast buffets in the Great House, and a place to sip a cold drink in the thatched-roof **Beauregard's on the Beach** on serene Grotto Beach. If you're looking for real solitude, simply walk around Hole #3 on the Buccaneer golf course and take the breezy seaside path to Whistle Point, a secluded white-sand beach with ocean views that go on forever. You and your extended clan can even stay at Whistle Point in the resort's six-bedroom **Beach House** complex, with a wraparound terrace and its own private pool.

5007 Estate Shoys. www.thebuccaneer.com. ✆ **800/255-3881** in the U.S., or 340/712-2100. 138 units. $529–$779 double, $893–$2,168 suite. Extra children 17 and under $40/night; extra adults $85/night. Rates include breakfast and welcome drinks. **Amenities:** 3 restaurants; 3 bars; babysitting; health club and spa; 2 outdoor pools; room service; 8 tennis courts; watersports equipment; free Wi-Fi.

Divi Carina Bay Beach Resort & Casino ★ This adults-only all-inclusive resort brought gambling to the U.S. Virgin Islands—and today remains the only casino in the island chain. But that's not its only perk (or downside, depending on your point of view). Opening onto a sugar-white beach, the Divi Carina's guest rooms and villa suites all offer unobstructed views of the Caribbean. Divi decor can be stodgy, but Carina Bay's beachfront and hillside rooms have gotten a pleasing design refresh, with blonde wood floors and a soothing sand palette with pops of ocean-blue accents. You'll have plenty of room to move around as well as private decks or balconies. The 20 hillside villas are across the street, but they're just a 3-minute walk to the sands—and they, too, offer those sumptuous ocean views. Another building has 50 oceanfront accommodations with balconies.

5025 Turner Hole Rd. www.diviresorts.com. ✆ **800/367-9352** in the U.S., or 340/773-9700. 180 units. Winter $448–$470 double; off-season $350–$412 double. Rates are all-inclusive, 7-night minimum. Children 15 and under stay free in parent's room. **Amenities:** 3 restaurants; 3 bars; casino; fitness center; mini-golf; pickleball; 2 outdoor pools; spa; tennis court; watersports equipment/rentals; free Wi-Fi.

MODERATE

As this book was going to press, the Chenay Bay Beach Resort—having suffered through bankruptcy, fire, and Category 5 hurricanes—was under new ownership and being refurbished and rebooted as **Bungalows on the Bay** (www.facebook.com/ChenayBay). The 50 barefoot-casual West Indian–style cottages (six of which are timeshares) already enjoy a location on one of the island's finest beaches for watersports activities (swimming, snorkeling, windsurfing). It's 3 miles east of Christiansted.

Grapetree Bay Hotel & Restaurant ★   In the footprint of a 1960s-era hotel that Hurricane Hugo put out of business in 1989, this breezy beach-side property opened in 2021 in an enviable spot on a beautiful East End beach. Like its swinging '60s predecessor, it has a cool seaside (saltwater) pool and an open-air restaurant. Rooms are absolutely massive, more than 700 square feet of space done in seafoam-blue hues and white linens, and all come with balconies with smashing ocean views. Configurations are king or double queen. This beach puts you close to a Nature Conservancy coastal preserve with trails that lead to two of the island's prettiest and most remote beaches (Jack's and Isaac's Bay). The Goat Hill trail takes you right to the historic monument at Point Udall (the hotel provides trail maps). The hotel was still working out some kinks at press time, but it looks like the **East End** restaurant and bar is open for dinner (daily 3–9pm) with such specials as Leatherback beer–battered fish and chips and carne asado tacos, and the poolside **Sea Terrace** is open for lunch (daily 11am–3pm).

5000 S. Grapetree Rd. grapetreebayhotel.com. ℭ **340/249-0700.** 18 units. $260–$340 double. Rates include breakfast. **Amenities:** Restaurant; bar; fitness center; saltwater pool; free Wi-Fi.

The Palms at Pelican Cove ★   Water-lovers take note: This casual 40-room resort is not only set on 7 acres and 1,400 feet of Pelican Cove beach, it also boasts one of the largest pools on the island—so you've got a lot of room to meander and privacy if you want it. Guest rooms are spacious, too, with solid wooden furniture and private oceanview lanais, and the rock showers are a cool touch. Social life revolves around a sprawling open-air lounge, bar, and restaurant with sea views—the Wednesday Caribbean Night features Moko Jumbies and fire dancers, and live music is on tap Saturday nights with R&B Connection. The beach is narrow, but the seas are calm and shallow, and coral reef lies just 100 feet offshore, making the Palms a favorite of snorkelers.

4126 La Grande Princesse, Christiansted. www.palmspelicancove.com. ℭ **340/718-8920.** 40 units. $200–$250 double. **Amenities:** Restaurant; bar; outdoor pool; watersports (including free scuba lessons); free Wi-Fi.

Tamarind Reef Resort, Spa & Marina ★   This sprawling low-rise property has a lot going for it. Although its sandy beach is lovely, the shoreline is rocky and not ideal for swimming—but the reef (and snorkeling trail) just offshore make for fine snorkeling. A sun-drenched oceanfront pool is next to the **Deep End Bar & Grill** with the blue seas stretching out on the horizon (ask to stay in a building away from the bar if you prefer peace and quiet). You stay in Tamarind Reef to take advantage of island-hopping trips offered by numerous day-sail and charter-boat operators at the adjoining **Green Cay Marina.** It's got one of the island's best and liveliest restaurants, the **Galleon,** right at your door. Refreshed rooms are comfortable and spacious, with tile floors and a tropical motif that's pleasant enough; all have fabulous

Boutique styling at the Waves Cane Bay.

ocean-facing patios or terraces so you can be reminded of why you picked the Tamarind in the first place.

5001 Tamarind Reef. www.tamarindreefresort.com. *℃* **800/619-0014** in the U.S., or 340/718-4455. 38 units. $199–$263 double. Extra person $35–$50. Children 6 and under stay free in parent's room. **Amenities:** 2 restaurants; bar; fitness center; marina; outdoor pool; spa; 4 tennis courts; watersports equipment/rentals; free Wi-Fi.

The Waves Cane Bay ★★   Given a transformational design overhaul and renaming in 2021, this 11-room North Shore hotel is making serious waves for its just-so boutique styling from designer/owner Chris Pardo. We're talking highly textural and comfortably organic: fiber matting on wood floors, filigreed straw lamps, macramé wall hangings, and nubby throws; wood and bamboo furnishings against pale-olive plaster walls; bold geometric tile flooring in bathrooms and on oceanfront balconies. Each of the 11 suites has a sweet private patio with mahogany windows; some have kitchens. You've got the sea at your door and mountains rising in the back and the coral reef just off the shoreline—you can famously scuba dive right off Cane Bay beach, a quick stroll next door (the snorkeling there is not bad either). Built over a stone grotto, the hotel's beachfront restaurant, **AMA,** is equally stylish and one of St. Croix's top choices. The grotto has a shallow natural pool you can even dip into when the restaurant is closed.

112c Cane Bay. www.thewavescanebay.com. *℃* **340/718-1815.** 11 units. $299–$399 double. From the airport, go left on Rte. 64; after 1 mile, turn right on Rte. 70; after another 1 mile, go left at junction with Rte. 75; after 2 miles turn left at junction with Rte. 80; follow for 5 miles. **Amenities:** Restaurant; bar; natural grotto pool; watersports equipment/rentals; free Wi-Fi.

INEXPENSIVE

Arawak Bay: The Inn at Salt River ★   Travelers praise this two-story North Shore B&B for its sweeping views of Salt River Bay; warm, accommodating staff; and its hearty, delicious home-cooked breakfasts (guaranteed to start your day off right). Each room has a king bed or two doubles with vintage-style quilts; you step out of your room onto a long, shared balcony with sea views (the second-floor balcony has better sightlines). Help yourself to a nice glass of wine in the kitchen honor bar or take a dip in the (miniscule) pool. You will have to drive to reach the beach or nearby restaurants.

www.arawakhotelstcroix.com. © **888/234-0416** or 340/772-1684. 14 units. $135–$180 double. Rates include breakfast. **Amenities:** Bar; outdoor pool; free Wi-Fi.

Christiansted

The game-changing revitalization and beautification of the Christiansted harborfront was in full swing at press time. Not only has the **King Christian Hotel** (p. 144) been bewitchingly reimagined by new owners, Neighborhood Establishment, but the group has also vacuumed up (for $3.65 million) the mustard-hued **Kings Alley Hotel** and an adjoining historic property into the King Christian complex, complete with a full refresh. When completed, the King Christian hotel will hold more than 100 hotel rooms, eight food and beverage and retail outlets, an event space, and two boat docks accommodating 20-plus vessels.

In another big development, the Neighborhood Establishment group is also planning a much-needed $55-million overhaul of the **Hotel on the Cay,** on the tiny isle of Providence Cay just opposite the Christiansted boardwalk. Work to transform the property into a hip 115-room hotel with a marina is expected to be completed by 2024.

MODERATE

Company House Hotel ★   Just a block or two from the downtown Christiansted waterfront, this good-value three-level inn is located in a vintage warehouse that once served the West Indies Company. It's within walking

Colorful tile murals bedeck the pool at the Company House Hotel, close to Christiansted's waterfront.

distance of the town's National Historic Site district. Although the public rooms have a historical elegance, the newly refreshed accommodations are simply outfitted (but roomy), with tile floors, wood furniture, and good-quality beds in crisp linens. Some bathrooms have been nicely updated with white subway tiles and pebble-floored showers. One suite has a kitchenette with a full-size fridge, while the King's Suite has amazing harbor views. The pool is small and narrow, but ya gotta love the colorful tile murals.

2 Company St. www.hotelcompanyhouse.com. ℂ **340/773-1377.** 35 units. $219–$239 double; $269 and up suite. Children 12 and under stay free in parent's room. Rates include breakfast. **Amenities:** Piano bar; outdoor pool; free Wi-Fi.

King Christian Hotel ★★ If the fantastic King Christian reno by designer Chris Pardo (who did the refresh on the Waves Cane Bay, p. 142) is any indication, the entire project to upgrade the Christriansted harborfront will be transformative. Fancy this is not; earthy, textural, smart is more like it. Rooms are done in wood and rattan, with sisal mats and orange-gold throws against whitewashed walls. Both bedrooms and bathrooms have beautiful patterned tile floors. Color streams in through framed windows and balconies: a robin's-egg sky stacked atop harbor blues, white walls burnished amber by the sun's buttery rays. Decor is determinedly not matchy-matchy: Each side of the bed has different lamps and different nightstands, but colors and textures are satisfyingly cohesive. All rooms have balconies, and four two-bedroom suites come with big wraparound open porches and full kitchens. The new lobby is a wine bar, where guests can sample and buy. The enhancement of the existing 21 rooms in the old Kings Alley Hotel will include the addition of a sushi bar on the first floor. A second-floor deck with bar overlooks the isle of Protestant Cay, and another deck overlooks the pool with fort views. You can take the water taxi over to Cay Beach and watch the boats skim the harbor.

1102 King's Wharf. www.kingchristianhotel.com. ℂ **340/773-6330.** 100 units. $209–$269 double; $309–$399 studio and 1-bedroom suite; $559–$779 2-bedroom suite. **Amenities:** 2 restaurants; wine bar; tiki room; coffee shop; ice cream shop, outdoor pool; free Wi-Fi.

Frederiksted & West End
MODERATE

Cottages by the Sea ★★ Guests keep returning year after year to this hospitable, restful, and meticulously managed family-run resort. Cottages by the Sea is neither fancy nor particularly stylish, just the kind of relaxing, homey place where everyone is either digging their feet in the sand or curling up in some nook with a good book. The beach is the thing here, idyllic and palm-fringed and with crystalline seas that are fine for snorkeling. Just outside Frederiksted (within walking distance), the eponymous cute-as-a-button cottages (and four hotel rooms) are painted in tropical hues, each with its own private patio or porch and all but four with fully equipped kitchens. Every cottage has a different configuration and design scheme; some have little dining nooks, others wainscoted walls. The four European hotel rooms have kitchenettes. This is excellent value for families—up to two children 17 and

Relaxing, homey rooms on a palm-fringed beach bring many repeat visitors back to Cottages by the Sea.

under stay for free in their parent's cottage—and the gorgeous beachfront locale can't be beat (look for sea glass on the beach). The adjacent restaurant (outside owned), **Beachside Café,** is a minute's walk from the cottages.

127A Estate. caribbeancottages.com. ⓒ **800/323-7252** or 340/772-0495. 27 units. Oceanview cottages $185–$375; gardenview cottages $130–$300. Extra person $20. Up to 2 children 17 and under stay free in parent's cottage. **Amenities:** Bikes; laundry; watersports equipment/rentals; free Wi-Fi.

The Fred ★★   Bringing sassy, elevated style to the West End in 2018, the Fred has a color-saturated South Beach vibe crossed with centuries-old Danish colonial flavor. It's a pet-friendly, adults-only beachside complex comprised of six restored historic 18th-century structures. The shiny gold crown motif—honoring Danish King Frederick V, for whom the town is named—is everywhere, from crown keychains in the perky gift shop to the painted crown at the bottom of the big blue saltwater pool (one of two pools). The larger pool is the resort's beating heart, framed by a hot tub, tropical greenery, and the swinging seaside alfresco cafe/bar (hosting weekend sushi nights from 4 to 9pm and a lively brunch from 10am to 3pm) with umbrella-topped tables looking out on the glittering bay. The 22 rooms are almost an afterthought, but they're plenty stylish and individually designed in jazzy tropical prints. Some have balconies overlooking the sea, and one even has a full kitchen. Set in the gingerbread-trimmed 1790 Totten House, the lobby/gift shop is all richly saturated color, with lime-green leather couches against royal-blue walls, portraits of roosters, and neon signs. The Fred fronts the beach, where you can snorkel and watch cruise ships roll in and out of Frederiksted Pier. When you're there during the day and the place is humming, music cranked and bronzed bodies lounging on the ocean deck, you might assume that the Fred is a 24/7 party-hearty hang. But at 10pm, the brakes go on, and everything blessedly becomes a noise-free zone till 8am.

605 Strand St. www.sleepwithfred.com. ℂ **340/777-3733.** 22 units. $248–$445 double. Day pass: $35 double, $25 single. **Amenities:** Restaurant/bar; gift shop; 2 outdoor pools; spa; watersports equipment/rentals; free Wi-Fi.

Sand Castle on the Beach ★★   This 21-room hotel has a dreamy strip of Frederiksted Beach sand at its back door. It's long known for its gay and lesbian following, but Sand Castle welcomes all, with friendly service and splendid sunset views. It has plenty of sociable public spaces, including two freshwater swimming pools (one clothing-optional) and the alfresco resort restaurant, **Beach Side Café,** a happening place to eat and drink (drag queen brunch, anyone?) and a popular spot for meltingly lovely sunsets. Accommodations range from newly refreshed beachfront villas with full kitchens and terra cotta–tile floors to roomy courtyard suites around a private pool. Budget travelers will appreciate the good-value garden or queen studios—they may lack views (or full kitchens or elbow room), but they're close to all the resort action. The beautiful beach has good snorkeling. The hotel is right next to Dorsch Beach, a popular seaside park that can get fairly active on "Sunday Fundays." The resort offers a limited number of cruise-ship day passes ($40/person) that include lounge chairs and beach umbrellas and use of the pools.

Veterans Shore Dr. sandcastleonthebeach.com. ℂ **340/772-1205.** 21 units. $224–$270 double; $289–$355 suite; $509–$550 villa. Rates include breakfast. **Amenities:** Restaurant; exercise room; 2 outdoor pools; watersports equipment/rentals; free Wi-Fi.

Victoria House ★   This three-story boutique property has genuine color and charm. It's in a Victorian-era house right on the downtown Frederiksted waterfront. Unlike most of the other Frederiksted lodgings, it's not directly on the beach, but a number of rooms have ocean views. The spacious, nicely renovated rooms and suites are done in vivid hues, all with comfy beds and large, walk-in showers. The third-floor suites share a wraparound gallery deck overlooking the sea, and the Starfish suite has a love seat with front-row views of the Frederiksted waterfront. Of the two two-bedroom suites, one, the Sunset, comes with a full kitchen. A cobblestoned outdoor courtyard has tables for games and snacking. No children.

7 Strand St. www.victoriahousevi.com. ℂ **340/692-8888.** 8 units. $189–$309 double. Ages 21 and older only. **Amenities:** Watersports equipment/rentals; free Wi-Fi.

Inns & Guesthouses

Feather Leaf Inn ★★   This enchanting 19-acre seafront property is new to the local lodging scene but already feels deeply rooted. The past is pungent here, where the 260-year-old ruins of Estate Butler's Bay, a Danish sugar plantation, have been repurposed as a gracious eco-inn, a 5-year labor of love by husband-and-wife owners Ryan Flegal and Corina Marks. Vintage

Right on the Frederiksted waterfront, the aptly named Victoria House has boutique color and charm.

hardwood floors had buckled, and little was functional, but the good bones were there. Original 2-foot-thick stone walls, wide open windows, and interiors with open airflow make for built-in natural temperature controls. At the Feather Leaf, guests are immersed in Caribbean history and ecology and the pleasures of slow living. With an emphasis on healthy, plant-based, sustainable practices (the inn is 100% solar-powered, and the grounds have been planted with a budding "food forest" of more than 100 fruit and nut trees), it's become popular as a yoga and meditation retreat. Rooms in the Main House have gleaming hardwood floors and mahogany louvered windows open to stunning sea vistas; many of the rooms here are furnished in Crucian antiques. The Dragonfly House has a shared kitchen and three bedrooms, making it a good choice for group stays; the beds' mahogany headboards were custom-built from estate trees uprooted by storms. The original 1,000-square-foot carriage house is now the Ocean House (sleeps five), with rubble stone walls, high ceilings, and a sea-facing patio. All rooms are open to the balmy trade winds, but two Deluxe Queen rooms are air-conditioned. The saltwater pool is edged in red brick, echoing the house's red-brick veranda and the scarlet shutters of the Main House Gallery Porch. In 2023, the inn will do pop-up dinners and planned events on the 40-seat terrace, which faces west for idyllic sunset views. Take the path beneath flamboyant trees to the small, rocky beach for good snorkeling in the shallows of Butler's Bay. Notable wreck dive sites (p. 164) are a short swim farther out. The Feather Leaf's sister hotel in Christiansted, **Sugar Apple Bed & Breakfast** (www.sugarapplebnb.com), is a historic 12-room property formerly known as the Pink Fancy Hotel.

325 Prospect Hill Rd., Frederiksted. www.featherleafinn.com. © **340/474-1358.** 9 units. $180–$358 double; $320–$498 Ocean House. Rates include breakfast. **Amenities:** Outdoor pool; free Wi-Fi.

Villas, Condos & Cottages

Renting a villa, condo, or house on St. Croix is an excellent option for vacationing groups, families, and couples. The island has a wide-ranging selection of options. Most, if not all, offer full kitchens, and many have pools.

St. Croix Rent a Villa (www.stcroixrentavilla.com; ✆ **340/690-3465**) gets high marks for personalized service and quality properties in arranging vacation rentals. Rentals range from honeymoon villas to family-friendly choices, both beachfront and hillside. It handles many of the rental villas at **Villa Madeleine** (see below). **Vacation St. Croix** (vacationstcroix.com; ✆ **340/718-0361**) offers some of the best accommodations on the island, specializing in lodgings directly on the beach (villas, condos, and private homes). **Premier Properties** (www.premierpropertiesusvi.com; ✆ **917/721-2727**) has an array of short- and long-term rentals, from standalone villas to condos.

The 43-unit **Villa Madeleine** ★, off Route 82, Teague Bay (www.villamadeleine-stcroix.com; ✆ **800/533-6863** or 340/690-3465; weekly: $1,700–$2,000 double, $2,300–$2,450 quad), is a real hideaway, with nicely furnished two-story condo villa suites in a lush tropical setting. Each villa has its own private courtyard and pool, many with views of the bay, but all are individually owned and differ when it comes to style and updated interiors. The beachfront all-suites **Colony Cove** ★, 3221 Estate Golden Rock (✆ **800/524-2025** or 340/718-1965; $140–$255; children 11 and under stay free in parent's unit), offers 60 units and is 1 mile west of Christiansted. Of all the condo complexes on St. Croix, Colony Cove is most like a full-fledged hotel, with a large staff on hand, an on-site watersports desk, and a swimming pool.

Popular owner-rental sites like **VRBO.com** and **Airbnb.com** advertise a number of properties on St. Croix.

Camping

Mount Victory Camp ★★ Just a 10-minute drive north of Frederiksted, this beautifully landscaped eco-resort gives visitors an opportunity to immerse themselves in one of St. Croix's lesser-known natural environments: the forested farm valley of the wild western coast, where nights bring cooling trade winds and the island's agricultural riches are being tapped once more. It's a refreshing departure from the beach scene, although you're only a 2-mile drive down the hill to a comely white-sand beach. Four of the five camp lodgings are rustic Arts and Crafts–style bungalows handcrafted by a shipwright using salvaged tropical hardwoods. The lone **Schoolhouse Apartment** ★★ was built around

> ### Ridge to Reef: Farm Stay
>
> A creative alternative to the typical seaside resort is a stay on an organic rainforest farm on the island's jungle-lush west coast. **Ridge to Reef Farm** (www.ridge2reef.org; ✆ **340/220-0466**) offers off-the-grid solar-powered lodgings, from tent camps ($35/night) to hostel-like bunk cabanas ($55/night) to private cabanas ($85/double/night)—hot water and Wi-Fi included. You can buy your food right off the farm and cook it in the community kitchen. You can even volunteer for farm work (like feeding the pigs).

the ruins of a historic old schoolhouse (ca. 1841); it's a wonderful mix of tropical hardwoods and native stone walls. Both the bungalows and the apartment accommodate four to six adults. You can also do tent camping ($30/two adults and two kids), but you'll have to bring your own gear. Each dwelling has basic cooking and eating facilities, and open-air showers use solar-heated water collected from a solar flat-plate thermal collector. A shady, breezy pavilion is the beating heart of the resort, its pitched slats fashioned from mahogany (using wood harvested from dead or dying trees—mahogany is a protected species). You'll need to bring in your food; fresh organic fruit and produce is sold at the island's farmers markets (p. 159). Outdoor activities include guided hikes into the rainforest and workshops in "ancestral skills" like stone toolmaking and palm-leaf basketry through **Caribbean Earth Skills** (see box, above). It even has a tortoise colony!

2 Mt. Victory, Frederiksted. www.mtvictorycamp.com. ✆ **340/201-7983.** 5 dwellings. Cabins $70-$90; apartment $90–$110 double. 2 kids free, extra person $15 ($10 kids). Payment through Venmo or PayPal only. **Amenities:** Public phone; picnic tables; free Wi-Fi.

WHERE TO EAT

Many people believe that St. Croix has the best dining scene in the Virgin Islands. It's certainly a dynamic one, helmed by forward-thinking chefs who have attracted world-wide acclaim with their sustainable practices. The sheer diversity of restaurants and cuisines is remarkable, from Crucian island food to East Indian to Latin-inflected menus catering to the island's large Puerto Rican population. And never discount that ramshackle beach bar or neighborhood chicken shack: Many of the island's local owner-operated spots offer some of the most delicious dining around. Sample a range of cuisines on a **guided tasting and cultural walking tour ★★** in St. Croix offered by **Virgin Island Food Tours** (www.vifoodtours.com; ✆ **866/498-3684;** $99 adults, $59 children 4–11).

The island's agricultural heritage is strong and undergoing a resurgence. St. Croix's mid-island agricultural belt is the site of the Annual Agricultural and Food Fair and home to two rum distilleries, a brewery, and a distillery turning

Virgin Islands Coffee Roasters is a popular hangout near the Christiansted waterfront (see box p. 152).

local breadfruit into award-winning vodka (p. 178). Tied in with this trend is the island's reputation as a health-and-wellness destination: St. Croix has more vegan cafes, juice bars, and organic farms than all the other Virgins combined.

The issue for most visitors—particularly those staying outside of Christiansted and Frederiksted—is often simply getting around at night. Many roads in St. Croix are badly lit, and driving on the left (for those used to driving on the right) can be challenging even during daylight hours. So don't drive; get a taxi. Taxi drivers are happy to deliver you to a restaurant and return for you when your meal is done. Have your hotel call a taxi for you, be sure to confirm the rate there and back with the driver before you set out, and get the driver's card for later trips if all is copacetic.

If you're staying at one of the small hotels or guesthouses in and around Christiansted, you'll likely be able to walk to your restaurant of choice. If you're at a hotel in Frederiksted, the night is yours. The cruise-ship crowds will have departed, and the small dining rooms here have a more down-to-earth (and less expensive) feel than those in Christiansted.

Keep in mind that most restaurants and hotels shutter during the height of hurricane season, often from late August or early September into early October.

North Shore

AMA Canebay ★★ INTERNATIONAL Getting raves for its refined menu and insanely gorgeous setting overlooking a rocky ocean ledge, AMA Canebay is one of the island's top choices. You and your party can share from a menu of small plates: a meltingly soft crab souffle, say, or the big Caesar salad with a kick (chipotle cashew dressing). Or choose from land-and-sea mains, from a sublime shrimp and grits to porcini and beef pappardelle in a brandy cream sauce. Finish with what the restaurant calls "crack pie" topped with whipped cream. Service is tiptop. Ask for a seat down in the Grotto and watch the surf turn from slate blue to silver as the sun goes down.

112c Cane Bay. www.amacanebay.com. ℭ **340/227-3432.** Reservations recommended. Entrees $22–$28. Tues–Sat 5–9pm.

Blues' Backyard BBQ & Grill ★★ BARBECUE/AMERICAN The kitchen is really cooking at this food truck and backyard barbeque grill, where you can listen to live music beneath spreading flamboyant trees and dine on award-winning slow-cooked barbecued brisket and ribs, chicken pot pies, and pulled-pork sandwiches. Sunday brunch features Southern-style biscuits and sausage gravy, *huevos rancheros* quesadillas, and sometimes a Creole

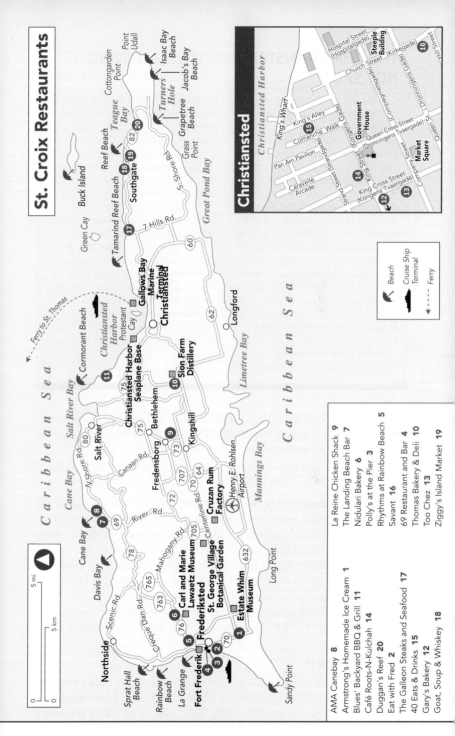

St. Croix Restaurants

AMA Canebay **8**
Armstrong's Homemade Ice Cream **1**
Blues' Backyard BBQ & Grill **11**
Café Roots-N-Kulchah **14**
Duggan's Reef **20**
Eat with Fred **2**
The Galleon Steaks and Seafood **17**
40 Eats & Drinks **15**
Gary's Bakery **12**
Goat, Soup & Whiskey **18**

La Reine Chicken Shack **9**
The Landing Beach Bar **7**
Nidulari Bakery **6**
Polly's at the Pier **3**
Rhythms at Rainbow Beach **5**
Savant **16**
69 Restaurant and Bar **4**
Thomas Bakery & Deli **10**
Too Chez **13**
Ziggy's Island Market **19**

Christiansted

THE CHRISTIANSTED boardwalk: DINING HOT SPOT

With the revitalization of the Christiansted harborfront, its boardwalk has become a one-stop spot for food and shopping. The King Christian Hotel expansion has added some super-stylish little cafes along Kings Wharf, including the tiki bar **Breakers Roar** (www.breakers roartikibar.com); a wine bar in the hotel's lobby; **Virgin Islands Coffee Roasters** (www.virginislandscoffeeroasters.com); the ice-cream shop **Cream & Co.** (www.creamandcoicecream.com), with kicky local flavors like mocha jumbie, mango lang-lang, and olive oil pecan; a darling breakfast spot, **Caroline's** (www.carolines breakfast.com), done up in *Eloise at the Plaza*–style pinks and tropical prints; and **El Leon** (www.elleonrestaurant.com), serving Oaxacan food.

Farther down the boardwalk, set inside an old sugar mill, **Mill Boardwalk Bar Brick Oven Pizza** ★ (www.facebook.com/themillboardwalkbar) serves interesting pies like a Clam Casino Pizza and a special spicy Cinco de Mayo pizza from scratch. It also has a tasting room featuring Mutiny vodkas, made from breadfruit at St. Croix's own Sion Farm (p. 178). **Shupe's on the Boardwalk** (www.shupes ontheboardwalk.com) offers burgers, pitchers of beer, hand-cut fries, pounding music, and chicken wings; its slightly less raucous sister property **Brew STX** ★ (www.brewstx.com), St. Croix's only microbrewery, add salads and vegan options to the upscale pub fare. Also on the waterfront: the open-air restaurant **RumRunners** (www.rumrunnersstcroix.com), with favorites like surf 'n turf, fish tacos, conch fritters, and baby back ribs.

shrimp-and-sausage frittata. Food is fresh-cooked, and even the slaw is home-made. Music is on tap on Wednesday, Thursday, and Friday from 4:30 to 7:30pm and Sunday brunch.

32K LaGrande Princesse (Rte. 70, Northside Rd). www.facebook.com/bluesbackyard-bbq. © **340/514-2541.** Entrees $6–$38. Daily noon–8pm; Sun brunch 10am–2pm.

The Landing Beach Bar ★ SEAFOOD/CASUAL   This is one of the island's most popular beach bars, where the good food—like yellowfin tuna tacos and mahi Reubens, and specials like curry conch stew—truly elevates it beyond pub-grub mediocrity (a not untypical phenomenon in the Virgins, we've found). Offering killer Cane Bay views, the expansive space is open to the elements and gentle sea breezes (peacocks strut the grounds). Live music on weekends.

110c Cane Bay. thelandingbeachbar.com. © **340/718-0362.** Burgers, sandwiches & wraps $12–$18; tacos $14–$16. Mon & Wed–Sat 11am–8pm; Sun 10am–6pm; closed Tues.

Christiansted

Many people, us among them, were heartbroken to hear that **Café Christine,** for many years a favorite lunch spot in a leafy courtyard in downtown Christiansted, had closed permanently in May 2022. Also up for sale at press time was **Galangal,** another favorite Christiansted longtimer.

EXPENSIVE

40 Eats & Drinks ★★ AMERICAN   A bistro reinvention of the restaurant 40 Strand Eatery, this casual, compact space has outsized ambitions when it comes to food, and what they cook up is awfully good. Dishes certainly *sound* good—the 40 Eats brain trust is genius in coming up with kicky creative pairings. Brunch choices are as flavorful as they sound, from a picadillo sloppy Joe to Painkiller French toast. The pimento-cheese burger warms the cockles of this old Southern heart. A typical dinner menu might start with curry carrot bisque or a steak-and-potatoes bruschetta and go on to the million-dollar meatloaf (made with beef, veal, foie gras, and cognac gravy) or seared mahi beneath a scallion shrimp cream sauce. Be sure to check the Facebook page; the restaurant's opening hours can be erratic. Outdoor seating is also available. 40 Easts also does the food at **Sion Farm Distillery** (p. 178).

40 Strand St. www.facebook.com/40StrandEatery. ⓒ **340/692-0524.** Reservations recommended. Entrees $22–$36. Mon–Fri 11:30am–7:30pm; Sat-Sun 9am–3pm.

Savant ★★★ CARIBBEAN/THAI/MEXICAN/FUSION   The best restaurant on St. Croix may just be the best restaurant in the Virgin Islands. And it *looks* good, the work of the former set-designing wife of the owner, who transformed this historic building into not one but two sexy set pieces. The front room feels like a speakeasy jewel-box, but the real action is in the main restaurant on the candlelit back patio, with native stone walls and plant-filled niches and a ceiling that's a swooping swath of sailcloth. You can pinball from potstickers and tuna poke to blackened shrimp-and-grits or hearty wild boar ribs atop peanut noodles and a sauteed cabbage mix; you can't go wrong with any of it. Finish, if you can, with the triple chocolate Amaretto cake or the pecan coconut pie. Savant has only 20 candlelit tables, so call for a reservation as far in advance as possible. A seat at the great-looking bar wouldn't be the worst thing in the world.

4C Hospital St. www.savantstx.com. ⓒ **340/713-8666.** Reservations required. Entrees $14–$39. Mon–Sat 6–10pm.

Too Chez ★★★ NEW AMERICAN Whenever we ask locals for restaurant recommendations, this spot is always high on everybody's list. Maybe it's because Crucians recognize and appreciate the power of culinary lineages. Dave and Jane Kendrick ran the much-loved Uptown Eatery, which closed in 2020, and the equally loved Kendricks before that. Too Chez is the domain of their son Dustin

Set in a charming West Indian cottage, Too Chez honors the culinary legacy of owner Dustin Kendrick and his parents Dave and Jane.

Kendrick, and he delivers with sensational flair. The menu is short and to the point: Start with elegant baked shrimp scampi, tuna poke, or Dave Kendrick's chipotle soup, then on to swordfish piccata or grilled baby back ribs. In the upscale burger wars, Too Chez may be the champ, with its version handmade with Angus ground filet mignon. Everybody loves the Key lime pie. And now the family has come home in a sense, as Too Chez is back in Kendricks' old location in the charming little Quin House, a West Indian cottage with tables inside and out.

2132 Company St. www.toochezstx.com. ℂ **340/713-8888.** Entrees $25–$40. Tues–Sat 5:30–8:30pm.

MODERATE

Cafe Roots-N-Kulchah ★ VEGAN   This 20-seat cafe on a Christiansted side street has outdoor seating in a shaded courtyard. Choices are limited (three entrees a day), but everything is thoughtfully prepared with top-quality ingredients and packed with flavor. Scribbled on a blackboard are the chef's specials

of the day: vegan lasagne rolls, a black-bean burger, a baked barbeque pumpkin. A vegan saltfish is made with hearts of palm and nori seaweed. All entrees come with yummy sides like banana fritters, stir-fried veggies, and arugula salad. Thirst-quenchable fresh fruit drinks might be lemon anise, blackberry ginger, and a blueberry basil iced tea, and organic vegan wine is also served. A native Crucian, Chef Kimba Kabaka is a culinary school graduate and has a masters in horticulture. He is also an artisan wood-turner, making beautiful bowls, platters, and even tables out of (largely) local woods.

Vegans are well served at Cafe Roots-N-Kulchah.

5 King St. ℂ **340/513-8665.** Entrees $16–$20. Tues–Sat 11:30am–6pm, plus seasonal dinner hours.

INEXPENSIVE

Gary's Bakery ★ BAKERY   Sample Gary's fresh baked goods, a selection of Crucian favorites that might include butter bread, titi bread, coconut rolls, and coconut tarts. Have a Gary's Crucian breakfast of saltfish or smoked herring with johnnycakes.

33 King St. ℂ **340/773-6361.** Breads and pastries $1–$4. Mon–Sat 5am–6pm; Sun 5am–noon.

Mid-Island

Also check out the excellent restaurant at the Sion Farm Distillery (p. 178), which is open for lunch, dinner, and cocktails.

Celebrating the foods and rich agricultural bounty of the island of St. Croix, the Memorial Day weekend **Agriculture & Food Fair (Agrifest)** ★★, now in its 50th year, is a foodie's paradise, featuring competitions for best crop farmers, farmers markets, and nurseries, as well as island classics like kallaloo, coconut sugarcake, crab and rice, *maubi* (a fermented beverage), dumbbread, and saltfish gundy. The Fairgrounds in Estate Lower Love are packed with food and refreshment booths and crop exhibits. The colorful annual posters alone are worth collecting. The fair is open for the 3-day weekend from 9am to 5pm ($6 adults, $5 seniors, $4 children 12 and under; festival passes available). For details, go to viagrifest.org.

MODERATE

La Reine Chicken Shack ★★ BARBECUE/CARIBBEAN   It's reputedly Martha Stewart's favorite restaurant on the island, and after you sample one of the shack's spit-roasted chickens, it might be yours too. La Reine Chicken Shack is known for its meltingly juicy, fall-off-the-bone roast chicken, but just try turning away the barbeque ribs or the curry chicken, all served with rice and beans and salad or johnnycakes. Specials might be a seafood kallaloo or a rib-sticking meat loaf. Despite surging poultry prices, La Reine was still good value at press time, when half a chicken, rice and peas, and a couple of johnnycakes put you out $15. Eat in the open-air restaurant or take out (you'll be dining on Styrofoam either way), but if you eat in, you can also sip a cocktail from the full bar.

24 Slob A-B Estate La Reine. ✆ **340/778-5717.** Entrees $15–$19.75. Mon–Sat 10:30am–8pm. Rte. 75 (Queen St.) just off Centerline Rd., next to La Reine Farmers Market.

INEXPENSIVE

Thomas Bakery & Deli ★ BAKERY/DELI   This local fave features Caribbean specialty breads like coconut rolls, pineapple and guava turnovers, saltfish pates, and the breakfast staple known as titi bread (a buttered bread so named for its breast-like puffiness).

4500 Queen Mary Hwy., Castle Coakley. ✆ **340/778-2625.** Bread and pastries 50¢–$2.50; pates $3.50. Mon–Fri 5:30am–7pm; Sat 5:30am–6pm; Sun 5:30am–1pm.

East End

EXPENSIVE

Duggan's Reef ★★ CONTINENTAL/CARIBBEAN   Duggan's is an island favorite. Owned by the same family since 1983, it's perched on a reef overlooking the sapphire seas of Reef Beach, where windsurfers and sailboats skim the water. Duggan's was walloped by Hurricane Maria in 2017 but rebuilt and reopened in 2018. Fresh Caribbean lobster is a star here, from the lobster egg rolls to lobster pasta gratin to the formidable Irish whiskey lobster. Local mahi is also very good, and they do the American classics (burgers, steak, fried chicken) to a T. Glad to have you back, Duggan's.

5A Teague Bay. www.duggansreefstx.com. ✆ **340/773-9800.** Reservations required for dinner in winter. Entrees $23–$39; pastas $19–$30. Mon–Sat 5:30–8:30pm; closed Sun.

The Galleon Steaks and Seafood ★★ AMERICAN/CARIBBEAN
This fizzy marina restaurant and bar is the domain of Chef Charles Mereday,
who electrified the Naples, Florida, restaurant scene with Mereday's Fine
Dining and served as executive chef of Old Stone Farmhouse on St. Thomas
back in the aughts. His smart revamp of the Galleon has been a raging success—the marina restaurant and bar is always packed with happy, chattering
diners. Among the myriad dining rooms is an outdoor deck overlooking the
marina, docking home to the U.S. Coast Guard and many Buck Island outfitters. Mereday is deft on his feet, upgrading the banal with flair and fresh-
sourced ingredients. Shrimp-stuffed Caribbean lobster glistens with unagi
mirin butter, a duck leg confit is encircled in a tangy tamarind sauce; the tuna
nachos are just right. A Kombucha Julep (Bullit bourbon, ginger-lime kombucha, and mint) is balm for head *and* tummy. The pastry chef is Erika Dupree,
featured on *Top Chef Just Desserts*. Also check out the Galleon's sister restaurant, **Parrot Fish** (parrotfishstx.com; ✆ 340/727-0231), 1113 Strand St., in
downtown Christiansted, with a wine bar, sports TVs, mezze plates, tacos, and
more.

5000 Estate Southgate, Green Cay Marina at Tamarind Reef Resort, E. End Rd. the
galleonstcroix.com. ✆ **340/244-6007.** Reservations recommended. Entrees $24–$48.
Tues–Sat 4–9pm. Go E. on Rte. 82 from Christiansted for 5 min.; 1 mi past the Buccaneer, turn left into Green Cay Marina.

Goat, Soup & Whiskey ★★ AMERICAN   The St. Croix outpost of a
Colorado ski-resort tavern known for solid grub and live music, Goat, Soup &
Whiskey has fast become a seasonal hot spot here on St. Croix's East End (it
also has another location in . . . Ohio?). The spacious, open-air dining room
has wonderful sea views (and yes, that's Buck Island) and a beamed wood
ceiling. A well-oiled kitchen supplements the straightforward menu (appetizers like lollypop lamb chops and pricey steak-centric entrees) with dishes in
tasty local flavors: curried goat soup, jalapeño corn chowder, and mahi tacos.
Pastas are the more affordable route, ranging from a creamy pesto primavera
($21) to seafood fettucine ($37).

5000 Estate Coakley Bay, East End. www.soupandwhiskey.com. ✆ **340/773-3333.**
Entrees $21–$51. Tues–Sun 11:30am–9pm; Sun brunch 10am–2pm. Open Dec 10–
April 11.

MODERATE

Ziggy's Island Market ★★ CARIBBEAN   It's a gas station, a convenience store, and an eating establishment all at once, with a chef overseeing an
irresistible menu that zigzags from Crucian-inspired dishes (crab and conch
fritters, coconut cilantro rice, mango ginger slaw) to ziti in a cheesy tomato
sauce to a mouthwatering Sunday brunch starring crab Rangoon Benedict,
green chili pork *huevos rancheros,* and mimosa fried chicken and waffles.
Other Ziggy's specialties include Italian paninis and what has been advertised
as the best roti east of C'sted. It's all over the map, but quite deliciously, and

Catch of the day at the East End's popular Goat, Soup & Whiskey.

this is a must-stop for visitors and locals alike. Get it to go with curbside takeout or dine in at the "Libation Station" with a cold beer in hand.

East End Rd., 5008 Estate Solitude. www.facebook.com/ZiggysIslandMarketSTX. ℂ **340/773-8382.** Entrees $16–$23. Mon–Fri 6am–8pm; Sun 8am–2:30pm (kitchen closes earlier). Libation Station Mon–Fri 3–9pm; Sat noon–8pm

Mahogany Road
INEXPENSIVE

Nidulari Bakery ★★ CARIBBEAN/INTERNATIONAL   It's billed as "St. Croix's only artisanal bakery and food truck in the rain forest!" and if you make it up this far along pot-holed Mahogany Road, you deserve a tasty snack. There's a kind of wood-fairy ambience up in this lush tangle of woods, and the little caravan "gypsy" cart feels straight out of a Black Forest fable. If your curiosity isn't piqued by the mashed-up menu of culinary traditions— from South Asian to island to Southern comfort food—I'm not sure what it takes to get you up the mountain. My friends, that little gypsy truck is where you can get a very tasty veggie curry plate, mac 'n' cheese, and coconut-butternut squash soup. The banana French toast is flambéed, for chrissakes! Sandwiches might be a Southern-style pulled pork or a vegetarian lentil fritter; and sweet goodies come in the form of hot cross buns, nutmeg cake, coffee bread pudding (with chocolate ganache!), and a lemon-lavender shortbread cookie. The refreshing drinks might be basil lemonade or ginger lemonade.

9 Little La Grange, about 1.3 miles up Mahogany Rd. from the West End. nidulari.com. No phone. Cash or PayPal only. Entrees and sandwiches $16–$17; breads $5; pastries and cake $1–$3. Wed noon–3pm; Sat–Sun 11am–3pm.

In & Around Frederiksted

Keep in mind that local establishments (including shops) may not keep full hours on non–cruise ship days. Sadly, the family-run **Villa Morales,** serving home-cooked Puerto Rican classics for nearly three-quarters of a century, closed in 2019.

EXPENSIVE

Eat with Fred ★★ AMERICAN/INTERNATIONAL   Dine on a beautiful deck overlooking the sea (and the sunset) at the house restaurant at Fred's boutique hotel. It's pretty impressive, with food that is beautifully prepared and responsibly sourced—and those views! Breakfast, lunch, and dinner are served here, and fresh sushi rolls—from California to spicy tuna to the Frederick (lobster, carrot, cucumber, melon!)—are offered every Saturday and Sunday (4–9pm). For lunch, the Fred Burger on a brioche bun is big, juicy, and tasty, and the local mahi sandwich is just right. For dinner, a straightforward set menu of small plates (chicken skewers, ceviche), salads, blackened or grilled fish, and steaks comes with local-centric sides like whipped cassava and green banana hash. Service can be creaky, but hopefully any post-pandemic staffing issues have been ironed out by the time you read this.

The Fred, 605 Strand St. www.eatwithfred.com. ℂ **340/777-3733.** Small plates $12–$22; entrees $20–$58. Mon–Fri 8am–9pm; Sat–Sun 11am–9pm.

69 Restaurant and Bar ★★ INTERNATIONAL   This lovely little courtyard restaurant off Strand Street brings special-occasion fine dining to downtown Frederiksted, something this town hasn't seen in a while. White tablecloths and twinkly fairy lights aside, 69 is making a real effort to create fresh and refined dishes. The menu has aspirations, and some say the talented kitchen is already meeting them. So, you might start with lamb meatballs or mahi cakes with a Creole remoulade. Tuna ceviche is marinated in locally squeezed fruit, and how the heck did New England clam chowder get on the menu? Mains include refined takes on Crucian fish, one served with roasted breadfruit and another drizzled with creamy braised leeks, and the ever-popular beef short ribs are braised and topped with a sprightly horseradish chimichurri sauce. Crucian fruit and locally raised veggies and greens figure prominently throughout.

69A King St. sixninestx.com. ℂ **340/772-6969.** Entrees $20–$48. Tues–Sat 11am–2:30pm and 5:30–9pm (oysters 5–9pm); Sun brunch 11am–2:30pm.

INEXPENSIVE

Armstrong's Homemade Ice Cream ★★ ICE CREAM   Since 1900, this family-run store has been making ice cream with local fruits from recipes handed down over three generations. It remains a must-visit. Flavors range from soursop to guava, coconut, and passionfruit. Armstrong's number-one seller? Gooseberry. A special guavaberry ice cream is a Christmas treat. Armstrong's, which also has a seasonal breakfast menu, is a 5-minute drive from downtown Frederiksted.

78-B Whim. www.facebook.com/armstrongshomemadeicecream. ℂ **340/772-1919.** Ice cream $3–$6. Tues–Sat 7am–7pm; Sun 11am–7pm.

PROVISIONING

On St. Croix, everyone should take advantage of the island's farm-fresh fruit and produce. You can do so at the following places, whether you're stocking a kitchen or just looking for a snack or pre-prepared meal. Here are some essential St. Croix resources:

o **Groceries: The Market STX** (formerly Plaza West; www.themarketvi. com; ☏ 340/719-1870), on Centerline Road near the airport, is stocked to the gills with, well, everything; it's open daily 6:30am-10pm. The big **Pueblo** (wfmpueblo.com) grocery chain has two locations in St. Croix: La Reine and Golden Rock. **Seaside Market & Deli** (☏ 340/719-9393), at 2001 Mt. Welcome in Christiansted, has groceries as well as a full-service gourmet deli (with hot foods) and a bakery; it's open daily 6am-9pm.

o **Fresh Seafood:** The revamped **La Reine Fish Market,** on Estate La Reine, reopened in 2021 with some 18 stalls and 12 cleaning stations.

o **Fresh Meat:** The family-run **Annaly Farms** (☏ 340/778-2229), on Route 72 at Lower Love, sells cut-to-order custom cuts of meat, including local hormone-free Senepol beef, as well as U.S. choice beef, pork, lamb, and even fresh vegetables. It's located on Route 72 on the way to the Carambola golf course. **Sejah Farm** (see below) raises chickens, goats, rabbits, and duck (the latter two to order) and sells fresh cuts from Thursday to Saturday at its farmstand.

o **Fresh Produce/Fruit:** The roads of St. Croix are dotted with **farm-stands.** Look for farmers selling fat avocadoes, bananas, papayas, beans, and more along Centerline Road and on roads in Estate Upper Love. **ARTFarm** (artfarmllc.com; ☏ 340/514-4873), a unique organic farm/art gallery, sells organic produce, fruit, and herbs 3 days a week, plus Saturday half-hour pop-ups (11:30am–noon) at its farmstand on South Shore Road. Look for ARTFarm's heirloom tomatoes, kale, squash, beets, and fantastical fruits. **Sejah Farm VI** (sejahfarm.com; ☏ 340/277-6046) sells fruits (mango, golden apple, sugar apple, pineapple), veggies (tomatoes, lettuces, peppers), and herbs (lemongrass, sage, basil, and more); it's on Casper Holstein Drive, near Frederiksted (they even accept farm volunteers). The **La Reine Farmers Market**, on Queen Street at Centerline Road, held Saturdays 6:30-11am, has fruits, vegetables, and herbs as well as herbal teas (like lemongrass and bush tea). **Ridge to Reef Farms** (www.ridge2reef.org; ☏ 340/473-1557) has a farm stand and also offers customized weekly CSAs filled with its organic fruits and vegetables; pickup is Saturdays noon-3pm at Leatherback Brewery or the Lawaetz Farm & Museum (p. 175). Sign up to receive notices of the farm's monthly **"Slow Down Dinners,"** held to support the farm's "Farm to School" efforts.

Polly's at the Pier ★★ COFFEE/INTERNATIONAL   In business since 2009, this centrally located Fredricksted cafe is many, many things: an internet cafe with free Wi-Fi; a gourmet coffee shop; a rotating art gallery; a breakfast and lunch cafe (making breakfast quesadillas, fresh salads, sandwiches, burgers, wraps, rice bowls); and an ice cream shop selling

Armstrong's Homemade Ice Cream (p. 158). It even hosts a Taco Tuesday with margaritas. The miracle is that Polly's does it all very well indeed.

#3 Strand St. pollysatthepierstcroix.com. *℃* **340/719-9434.** Sandwiches, wraps, and quesadillas $9.25–$16; breakfast entrees $7–$12.75. Mon–Sat 8am–3pm; Sun 8am–1pm.

Rhythms at Rainbow Beach ★★ ISLAND/SEAFOOD   Located at the south end of Rainbow Beach, about a mile from the cruise-ship pier, this oceanfront bar/restaurant caters to the splash-and-sun set at Rainbow Beach (and cruise-ship hordes on beach excursions) and then shuts down just before twilight. It's a buzzy daytime spot with gas-fumey jet-skiers sharing the seas with paddle boarders and kayakers—little wonder, since **West End Water Sports** (wewatersports.com; *℃* **340-277-8295**) and all its toys are right next door. In spite of the sometimes-frenzied tourist action, here's the dirty little secret of Rhythms: The food is really, really good, including a seriously delicious grouper sandwich, coconut shrimp, and an array of tasty tacos.

Rainbow Beach. www.rainbowbeachstx.com. *℃* **340/690-9282.** Entrees $9–$17; tacos $12–$17. Daily 11am–6:30pm; bar open to 7pm.

EXPLORING ST. CROIX

Beaches

Beaches, and the lacy reefs that protect them, are St. Croix's big attraction. Renting a car is a great way to hit the beaches—and see the island's attractions.

The most celebrated beach is offshore **Buck Island ★★★**, part of the U.S. National Park Service network. A volcanic islet surrounded by stunning underwater coral gardens, it has idyllic white-sand beaches and superb snorkeling. A number of operators run excursions to Buck Island, leaving from the Christiansted boardwalk; for details, see "Side Trip to Buck Island," p. 185.

The main beach at the Buccaneer Resort on the North Shore east of Christiansted, **Mermaid Beach ★**, is a pretty crescent shaded by swaying palms. **Shoy's Beach ★**, down a road to the right of the Buccaneer entrance, is a local favorite. Park in the parking lot, take a stroll through a lacy canopy of tree branches, and you're there—bring snorkel and mask.

Your best choice for a beach in Christiansted is the one at **Protestant Cay ★**. This palm-shaded island has a surprisingly sweet white-sand strip, calm seas, and surprisingly good snorkeling on the north side of the cay (turtles!!). To get here, take the ferry from the fort at Christiansted; it runs every 10 minutes from 6am to midnight. The 4-minute trip costs $3 round-trip. (The former timeshare Hotel on the Cay is being transformed into a luxury resort with a marina, scheduled to open in 2024.)

Five miles west of Christiansted is the **Palms at Pelican Cove ★★**, where some 1,200 feet of white sand shaded by palm trees attracts a gay and mixed crowd. A reef lies just offshore, so snorkeling conditions are ideal.

Also recommended on the North Shore are **Davis Bay ★★** and **Cane Bay ★★**, each with swaying palms, white sand, and good swimming. These beaches are often windy and currents can be strong, so their waters are not

Day excursions to Buck Island (p. 185) often focus on its underwater snorkeling trails, boasting some of the Caribbean's most stunning undersea views.

always calm, but when the surf isn't stirred up, the snorkeling at Cane Bay can be well worth your while; you'll see elkhorn and brain corals, all some 750 feet off the Cane Bay Wall. Cane Bay adjoins Route 80 on the North Shore. Close to the Carambola Beach Resort, Davis Beach doesn't have a reef; it's more popular among bodysurfers than snorkelers.

On Route 63, a 4-minute drive north of Frederiksted, lies **Rainbow Beach ★**, with white sand and ideal snorkeling conditions—it has a good restaurant (**Rhythms;** p. 160) and offers all kinds of beach and watersports rentals. Nearby, also on Route 63, about 5 minutes north of Frederiksted, is another good beach, called **La Grange ★**. Lounge chairs can be rented here, and there's a bar nearby.

The blinding white sand and deep blue seas of **Sandy Point ★★**, directly south of Frederiksted (a 7-min. drive away), starred in the final scene of the movie *The Shawshank Redemption*. It's the largest beach in all the U.S. Virgin Islands, but it's open to the public only on weekends from 10am to 4pm. Its waters are shallow and calm, perfect for swimming. Zigzagging fences line the beach to help prevent beach erosion. Sandy Point is protected as a nesting spot for endangered sea turtles. Continue west from the western terminus of the Melvin Evans Highway (Rte. 66). For more on visiting the refuge, see p. 179.

Two of the island's prettiest and least crowded beaches, **Jack's Bay ★★** and **Isaac's Bay ★★** on the East End, are somewhat difficult to get to and accessible only on foot, via a fairly easy 1.2-mile trek through protected wilderness from the trailhead near the Millennium Monument at Point Udall. The terrain is unshaded dry scrub and rocky paths, and signage helps lead the way. You'll reach Isaac's Bay Beach first. A little farther down the same path and up over a hill is Jack's Bay Beach, equally beautiful, with soft sand and clear seas. Both have sparkling turquoise seas that offer excellent snorkeling.

Windsurfers like **Reef Beach,** which opens onto Teague Bay along Route 82, East End Road, a half-hour ride from Christiansted. You can get food at **Duggan's Reef** (p. 155). Farther east on East End Road, **Cramer Park,** a special public park operated by the Department of Agriculture, is lined with sea grape trees and has a delightful picnic area, a restaurant, and a bar. Take Route 60 (S. Shore Rd.) to wide and sandy **Grapetree Beach,** with calm water. The beach is flanked only by a few private homes and the newly revived Grapetree Resort (p. 141).

Watersports & Outdoor Adventures

St. Croix is packed with outdoor adventures. In the east, the terrain is rocky and arid, getting little water. But the western part of the island is lush, including a small "rain forest" of mango, tree ferns, and dangling lianas. Between the two extremes are beautiful sandy beaches, rolling hills and pastures, and roads lined with mahogany and colorful flamboyant trees. Watersports galore abound, including boating, sailing, diving, snorkeling, fishing, hiking, and windsurfing.

Caribbean Sea Adventures ★ (caribbeanseaadventures.com; ✆ **340/773-2628**) is a solid all-round choice for snorkeling, sailing, fishing, sunset cruising, and parasail adventures around St. Croix. Among its excursions are a Buck Island half-day powerboat trip ($85 adults, $65 ages 18 and under); a 6-hour sportfishing charter on a 32-foot Boston whaler for marlin, wahoo, and tuna; sunset sails on a luxury catamaran ($40/person); and private charters.

Tan Tan Tours (stxtantantours.com/tours; ✆ **340/773-7041**) has been offering scenic guided off-road Jeep tours for more than 20 years. One thing these half- or full-day tours have in common: All lead to the famed Annaly Bay tide pools for a cool swim. Full-day tours (lunch included) take you from the East End of the island to the West ($255/person), while half-day tours include a 4-hour trip to the West End ($175/person) or a 3-hour hike and swim at the Annaly Bay tide pools ($145/person).

Sportfishing charters with Caribbean Sea Adventures.

OUT ON THE bio BAY

Seeing St. Croix's magical bioluminescent bays by kayak is a nighttime thrill. At night, waters in the Salt River Bay National Historical Park & Ecological Reserve literally shimmer from the light of microscopic bioluminescent organisms known as dinoflagellates (*Pyrodimium bahamense*). These cousins to fireflies glow in response to movement, a shimmering blue finger of light tracing the dip of a paddle. Kayak tours into St. Croix's two bioluminescent bays are best on cloudy, moonless nights. **Virgin Kayak** (see below), **BushTribe Eco Adventures** (below), and **Sea Thru Kayaks VI** (seathrukayaksvi.com; ☏ **340/244-8696**) explore the island's bio bays by ocean kayaks and see-through kayaks. Cost for an average 90-minute tour is $50 to $60 per person.

WATERSPORTS

FISHING   The fishing grounds at **Lang Bank** are about 10 miles from St. Croix. Here you'll find kingfish, dolphin fish, and wahoo. Using light-tackle boats to glide along the reef, you'll probably turn up jack or bonefish. Serious sport fishermen can angle for big marlin with **Caribbean Sea Adventures** (see above) or **Hook and Son Fishing Charters** (www.hookandsunfishingstcroix.com; ☏ **340/227-9650**). Offshore deep-sea fishing charters for six passengers cost around $900 for 4 hours and $1,200 for 6 hours with bait and tackle and drinks included.

At **Clover Crest,** in Frederiksted, local anglers fish right from the rocks. For more information on legal shore-fishing spots around the island, contact the tourist office in Christiansted or Frederiksted.

KAYAKING   The beauty of St. Croix is best seen from a **kayak.** You can explore the waters of Sandy Point, Shell Island, and Salt River Bay National Park (see "Out on the Bio Bay," above) or kayak over the steep underwater wall at Cane Bay on half-day, full-day, and weeklong tours offered by **Virgin Kayak Tours ★** (www.virginkayaktours.com; ☏ **340/514-0062**). (Virgin also rents foot-operated pedal kayaks.) **BushTribe Eco Adventures** (www.bushtribe.com; ☏ **340/277-2503**) offers a range of kayak trips, including nighttime tours of Salt River Bay National Park. At Rainbow Beach, **Sea Sport St. Croix** (seasportsstcroix.com; ☏ **340/244-9011**), a partner with West End Water

BushTribe Eco Adventures offers a range of kayak trips around St. Croix.

Sports, rents single ($20/hr.) and double ($30/hr.) kayaks as well as paddle-boards and floats.

KITEBOARDING **Kite St. Croix** (www.kitestcroix.com; © **340/643-5824**), in Cotton Valley on the north shore of the island's East End, offers kiteboarding lessons ($150–$225) and rentals on-site. The best times for kiteboarding winds are December through March and June through August.

SAILING/BOAT EXCURSIONS **Lyric Sails** ★ (lyricsails.com; © **340/201-5227**), operating out of Frederiksted, gets a lot of love (and repeat book-ings) for its day sails, sunset sails, full moon sails, and Sunday Funday sails accompanied by live music aboard its 63-foot sailing catamaran, *Jolly Mon*, which can hold up to 49 passengers.

For kids of all ages who love pirates, a private 2-hour sailing-adventure tour with local historian, shipwreck diver, and sailor Stanford Joines on his **St. Croix Sailing Adventure Tours** ★ (stanfordjoines.org/tours/; © **340/332-2472**) is fun and highly informative. Joines, the author of *The Eighth Flag,* a pirate history of St. Croix and the Caribbean, sails his boat, *Folly,* and regales passengers with local pirate lore as the boat cruises St. Croix's North Shore, maybe even stopping at the offshore *John and Martha* shipwreck to see real pirate cannons. Excursions cost $75 adults, $45 for ages 12 and under.

SCUBA DIVING & SNORKELING ★★★ Sponge life, black coral (the finest in the West Indies), and steep drop-offs near the shoreline make St. Croix a snorkeling and diving paradise. The island is protected by the largest living reef in the Caribbean, including the fabled North Shore wall that begins in 25 to 30 feet of water and drops to 13,200 feet, sometimes plunging straight down. See "Beaches," p. 160, for recommended snorkeling spots.

Buck Island ★★ is a major scuba-diving site, with a visibility of some 100 feet and an underwater snorkeling trail. Practically all outfitters on St. Croix offer scuba and snorkeling tours to Buck Island. For more information on the island, see "Side Trip to Buck Island," p. 185.

Cane Bay ★★ is famed for shore dives along **The Wall,** a steep underwater offshore drop-off that at its deepest point plunges down to 13,000 feet. The Wall is more or less the edge of the vast 28,000-foot-deep Puerto Rico Trench, the boundary between the Atlantic and the Caribbean seas. You can take a dive boat to the Wall, but the easiest access is right from shore, about a 250-yard surface swim from the west side of the old Cane Bay boat ramp to the moor-ing buoy. Once you descend, you'll see formations of pillar coral, sea fans and sponges, and plentiful reef fish before the sea floor slopes into the black abyss. The Wall is home to pelagic fish like sharks, and divers say you can hear the music of humpback whale song in late winter. Snorkeling Cane Bay is also rewarding when seas are calm. A little further west, **Davis Bay** is also near the Puerto Rico Trench, and **Northstar Reef** ★★, at the east end of Davis Bay, is a spectacular wall dive, recommended for intermediate or experienced divers only. The wall here is covered with stunning brain corals and staghorn thickets. At some 50 feet down, a sandy shelf leads to a cave where giant green moray eels hang out.

Other favorite dive sites include the historic **Salt River Canyon** ★★ (northwest of Christiansted at Salt River Bay), for advanced divers. Submerged canyon walls are covered with purple tube sponges, deep-water gorgonians, and black coral saplings. You'll see schools of yellowtail snapper, turtles, and spotted eagle rays. We also like the gorgeous coral gardens of **Scotch Banks** (north of Christiansted) and **Eagle Ray** (also north of Christiansted), the latter so named because of the rays that cruise along the wall there.

The coral-encrusted **Frederiksted Pier** ★★, in historic Frederiksted, is big fun for both diving *and* snorkeling, where massive undersea pillars attract banded shrimp, plume worms, sea horses, octopus, and sea turtles. Good sites farther out from the pier include **Aquarium Reef, Sugar Reef,** and **Armageddon,** a reef created from the remains of the old Frederiksted Pier, destroyed by Hurricane Hugo in 1989. Pier snorkeling is highly rewarding—just enter the shallow water at the concrete blocks to the left side of the pier and snorkel along the rocks to your right to the pier. Parts of the old pier lying in the water are also good spots for fish. Of course, do not dive or snorkel here when cruise ships are in.

The wrecks at **Butler Bay** ★★, north of Frederiksted on the west shore, include the submerged ruins of three ships: the *Suffolk Maid* trawler, the *Northwind* tugboat, and the 177-foot *Rosaomaira,* the latter sitting in 100 feet

Nep2une's Divers (p. 166) leads excursions to explore the underwater beauty off Frederiksted.

of water. These wrecks form the major part of an artificial reef system that also contains abandoned trucks and cars. This site is recommended for intermediate or experienced divers. The wrecks are about 400 to 600 feet offshore and can be reached by boat or swimming in from the beach. The beach at Butler Bay is small and rocky, but the reef is good for both diving and snorkeling.

Outfitters

In Cane Bay, the family-owned and -operated **Sweet Bottom Dive Center** (www.sweetbottomdive.com; ✆ **340/7733483**) is a PADI five-star outfit that offers personalized guided shore and boat dives for small groups and also dive certification training. Sweet Bottom also leads night dives along the Frederiksted Pier and has a second location at the Carambola resort. In Frederiksted, a top outfitter is **Nep2une's Divers** (neptunestx.com; (✆ **340/227-1915**), which offers guided boat, shore, and night dives with a seasoned staff as well as dive instruction. Its dive shop, at 202 Custom House St., within yards of the Frederiksted pier, has rentals as well as underwater photography and videography services. Another recommended Frederiksted outfitter, the **Cane Bay Dive Shop** (www.canebayscuba.com; ✆ **340/772-0715**) is at 2 Strand St., across the street from the pier. The sheer variety of dive sites near the pier means you can do some serious diving without having to take a long boat ride. Packages go all the way up to a 10-tank boat package for $580. All outfitters have all the gear you need, both rentals and sales.

Most beachside resorts offer complimentary snorkeling equipment. You can also rent a complete snorkel set for $15 per day at **Cane Bay Dive Shop** (see above). For snorkeling gear and other water toys at Rainbow Beach, **Sea Sport St. Croix** (seasportsstcroix.com; ✆ **340/244-9011**), a partner with West End Water Sports, rents snorkel sets ($20/hr.) and fins ($10/hr.) as well as paddleboards and floats.

Finally, check out the inspiring dive videos created by the celebrated St. Croix dive family, the Dykstras, for their clothing company, **Triton's Realm** (www.tritonsrealm.com).

STANDUP PADDLEBOARDING **Sea Sport St. Croix** (see above), a partner with West End Water Sports, rents stand-up paddleboards ($20/hr.) at Rainbow Beach.

OUTDOOR ADVENTURES

BICYLING St. Croix is a very bike-friendly island, with miles of relatively flat roadways punctuated by the occasional lush hill. **Island Life Adventures**, 2 Strand St., Frederiksted (www.island-life-adventures.com; ✆ **340/725-7433**), offers bike rentals and guided bike tours of the island, including visiting newly created trails in Salt River and Windsor Farm that cut through rugged forest.

GOLF St. Croix has long been known to have the best golf in the Virgin Islands, and when this book was going to press it was no contest, considering the fact that the Mahogany Run golf course in St. Thomas was still languishing without a new owner and St. John has no course to begin with. But St. Croix's most celebrated course, the par-72 **Carambola Golf Club,** on the northeast side of St. Croix (www.golfcarambola.com; ℭ **340/ 778-5638**), was also in limbo at press time, still closed for renovations in the wake of the devastating 2017 hurricanes. A wondrous "botanical garden" of a course, Carambola was the 1966 work of Robert Trent Jones, Sr. Hopefully, by the time you have this book in hand, Carambola (and its connecting Rockefeller resort) will be fully open for business.

St. Croix has the U.S.V.I.'s best golf, with the East End's Reef Golf Course a top site.

The **Buccaneer,** Gallows Bay (ℭ **340/712-2144;** p. 138), 3 miles east of Christiansted, has a challeng-ing 5,668-yard, par-70, 18-hole course with panoramic vistas. Call about non-guest greens fees. The **Reef Golf Course** (www.reefgolfstcroixusvi.com; ℭ **340/773-8844**), a recreational complex on the island's East End at Teague Bay, has a par-35 9-hole course; greens fees are $20 for 9 holes, $30 for 18 holes. Golf carts can also be rented ($30 for 9 holes, $50 for 18 holes). Twi-light rates ($15–$25) start at 3:30pm. Tennis and pickleball courts and 18-hole disc golf are also available. Put in an afternoon of golf and then celebrate with a seaside dinner at **Duggan's Reef** (p. 155) next door.

HIKING   Scrub-covered hills make up much of St. Croix's landscape. The island's western district, however, includes a dense, 15-acre forest known as the **Rain Forest** (actually, it's subtropical rain forest). A network of footpaths here offers fantastic nature walks. The area is thick with mahogany trees, *kapok* (silk-cotton) trees, and *samaan* (rain) trees. Sweet limes, mangoes, hog plums, and breadfruit trees, all of which have grown in the wild since planta-tion days, are here. The Rain Forest is private property, but visitors are wel-come to go inside to explore. To experience its charm, some people simply opt to drive along Route 76—aka **Mahogany Road,** a potholed two-laner show-casing some of the island's most impressive mahogany trees, though many were toppled by the 2017 hurricanes. Drive slowly: This corkscrew road is in dire need of some infrastructure TLC. Our favorite Rain Forest trail, **Creque Dam Road** (Rte. 58/78), takes about 2½ hours one-way. From Frederiksted, drive north on Route 63 to Creque Dam Road, where you turn right, park the car, and start walking. A mile past the Creque Dam, you'll be deep within the forest's magnificent flora and fauna. Continue on the trail until you come to the Western Scenic Road. Eventually, you reach Mahogany Road (Rte. 76), near St. Croix LEAP Project. The trail is moderate in difficulty.

BushTribe Eco Adventures (www.bushtribe.com; © **340/277-2503**) offers fascinating ecological hikes led by knowledgeable and enthusiastic guides. Sign up for hikes through tropical woodlands to the Annaly Bay Tide Pools; to the Danish-built Hams Bluff Lighthouse; or through marine parkland to Isaac's Bay on the island's East End (each hike $50/person). **Crucian Heritage & Nature Tourism** (CHANT; www.facebook.com/CHANTVI; © **340/772-4079**) offers hikes to the crystalline tidal pools and saltwater baths of Annaly Bay ($50/person), as well as historical walking tours in Christiansted and Frederiksted. **St. Croix Environmental Association** (www.stxenvironmental.org; © **340/773-1989**) hosts free nature hikes with UVI ecologists. Check the association's Facebook page for the latest.

HORSEBACK RIDING   **Paul & Jill's Equestrian Stables,** 2 Sprat Hall Estate, Rte. 58 (www.paulandjills.com; © **340/332-0417**), is known throughout the Caribbean for the quality of its horses and trails. It's set on the sprawling grounds of the island's oldest plantation, Sprat Hall. Scenic trail rides travel through the forests, along the beach, and past ruins of abandoned 18th-century plantations and sugar mills. A 2-hour, 4-mile trail ride costs $150; beginners and experienced riders alike are welcome. Tours usually depart daily in winter at 11am, with slight variations according to demand. Call and reserve at least a day in advance. Stephen O'Dea ("Cowboy Steve") and **Equus Rides** (www.horsebackridingstcroix.com; © **340/513-4873**) lead 2-hour horseback rides past historic ruins and onto beaches (and in the water) along the island's North Shore, for $145 per rider (all levels welcome); the meeting place is the Off the Wall restaurant in Cane Bay. Both operators have strict weight limits of around 220 pounds.

TENNIS   Some authorities rate the tennis at the **Buccaneer ★★★**, Gallows Bay (© **340/773-3036**; p. 138), the best in the Caribbean. The resort offers a choice of eight courts, two lit for night play, all open to the public. Non-guests pay $18 per hour daytime, $22 nighttime; you must call to reserve a court at least a day in advance. A tennis pro is available for lessons, and if you're looking for tennis partners, they are happy to match you up for singles or doubles.

ZIP LINING   The **Carambola Zip Line** (www.carambolazipline.com; © **340/244-1464**) slashes through some of the lushest forests on St. Croix. A 30-minute Safari Bus ride takes you to the zip line, with three zip lines that include the half-mile Gauntlet and the 40 mph Carambola Run, which zips you down the mountain. Minimum age is 10; participants must weigh between 75 and 275 pounds. The three-line Zipline Adventure Tour costs $88 to $108; call ahead to reserve your spot.

Seeing the Sights

Christopher Columbus named the island Santa Cruz (Holy Cross) when he landed on November 14, 1493. He anchored his ship off the North Shore but was quickly driven away by the spears, arrows, and axes of the Carib Indians. The French laid claim to the island in 1650; the Danes purchased it from them in 1733. Under their rule, the slave trade and sugar-cane fields flourished until the latter half of the 19th century; Danish architecture and influence can still be seen on the island today. In a shrewd purchase deal with the Danes, the U.S. acquired the islands in 1917.

Although the 21st century has definitely invaded St. Croix, with subdivisions, condo complexes, shopping centers, and modern strip malls, evidence of the past is everywhere across its 84 square miles, especially in the nostalgic ruins of some 100 slave-driven plantations where sugar cane was once grown. Take the time to explore Christiansted and Frederiksted, where the island's Danish roots can be seen everywhere.

One of the best ways to explore St. Croix is on a **taxi tour ★★** with a local driver. For entertaining and insightful sightseeing tours, see our list of recommended St. Croix taxi drivers (p. 135). In general, a 3½-hour island tour for one to four persons costs around $150; a 6-hour tour is $300. The fare should be negotiated in advance. Expect to pay admission fees if you visit the St. George Village Botanical Garden ($10; p. 178) or the Cruzan Rum Factory ($5; p. 177).

ALEXANDER HAMILTON'S st. croix

The influential American statesman (and eponymous star of the celebrated 2015 Broadway musical) Alexander Hamilton served brilliantly in the American Revolution and wrote many of the articles contained in the *Federalist Papers*. He became secretary of the treasury under George Washington and was famous for both his literary and oratorical skills. But this American icon wasn't a native-born American. Born on the island of Nevis, Hamilton spent a formative youth and adolescence here on St. Croix. After his father abandoned his young family in 1766, Hamilton lived with his mother, Rachel, and brother, James, Jr., above their shop at **No. 34 Company Street** in Christiansted. The "unusually precocious" 11-year-old boy was hired as a clerk of an import-export mercantile firm located on **Nos. 7 and 8 King Street,** and Hamilton spent 8 years doing business along the **Christiansted wharf.** As he later acknowledged, this youthful immersion in international trade was "the most useful part of my education." Recognizing the young man's talents, local leaders raised monies for Hamilton to go to college on the American mainland. He left the island in 1773, matriculating at King's College (now Columbia University) and went on to a thriving law career in New York before becoming secretary of the treasury under President George Washington. He was shot in a duel with Aaron Burr in 1804 and died at the age of 50, never having returned to his St. Croix home.

Walk in the St. Croix footsteps of Hamilton on the 2½-hour **Hamilton Walking Tour** with **Crucian Heritage & Nature Tourism** (CHANT; chantvi.org; ✆ **340/772-4079**), offered on Tuesdays at 9am ($35/person).

Note: You may want to concentrate on the island's East End for one trip and the West End on another.

HERITAGE & CULTURAL TOURS

St. Croix's cultural riches are explored on tours run by **Crucian Heritage & Nature Tourism** (CHANT; chantvi.org; © **340/772-4079**). In addition to **historic walking tours** of the colonial towns of Christiansted and Frederiksted, CHANT offers a nature-rich "Bushman" hiking tour along the Annaly Ridge to the Annaly tide pools as well as underwater photography classes and oral-history workshops. Also check out the goings-on at the **St. Croix Landmarks Society** (www.stcroixlandmarks.org).

CHRISTIANSTED ★★

The largest town on St. Croix, Christiansted is where the action is. Some of the best restaurants in the Virgin Islands are found along its narrow one-way streets, not to mention artisan jewelers making fabulous versions of the famed Crucian hook bracelet. With courtyard bistros and historic buildings lining every street, it's a cool place to explore. The **Christiansted harborfront** underwent a major overhaul in 2022, with the addition of snazzy new restaurants and shops (tiki bar, ice-cream shop, coffee roaster, Oaxacan resto) affiliated with the renovated, thoroughly reimagined, and greatly expanded **King Christian Hotel** (p. 144). The boardwalk buzzes these days, a lively scrum that includes a brewery, assorted shops, and roving bands of colorful chickens. By the time you read this, Providence Cay and its little inn will be reopened as a marina resort with a stylish reboot of its own.

WALKING TOUR: CHRISTIANSTED

START:	**The Visitors Bureau**
FINISH:	**Christiansted's harborfront**
TIME:	**1½ hours**
BEST TIMES:	**Any day from 10am to 4pm**
WORST TIMES:	**Monday to Friday 4 to 6pm**

Christiansted still has many traces of its Danish heritage. Constructed by the Danish West India Company, the heart of town is still filled with many imposing old buildings, mostly former warehouses, from the 18th century. Today they are registered as a U.S. National Historic Site. Across a small park stands **Fort Christiansvaern,** which the Danes built on the fortifications of a 1645 French fort. From its precincts, some of the best views of the harbor can be seen. Christiansted is best seen by walking tour.

1 The Old Scale House

Located near the harborfront, this yellow-sided building with a cedar-capped roof was built in 1856 to replace a similar structure that had

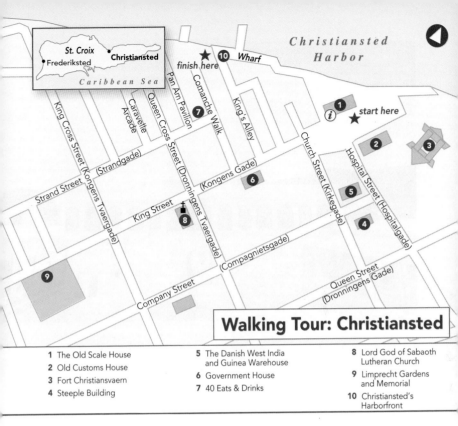

burned down. In its heyday, all taxable goods leaving and entering Christiansted's harbor were weighed here. In front of the building lies one of the most charming squares in the Caribbean, its old-fashioned asymmetrical allure still evident despite the mass of cars. Inside is an information center and a bookstore and gift shop.

With your back to the Scale House, turn left and walk through the parking lot to the white-sided gazebo-like band shell that sits in the center of a park (named after Alexander Hamilton—see "Alexander Hamilton's St. Croix," p. 169). On your right, the yellow-brick building with the ornately carved brick staircase is the:

2 Old Danish Customs House

The gracefully proportioned 16-step staircase was added in 1829 as an embellishment to an older building dating back to 1734. During the island's Danish occupancy, this is where merchants paid their taxes. (There are public toilets on the ground floor.)

Walk uphill to the massive, yellow-painted walls of:

3 Fort Christiansvaern

The best-preserved colonial fortification in the Virgin Islands, this seafront structure—maintained as a historic monument by the National Park

Colonial power in Christiansted was personified in the imposing Fort Christiansvaern.

Service—dates back to 1738. Its original four-sided, diamond-shaped design was in accordance with the most advanced military planning of its era. Use the self-guided-tour map provided at the gate to look around. The fort was built to defend against piracy, but it was also a slave market and a jail that, when it came to race, had its own cruel hierarchy. The fort is open Monday through Friday from 8:30am to 5pm, and the entrance fee (good for 3 days) is $7 adults, free for children 15 and under. For information, call © **340/773-1460.**

Exit from the fort, and head straight down the tree-lined path toward the most visible steeple in Christiansted. It caps the appropriately named:

4 Steeple Building

Completed in 1753, the Steeple Building was embellished with a steeple between 1794 and 1796. For a time, it served as the headquarters of the Church of Lord God of Sabaoth, the island's first Lutheran church (see stop #8, below). Inside are exhibits on plantation life on the island.

Across Company Street from the Steeple Building is.

5 The Danish West India & Guinea Warehouse

Built in 1749 as the warehouse for the Danish West India and Guinea Company, this structure was once three times larger than it is today and included storerooms and lodging for staff. Go to the building's side entrance, on Church Street, and enter the rear courtyard. For many years, this was the site of some of the largest slave auctions in the Caribbean.

Continue on Church Street to King Street, where you'll see the King Christian Hotel in front of you. Turn left and walk to the unmarked arched iron gateway on your left, set beneath an arcade. Enter the charming gardens of:

6 Government House

This grand Danish Colonial building was formed from the union of two much older town houses in the 1830s. It was used as the Danish governor's residence until 1871, when the Danish West Indies capital was moved to Charlotte Amalie, on St. Thomas. The European-style garden here contains a scattering of trees, flower beds, and walkways. The gardens are open Monday to Friday 8am to 5pm.

7 40 Eats & Drinks ☕

If you need refreshment, continue up King Street a few yards and turn right onto Strand Lane. Follow it around the bend to find **40 Eats & Drinks,** at 40 Strand St. (℃ **340/692-0524**), a casual bistro with a delicious, eclectic menu (p. 153).

Exit 40 Eats, take a left onto Strand Street and head to Queen's Cross. Turn left on Queen's Cross and walk 1 block to King Street. At the corner of King Street and Queen's Cross you'll see the square tower of the:

8 Lord God of Sabaoth Lutheran Church

This neoclassical church, built sometime before 1740, was originally the site of the Dutch Reformed Church; in 1834 it was turned over to the Lord God of Sabaoth congregation (see stop #4, above), who added the Gothic Revival tower. Much inside predates the Lutheran occupation, including the tower bell, cast in Copenhagen in 1793, and an impressive 18th-century picture frame fashioned of local mahogany that resides behind the altar.

Turn right and walk up King Street. Within 2 blocks on your left, you'll see the gate to:

9 Limpricht Park

For 20 years (1888–1908), Peter Carl Limpricht served as governor of the Danish West Indies. Today, an occasional chicken pecks at seedlings planted near a Danish-language memorial to him.

Leaving the park, retrace your steps down King Street until you reach Strand Lane. Turn left and go to the bend in the street where you can head right under the archway into King's Alley Walk. Follow the meandering curves of King's Alley until you reach:

10 Christiansted's Harborfront

End your tour here by strolling the boardwalk of the waterside piers and watching sailboats bob in the harbor. The area got a serious reboot in 2022, and the waterfront now feels like the place to be. Big tarpon linger at the boardwalk edge for impromptu feedings.

FREDERIKSTED ★

This former Danish settlement at the western end of the island, about 17 miles from Christiansted, is a waterfront village of under 1,000 people that really comes to life when cruise ships dock at its pier—this is the only port stop on the island. It's a sun-splashed little town with a rich history. Frederiksted was the site of the Emancipation Revolt by some 8,000 slaves in 1848—hence its nickname, "Freedom City"—and an incendiary 1878 labor revolt that literally burned down the city. The citizens rebuilt by putting Victorian wood frames and clapboards atop old Danish stone and yellow-brick foundations. The 7-block harborfront historic district and Frederiksted pier are the main attractions, but stellar beaches like Rainbow and Sandy Point are a short drive away (see "Beaches," p. 160). The harborfront is a bewitching hodgepodge of faded architecture, tucked-away courtyards spilling over with bougainvillea, and lots of skittering chickens. Venture beyond the waterfront, however, and you'll see signs of an impoverished town still in recovery from the 2017 hurricanes. Frederiksted's fortunes should rise

Frederiksted's 1848 Emancipation Revolt is commemorated with a statue in front of the Customs House.

considerably in 2023, when cruise-ship activity is expected to triple, and the government has committed to making substantial investments toward rebuilding the town.

A pretty greensward, the **Verne I. Richards Memorial Park,** separates the sea from the harborfront boulevard, **Strand Street.** Be sure to take a stroll along the deep-water cruise-ship **Frederiksted Pier** (officially the Ann E. Abramson Marine Facility; www.viport.com/ann-e-abramson-marine-facility), a 1,526-foot pier that can accommodate Voyager Class vessels. When the big ships are not in dock, it's a popular diving and snorkeling destination (see "Scuba Diving & Snorkeling," p. 164). The pier was named for an influential local matriarch known as the "Iron Lady" of St. Croix, a business owner, building contractor, and civic leader who ran the town's taxi and bus fleets.

The **Customs House,** just east of Fort Frederik (see below), is an 18th-century building with a 19th-century two-story gallery. In front of the Customs House is a **statue of a slave blowing a conch** to proclaim the 1848 uprising. To the south of the fort is the **visitor bureau** at Strand Street (© **340/772-0357**), where you can pick up a free map of the town.

Fort Frederik ★★ HISTORIC SITE   This russet-hued masonry fort, completed in 1760, trains its black cannons on the deep-water bay. Returned to its 1780 configuration in a 1976 restoration, the fort today has an evocative sort of dilapidated, paint-peeling grandeur. A $6.2-million FEMA restoration effort to repair 2017 hurricane damage (and remedy mistakes made in the subpar 1976 restoration) was finally underway at press time. The National Historic Landmark is said to have been the first fort in the Caribbean to salute the flag of the new United States. In 1776, when an American brigantine, anchored at port in Frederiksted, hoisted a crudely made Old Glory, the head of the fort fired a cannonball in the air to honor the Americans and their new independence (an act that violated the rules of Danish neutrality). It was at this same fort, on July 3, 1848, that Governor-General Peter von Scholten emancipated the slaves in the Danish West Indies in response to a slave uprising led by a young man named Moses "Buddhoe" Gottlieb. In 1998, a bust of Buddhoe was unveiled here. A self-guided-tour map of the fort is available at the **Fort Frederik Museum** ★ inside the fort. Exhibits have included collections of Crucian mahogany furniture and a display of the wreck of the *Fredensborg*, which sank off Norway after delivering slaves to St. Croix.

At N. end of Frederiksted next to Frederiksted pier. www.nps.gov/places/fort-frederik-sted-usvi.htm. 🕐 **340/772-2021.** Admission $5; free for ages 15 and under. Mon–Fri 8:30am–4pm (Sat 1–4pm on cruise-ship days).

Caribbean Museum Center for the Arts (CMCArts) ★★ MUSEUM

This very worthy nonprofit is full of delightful surprises. A recent exhibition took a spirited dive into the art and craft of Moko Jumbies, those iconic Carnival stilt dancers with spiritual meaning in African lore. Displays included Moko Jumbie dolls in colorful costumes, masks of copper and brass, a clay Moko Jumbie vase, paintings, sculptures, the works. Located in an airy two-story 18th-century Danish building with big rectangular windows upstairs letting in harborfront breezes, CMCArts was created in 1994 as an arts outreach for disaffected island youth. Its mission these days is to showcase and celebrate the region's cultural and artistic heritage. In addition to a fabulous permanent collection of Crucian art and rotating exhibits, CMCArts offers art classes and music and theater workshops, and is heavily invested in educational outreach. A block-deep cobblestone courtyard in back is the site of everything from face-painting days to orchid workshops to weddings.

10 Strand St. www.cmcarts.org. 🕐 **340/772-2622.** Tues–Sat 9am–4pm. Donations welcome.

Little La Grange Farm & Lawaetz Museum ★★ ORGANIC FARM/

HISTORIC SITE   This 1750 La Grange valley farmstead was built as a sugar plantation but was converted to a cattle ranch after it became the home of Danish farmer Carl Lawaetz in 1896. Here he and his wife, Marie, raised Senegal cattle and seven children. Now under the management of **Ridge to**

DRIVING THE ST. CROIX heritage trail

A trail that leads into the past, **St. Croix Heritage Trail** traces the island's Danish colonial heritage. All you need are a brochure and map, available at the tourist office in Christiansted (p. 132). This 72-mile itinerary includes a combination of asphalt-covered roadway, suitable for driving, and narrow woodland trails which must be navigated on foot. Many aficionados opt to drive along the route whenever practical, descend onto the footpaths wherever indicated, and then return to their cars to continue the tour. En route, you'll be exposed to one of the Caribbean's densest concentrations of historical and cultural sites. The route connects Christiansted and Frederiksted, going past the sites of former sugar plantations, and traverses the entire 28-mile length of St. Croix. The brochure identifies everything you're seeing: cattle farms, suburban communities, even industrial complexes and resorts. It's not all manicured and pretty, but much is scenic and worth the drive. Allow at least a day for this trail, with stops along the way, including **Point Udall,** the eastern-most point under the U.S. flag in the Caribbean, and the two highlights of the trail: the ruins of **Estate Mount Washington** (now in private hands, but you can see the ruins from the road); and **Estate Whim,** one of the best of the restored great houses (currently closed for hurricane repairs; p. 179).

Reef Farms (www.ridge2reef.org), the estate has a working organic farm on-site. You can take a 45-minute guided tour of the National Historic Register estate house, filled with turn-of-the-20th-century antiques and family heirlooms, or stroll around the 19-acre grounds, which hold the ruins of the plantation's old sugar mill alongside orange-flamed flamboyant trees and roaming peacocks. Currently, the site is only open 2 days a week. A farmstand sells organic fruit and vegetables from the farm as well as local gifts on Wednesday and Saturday from 11am to 3pm.

Mahogany Rd., Rte. 76, Estate Little La Grange (about 1.5 miles NE of Frederiksted). www.llgfarm.com. © **340/220-0466.** Admission $15. Wed and Sat 11am–3pm.

ATTRACTIONS AROUND THE ISLAND

On the north coast, a top attraction for visitors is the jagged estuary of the **Salt River,** where Columbus landed on November 14, 1493. Marking the 500th anniversary of Columbus's arrival, in 1992 former President George H. W. Bush signed a bill creating the 912-acre **Salt River Bay Historical Park & Ecological Preserve** ★★ (www.nps.gov/sari). The park contains the site of the original Carib village explored by Columbus and his men, including the only ceremonial ball court ever discovered in the Lesser Antilles. Within the park is the largest mangrove forest in the Virgin Islands, sheltering endangered animals and plants, plus an underwater canyon attracting divers from around the world. *Note:* As this book was going to press, the preserve was closed for major hurricane repairs; a new visitor center was in the works.

Point Udall (see box, below) is the easternmost point of the United States.

Check the park website for updates. You can still kayak the preserve with several outfitters; go to "Kayaking," p. 163, for details.

Cruzan Rum Factory ★ FACTORY   This vintage factory distills the famous Virgin Islands rum that some consider the finest in the world, although the stuff now detours through a Jim Beam bottling factory in the U.S. before it reaches your favorite beach bar. The grounds are serenely bucolic, with offices ensconced in an 18th-century plantation house and a magnificent ficus tree spreading its boughs on the lawn. Charmingly low-tech guided tours include a factory visit and the chance to peer into giant vats of bubbling

---

Where the Sun First Shines on the U.S.A.

The rocky promontory of **Point Udall,** jutting from St. Croix's East End into the Caribbean Sea, is the easternmost point of the United States, marked with a stone plaza topped by a giant sundial. Diehards go out to see the sun rise, but considering the climb via a rutted dirt road, you may want to wait until there's a bit more light before heading here. Once at the top, you'll be rewarded with one of the best scenic views in the U.S. Virgin Islands. Point Udall is reached along Route 82 (it's sign-posted).

---

molasses—the scent is pure sugar perfume. *Note:* Visitor tours were on hold at press time; call ahead for updates.

Estate Diamond 3, W. Airport Rd., Rte. 64. www.cruzanrum.com. ℂ **340/692-2280.** Admission $5 adults, $1 children 18 and under. Tours Mon–Fri 9am–4pm; Sat 10am–2pm.

Sion Farm Distillery ★★ DISTILLERY The first vodka distillery in the Caribbean crafts the spirits from breadfruit—one of the most sustainable food plants in the world. It's a win-win-win kind of formula. Breadfruit trees capture more carbon dioxide than just about any other tree on the planet—and one tree can feed a family of four. Now the distillery is planting breadfruit trees all over the islands. Founded in 2019, Mutiny Island Vodka—named after the *Mutiny on the Bounty* crew, who survived their island odyssey by eating breadfruit—took home the 2022 gold medal at the San Francisco Spirits Competition for its exceptional flavors. Tours of the distillery, held every half-hour, include a tasting session. (Sion makes locally infused rum as well.) The **distillery restaurant,** from the people behind 40 Eats & Drinks restaurant in Christiansted, is open for lunch, dinner, and cocktails, serving sandwiches, snacks, and entrees like guava roast pork and spicy Voodoo Shrimp. There's also a **Sion Farm Tasting Room** at the beautiful Mill on the Christiansted boardwalk (open Monday–Friday noon–5pm).

4000 Sion Farm, Mid-Island. www.sionfarmdistillery.com. ℂ **340/692-2874.** Free admission. Distillery Mon–Fri 11am–7:30pm; happy hour 4–5:55pm. Tours 11:30am–5pm.

St. George Village Botanical Garden ★★★ GARDEN This remarkable garden sprawls over 16 acres of what was Estate St. George, a circa-1760 sugar factory. An active sugar factory until 1918, the land fell into wild ruins and eventually was donated to the St. Croix Garden Club in 1972. If one place can tell the story of devastation and rebirth, it's here. As tour guide Denise Young puts it: "The garden is very special; you peel one layer away and keep finding more." A section of St. George is still an active archaeological site, and many artifacts in the little **St. George Village Museum** (housed in a colonial-era workers' cottage) came from the dig, including pottery shards and pre-Columbian finds. There's even a Danish cemetery on the grounds, containing the grave of President James Monroe's sister-in-law: Sarah Kortright Heyliger, wife of a prominent Danish sugar-cane factory owner.

The garden now has some 1,500 plant varieties—from West Indian mahogany, one of the hardest woods in the world, right down to the perfumed needle flower. Specialty gardens include a rain forest, a fragrant garden (the scents are strongest at night), and an African Provisions Garden, growing the plantains, sweet potatoes, and taro of a starchy diet needed to power enslaved peoples through heavy labor. The garden also hopes to memorialize the names of the thousand or so enslaved people who lived, worked, and died on Estate St. George—a quite doable project, says garden director Isidor Ruderfer, thanks to the Danes' meticulous inventory record-keeping.

Estate Whim

Repairs finally began in earnest in summer 2022 on the **Estate Whim Museum, Library, and Archives ★★**, extensively damaged in the 2017 hurricanes. Dating from the 1740s, the island's oldest sugar plantation has been under the management of the St. Croix Landmarks Society since 1954, which rescued it from dilapidated ruins tangled in tropical vines. The 12-acre plantation includes a furnished Great House with 3-foot-thick walls of coral, stone, and molasses; a cookhouse; and three cane-processing mills. The estate will be closed to the public until repairs are finished; check ahead for updates (www.stcroix landmarks.org; ✆ **340/772-0598**). It's located 2½ miles southeast of Frederiksted on Centerline Road.

Today the gardens are still recovering from the devastation wrought by Hurricane Maria in 2017, when two workers who rode out the storm awoke to 15 feet of vegetation piled high in the courtyard. It's hoped that the 1,000 Orchid Project, in the rubble of sugar-factory ruins, will reestablish the decimated orchid population. But the grounds are full of other tropical flora and alive with butterflies, geckos, and anole lizards. When we visited, a massive iguana dropped out of a tree branch to comfortably plop in a dense tangle of rainforest palms. Vines coil around the ruins of a boiling house, a curing house, a stillhouse, and the oldest operating blacksmith shop (ca. 1846) in the U.S.V.I. In a thicket of woods are the remnants of the plantation's ingenious flume irrigation system—evidence, Ruderfer says, that the colonists were certainly clever, "but they did it with free labor."

127 Estate St., 1 St. George (just N. of Centerline Rd.), 4 miles E of Frederiksted. sgvbg. org. ✆ **340/692-2874.** Admission $10 adults, $2 ages 12 and under; donations welcome. Daily year-round 9am–3pm.

Sandy Point Wildlife Refuge ★★ NATURE PRESERVE   St. Croix's rarely visited southwestern tip is composed of salt marshes, tidal pools, and low vegetation inhabited by birds, turtles, and other wildlife. More than 3 miles of ecologically protected coastline lie between Sandy Point (the island's westernmost tip) and the shallow waters of the West End Salt Pond. This national wildlife refuge is one of only two nesting grounds of the leatherback turtle in the United States—the other is on Culebra, an offshore island of Puerto Rico. It's also home to colonies of green and hawksbill turtles, and thousands of birds, including herons, brown pelicans, Caribbean martins, black-necked stilts, and white-crowned pigeons. As for flora, Sandy Point gave its name to a rare form of orchid, a brown/purple variety. The area consists of 360 acres of subtropical vegetation, including the largest salt pond in the Virgin Islands.

Park rangers are determined to keep the area pristine, and in doing so they have to face such problems as the poaching of sea turtles and their eggs, drug smuggling, dumping of trash, and the arrival of illegal aliens. Even the mongoose and feral dogs are a menace to the nesting female turtles. If Sandy Point's rules and regulations seem a little stringent, then you haven't met a **leatherback sea turtle.** The largest of its species, it can measure some 6 feet in length and weigh more than 1,000 pounds. Every 2 or 3 years, the turtles come back to this refuge to nest from March to July. The average female will deposit anywhere from 60 to 100 eggs in her nest. The survival rate is only 1 in 1,000 hatchlings. The refuge is also home to the **green sea turtle,** which can grow to a maximum of 4 feet and weigh about 400 pounds. These turtles come here only from June to September, when the females lay from 75 to 100 eggs. Birders also flock to Sandy Point to see some **100 species of birds,** five of which are endangered. Brown pelicans, royal terns, Caribbean elaenias, bananaquits, and yellow warblers are among the birds that call Sandy Point home.

Sandy Point, at end of Rte. 66 (Melvin Evans Hwy.). www.fws.gov/refuge/sandy-point. *©* **340/773-4554.** Admission free. Sat-Sun 10am-4pm. Beach closed mid-Apr-Aug. Call ahead for guided visits.

ST. CROIX SHOPPING

Christiansted's shopping scene may pale in comparison to the turbo-charged duty-free-for-all tourist rumble in Charlotte Amalie on St. Thomas, but we find it much more fruitful and satisfying. You can get great stuff here. Many of the goods sold on St. Croix are original and artisanal, reflecting the crafty, handmade spirit of the island. Most are boutiques compressed into the half-mile or so of downtown Christiansted between Company Street and the harbor, occupying courtyards, antique buildings, and arcades; some even have a hole-in-the-wall vibe. Along the boardwalk is the **King's Alley Complex,** a pink-sided compound filled mainly with generic tourist shops (with some exceptions; see below).

  Frederiksted has a sprinkling of shops appealing to cruise-ship passengers arriving at Frederiksted Pier.

  Keep in mind that shopping in St. Croix is duty-free, and U.S. citizens enjoy a $1,600 duty-free allowance (even children) per person every 30 days.

Christiansted
ARTS & CRAFTS
Many Hands ★★ This shop has been selling local artworks for almost 50 years. The collection of local one-of-a-kind paintings is intriguing, as is the pottery and handmade jewelry. It's open daily 10am–6pm. 110 Strand St. *©* **340/773-1990.**

BOOKS
Undercover Books & Gifts ★ This little independent bookstore has popular fiction, a good selection of kids' books, books on Crucian history and

culture, cookbooks, plus gifty stuff like woven baskets, jewelry, candles, and puzzles. It's located near the ferry dock in Gallows Bay and is open Monday–Friday 9am–5pm and Saturday 10am–4:30pm. 5030 Anchor Way. www.undercover booksstcroix.com. © **340/719-1567.**

CLOTHING/GIFTS

Asha World Designs ★★ An island offshoot of a Breckenridge, Colorado, company, Asha fits right in with its artisanal compatriots up and down Company Street. Made from textiles and hand-woven fabrics sourced throughout Southeast Asia, India, and Nepal, Asha's light and flowy print dresses are ideal for St. Croix's semi-tropical heat. Look for smart bags and elegant jewelry in this spare, calming duplex space. It's open Tuesday–Saturday 9:30am–5:30pm (until 5pm Thurs). 2110 Company St. www.ashaworld designs.com. © **340/690-6512.**

From the Gecko Boutique ★ This store is crammed with good stuff, from beachy dresses to jewelry to candles. It sells upcycled aluminum-can gecko ornaments and Bottles Reimagined, local candles made with essential oils (in scents like Crucian rum and lavender) and soy and placed in halved floral-embossed champagne bottles. 2106 Company St. fromthegecko.com. © **340/778-9433.**

Ginger Thomas ★ This chic shop on the Christiansted boardwalk specializes in highly curated workout and yoga wear, from the likes of Venus Williams and Beyond Yoga, as well as some beachy coverups, dresses, and tennis wear. It sells men's sportswear, too. The store's name comes from the official flower of the U.S.V.I., the Ginger Thomas, which blankets the hillsides in a golden yellow. 2106 Company St. shopgingerthomas.com. © **340/513-5553.**

Molly's Tropical Boutique ★ Our daughter snagged a beautiful, one-of-a-kind dress here. Molly's is packed with a nicely curated assortment of beachy dresses, shirts, and bathing suits in tropical prints, as well as island shoes and sandals (including Havaianas flip-flops), beach bags, water bottles, and sunglasses. 1104 Strand St. www.stcroixmollys.com. © **340/773-5739.**

JEWELRY

Chaney Chicks ★ This shop specializes in "chaney": vintage china shards that island kids traditionally gather from beaches, round out, and use as money (the name is a mash-up of "China money"). Here chaney is used to make one-of-a-kind necklaces, earrings, you name it. 4 Strand St. www.chaney chicks.com. © **305/896-3135.**

Crucian Gold ★★ This jewelry studio was founded by island-born Brian Bishop, whose gold and silver creations included the distinctive Crucian bracelet with a "true lovers' knot" design. It's now run by the Bishop family and a team of gold and silver artisans. Pendants framed in gold or silver encase shards of "chaney" (see above). Note that 20% of the shop's turtle collection is donated to sea turtle conservation through the **St. Croix Environmental Association's EcoFund** (www.stxenvironmental. org). 1112 Strand St. cruciangold.com. ℂ **340/244-2996.**

ib Designs ★★ Local metalsmith Whealan Massicott has been crafting Caribbean-inspired jewelry in delicately wrought designs since 1999. Whealan's wife, Kris, describes his work as "organic and heartfelt." His sons have since joined him in his Company Street shop; Whealan also plays guitar in local cafes. Note that 10% of the shop's fan-coral collection is donated to marine education through the **St. Croix Environmental Association's EcoFund** (www.stxenvironmental.org). Also look for Massicott's one-of-a-kind pieces at Lovango Cay and in St. John. 2108 Company St., at Queen Cross St. www. ibdesignsvi.com. ℂ **340/773-4322.**

"Chaney"—vintage china shards scavenged from beaches—are turned into fun jewelry at Chaney Chicks (p. 181) in Christiansted.

Joyia ★★ The working studio of local jewelry artist Joyia Jones, this wonderful shop is filled with her elegant handcrafted pieces of gold, silver, copper, and precious stones. Joyia Jones arrived in St. Croix 9 years ago from Charlottesville, VA, and married a fourth-generation Crucian; her works are timeless and built to last. 2220 Queen Cross St. joyiajewelry.com. ℂ **340/713-4569.**

Sonya Ltd. ★★ In 1964, designer Sonya Hough created the original St. Croix C-clasp hook bracelet, now an unofficial symbol of the island. There's symbolism to the design: If the "C" is turned inward, toward your heart, it means you have a significant other; those on the hunt wear the "C" turned out (many locals won't leave the house without putting on this piece of jewelry just right). Sonya retired from the business in 2021, but her downtown office continues to sell rings, earrings, and necklaces, all handmade to order. It's open Monday–Friday 10am–3pm. 1 Company St. www.sonyaltdstore.com. ℂ **340/773-8924.**

Frederiksted and Beyond

At press time, the wonderful **Estate Whim Museum Store,** along with the museum, was closed (see box, p. 179). But with repairs in the works, the entire complex may be up and running by the time you read this. The museum's eclectic inventory of jewelry, Madras cloth, art prints, and local Guavaberry liqueur is worth a good poke-around. 52 Estate Whim Plantation, E. of Frederiksted on Centerline Rd. ✆ **340/772-0598.**

Caribbean Museum of the Arts Gift Store ★★   The arts museum shop sells original works by local artists, prints, handmade gifts, books, calendars, T-shirts, the works! It's open Tuesday–Saturday 9am–4pm. 10 Strand St. www.cmcarts.org. ✆ **340/772-2622.**

Franklin's on the Waterfront ★★   This fabulous gift and home-furnishing emporium stands out in little Frederiksted. Franklin's sells a thoughtfully curated selection of beautiful works made by local artisans, from high-end candles to Caribbean bath and body products and more. Open Monday–Saturday 8am–5pm and Sunday 8am–3pm. 217 Strand St., #4. www.facebook.com/franklinsonthewaterfront. ✆ **340/473-0222.**

SUNDAY funday

Sunday is the traditional day for many Crucians (and all Virgin Islanders) to chill out recreationally after church—which often involves some mellow beach and brunch time. From this, **Sunday Funday** evolved, and at many spots around the island the scene is anything but mellow. As one local said, "You will always find a crowd when there is music, especially on Sundays."

Things get particularly boisterous on the West End beaches. In Frederiksted, **Rainbow Beach** has volleyball games in addition to the ongoing water parade of boats and jet skis. **Sand Castle on the Beach** offers a day pass that allows beachgoers access to their freshwater pool and resort facilities as well as a chair ($10/person for beach lounger and access); locals fill adjacent **Dorsch Beach. The Fred** (p. 145), on the Frederiksted oceanfront, is always a fizzy daytime party scene.

On the North Shore, **Cane Bay** in particular can be a party zone, with loads of people (and families) enjoying music and cookouts on both sides of the road along the beach and at **The Landing Beach Bar** (p. 152). Look for a soca/reggae band and pig roast at breezy, laidback **Calvin's Spratnet Beach Bar & Grill** (✆ 340/719-8485) on Cane Bay, which has more than decent food to match its beachfront setting.

In Christiansted, the **New Deep End Bar & Grill** (www.newdeepend.com; ✆ 340/718-7071), at the Tamarind Reef Resort (p. 141), has live music during brunch and crab races. Sunday brunch at **La Reine Chicken Shack** (p. 155) features DJ soca and Latin music. The food truck and backyard beach bar known as Blues' Backyard BBQ & Grill (p. 150) has live music every Wednesday, Thursday, and Friday from 4:30 to 7:30pm and Sunday brunch as well as annual family-friendly cornhole tournaments (to benefit the St. Croix Animal Welfare Center).

Don't miss a chance to see traditional Quadrille Dancers perform (p. 185).

Fred's ★★   The Fred hotel's boutique cheekiness carries over into its gift shop, in Fred's ultra-colorful lobby. It's loaded with high-end beach clothing, sparkly jewelry, pet paraphernalia, and even sparklier Fred swag (towels, beach bags, keychains), bearing the Fred crown logo. Definitely a fun place to shop. 605 Strand St. www.sleepwithfred.com. © **340/777-3733.**

ST. CROIX AFTER DARK

Find out what's happening while you're on island with *St. Croix This Week,* distributed free and available at hotels, restaurants, and the tourist office. Most **hotels and resorts** offer regular live music. *Note:* Take care leaving bars alone at night in Christiansted or Frederiksted. A taxi ride back to your hotel is a safer choice than walking dark, empty streets.

BARS, MUSIC & FOOD

Brew STX ★   This microbrewery/restaurant on the Christiansted harbor-front has something happening most nights from 6 to 9pm, from live music to DJs spinning to Monday night crab races. 55 A&B King's Alley, Christiansted. www.brewstx.com. © **340/719-6339.**

Leatherback Brewery ★★   Founded in 2017, St. Croix's first craft-beer brewery has been such a hit that you can now find Leatherback beers in grocery stores, markets, and restaurants throughout the Virgins (both U.S. and B.V.I.). In 2020 it even opened a taproom on St. Thomas (near Havensight). Leatherback's beers include IPAs, lagers, farmhouse ales, and smoked porters; the secret sauce is rainwater, which flows into a cistern and is run through an advance purification system. See how they do it (and taste a few brews in the indoor/outdoor tasting room) with a visit to the brewery, which incidentally also makes dynamite pizzas. Sunday Funday is a big deal here. It's open Monday–Saturday 11:30am–8pm, Sunday noon–7pm. 9902 Industrial Park, Mid-Island, just off Rte. 66 (Melvin H. Evans Hwy). leatherbackbrewing.com. ℂ **340/772-2337.**

Levels ★   This Christiansted joint has some of the best live music, performances, and cultural events on island. "Playlist Thursdays" features music curated by celebrated DJs. 54B Company St., Christiansted. www.levelsvi.com. ℂ **340/277-2727.**

Off the Wall ★   This laidback open-air Cane Bay bar is a favorite sunset spot with spectacular views and good, affordable pizzas. Things really get percolating every Tuesday and last Saturday of the month, from 6 to 7:30pm, when Off the Wall hosts a **Bingo Night** ★ ($5/card for 5 games). Get there early to snag a seat. The bar's open 11am–9pm daily (closed Wed). Cane Bay. otwstx.com. ℂ **340/718-4771.**

The Palms at Pelican Cove ★   The beachside restaurant at the Palms resort (p. 141) has live music on Wednesday and Saturday nights 6–9pm. Christiansted. ℂ **340/718-8920.**

SIDE TRIP TO BUCK ISLAND ★★★

The crystal-clear waters and white-coral sands of **Buck Island Reef National Monument** are legendary—some call it the single-most-important attraction of the Virgin Islands. Only about a half-mile wide and a mile long, 850-acre Buck Island lies 1½ miles off the northeastern coast of St. Croix, where a vibrant barrier reef shelters a constellation of colorful reef fish, including queen angelfish and smooth trunkfish.

Buck Island's greatest attraction is its underwater **snorkeling trails,** which ring part of the island and are maintained by the National Park Service.

Join in the Quadrille

If at all possible, try to catch a performance of **Quadrille Dancing** ★★★, a genuine cultural treat. Native to the Virgin Islands, quadrille dances have changed little since plantation days. The women wear long dresses, white gloves, and turbans, and the men wear flamboyant shirts, sashes, and tight black trousers; they dance to *quelbe*, the official folk music of the Virgin Islands. When you've learned their steps, you're invited to join the dancers on the floor. Ask at your hotel if there are any local performances happening while you're on island—it's a charming experience you won't forget.

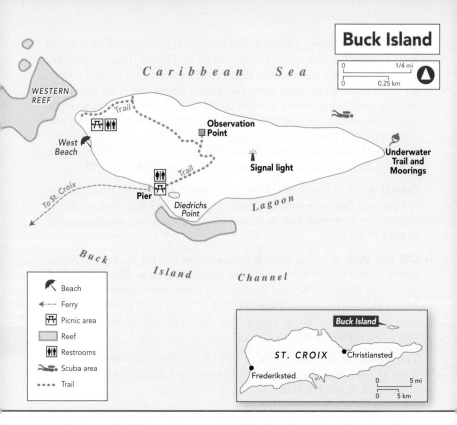

Buck Island

Caribbean Sea

WESTERN REEF

West Beach

To St. Croix

Pier

Diedrichs Point

Trail

Trail

Observation Point

Signal light

Lagoon

Underwater Trail and Moorings

Buck Island Channel

Beach
Ferry
Picnic area
Reef
Restrooms
Scuba area
Trail

Buck Island

ST. CROIX

Christiansted

Frederiksted

5 mi
5 km

Equipped with a face mask, swim fins, and a snorkel, you'll glide through a forest of elkhorn coral and be treated to some of the most beautiful underwater views in the Caribbean. Plan on spending at least two-thirds of a day here.

You can also hike the trails that twist around and over the island; circumnavigating the island takes only a couple of hours. Trails meander from several points along the coastline to the sun-flooded summit, affording views over nearby St. Croix. *Warning:* The island's western edge has groves of poisonous manchineel trees, whose leaves, bark, and fruit cause extreme irritation when they come into contact with human skin. Plus, always bring protection from the sun's merciless rays—including a hat and sun block. The sandy beach has picnic tables and barbecue pits, as well as restrooms and a small changing room. There are no concessions on island.

Six tour operators designated by the NPS offer regular excursions to Buck Island, providing snorkeling equipment, drinks, and all-you-can-eat island barbecue lunches (fish, burgers, hot dogs). Of these, we recommend **Big Beard's Adventure Tours,** in Christiansted (www.bigbeards.com; ✆ **340/773-4483**), which offers full- and half-day Buck Island excursions. Mutiny vodka punch and other libations are served, but these are no music-thumping booze

Roll the Dice

In 1996, U.S. senators agreed to allow the opening of gambling casinos in the U.S. Virgin Islands. In a bow to the islanders, senators agreed that majority ownership of the casino hotels would be reserved for locals. It hasn't exactly been a casino bonanza since then. St. John has a casino, the Parrot Club (p. 231), in Wharfside Village, and St. Thomas has a handful of "gaming centers" with slots. St. Croix has two gambling locations. The 10,000-square-foot **Divi Carina Bay Casino** (Divi Carina Bay Resort; carinabay.com; ✆ **340/773-7529**) has 20 gaming tables and 250 slot machines and is open daily 11am to 1am. A small, slots-only gaming center, the **Caravelle Hotel & Casino** (www.hotelcaravelle.com), located in downtown Christiansted (adjacent to Rum-Runners restaurant), is open Monday to Thursday 4pm-midnight and Friday to Sunday 2pm-midnight. No passport is needed to enter either casino, but you do need some form of ID (21 and older only).

cruises. The 42-foot catamaran *Renegade* can accommodate up to 39 passengers. Big Beard's full-day sails to Buck Island go from 9:30am to 3:30pm and cost $120 adults, $90 children 6 to 12, and $28 children 5 and under.

You can also moor your private boat at Buck Island, but you'll have to apply for a permit to do so at the NPS Visitor Center fee booth at Fort Christianvaern in downtown Christiansted (www.nps.gov/buis); it also has maps, pamphlets, and brochures. Buck Island is open daily from 7am to 5pm and has no entrance fee.

ST. JOHN

The smallest and most serene of the U.S. Virgin Islands is a natural wonder of luminous bays and pristine parkland. Roads trace racy arabesques around green peaks, and the vistas from on high are utterly ravishing. Forests are richly tinted with tones of green and turquoise and liberally accented with flashes of silver and gold from the strong Caribbean sun. The island has probably the most gorgeous, pristine beaches per capita of the Virgin Islands. It has a sleepy, secluded feel—if you can't chill here, well, you may need some therapy. In fact, St. John is where St. Thomas locals come to "plug out." They don't call the island "Love City" for nothing.

St. John is no mere pretty face, however. It has in the ruins of 18th-century sugar plantations a landscape dotted with its own trail of tears. It's got churches: 18 at last count. It's got rugged hiking trails leading to waterfalls and petroglyphs, the carvings of Taino civilizations from pre-Columbian times.

But what's equally notable is what St. John *doesn't* have. This 19-square-mile island has no airport and no cruise-ship pier. It's practically a one-road island, where the main road (Centerline) travels nearly coast to coast and another traces the North Shore. No matter: This may be the most popular day trip destination for visitors from nearby islands and ferry excursions for cruise-ship passengers from St. Thomas—meaning that the most touted beaches (we're looking at you, Trunk Bay) can get a little crowded in high cruising season (October–May). But know that just around the bend is another perfect beach, and down from that another, and so on. Plug out and discover your own.

ESSENTIALS

Arriving

BY PLANE

St. John has no airport. A number of major airlines have regularly scheduled nonstop air service from cities all over North America into St. Thomas, the major international gateway to the Virgins (p. 61). From St. Thomas, you'll take a ferry to St. John.

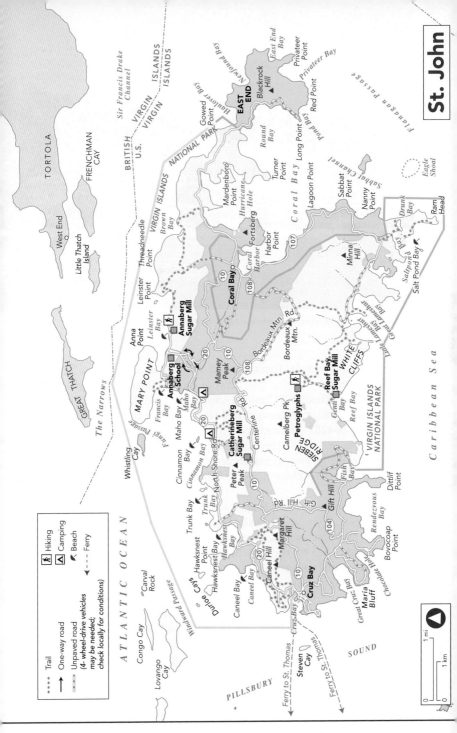

St. John

Ferries from St. Thomas arrive in St. John's laid-back capital, Cruz Bay.

BY FERRY

Public ferries between St. Thomas and St. John run at regular times all day long. Passenger ferry service runs between two St. Thomas terminals (Red Hook, on the East End; and Charlotte Amalie) and Cruz Bay in St. John. The 20-minute ferries traveling between **Red Hook** and Cruz Bay (stjohnticketing. com; © **340/776-6282**) run much more frequently, every hour on the hour, and cost $8.15 per person ($1 children) one-way. Ferries from **Crown Bay** in Charlotte Amalie (www.interislandboatservices.com; © **340/776-6597**) cost $20 per person ($10 children 3–11; $5/bag) and take approximately 45 minutes.

The Red Hook ferry dock is approximately 10 to 12 miles from the St. Thomas airport. If you've just landed on St. Thomas, your best bet is to take a taxi from the airport, which, depending on traffic, could take 30 to 45 minutes, at a fare of $23 for one passenger, $17 per passenger for two or more (plus $3/bag). Build taxi time into your schedule when planning your itinerary and book your ferry tickets in advance.

Car ferries also run between Red Hook and Cruz Bay, running regular routes from 7am to 7pm; book ahead on one of three carriers: **Love City Car Ferries** (www.lovecitycarferries.com; © **340/779-4000**); **Big Red Barge Co.** (www.bigredbarge.co; © **340/227-0918**); or **Global Marine** (© **340/779-1739**). All make daily runs except for Global Marine, which only travels weekdays. Car-ferry rates cost $65 round-trip and apply to cars, SUVs, and small trucks. Motorcycles are $25 round-trip. Arrive at least 15 minutes before departure.

You can also get to St. John via **private water-taxi service.** Longtime operator **Dohm's Water Taxi** stopped operation after the 2017 hurricanes. **Dolphin Water Taxi** (www.dolphinshuttle.com; ⓒ **340/774-2628**) offers land-water taxi services from the St. Thomas airport to Cruz Bay, at a cost of $78 per person (airport taxi transfer to Red Hook $19, plus $59 for water taxi from Red Hook to Cruz Bay). **SeaHorse Water Taxis** (seahorsevi.com; ⓒ **833/340-0340** or 340/474-4905) also offers personalized land-water taxi services in the U.S.V.I. and B.V.I.

Visitor Information

A small **Virgin Islands Department of Tourism** office (www.visitusvi.com; ⓒ **340/776-6450**) is located a short walk from the ferry dock in Cruz Bay. It's open Monday to Friday from 8am to 5pm. The visitor center and headquarters for the **Virgin Islands National Park** (www.nps.gov/viis; ⓒ **340/776-6201**) is also in Cruz Bay, offering information, maps, sundries, and wall-mounted wildlife displays, plus a video presentation about the culture of the Virgin Islands; it's open Monday through Friday 9am to 1:30pm.

St. Thomas + St. John This Week is distributed free throughout the islands. **St. John Source** (stjohnsource.com) is an independent online newspaper. An online blog, **News of St. John ★★** (newsofstjohn.com), is utterly invaluable in providing updates on restaurants, activities, you name it—it has its ears to the ground on everything St. John; sign up to get regular updates on the island's daily happenings.

Island Layout

Most visitors arrive on St. John at **Cruz Bay,** on a ferry from St. Thomas. This charming little village, with its few restaurants and shops, is quite the departure from the bustle of Charlotte Amalie. Cruz Bay is also the first stop on any trip to **Virgin Islands National Park,** which sprawls through the interior and encompasses almost all the coastline.

Route 20 leads north out of Cruz Bay, then swings east along the north coast, passing the beaches at Caneel, Hawksnest, Trunk, Cinnamon, and Maho bays. At the far north, Route 20 leads to the start of the **Annaberg Trail,** a historic hike through the ruins of 18th-century sugar plantations. Route 10, Centerline Road, cuts west-to-east through the center of the island. Dozens of foot trails lead off this road, making for easy exploration of the peaks and mountains.

On the East End of the island is **Coral Bay,** the island's original settlement and the highest point of elevation in the U.S. Virgin Islands. It's home to a smattering of small restaurants and bars, beautiful beaches, and free-roaming donkeys and goats. Crumbling ruins of forts and plantations also dot the coastline here. The far East End of the island is undeveloped and pales in comparison to the lush greenery of the park.

The **south coast** is a favorite hideaway for locals, but little known by visitors. The coastline here is sweeping and tranquil, yet rocky in parts and

A perfect fit for the relaxed vibe of "Love City," Coral Bay Harbor's popular floating taco bar, Lime Out (see box p. 214), can be reached only by boat.

punctuated with a handful of small protected bays and secluded surfing spots like Fish Bay.

Getting Around

The 20-minute ferry ride from St. Thomas will take you to **Cruz Bay,** the capital of St. John, which seems a century removed from the life you left behind. Cruz Bay is so small that its streets have no names, but it does have a number of lively seaside restaurants and cafes, shops, and a small park.

BY BUS

The local **Vitran** bus service (www.vitranvi.com; (C) **340/774-0165**) runs buses between Cruz Bay and Coral Bay, along Centerline Road about once an hour, costing $1 for adults and 55¢ for seniors.

BY TAXI

You'll have no trouble finding taxis to take you anywhere in St. John. Taxis meet the ferries as they arrive in Cruz Bay; you can also hail one if you see one. Many taxi drivers operate multi-passenger **taxi van shuttles** or open-air **safari vans** (converted truck beds with open-air seating). Taxi vans are equipped to transport approximately 8 to 12 passengers to multiple destinations on the island, while safaris can often fit up to 26 people. It's cheaper to hop on a van or safari than ride a taxi on your own if you're going between your hotel and Cruz Bay, but keep in mind you will be making stops along the way. We've hailed down safari vans at popular beach drop-offs (like the spur trails for Honeymoon and Salomon beaches) for rides back into Cruz Bay for a nominal fee.

Taxi rates are set by the island's Taxi Association and fares are widely posted; check out the official fares in the free *This Week* magazines. Typical fares from Cruz Bay to Trunk Bay are $12 ($9 each for 2 or more passengers), $14 to Cinnamon Bay ($11 each for 2 or more), and $25 to Coral Bay ($15 each for 2 or more). Waiting charges are $1/minimum per minute after the first 5 minutes.

It's easy to find taxi drivers, and they often double as tour guides. We highly recommend taxi driver **Kenneth Lewis** (✆ **340/776-6865**), who will meet you at the ferry terminal in St. John for hotel or villa transfer and is also a wonderful **sightseeing guide.** Expect to pay about $55 for a single-passenger tour or $25 per person for two or more passengers for 2 hours of sightseeing in a shared car. Kenneth's vehicle can accommodate up to 18 passengers.

BY CAR OR JEEP

One of the best ways to see St. John is by car, which you can rent on island. Four-wheel-drive jeeps are the name of the game here on mountainous St. John; most agencies have two- and four-door Jeep Wranglers and Jeep Chero-kees but often also have Bronco Sports and Toyota Highlanders. It is essential in these post-pandemic days to **reserve your rental car as soon as you've made your villa or hotel reservation**—St. John tourism is on the upswing, and inventory is limited. This is especially crucial during the high season between December and May, but summer rentals are getting booked up fast as well. Recommended local agencies include **St. John Car Rental,** across from the Catholic church in Cruz Bay (www.stjohncarrental.com; ✆ **340/776-6103**), operating on the island since 1974; **Aqua Blu Car Rental** (www.aquablucar rental.com; ✆ **340/776-2782**); **Sunshine's Jeep Rental** (✆ **340/690-1786**), and **Mr. Piper's Jeeps** (www.mrpipersjeeps.com; ✆ **340/693-7580**).

Remember: Drive on the left and follow posted speed limits, which are generally very low.

St. John has only two gas stations: **E-C Gas and Service Station** (✆ **340/776-6046**), at 5 Enighed, in Cruz Bay, and **Mid Way Gas Station**, on Center-line Road before Mile 3 (if you're driving from Cruz Bay), which also has a grocery and deli.

Parking is very limited in Cruz Bay, but a handful of local parking entrepre-neurs can help you out in a pinch. Slim Man and his team at **Slim Man's Parking** (✆ **340/344-3836;** $5/hr.) have the uncanny ability of finding a slot for your car in his space-challenged lot behind Wharfside Village. (Slim Man also rents jeeps.) **L&L Jeep Rental** (www.bookajeep.com; ✆ **340/776-1120**) has a paid-parking lot in its small but central Cruz Bay location, on Prince Street near the police station.

[FastFACTS] ST. JOHN

Banks **FirstBank Virgin Islands** (www.1firstbank. com/vi; ☏ **866/695-2511**) has a full-service bank and ATM in the Marketplace in Cruz Bay. **Oriental** (formerly Scotiabank; orientalbank. com/en/vi; ☏ **800/981-5554** or 340/774-0037) has an ATM in Cruz Bay. **Banco Popular** (www.popular.com/ vi; ☏ **800/724-3655**) also has an ATM in Cruz Bay.

Business Hours Stores are generally open daily 9am to 5pm; some shops close on Sunday.

Dentists The **Virgin Islands Dental Association** (www.virginislandsdental. org) is a member of the American Dental Association and is also linked with various specialists.

Doctors Call ☏ **911** for a medical emergency. Otherwise, go to **Myrah**

Keating Smith Community Health Center, 3B Sussanaberg (www.srmedicalcenter. org; ☏ **340/693-8900**), a primary healthcare facility with 24-hour emergency services. Patient transfers to the nearest hospital, **Schneider Regional,** in St. Thomas, are via a 15-minute ride on the Star of Life ambulance boat.

Drugstores **Chelsea Drug Store,** Marketplace Shopping Center, Rte. 104, Cruz Bay (chelseadrug storeredhook.com; ☏ **340/776-8300**), is open Monday to Saturday 8:30am to 6:30pm and Sunday 9:30am to 4:30pm.

Emergencies For the police, an ambulance, or in case of fire, call ☏ **911.**

Post Office The **Cruz Bay Post Office** is at 100 Vester Gade in Cruz Bay (☏ **340/779-4227**).

Safety There is some crime here, but it's relatively minor compared to St. Thomas. Most crime against tourists consists of muggings or petty theft, but rarely violent attacks. Precautions, of course, are always advised. You are most likely to be the victim of a crime if you leave valuables unguarded on Trunk Bay, as hundreds of people seem to do every year.

Taxes The only local tax is a 12.5% surcharge added to all hotel rates.

Telephone All island phone numbers have seven digits. It is not necessary to use the 340 area code when dialing within St. John. Make long-distance, international, and collect calls as you would on the U.S. mainland by dialing 0 or your long-distance provider.

WHERE TO STAY

The number of accommodations on St. John is limited, and that's how most die-hard fans would like to keep it. There are four basic types of choices here: resorts, villas, guesthouses, and campgrounds. Of these, rental villas are by far the most prevalent option. Prices are often slashed in summer by 30% to 60%, but this is less a given than ever before—St. John is increasingly a year-round destination, and if you plan on finding a villa to rent, you'll need to do so months in advance. However, know that **most St. John lodgings and restaurants are closed during the early fall "slow season"** from around late August into October (high hurricane season).

Most of the island's eateries and shops are in or around Cruz Bay, making it the most convenient place to stay and an easy stroll to restaurants, bars, and shopping.

Keep in mind that lodgings tack on a government room tax of 12.5%.

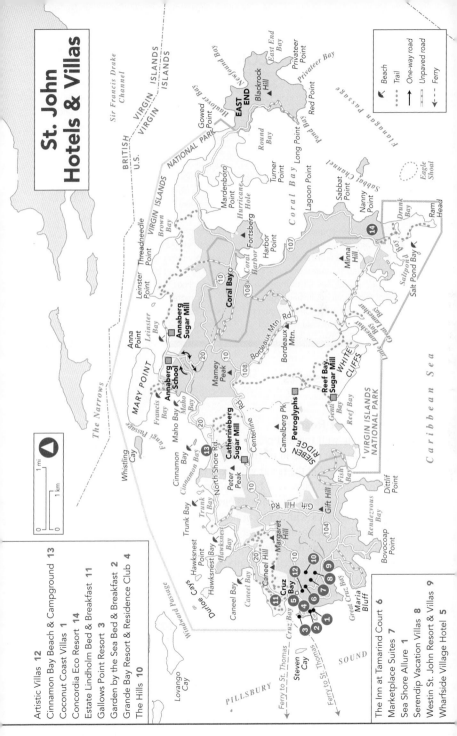

THE caneel bay CONUNDRUM

Ah, the trials of Caneel Bay, the legendary resort opened by Laurance S. Rockefeller in 1956 and beloved by generations in the years hence. One of the top luxury lodgings in the world, Caneel Bay famously shunned showy glitz and high-tech toys, disdained phones and TVs in the rooms, and of course, fronted some of the most fabulous beaches on the island (and in the Caribbean). The region's first eco-resort, it was lauded for its low-rise, low-impact development.

But Caneel Bay was no match for the twin Category 5 hurricanes of 2017. It has remained shuttered since, its shattered villas overgrown, its future the subject of numerous public hearings, a detailed National Park Service plan of action, and general palavering and wringing of hands. A 20-year lease granted in 2004 to CBI Acquisitions to maintain the property is up in 2023, and many people would like to see the property revert to national parkland, or at least replaced with a scaled-down resort and its beautiful beaches made more accessible to the public.

One positive from the Caneel Bay shutdown: The resort's bays are flourishing—alive with massive green turtles and stingrays, starfish, even dolphins!—as access to the beaches is severely restricted and beach moorings are prohibited by the National Park Service police. The coral is thriving.

For more on Rockefeller and St. John, see "Sustainable St. John: A Rockefeller Dream," p. 224.

Hotels & Resorts
CRUZ BAY
Expensive

Gallows Point Resort ★ Set out on a peninsula on the southern end of Cruz Bay, this well-run and nicely renovated resort is one of the first sights you see when you cruise in on the ferry. It's just a short stroll from the Cruz Bay ferry landing, but the resort will greet you at the dock with a complimentary arrival shuttle. New is a beautiful coastal pool, and a spa and fitness center. All rooms are sunny, spacious one-bedroom ocean view suites with full kitchens and terraces with ocean or harbor views. Each can accommodate up to five people, making this a great choice for families. You can stay on the one-story lower floors or duplex upper floors, but we recommend the latter, as the duplex living rooms are bright, airy, and high-ceilinged. A new fine-dining restaurant, **Ocean 362** (ocean362.com; ⓒ **340/776-0001**), offers sunset dinners 5 nights a week; a third-story bar has breathtaking Cruz Bay views. **One caveat:** The beach nearby is small and rocky.

3 AAA Gallows Point Rd. gallowspoint.com. ⓒ **340/693-7730.** 60 units. Winter $495–$695 suite; off-season $265–$495 suite. No children 5 and under. **Amenities:** Restaurant; bar; pool (outdoor); sundecks; free Wi-Fi.

Grande Bay Resort & Residence Club ★ Set in a stellar location above Cruz Bay and the harbor, these standard and club condo suites come in studio and one-, two-, and three-bedroom configurations with lockout capability, making this a good choice for groups or families. Most of the units are fractional timeshares in the rental pool, and each is individually decorated, so

The Westin St. John Resort rambles over 47 bayside acres, centered around a grand half-acre swimming pool.

you never quite know what the decor will look like. But all are comfortably laid out, complete with full kitchens with granite countertops, balconies, and washer/dryers. You can rent a full-size, four-door Jeep Wrangler on-site for $95 a day.

3 AAA Gallows Point Rd. grandebayresort.com. © **340/693-4668.** 73 units. $325–$778 condos. Minimum-stay requirements in high season. **Amenities:** Restaurant; fitness center; pool; spa; free Wi-Fi.

Westin St. John Resort & Villas ★★   Now part of Marriott's Vistana Experiences, this resort comprises Westin Vacation Ownership timeshare villas and townhouses that move in and out of the rental pool. The resort is on a sprawling 47 acres and fronts a gentle bay. The grounds are so spread out that golf-cart shuttles are there to assist guests in getting around, and the air-conditioned rooms are hermetically sealed off from the balmy trade winds. Choose from nicely furnished, meticulously maintained villas and lofts—all have those super-comfy Westin Heavenly beds. Two- and three-bedroom villas and two-bedroom lofts come with full kitchens. Although none are on the beach (admittedly, it's not St. John's best beach and manmade at that), all have lovely bay views, some from hillside perches—so be sure to ask for a unit with a balcony. But it does have the **grandest pool ★★** on St. John, the resort's beating heart. This half-acre beaut has towering palm trees, private cabanas, and **Snorkels Bar and Grill.** The bay is dotted with sailboats and excursion boats; **Cruz Bay Watersports** is here for all your island-hopping needs. The resort has a small deli-grocery, **Mango Deli** (daily 7am–9pm), but you can also walk to the much better (and less pricey) **Dolphin Market,** on Chocolate Hole Road (the resort will pick up you and your groceries from the store). An on-site **Westin Family Kids Club** (daily 8:30am–10pm) offers a range of sessions to keep kids 3 to 12 happily occupied. The Westin ferry shuttles guests from Red Hook to Cruz Bay ($127/person round-trip). Westin timeshare villas can be rented through Vistana and numerous other agencies, but a local agency, **St. John Condos** (www.stjohncondos.com; ✆ **713/319-4686**) has long specialized in Westin St. John villa rentals (direct from owners), with some 300 units in its rental inventory, many of which allow for a more flexible arrival and departure rate, and competitive fees.

Chocolate Hole Rd. www.vistana.com/destinations/the-westin-st-john-resort-villas. ✆ **340/693-8000.** 367 units. $419–$520 studio; $399–$637 one-bedroom; $592–$1,167 two-bedroom; $1,383–$1,783 three-bedroom villa. Round-trip shuttle and private ferryboat transfers from St. Thomas airport $127/person, $85 ages 4–12. **Amenities:** Restaurant; bar; deli/shop; children's playground; children's programs; concierge; kids' club; outdoor pool; room service; in-villa spa treatments; 4 tennis courts; watersports equipment/rentals; free Wi-Fi.

Moderate

Marketplace Suites ★ Staying in what is essentially a shopping-mall complex on your vacation in one of the great beach destinations in the Caribbean may seem . . . *counterintuitive,* but these 12 hotel suites on the third floor of the Marketplace Plaza offer modern, neatly furnished lodgings with (small) kitchens and comfortable beds at economical rates. You're in a central Cruz Bay location, within walking distance from Cruz Bay's restaurants, beach bars, and shopping. Marketplace Suites comprise four studio units, seven one-bedrooms, and one two-bedroom, each of which comfortably sleeps two to four guests. No, you won't have much of a view (windows are scarce), but a full-service grocery store/deli, drugstore, cafe, smoothie joint, and art gallery are on the first and second floors.

5000-4A Estate Enighed. marketplacesuitesusvi.com. ✆ **800/727-6610.** 12 units. $125–$250 lower suites; $395–$765 upper suites. **Amenities:** Cafe; shops; free Wi-Fi.

Wharfside Village Hotel ★★ Rebuilt, retooled, reimagined—Wharfside Village has emerged as a sleek 15-room boutique hotel with all the trimmings. It's always enjoyed a prime location, in the heart of the waterfront action at the ferry dock. But after picking up the pieces from its bout with Hurricane Irma in 2017, Wharfside 2.0 is giving people more good reasons to stay here. That includes three extremely stylish beach bar/restaurants on the first floor (**Joe's Rum Hut, La Tapa Plage,** the **Beach Bar**), a casino (the **Parrot Club**), Wharfside Water Sports, and shops (the latter still not completely filled at press time). Located on the complex's second and third floors, the rooms and suites (sleeping two) are island minimalist, with straw lamps, mahogany beds (king or queen), and outdoor patios to take in those Cruz Bay breezes. Smart little touches include all-important "sound barrier" walls, keyless touchpad entry, retro mini-fridges and Nespresso machines, and welcoming snacks. Rooms are on the small side, but West Indian–style pitched wood ceilings in some give it an airy feel. The four king suites are large and come with en suite sitting areas; the King Master Suite has the property's largest beachfront patio. If you're seeking good value, choose a room with a street view—you'll be hanging out downstairs or on the beach anyway.

Cruz Bay waterfront. thewvhotel.com. ℭ **340/714-2789.** 15 units. $260–$444 double; $380–$476 suite. No children 5 and under. **Amenities:** 3 restaurants; 2 bars; casino; shops; watersports equipment/rentals; free Wi-Fi.

CORAL BAY
Moderate/Inexpensive

Concordia Eco Resort ★ This 40-year-old pioneer in sustainable tourism reopened post-hurricanes in 2022. Much has been remodeled and refreshed, but Concordia is still living by the same ethos, drawing electricity from photovoltaic power and collecting (and filtering) water in cisterns. Shower tanks are solar-heated, and eco-tents use composting toilets. But don't stay here just to be virtuous; do so because the views are wonderful (Concordia's elevated structures cling to 50 acres of cliffside), the staff is lovely, and the prices are reasonable (for St. John). Doubles come in a range of lodging styles, from eco-tents to full-kitchen lofts to resort-style studios. The wood-framed, soft-sided eco-tents (and premium eco-tents) are set on the hillsides and have a treehouse feel, with cooling breezes (no A/C, of course) and those phenomenal views. Eight eco-studios are newly and simply furnished, with tile floors and kitchenettes with two-burner stovetops.

Near Coral Bay. concordiaecoresort.com. ℭ **340/690-0561.** 42 units. Winter $175–$289 double, $268–$289 quad; off-season $126–$232 double, $175–$185 quad. **Amenities:** Restaurant (seasonal); laundry; pool (outdoor); watersports equipment rentals; free Wi-Fi.

Condos & Villas

More than any other U.S.V.I., St. John specializes in furnished villa rentals—the island actually has more villas and condos available than hotel beds. What you get is spaciousness and comfort, as well as privacy and freedom, and most come with crazy-gorgeous views from breezy patios. Rentals range from large multiroom resort homes to simply decorated one-bedroom condos. Full kitchens are generally a given, and many rentals come with pools and even house jeeps. Standard amenities include the little necessities of St. John life: totable beach chairs, beach towels, coolers, hiking backpacks, snorkels and masks, and barbecue grills.

Keep in mind that since coming out of the pandemic, St. John has become a hot, hot rental market—so find your villa early and lock it in.

Also keep in mind that most people renting villas also rent vehicles, and driving St. John's crazy quilt of switchback roads can be challenging enough by day, and potentially dangerous at night (especially in the rain). It's a big reason why many people prefer to be within a 15-minute drive of the dining and shopping in Cruz Bay. Others love staying in the heights around Coral Bay, where the views can be truly stupendous (and Coral Bay has its own good restos and bars), but driving can be equally nerve-wracking. Wherever you're staying, if you venture out from your villa at night, it's never a bad idea

Rental villas are a popular choice on St. John, offering extra space and seclusion. At Coconut Coast Villas (p. 202), for example, units feature breezy private porches.

to use a taxi. The range of rental rates is all over the map; a two-bedroom villa can cost anywhere from $2,000 up to $36,000 (and more) a week.

- **Caribbean Villas of St. John** ★★ (www.caribbeanvilla.com; ✆ **800/338-0987** or 340/776-6152), the island's biggest real estate agency, is an excellent choice if you're seeking a villa or private home.
- **Destination St. John** (www.destinationstjohn.com/villa-rentals; ✆ **800/562-1901** or 340/779-4647) is another good agency with a choice stable of villas.
- Another high-end agency is **Blue Sky Luxury Travels** (blueskyluxury travels.com; ✆ **615/604-2447**), which also rents charter luxury planes and yachts if you're in the market.
- **St. John Condos** (www.stjohncondos.com; ✆ **713/319-4686**) is a longtime Westin St. John villa-rental specialist, with some 300 units in its rental inventory and competitive fees.
- When it comes to villas and houses, bargain gems don't come easy on St. John, but if you're going to find one it might be through popular owner-rental sites like **VRBO.com** and **Airbnb.com** (in addition to the lodgings listed below).

EXPENSIVE

Artistic Villas ★★   Owned and managed by local potter Donald Schnell (p. 229), each of these villas is its own incredible artistic creation. All six are in different locations—Gifft Hill, Chocolate Hole, Great Cruz Bay—but three are upstairs in the Amore building where Schnell's studios are located. All are within a 10-minute drive of the shops and dining in Cruz Bay. The gorgeous

European-inspired villas bear the unmistakable hand of Schnell in ceramic wall sconces, weave lights, and stone planters. Many have Italian plastered walls and island-stone showers. The Beach Villa, its main room sheathed in Caribbean stone walls, has tropical sculpture gardens and a seafront pool (and a piano!). The Beach Estate is equally luxurious, the work of local architect Glen Speer, who built the Mongoose Junction complex. It has a vintage palazzo feel, with an outdoor garden full of Italian statues; a breezy patio overlooking Great Cruz Bay features a 12-person Italian marble stone table. Ocean Garden is tucked into a flower-filled hillside looking out onto Chocolate Bay. The two-person Amore villas have many of the same charming design touches but at more affordable rates. All but the Amore Loft Suite and the Amore Loft Studio have full kitchens.

Cruz Bay. artisticvillasusvi.com. ℂ **800/253-7107** or 340/776-6420. 6 units. Amore villas (sleeps 2) $195–$385 nightly, $1,365–$2,695 weekly; Ocean Garden (sleeps 6) $475–$565 nightly, $2,695–$3,955 weekly; Beach Villa & Beach Estate (sleep 10–12): call for rates. Extra person $15–$45. **Amenities:** Pool (in some); free Wi-Fi.

The Hills ★★ These 22 European-style villa/condos bring a level of spacious sophisticated luxury to St. John's little harbor village. Overlooking Cruz Bay, a variety of two-, three- and four-bedroom condominium-style villas comfortably accommodate up to eight guests. Each villa features a fully equipped chef's kitchen, washer/dryer, and a private veranda. Several villas have their own private pools. The poolside Clubhouse serves lunch and dinner (Mon–Sat noon–9pm). *One caveat:* The Hills is indeed high in the hills overlooking Cruz Bay, and the walk up is more challenging than the walk down (although it's pretty steep either way). Management suggests getting taxis or driving to get to Cruz Bay restaurants and shops. *One more caveat:* The

Several luxury villas at The Hills have their own private pools with hillside views over Cruz Bay.

website reservations system is unnecessarily convoluted. Until it's streamlined, you might want to book through the toll-free number.

11 Enighed, Cruz Bay. thehillsstjohn.com. ☏ **800/727-6610.** 22 units. $575 and up 2-bedroom villa; $645 and up 3-bedroom villa; $745 and up 4-bedroom villa; $1,200 and up 6-bedroom villa. Extra person $150/night. **Amenities:** Restaurant; bar; fitness room; pool; free Wi-Fi.

Sea Shore Allure ★★   These eight elegant marble-clad villa suites are a pretty sweet addition to the lodgings pool near Cruz Bay. All are well-stocked, with porches with ocean views and full kitchens with stainless steel appliances; bathrooms have bidets and rain-forest showers. Some one-bedroom suites come with luxuriously large spa bathrooms. It's all pretty high-end (and immaculate to boot), but never stuffy. A small saltwater pool comes with a cheeky tiki bar, and the resort's private beach (and free snorkeling equipment) lets you tootle around St. John's Bay in flippers and mask. The location feels secluded and tucked away, but you're just a short stroll (and less than half a mile away by car) from the shops and eateries of Cruz Bay. High marks go to the topnotch staff, who will provision your villa with advance notice, and the welcome basket of snacks and stuff is a nice touch. Families often rent out the whole place. The one drawback: Your views of sea and sky include the active car ferry.

271 and 272 Fish Fry Dr., Cruz Bay. www.seashoreallure.com. ☏ **340/779-2800.** 8 units. $520–$710 1-bedroom suite; $710–$956 2-bedroom suite; $1,240–$1,344 3-bedroom suite. Extra person $150/night. Minimum stay requirements. **Amenities:** Bar; babysitting; BBQ grills; laundry; pool; free Wi-Fi.

MODERATE

Coconut Coast Villas ★   Guests come back year after year to this family-run boutique villa complex. And why not? Each of its units (studio doubles and two- and three-bedroom condos) faces the waterfront and is fully equipped with a kitchen, private en suite bathrooms, breezy private balcony, grills, and all you need to go beach-hopping: beach chairs, coolers, and beach towels. You will likely be beach-hopping, as Coconut Coast's own beach is rocky. But you're just a 5-minute walk to nearby Frank Bay, where you can swim and snorkel off a sandy beach, and just a 10-minute stroll from all the food, nightlife, and shopping action on Cruz Bay. The condos can be on the smallish side, and the kitchens, while fully equipped, have a New York apartment coziness. But this is very good value for St. John.

Turner Bay. coconutcoast.com. ☏ **800/858-7989** or 340/693-9100. 9 units. $267–$389 studio suites; $367–$499 2-bedroom suites; $533–$685 3-bedroom suites. 3-day minimum required in high season. **Amenities:** Outdoor pool; free Wi-Fi.

Serendip Vacation Condos ★   This well-managed, good-value hideaway offers nine clean, newly renovated condo apartments, each with a fully equipped kitchen and a big, covered veranda (up to 300 sq. ft.!), with smashing sunset views. It's not on the beach but set on a hillside atop Jacob's Ladder, less than a mile from downtown Cruz Bay. Book here early; Serendip gets a lot of repeat business. Each of the seven one-bedroom apartments can comfortably accommodate four people (the Alpha and Echo apartments sleep up to six).

9–7 Serendip Rd. www.serendipstjohn.com. ℂ **340/776-6646.** 9 units. $249–$399 studio apts; $299–$499 1-bedroom apts. Extra person 4 and older $35; children 3 and under stay free in parent's apt. Cleaning fee $50. 5-day minimum in high season; 3-day minimum low season. **Amenities:** Outdoor pool; grills; free Wi-Fi.

Inns & Bed & Breakfasts
MODERATE/EXPENSIVE

Estate Lindholm Bed & Breakfast ★★ Overlooking Cruz Bay harbor, this is the island's best B&B. It was once part of an 18th-century sugar estate, and one room, the Plantation Cottage, is sheltered in the 18-inch-thick walls of the old Danish ruins. This elegant adults-only guesthouse has 17 guest rooms, each with private covered balconies (and wooden rockers) and many with four-poster beds, Tiffany-style lamps, and big wooden armoires. Some have tropical garden views; others have views out over the harbor. Some of the best vistas are from two new penthouse rooms, Salomon and Haulover. You're just a 10-minute walk from Cruz Bay

N. Shore Rd. estatelindholm.com. ℂ **340/227-4724.** 17 units. $265–$590 double. Rates include breakfast. **Amenities:** Restaurant; exercise room; outdoor saltwater pool; free Wi-Fi.

Garden by the Sea Bed & Breakfast ★★ Overlooking the Caribbean, this colorful and quaint three-suite B&B is just a 10-minute walk from Cruz Bay. A classic West Indian cottage, it's done up in green and lavender hues, with a veranda shaded by genip trees and palm fronds. Both the Garden Suite and the Wild Ginger Room have fabulous outdoor tropical garden showers, with shower walls made of native stone. The Terrace View Room is upstairs, with views of the sea and a private veranda. (White-sand Frank Bay is a minute's walk from the B&B.) All are air-conditioned. Breakfasts are home-cooked, with fresh juices and fruit and hearty dishes like quiche, eggs Benedict, and Pina Colada French Toast. You can also rent the **Rendezvous by the Sea villa ★**, a charming three-bedroom villa overlooking the Caribbean (weekly rates $4,950–$5,350 in winter, $2,900–$3,900 in summer). The inn only accommodates ages 16 and older.

Pickering St., Cruz Bay. www.gardenbythesea.com. ℂ **340/779-4731.** 3 units. $295–$425 double. No children 15 and under. Rates include breakfast. **Amenities:** Free Wi-Fi.

Garden by the Sea invites guests to stay in a classic West Indian cottage.

INEXPENSIVE

The Inn at Tamarind Court ★   For casual comfort at economical rates, a warm, friendly welcome, and a very convenient (5-min. walk away) Cruz Bay location, you can't beat this 20-room inn. An effort has been made to give these rooms a little pizzazz, with crisp linens and tile floors. The Grand Suite and the Apartment can sleep four people comfortably. Standard rooms have twin or queen beds and private bathrooms. The inn has six rooms for single travelers that share two bathrooms.

Cruz Bay. www.tamarindcourt.com. ⓒ **800/221-1637** in the U.S., or 340/776-6378. 20 units, 14 w/bathroom. Winter $75 single w/shared bathroom, $148 double w/bathroom, $240 apt for 4 w/bathroom; off-season $60–$65 single w/shared bathroom, $110–$120 double w/bathroom, $170–$190 apt for 4 w/bathroom. Rates include breakfast. **Amenities:** Restaurant; bar; free Wi-Fi in the courtyard.

Campgrounds

Along with the listing below, consider the eco-tents and tent-cottages at **Concordia Eco Resort** (p. 199). Sadly, two of St. John's most popular campgrounds, **Maho Bay** and **Harmony Studios,** closed in 2013.

Cinnamon Bay Beach & Campground ★★   This National Park Service beach property is a dream of a campground, with lush forests at your back and the cerulean blue seas of Cinnamon Bay before you. It even holds historic ruins from the time of Danish colonial rule. And now the campground has gone a tad upscale, with updated cottage and glamping eco-tents. No more are cottages just a couple of concrete and screen walls; they're still somewhat bare bones, but elegantly so, with wooden platform beds, ceiling fans, and louvered windows (some have oceanside terraces). The big, comfortable eco-tents have roll-down canvas walls, platform beds, and Adirondack-style chairs. Bring your own tents and camping equipment to the primitive bare sites. Lavatories and showers are in four communal bath houses (no hot water, though). The **Raintree Café** serves daily breakfast, lunch, and dinner, and a camp store sells prepared foods, ice, charcoal, drinks, and toiletries (including reef-safe sunscreen). The campground is closed to non-guests, and quiet hours start at 10pm and last till 7am—no music or parties, people. Watersports rentals are available on-site.

Cinnamon Bay. www.cinnamonbayvi.com. ⓒ **340/776-6330.** 126 units, all w/shared bathroom. Cottages $416–$562; eco-tents $350–$416; bare sites $100. **Amenities:** Restaurant; store; watersports equipment/rentals; free Wi-Fi in restaurant.

WHERE TO EAT

St. John has a happy high/low mix of dining establishments, where casual spots preparing island classics put the same level of loving care into their meals as fancier places. The food here is generally fresh and exceptional. You'll find restaurants serving everything from Continental standards to Asian

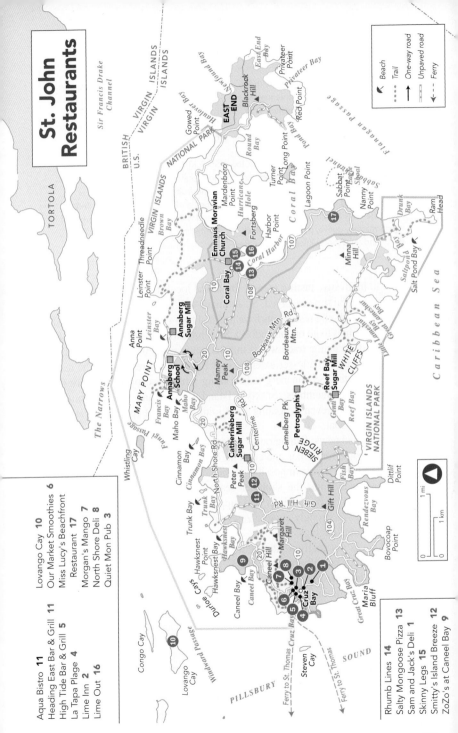

St. John
Restaurants

TORTOLA

Sir Francis Drake Channel

BRITISH
VIRGIN ISLANDS

U.S.
VIRGIN ISLANDS

VIRGIN ISLANDS

EAST END

Legend:
- Beach
- Trail
- One-way road
- Unpaved road
- Ferry

Aqua Bistro **11**
Heading East Bar & Grill **11**
High Tide Bar & Grill **5**
La Tapa Plage **4**
Lime Inn **2**
Lime Out **16**

Lovango Cay **10**
Our Market Smoothies **6**
Miss Lucy's Beachfront
Restaurant **17**
Morgan's Mango **7**
North Shore Deli **8**
Quiet Mon Pub **3**

Rhumb Lines **14**
Salty Mongoose Pizza **13**
Sam and Jack's Deli **1**
Skinny Legs **15**
Smitty's Island Breeze **12**
ZoZo's at Caneel Bay **9**

205

St. John Fruit Smoothies & Fresh Fruit

Nobody should leave St. John without sampling a fabulous smoothie made fresh at **Our Market Smoothies** ★★ (aka Thomas's stand), directly across from the Post Office in Cruz Bay. Fruit combos range from mango soursop to passionfruit banana, and you can ask for yours with a shot of rum. It's open daily 7am to 9pm. For freshly squeezed juices, **a stand in the Cruz Bay Market** near the ferry landing sells bottles of fresh mango, guava, passionfruit, and tamarind (and more) juices. In Coral Bay, a local vendor, **The Friendly Spot,** sells refreshing juices (mango, papaya) on the road past the parking lot to Salt Bay Pond. If you're looking for fresh fruit to buy in Cruz Bay, a **fruit stand** on the corner by the Lutheran Church (Prince St. & King St.) in front of the Connections building has some of the freshest island fruit around, as well as local honey and hot sauce. **Another fruit stand** is usually set up at the corner of Centerline and Gift Hill.

fusion to innovative tasting menus. Do as the locals do, and sample them all. If there's a good time involved, St. Johnians will be there!

Even the high-end restaurants have a casual feel—you certainly don't need to dress to the nines to go out on laidback St. John. Most all restaurants on St. John are open to the gentle trade winds that keep things comfortable year-round.

Cruz Bay and, to a lesser extent, Coral Bay, are where most of the restaurants are located. Sussanaberg is becoming a hot spot for local eateries and bars, including Shambles, Smitty's Island Breeze, and the Windmill Bar (p. 232). There's even a floating food joint, Lime Out (p. 214), that's only accessible by boat.

Now the bad news: Dining out is expensive anywhere you go, which is why so many people rent villas and cook in. But they obviously don't eat in every night, because it's near impossible to snag a reservation at the last minute in high season and into the shoulder seasons. Restaurants are reporting full bookings, even for bar seatings, and supply and service challenges aren't helping matters. We strongly suggest reserving your restaurant tables as soon as you book your lodgings.

St. John is not really a late-night kind of place. Most places close early, around 9pm (especially in Coral Bay).

Very important to note: Most restaurants close around late August and reopen sometime in October (some close even earlier and others don't open until Nov). This is hurricane season but also a chance for the businesses to recharge and make improvements.

Cruz Bay

A handful of lively and good-looking beachside restaurants have been reborn in Wharfside Village along the Cruz Bay harborfront. The **Wharfside Village Hotel** complex (p. 198), right on Cruz Bay Beach, reopened in 2022 following a transformative revamp after the 2017 hurricanes and hosts lively crowds at

groceries, markets & more: **ST. JOHN**
PROVISIONING

If you're doing any cooking on the island, you'll need to know where to stock your pantry and source fresh local food. Even if you don't have a kitchen, you'll want to buy snacks, drinks, and prepared foods. A full-service provisioning company, **Landlubber Logistics** (www.landlubberlogistics.com; ✆ 340/514-9343), partners with Starfish Market (see below) to stock villas for arriving renters. Here are some other essential St. John resources:

o **The Works:** Many people who rent cars at the St. Thomas airport stock up on the way to Red Hook on money-saving bulk grocery items, produce, fresh meats, and liquor and wine at **Cost U Less** (www.shopcostuless.com/stores/st-thomas-cost-u-less; ✆ **340/777-3588**), a Costco-type warehouse at 4400 Weymouth Rhymer Hwy. in St. Thomas, about a 20-minute drive from Red Hook. It's open Monday to Saturday 8am to 9pm and Sunday 8am to 7pm.

o **Deli/Prepared Foods: Sam and Jack's Deli** (p. 211) offers sandwiches, grab-and-go dinners, deli meats and cheeses, breads, pastries, and more.

o **Groceries: Starfish Market** (✆ 340/779-4949), the island's largest grocery store, is located on the first floor of the Marketplace in Cruz Bay; it has a good selection of quality meats (steaks in particular) and a deli with prepared foods. A well-curated grocery, **Dolphin Market** (✆ **340/779-6001**), has two locations in Cruz Bay—right in the heart of Cruz Bay and at Chocolate Hole Road near the Westin resort—and one small location in Coral Bay on the second level of Aqua Bistro in Cocoloba Plaza. All offer online shopping and grocery pickup and wine, beer, and alcohol. In Coral Bay, Dave's Homemade Meals to Go has merged with a boutique grocery to become the new **Coral Bay Fresh Market** ★, opened in 2022 (daily 7am–8pm) in the Isola building, offering fresh vacuum-packed meats, fresh produce, and delicious hot homemade meals to go. Locally owned **Calabash Market** (✆ 340/775-7172), also in Coral Bay, gets raves for its hand-cut meats (rib-eyes, strips) and seafood, fresh produce, deli sandwiches, and house-made Middle Eastern spreads like babaganoush and hummus.

o **Fresh Seafood: Calabash Market** (see above) in Coral Bay always has fresh seafood, including mahi, wahoo, tuna, shrimp, and scallops.

o **Fresh Produce/Fruit:** Vendors sell local fruits (papaya, bananas) and vegetables (tomatoes, okra) in the Marketplace at the Cruz Bay ferry harbor. Also see p. 206 for recommended local fruit vendors.

o **Water:** Water on the island is scarce. Buy a jug or two of water when you arrive and refill (60¢/gal.) at the water machine at Provisions Bakery and Kilroy's Dry Cleaners near the roundabout in Cruz Bay.

its **waterfront restaurant/lounges** ★★, including **La Tapa Plage** (see below); the **Rum Hut** (rumhutstjohn.com; ✆ **340/775-5200**), with tables in the sand and a great little menu of tacos, sliders, and big salads; and the **Beach Bar** (beachbarstjohn.com; ✆ **340/777-4220**), an open-air St. John landmark, which flies the flags of a thousand places and packs 'em in with live music, solid pub food, and spine-stiffening drinks.

EXPENSIVE

La Tapa Plage ★★ CONTEMPORARY MEDITERRANEAN/WINE BAR   In its sexy new beachside home on the Cruz Bay waterfront, part of the Wharfside Village complex, La Tapa is still serving up a smart, inventive menu with a locavore bent. The food is cooked to order by the talented chef/owner. Order a few *platos pequenos* (small plates) for the table, like rosemary-tempura fried Coral Bay eggplant, or a fine lobster bisque. Big plates—*platos grandes*—include a West Indian chicken pot pie or a classic paella with saffron risotto.

Strand Gade, Cruz Bay. www.latapastjohn. com. ✆ **340/693-7755.** Reservations recommended. Tapas $8–$19; entrees $34–$48; paella $72. Daily 5:30–10pm.

Dreamy waterfront views accompany an inventive locavore menu at La Tapa Plage.

Lime Inn ★★ CARIBBEAN/PACIFIC RIM   Fresh and sophisticated flavors rule at this perennial favorite (going on 40 years old!), a colorful open-air space splashed out in tropical hues of lime, butter yellow, and cornflower blue. Choose your dishes from the nightly four- or six-course tasting menu (you can only eat a la carte at the bar). Using island flavors and foods as a sturdy springboard, the kitchen cooks up instant classics like rare-seared yellowfin tuna in a lemony red-onion vinaigrette and curried spinach empanadas with pineapple chutney. Baby back ribs get a kick from the rum barbecue sauce, and what might have been a ho-hum grill of typical "ground provisions"— parsnips and butternut squash—hits another level with a rich red-wine guava glaze. Because all diners must pay the full price for set menus, this may not be the best place to bring small children. Wine pairings are extra.

20 Cruz Bay Quarter, Cruz Bay. thelimeinn.com. ✆ **340/776-0303.** Reservations recommended. Tasting menus $75 (4-course), $105 (6-course). Mon–Sat 5–9:30pm.

Morgan's Mango ★★ NEO-CARIBBEAN   This fine-dining spot has a sociable drink scene, with a big bar and a lengthy list of frozen concoctions, many made with the juice from fresh island fruits. But Morgan's gets a lot of love for its gourmet Caribbean food as well, covering a broad range of island styles. That might include a Caribbean take on tuna tartare, with a sesame orange vinaigrette, or a quinoa risotto. The St. John yellowfin tuna salad

comes with local organic baby greens and local tuna. We also like the grilled mahi served with a Crucian rum and mango sauce, or Poppas Pickapeppa Steak, marinated in peppercorn-infused Pickapeppa sauce (the famous Jamaican condiment).

Cruz Bay (across from the National Park dock and next door to Mongoose Junction). www.morgansmango.com. ☏ **340/ 693-8141.** Reservations recommended. Entrees $25–$45. Daily 5:30–10pm.

ZoZo's at Caneel Bay ★★★

ITALIAN This 2013 marriage of superstars installed what was then the island's best restaurant in a phenomenal location: atop the ruins of an 18th-century sugar mill at Caneel Bay resort. This thrilling mash-up was too good for this world: The restaurant was demolished by Hurricane Irma in

Morgan's Mango puts a gourmet spin on island food.

2017. Fast-forward to 2022: The future of Caneel Bay is still unknown, but ZoZo's has somehow slipped under the chicken wire of the resort ruins and re-emerged on a seasonal basis, serving a genteel lunch and dinner in the resort's old Beach Bar and Grill, facing the serene and sparkling waters of Caneel Bay—an area largely reachable only by boat. The menu is short and sweet, including a zuppa di pesce loaded with local mahi, seared tuna with buckwheat soba noodles, a lobster roll (stuffed with Caribbean lobster), watermelon salad, and an antipasti plate. A boutique shop is also on the premises. Guests arrive through the old Caneel Bay security gates, where you can park and take a complimentary round-trip shuttle to the restaurant (with a reservation), or you can go by boat—a number of outfitters include lunch here in their day charters and do a "touch and go" drop-off at the dock. Those arriving in their own boat will need reservations to dock. We're still not sure how they're doing this, and seasonal hours are short and erratic, but check ZoZo's Facebook page for the latest.

Caneel Bay, just outside Cruz Bay. www.zozosatcaneelbay.com. ☏ **340/693-9200.** Reservations recommended. Entrees $38–$46. Thurs, Fri & Sun 11:30am–2pm; 3–5pm and 5:30 and 6:30pm dinner seatings.

MODERATE

High Tide Bar & Grill ★★ SEAFOOD/AMERICAN On our last trip to St. John, we kept coming back to this centrally located, open-air beachfront spot. High Tide may be slightly scruffy (and proudly so), but it also feels like

Dining on Lovango Cay

Skimming the inky-black seas on a starry night to dine on a fabulous offshore cay sounds dreamy, right? It is. In the very short time since the resort has been open, taking a **boat to dinner** ★★ or lunch at **Lovango Resort & Beach Club** (www.lovangovi.com; ⓒ **340/625-0400**; p. 80) has become almost a ritual for St. John (and St. Thomas) visitors. Good thing the resort restaurants truly feel

like destination spots, in particular the romantic waterfront restaurant, serving refined Caribbean dishes. The **Lovango Ferry** ($25/person round-trip) does pick-up and drop-off at both Cruz Bay (10-min. ride) and Red Hook (20-min. ride) for waterfront dinners (Mon, Wed, Fri, Sat), lunch (daily), and Beach Club parties (Tues, Thurs, Sun).

the beating heart of the Cruz Bay waterfront. It's not just the excellent feng shui (it's pretty cool to pass through walls of original rubble stone on your way to the bathroom), or the fringe of sea grape trees, or the sun-dappled deck. High Tide knows what you need to get through the day. It makes the best breakfast in town, a very decent lunch (burgers, tacos, wraps), a more than decent dinner (tropical mahi, chimichurri rib-eye, conch fritters), and doesn't quit until quitting time. Neither does the bar. It's open year-round.

Cruz Bay waterfront. www.hightidevi.com. ⓒ **340/714-6169.** Reservations required for groups of 6 or more. Entrees $14–$19 lunch, $20–$39 dinner. Daily 8am–9pm.

INEXPENSIVE

North Shore Deli ★ AMERICAN   This family-run deli in Mongoose Junction is a find, with a refined and delicious menu of slow-roasted meats and tasty sides to go that make instant gourmet meals for your St. John villa life. Watch the faces of fellow beach-goers as you pull Asian peanut noodles (vegan), curry chicken salad, and turkey pesto sandwiches out of your beach bag. Breakfasts (7:30–11am) are excellent; try the North Shore scramble with eggs, sausage, cheddar, onions, peppers, and spinach.

Mongoose Junction, Cruz Bay. www.north shoredelistjohn.com. ⓒ **340/777-3061.** Sandwiches $12–$14. Daily 7:30am–4pm.

Quiet Mon Pub ★ AMERICAN In a song called "Be as You Are," country singer Kenny Chesney sings about hanging with the locals at this atmospheric Irish pub. Chesney, whose hillside Peter Bay mansion was flattened by the 2017 hurricanes, used

Bringing Irish pub fun to Cruz Bay, the Quiet Mon Pub hosts a short but festive St. Patrick's Day parade every March.

to pop in from time to time. Did he come for the food? Good question. The limited menu includes stuff like chili, chicken sandwiches, and a couple of hot dog options. Maybe he came for the memorabilia, flags, and green ferry lights strung from every niche and crevice. As for us, we come for the atmosphere, all fizzy fun, so it makes our list.

Cruz Bay. www.quietmonpub.com. ✆ **340/779-4799.** Lunch plates $6–$9. No credit cards. Mon–Sat 1–11pm; Sun 2–11pm; lunch served 1–6pm.

Sam and Jack's Deli ★ AMERICAN   Under new ownership in 2022, Sam and Jack's is back, offering the same thoughtfully curated gourmet grab bag of prepared dinners, deli meats, cheeses, pastas, sauces, sweets (cookies, brownies, cheesecake), beer, wine, and cocktails. Specialty sandwiches—like a meatball-and-marinara sub or a crispy fried shrimp with spicy Cajun remoulade on a toasted baguette—are no-brainers for beach picnics. Salads include tuna, antipasti, shrimp, and tofu—in fact, Sam and Jack's is big on vegetarian choices. Take the house-made lasagna and a fresh salad back to your villa and call it a day. It's on the third floor of the Marketplace building in Cruz Bay.

The Marketplace, Cruz Bay. samandjacksdeli.com. ✆ **340/714-3354.** Sandwiches $14–$17. Mon–Fri 8am–4pm; Sat 8am–3pm.

East of Cruz Bay/Gifft Hill
INEXPENSIVE
Heading East Bar & Grill ★ CARIBBEAN/LOCAL   Opened in November of 2020, this open-air space has picnic tables, folks playing dominos, and delicious island fare. Weekday entrees might be a yummy stew chicken, fry fish in Creole sauce, or mutton. Sides range from seasoned rice to red beans to fried plantains. Sunday breakfast (starting at 8am) is an immersion in West Indian traditions, with dishes like saltfish, souse, smoked herring, and fresh titi bread. Locals rave about Bobby's chicken soup and conch soup—if it's advertised as a special on Heading East's Facebook page, come and get it. Preorder dishes or eat in.

Centerline Rd., 28 Susannaberg (3.4 miles E. of Cruz Bay). www.facebook.com/heading eastllc. ✆ **340/201-2658.** Entrees $5–$12. No credit cards. Daily 7am–late.

Smitty's Island Breeze ★★ CARIBBEAN   Opened in late 2020 in a converted shipping container, Smitty's is the domain of Alvis Smith, a long-time former chef at Caneel Bay (and later at Miss Lucy's and High Tide). Smitty knows his stuff. His flavorful and authentic island dishes are made to order and come in generous portions with sides like okra fungi, plantains, and red peas and rice. Think chicken pilau (with rice), seafood stew, curried chicken, Thursday oxtails. Saturday is soup day, when Smitty makes kallaloo, pea soup, or a goat stew known as Goat Water, here with dumplings. Smitty's pates (both saltfish and beef; $4) and johnnycakes ($1) are steaming-hot and delicious. Come for the weekend barbecues (Fri night, Sun afternoon) when Smitty cooks up an array of grilled meats. Have a seat at the sprinkling of tables and sample fresh-squeezed juices, Smitty's homemade ginger beer, or a local drink known as peanut punch, here made with sorrel, sea moss, and tamarind. Or go for something stronger.

Centerline Rd., at the entrance to the Windmill Bar (just E. of Cruz Bay). No phone. Entrees $8–$15. Daily 11am to 9 or 10 pm (closing varies).

Coral Bay
EXPENSIVE

Aqua Bistro ★ AMERICAN/CARIBBEAN   Beneath big umbrellas and coconut palms, Aqua Bistro looks out onto Coral Bay Harbor. The bar occupies a center spot in the space and makes a pleasant spot for an island tipple. But the food is well worth a visit, too. Start with the house-made conch fritters or the hummus platter, then try the blackened mahi or the herb-grilled shrimp. Its menu of "hand helds" includes tacos; shrimp, mahi, or jerk chicken sandwiches; and Aqua's Smash Burger, made with Black Angus beef.

Cocoloboa Plaza, Coral Bay. www.aquabistrostjohn.com. ⓒ **340/776-5336.** Reservations recommended. Entrees $19–$31; burgers and sandwiches $16–$18. Sun–Thurs noon–8pm; closed Fri and Sat.

Rhumb Lines ★★ CARIBBEAN/PACIFIC RIM   Now located across the island in Coral Bay, in the former site of its sister restaurant, Indigo Grill, Rhumb Lines still roams the Pacific Rim with its Asian fusion menu. In a pretty courtyard setting, with twinkly lights and big umbrellas, Rhumb Lines cooks up a terrific pad Thai, but the shareable Pacific Rim pupu plates (chicken peanut sate skewers, Thai spicy rolls) make this fun for groups. The good appetizers include mango gazpacho and Indonesian fries.

3 Estate Emmaus, Coral Bay. www.facebook.com/rhumblinesstjohn/. ⓒ **340/776-0303.** Reservations recommended. Main dishes $30–$48. Thurs–Mon 4–9pm.

MODERATE

Miss Lucy's Beachfront Restaurant ★★ CARIBBEAN   This legendary spot is worth the wait for a table—the views of Friis Bay are lovely, so settle in and have a drink. You'll be glad you did, and don't mind the neighborhood sheep and goats. Pioneering Miss Lucy was St. John's first female taxi driver before she started this beloved eatery. Although Miss Lucy died in 2007, Sonja has been cooking up a storm in the kitchen for the past 11 years. The conch fritters, which come with a "mango boom" dipping sauce, are state-of-the-art, and you can't go wrong with the fish fry, seafood kallaloo, roti, or the incredible grouper Reuben. Main dishes come with sides like rice and peas, a spicy sweet potato mash, or fungi, a local cornmeal dish cooked here with okra and garlic. Johnnycakes come hot with honey and butter. If you're lucky, dessert will be a mango-passion cheesecake. Open-mic nights on Thursday.

Salt Pond Rd., near Estate Concordia. www.facebook.com/misslucys. ⓒ **340/693-5244.** Reservations recommended. Entrees $10–$25. Tues–Sat noon–4pm (Thurs noon–2pm) and Thurs 5:30–9pm.

Salty Mongoose Pizza & Rum Beach Bar ★ PIZZA   In a sunny waterfront location, the "Goose" specializes in delicious brick-oven pizzas made with fresh and select ingredients, including a whole-milk mozzarella, provolone, and parmesan cheese blend with herbs and greens grown by Josephine's Greens here on St. John. The pizza-centric menu will reportedly grow to include salads, pasta dishes, and daily sandwich specials. Live music is often on tap on weekend evenings.

In the Isola Shops, Coral Bay. www.salty mongoose.com. ⓒ **340/643-8486.** Build-your-own pizza $20–$24, extra toppings $3–$4; artisanal pizza $28–$36. Cash or Venmo only. Fri–Tues noon–8pm; Wed 4pm–close.

Delicious brick-oven pizza by the sea, courtesy of the Salty Mongoose.

INEXPENSIVE
Skinny Legs ★★ BURGERS/PUB GRUB   Don't let the chicken-pecked floors and ceilings hung with license plates fool you: This is the place to come for good food, good company, and the island's **best burgers.** Skinny Legs has been around Coral Bay long enough (30 years) to reach icon status. Consider the merch alone: T-shirts, hoodies, coozies, dog collars, tie-dye bucket hats. Just keep your eyes trained on those juicy half-pound burgers. The homemade chili warms you up on rainy days (sunny ones, too), and the salads are piled high with fresh, yummy veggies and organic greens raised here on St. John. The fish sandwiches are as good as any on the island. A family-friendly, community-minded spot, Skinny Legs usually has something cooking, from live music to horseshoe contests to Derby Day parties.

Skinny Legs serves what most agree is the island's best burger.

Emmaus, Coral Bay, beyond the fire station. www.skinnylegsvi.com. ⓒ **340/779-4982.** Burgers and sandwiches $7.50–$15. Tues–Sat 11am–8pm.

FLOATING restaurants

If it floats, it cooks, is the motto of no one nowhere. But here in the Virgin Islands, where people spend half their lives on the water, there's a lotta love for what are more or less floating food trucks. St. John has its own floating taco bar in **Lime Out ★** (www.limeoutvi.com; *©* **340/643-5333**), in Coral Bay Harbor. Half the fun is getting there by boat (and it's the only way to get there). You can even eat in: Lime Out has circular lime-green floats for your floating pleasure. The inventive made-to-order tacos ($9–$13), the creation of Chef Amaro Rivera from sister resto Lime Inn (p. 208), range from a mahi ceviche to slow-braised short-rib to a curry chicken. Lime Out is open Sunday to Friday from 11am to 5pm. Closer

to St. Thomas, **Pizza Pi ★** (pizza-pi.com; *©* **340/643-4674;** VHF 16) is a 37-foot motorized sailboat anchored in the protected waters of Christmas Cove. You pull up beside it, they take your order, and in no time at all you're eating 'za as the ocean breezes blow. And it's not like they're warming up cold pizza from some slice shop in Miami. No, Pizza Pi has a genuine pizza oven in its hold, producing excellent pizza like the Asian Chicken (with chicken, green onions, and bell peppers) and the Georgia Peacharia (with peaches, basil, and feta). Sixteen-inch pizzas run $23 to $33. If you're already anchored in Christmas Cove, Pizza Pi will deliver right to your boat. It's open daily 11am to 6pm in season.

EXPLORING ST. JOHN

Two-thirds of St. John is national parkland, with the lushest concentration of flora and fauna in the U.S. Virgin Islands. The **Virgin Islands National Park ★★★** (www.nps.gov/viis; *©* **340/776-6201**) totals 12,624 acres, including submerged lands and water adjacent to St. John, and has more than 20 miles of hiking trails to explore (see "Hiking," p. 223). From pelicans to sandpipers, from mahogany to bay trees, the park abounds in beauty, dotted with colorful accents from the blooms of tamarind and flamboyant trees. The mongoose also calls it home. Park guides lead nature walks through this park that often take you past ruins of former plantations. Admission is free, except for $5 admission fee for Trunk Bay.

Beaches

St. John has so many fantastic beaches it's hard to find a favorite, but the North Shore beaches are a superstar lineup. Where you go depends largely on where you can find a parking space—beach parking is limited everywhere. You can often snag a space if you arrive early in the morning or in the early afternoon (when the cruise-ship visitors are leaving), but it's really a matter of luck and the season. Moorings fees are required for overnighting in any of the island's bays; for more information, go to **www.nps.gov/viis/**.

NORTH SHORE

Starting from west to east, these are the best of the North Shore:

The former stomping ground of the rich and famous, the **Caneel Bay resort** had an embarrassment of beautiful beaches, seven stunners on its 170 acres.

Although the status of the shuttered resort remains up in the air (see "The Caneel Bay Conundrum," p. 196), you can visit Caneel's lovely **Honeymoon Beach ★★★** either by boat or by walking the 1.1-mile **Lind Point Trail** from the NPS headquarters (20 min.) or from the **Lind Point Spur Trail** off North Shore Road (11 min.). The ridge trail has upper and lower portions (and the Lind Overlook) and mostly a gentle slope but can be rocky and steep in patches, so good shoes are advised. Honeymoon is a favorite lounging and snorkeling beach, with shade from low-lying sea grape trees and the occasional palm. The other Caneel Bay beaches are closed to the public, although you can snorkel from Honeymoon around the bend to **Caneel Bay ★★**; it's otherwise only accessible by boat. **Salomon Beach ★★**, reached just before Honeymoon Beach off the Lind Point Trail, is a smaller but equally sweet white-sand crescent with shady palms, calm seas, and good snorkeling. You can return by taking the Lind Point Spur Trail to N. Shore Road and hailing a safari van into Cruz Bay. **Virgin Islands Ecotours** (viecotours.com; ℂ **340/779-2155**) offers an easy half-day guided kayak and snorkel tour of Honeymoon Beach and Henley Cay for $75 per person (snorkel gear and kayaks provided). A concession on Honeymoon Beach offers lounge chairs, towels, and a snack bar.

Just east is beautiful **Hawksnest ★★**, another beach administered by the NPS, with parking spaces, changing rooms, 24-hour restrooms, grills, and picnic tables.

The picture-perfect shoreline of **Trunk Bay ★★** is one of St. John's biggest attractions. Administered by the National Park Service, this heart-shaped bay has a bathhouse, beach-chair and snorkel-gear rentals, and a snack bar (but no lifeguards on duty). When conditions are optimal, the beach is ideal for snorkeling, swimming, and sailing. But erosion can be a problem in spots, and crowds can inundate the beach, especially when cruise-ship passengers from St. Thomas arrive en masse. Among the beach's many wonderful aspects is the underwater marked snorkeling trail near the shore, great for beginners: The **National Park Underwater Trail** (ℂ **340/776-6201**) stretches for 650 feet and helps you identify what you see—everything from false coral to colonial anemones. Trunk Bay is the only St. John beach that charges an admission fee: It's $5 for adults 16 and over ($20

Sea grape trees shade the white sands of Hawksnest Beach.

SEEING ST. JOHN ON A guided tour

The best way to see St. John quickly, especially if you're on a cruise-ship lay-over, is to take a 2-hour **taxi tour.** Most local taxi drivers offer these tours in multi-passenger safari vans. We highly recommend **Kenneth Lewis** (© 340/776-6865), a former cop from Dominica who is one of the best guides on the island; he can also arrange ferry pickup and transfer if you aren't renting a car. If he can't accommodate you, he can refer you to someone who can. You can also contact the **St. John Taxi Association** (© 340/693-7530).

For a jeep tour with a super-knowledgeable insider, **Explore STJ** ★ offers half- and full-day **island tours** (explorestj.com; © 203/376-3786) for up to four people. Guide Jenn Manes, former publisher of the popular and informative "News of St. John" blog and creator of the **Johnopoly** board game featuring all

things St. John, gives customized tours of the island in a Jeep Wrangler that might visit historical ruins, beaches, hiking trails, or do a little snorkeling with turtles—you choose your own adventure. Half-day tours are $325 per person, $475 for a full day.

Island Buddy ★ (islandbuddy.net; © 340/239-7084) does private jeep tours of island highlights and off-the-beaten-path sights outside the national parkland that might have you hanging with donkeys at remote plantation ruins, toasting to the insanely panoramic views at the Windmill Bar, or taking guided snorkels of the reef at Hansen Bay, a lovely locals' beach on the island's East End. Half-day jeep tours (for up to four guests) are $275; fee is $425 for full-day tours. Pickup is at the Cruz Bay ferry dock or your hotel/villa.

annual pass), and the beach is open from 8am to 4pm. A National Parks Pass also covers the fees.

For those craving privacy, adorable little **Jumbie Bay** ★★ looks out at Trunk Bay from across the waters but has nowhere near the scrum of visitors or a whisper of an amenity. This is partly by design—the cove is smallish, and the parking lot has room for only four vehicles. But it's a seriously dreamy spot to while away an afternoon. The waters are lovely, but the current gets stronger the farther you venture out.

Cinnamon Bay ★★ is one gorgeous strip of white sand, complete with hiking trails, great windsurfing, and laidback wild donkeys (don't feed or pet them). Administered by the NPS, the beach has a **campground** right on the beach (p. 204). The campground store rents out watersports equipment (snorkel gear, kayaks), even to non-guests. Snorkeling is popular here; you'll often see big schools of purple triggerfish. This beach is best in the morning and at midday, as afternoons can be windy. A marked **nature trail,** with signs identifying the flora, loops through a tropical forest on even turf before leading up to Centerline Road.

In 2014, **Maho Bay Beach** ★★ and its forested hillsides became the newest addition to the National Park Service collection of St. John beaches through a $2.5-million deal made by the nonprofit conservation group Trust for Public Lands. It's just east of Cinnamon Bay. With calm green waters, it's ideal for standup paddleboarding, and snorkelers are almost always guaranteed to see turtles grazing on the grassy bottom. It's a popular beach with boat charters and cruise-ship passengers. Traveling eastward along St. John's gently curving coastline, you'll come to **Francis Bay Beach ★★**, a lovely North Shore beach and often less crowded than its neighbors, and **Leinster Bay ★★**, the latter ideal for those seeking the solace of a private sunny retreat.

SOUTHEAST & SOUTH COAST

On the island's southeast shores, remote and tranquil **Salt Pond Bay ★★** lies adjacent to **Coral Bay.** It's one of the few beaches with good-shade sea grapes limning the white sand and a good-size parking lot. You'll have to walk down (and then back up) a quarter-mile sloping, rock-strewn path from the parking lot to the beach. The snorkeling is good a bit far out and along the bay's eastern shore. Facilities are limited but when we were there an enterprising roadside vendor, the Friendly Spot, was selling island specialties like fry fish and barbeque chicken as well as refreshing juices (mango, papaya, guava) on the road past the Salt Pond parking lot.

If you want to escape the crowds, head for **Lameshur Bay Beach ★★**, along the rugged south coast, west of Salt Pond Bay and accessible only via a bumpy dirt road. The sands are beautiful, and the snorkeling is excellent. You can also take a 5-minute stroll down the road past the beach to explore the nearby ruins of an old plantation estate that was destroyed in a slave revolt.

A local iguana saunters down to the calm green waters of Maho Bay Beach.

IT'S THE law

- **Reef-Safe Sunscreen:** It's against the law to use anything but reef-safe sunscreen in the U.S. Virgins. Look for the Reef Safe designation on package labeling, but double-check to ensure that any reef-damaging, coral-bleaching substances (such as oxybenzone, octocrylene, octinoxate, butylparaben, or 4-methylbenzylidine camphor) are not included. Use "non-nano" mineral sunscreen containing zinc oxide or titanium dioxide.

- **Keep Your Shirt On:** Local customs and law on St. John require that cover-ups or T-shirts and shorts be worn over bathing suits except on the beach. Men cannot appear bare-chested in public.

- **Petroglyphs:** Do not chalk or scratch petroglyphs—this kind of defacement can cause irreversible

damage and is a federal crime.

- **Shells:** It's illegal to remove shells from the beach in any U.S.V.I. waters.

- **Don't Feed the Wildlife:** It's not against the law to feed the island donkeys, goats, chickens, or iguanas, but for their own health and safety, it should be, says Hillary Bonner from the popular St. John blog "News from St. John." "The pictures of people petting and feeding donkeys on the roadsides of St. John are super cute, but it is not good at all for the animals—especially if they are fed something outside of their natural diet," Bonner writes. Even worse, when these animals become conditioned to approach vehicles for food, they cluster near roads and are in real danger of being hit by a car, says Bonner.

Watersports & Outdoor Adventures

St. John offers some of the best snorkeling, scuba diving, swimming, fishing, hiking, sailing, and underwater photography in the Caribbean. Scuba connoisseurs know that the diving here is highly rewarding, with a natural wall just 15 minutes offshore. **Island-hopping boat excursions ★★★** via captained sailboats or powerboats/yachts are the top activities in the Virgins, with half- and full-day sail/snorkels and sunset sails the most popular outings.

WATERSPORTS

BAREBOATING This is a beach-hopping paradise, and bareboating companies throughout the Virgins are almost too numerous to name. The following recommended companies are based on St. John. **Ocean Runners** (oceanrunnersvi.com; ℂ **340/693-8809**) rents Boston whaler powerboats from $395 per day. **Wharfside Watersports** (wharfsidewatersports.com; ℂ **340/201-6881**), on the Cruz Bay waterfront in Wharfside Village, rents Zodiacs ($395 half-day) and inflatable power dinghies ($195 half-day, $249 full day). **Cruz Bay Watersports** (see below) also has bareboat rentals.

DAY SAILING & BOAT EXCURSIONS Most boat charter companies in St. John are owner-operated, and there are a lot of excellent ones. Under a new 2022 agreement between the B.V.I. and U.S.V.I. governments, complicated pandemic-era regulations have been eased for the charter boat industry, allowing U.S.V.I. and B.V.I. charter vessels once again to move more freely between the two territories. The following are a few recommended operators, in no particular order, all based on St. John (for excursions departing from St. Thomas, see p. 97 in chapter 4).

Sunshine Daydream (sunshinedaydreamvi.com; ☏ **340/776-0928**) offers private captained 12-person charters on 32-foot World Cat powerboats with pick-up and drop-off at the National Park Dock in Cruz Bay; full-day charters are $800 to $950; half-day (4 hr.) are $600 to $750.

With nearly 25 years of maritime experience, **Flyaway Charters** (flyaway chartersvi.com; ☏ **340/514-9627**) offers customized half- and full-day snorkel sails out of Coral Bay. Flyaway takes passengers to interesting and less-trammeled places along St. John's eastern shore, including Witch Island and Nye Bay. A full-day trip might include lunch at Lovango Cay, ZoZo's at Caneel Bay, or Lime Out. Rates are $625 for a half-day sail for up to six passengers and $945 for a full-day trip for up to six passengers ($50/add'l passenger).

Big Blue Excursions (www.bigblue-usvi.com; ☏ **340/201-3045**) offers small, private customized half- and full-day sailing and powerboating charters for up to 12 passengers aboard the *Gypsea King,* a 41-foot Calypso marine powerboat; *Sweet Revenge II,* a 47-foot crewed catamaran; or *Cat's Eye,* a 45-foot Leopard sailing vessel.

Snorkelers hit the water with Big Blue Excursions.

Soulshine Charters (www.soul shinecharters.com; ☏ **340/776-0928**) offers private captained charters on its Lagoon 440 cruising catamaran *Sunshine.* The charter company is currently one of the few U.S.V.I. outfitters licensed to take passengers into B.V.I. waters. Call for rates.

Ocean Runners (see "Bareboating," above) offers 10- to 12-person captained charters on speedboats, power catamarans, and luxury yachts.

Sail Helios (sailhelios.com; ☏ **340/ 244-3290**) sails the classic 48-foot Hinckley Yawl *Helios* on personalized and all-inclusive half- and full-day trips for up to 12 people out of St. John to some of the prettiest bays on the island (Francis, Maho, Cinnamon, Honeymoon, and Salomon beaches) as well as fetching and secluded cays and coves beyond, like Thatch Cay, Lovango Cay, and Christmas Cove

($600–$1,200). Two-hour sunset sails for up to four people are $400. The boat leaves from the Cruz Bay waterfront in front of the High Tide Bar & Grill.

Intimate half- or full-day sailing cruises with **Sail Asante** (www.sailing asante.com; ☎ **404/408-9077**) come highly recommended. *Asante* is a 44-foot monohull sailboat, circa 1989. The boat will pick you up at the ferry dock in Cruz Bay. The excursions travel the waters between St. John and St. Thomas and stop for snorkels and beach time on both islands and in and around Jost Van Dyke. Private charters (up to six people) are $500 for half-day sails; half-day shared charters are $400 (up to four people) and $100 per person for each additional guest (six people max). *Asante* also does 2-hour sunset sails ($300 minimum up to four people; $75/person each add'l guest, up to six people max) and can even deliver you by sail to dinner at places like Zozo's or the Lovango Cay Resort.

Cruz Bay Watersports (cruzbaywatersports.com; ☎ **844/668-8753** or 340/776-6234), with a location at the Westin Resorts & Villas in St. John, has a fleet of 50-passenger luxury catamarans that operate some of the best and most professional **snorkel sails** in the Virgins. The 65-foot *Lady Lynsey II* can carry up to 80 passengers. All come with swim platforms, waterslides, easy boarding ladders, and all snorkel gear and flotation devices. Snorkel sails often offer snorkels to places like Maho Bay (sea turtles) and Caneel Bay, followed by a delicious picnic lunch either aboard the boat or at places like Pizza Pi or Lime Out. Five-hour snorkel sails range in price from $129 to $149 ($89–$99 children 3–12).

Bad Kitty & Calypso Charters (www.calypsovi.com; ☎ **340/777-7245**) offers sails aboard its 40-foot catamaran *Calypso,* a 26-foot power catamaran, *Tropicat,* and *Cat5,* a 36-foot power catamaran. Ride on customized private charters on the 49-foot wave-piercing catamarans *Bad Kitty* and *Bad Kitty2*. All are available for half- and full-day cruises and sunset sails to places like Waterlemon Cay and Jost Van Dyke. With a carrying capacity of up to 32 people, *Calypso* runs half-day snorkel trips at $100 per person ($90 children 12 and under); full-day snorkel sails aboard *Calypso* are $155 per person ($120 children 12 and under).

FISHING Led by Captain Robert Richards, the fleet of *Mixed Bag* boats of **Offshore Adventures** ★★ (sportfishingstjohn.com; ☎ **340/513-0389**) leave from the dock at the Westin resort and the National Park Dock in Cruz Bay. Count on spending from $650 to $700 per party for a custom-designed half-day of fishing in a 32- or 40-foot boat; it's around $1,200 for a full-day sport-fishing charter.

Local Flavor ★ (localflavorcharters.com; ☎ **340-513-1431**) is helmed by St. John native Captain Cleve, son of Vie of the late lamented Vie's Snack Shack. He does inshore fishing charters on one of three boats, including the 26-foot Angler Limited Edition *Local Flavor*. Captain Cleve's specialty is catching yellowtail snapper, bonito, red hinds, and jacks. Filleting service is provided. A half-day fishing charter for up to six passengers is $675, fuel o **Arawak Expeditions** (see "Kayaking," below) has a retail shop in Mongoose Junction that rents snorkel gear at reasonable prices ($5/day, $25/week) as well as dry bags, cellphone cases, and other little necessities for your watersports outings.

o Renting SUPs, surfboards, skimboards, and snorkel gear, **SUP St. John** (see "Stand-Up Paddleboarding," p. 223) will deliver straight to your villa.

o **Low Key Watersports** (see "Scuba Diving," p. 222) in Cruz Bay offers excellent-quality snorkel and scuba rentals (including prescription masks); a full snorkel setup starts at $9 a day ($45/week). They also rent beach tents and standup paddleboard rentals made by SIC Maui, delivered directly to your villa or beach. **Virgin Islands Ecotours** (see "Kayaking," below) offers SUP rentals.

o In Coral Bay, **Crabby's Watersports** (www.crabbyswatersports.com; ℂ **340/626-1570**) rents kayaks for exploring Hurricane Hole ($75/day, includes delivery and pick-up at Hurricane Hole).

o **On the beach:** Snorkel gear ($5/day), beach chairs ($5/day), and umbrellas ($10/day) are available to rent at the NPS concession at Trunk Bay. **Cinnamon Bay Campground,** on Cinnamon Bay Beach (wwwcinnamonbayvi.com; ℂ **340/714-7144**), has kayaks ($25–$30/hr.), glass-bottom kayaks ($35/hr.), snorkels ($10/day, $50/week), SUPs ($35/hr.), and beach chairs ($5/day) for rent right on the beach. Ask about daily packages. On Maho Bay beach, **Reef2Peak** (reef2peak.com/rentals; ℂ **617/378-5745**) rents snorkel gear ($10/day), beach chairs ($5/day), and umbrellas ($10/day) 7 days a week from 10am to 4pm. Call ahead to book their kayaks and SUPs.

included. Captain Cleve also does snorkeling charters to Lovango and Congo cays and sunset sails. A full-day combo fishing/island-hopping excursion for six people is $750.

Fly-fish the crystalline inshore waters of St. John with **Arawak Expeditions** (see "Kayaking," below) on charters (max. 3 passengers) into the St. John shallows in a 20-foot powerboat. You'll be angling for delicious mutton snapper and big tarpon. April and May is high season for bonefish, and Arawak takes to the island's saltwater flats to chase the elusive "gray ghost." Fly reels and rods provided, or bring your own.

Fishermen can use hand-held rods to fish the waters in Virgin Islands National Park.

KAYAKING **Arawak Expeditions** ★ (arawakexp.com; ℂ **340/693-8312**), which has been operating on St. John since 1993, provides half- and full-day kayak and snorkel outings to places like Hurricane Hole and Henley Cay, an uninhabited island in the Virgin Islands National Park. Trips cost $75 and $110–$120, respectively. Multiday excursions with camping are also available, ranging in price from $1,395 to $2,495.

Virgin Islands Ecotours ★ (www.viecotours.com; ✆ **340/776-2155**) offers some of the best kayak and snorkel adventures in North Shore and National Park waters. You can paddle from Honeymoon Beach to Scott Beach (former Caneel Bay resort beaches) and snorkel the gin-clear bays on a 2-hour Kayak and Snorkel with Sea Turtles tour ($75/person and up). A full-day Hurricane Hole excursion exploring the mangroves of the Coral Reef National Monument is $120 and up. Virgin Island Eco-Tours operates out of Cruz Bay and also has SUP rentals.

Reef2Peak ★ (reef2peak.com/rentals; ✆ **617/378-5745**) offers excellent half-day guided kayak and SUP paddling excursions for all ages to Hurricane Hole and Haulover Bay ($95–$120/person).

SCUBA DIVING ★★ Like its sister islands, St. John is a diving paradise, with some 25 dive sites within a 15-mile radius. One of the best dive operators on island is PADI five-star **Low Key Watersports** ★, 1 Bay St., Cruz Bay (divelowkey.com; ✆ **340/693-8999**). All wreck dives offered are two-tank/two-location dives and cost $155. Low Key also offers full-day trips that include two morning dives, one snorkel, and a stop for lunch at places like Pizza Pi and Lime Out (both only reached by water) or the gorgeous restaurant at Lovango Cay Resort. These 7-hour trips cost $255 for certified divers and $95 snorkelers, with all equipment provided (the cost of lunch is on you).

SNORKELING ★★★ St. John has so many great snorkeling sites it's impossible to list them all. The most popular spot for snorkeling is **Trunk Bay** (see "Beaches," p. 214), for its Underwater Snorkel Trail, but the other North Shore beaches (Francis, Maho, Cinnamon, Hawksnest, Honeymoon, and Salomon beaches) all have good snorkeling. For snorkel rentals, see "Watersports Rentals," p 221.

An excellent snorkeling spot is **Leinster Bay/Waterlemon Cay** ★★, just past the Annaberg Plantation ruins. You can swim in the bay's shallow water or snorkel over the spectacular and colorful coral reef, perhaps in the company of an occasional turtle or stingray. A tiny cay in one of Leinster's inner bays, **Waterlemon Cay Beach** ★★ has some of the island's best snorkeling, with hawksbill turtles dining on seagrass and big starfish stretching along the sea bottom. You can also walk along the Leinster Bay Trail to reach the island. The water is calm, clear, and filled with brilliantly hued tropical fish.

Haulover Bay ★★ is often deserted, and the waters are often clearer than in other spots around St. John. **Salt Pond Bay** ★ has some good snorkeling along the bay's eastern flank.

Another amazing spot to snorkel is the mangrove stands at **Hurricane Hole** ★. Here coral grows in abundance on the mangrove roots—attended by huge starfish, sponges (and the hawksbills that eat them), and anemones. Seas are calm and gin-clear, and it's magical. It's best reached by boat.

Also check out snorkel trips with **Flyaway Charters, Cruz Bay Watersports,** and **Calypso Charters** under "Day Sailing & Boat Excursions," p. 218; kayak and snorkel outings with **Arawak Expeditions** and **Virgin**

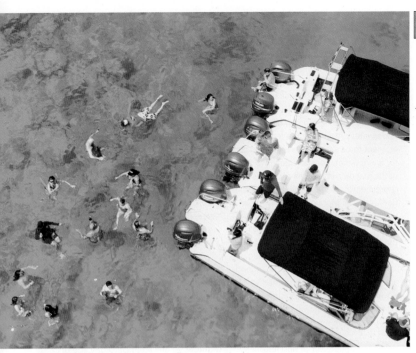

Flyaway Charters (p. 219) leads a variety of customized snorkel sails out of Coral Bay Harbor.

Islands Ecotours under "Kayaking," p. 221; and the Snorkel, Dive, and Dine trips offered by **Low Key Watersports** (see "Scuba," p. 222).

STAND-UP PADDLEBOARDING (SUP) St. John has a wealth of calm, protected waters that are ideal for stand-up paddleboarding. **SUP St. John ★** (www.sup-stjohn.com; ✆ 340/514-5527) has an extensive collection of some 50 paddleboards for all ages, abilities, and purposes (a yoga SUP!); they offer free delivery and pickup right to your villa with the weekly rental of two SUPs ($250/week for first board; $200/week per board for additional boards), and day rentals ($75/day, one board) to anywhere on the Cruz Bay side of the island. They also offer **2-hour private SUP lessons** ($75/person for 1–2 people; $65/person for 3 or more) and rent surfboards ($150/week), skimboards ($75/week), and snorkel gear ($35–$50/week). **Reef2Peak ★** (see "Kayaking," p. 221) offers half-day guided SUP and kayak paddling excursions for all ages to Hurricane Hole and Haulover Bay ($95–$120/person). You can also rent paddleboards at Cinnamon Bay at the **Cinnamon Bay Campground** and at Maho Bay beach with **Reef2Peak** (see "Watersports Rentals," p. 221).

OUTDOOR ADVENTURES

HIKING ★★★ Carved into St. John's rocky coastline are beautiful crescent-shaped bays and white-sand beaches. But the interior is no less

sustainable ST. JOHN: A ROCKEFELLER DREAM

In 1952, multimillionaire Laurance Rockefeller sailed around St. John with friends on his yacht. Rockefeller was so enchanted that he eventually donated 9,500 acres of rolling green hills and an underwater preserve to the federal government to be set aside as a national park for future generations to enjoy. Two-thirds of the island's surface area and the island's shoreline waters (the Virgin Islands Coral Reef National Monument) today make up the **Virgin Islands National Park** (www.nps.gov/viis; ℂ **340/776-6201**). Of the land that Rockefeller donated as national parkland, he held back roughly 150 acres for the creation of the legendary Caneel Bay resort. Farsightedly advertised in the 1960s as a low-impact "destination in harmony with its natural environment," Caneel Bay largely fulfilled that promise until 2017, when Hurricane Irma put it out of business.

To islanders, Rockefeller's legacy is a little more complicated, his altruism interpreted as a power move by outside interests. Even though Caneel Bay was St. John's largest employer for years, a number of islanders felt that the most recent owner (a private equity firm, CBI Acquisitions, whose lease is up in 2023) left employees high and dry. Many would be happy to see the entire 170 acres rolled into national parkland and its beaches left free from development—or, if a resort is ultimately approved, the property re-envisioned with a smaller footprint, green infrastructure, and greater public access. (Only two of its glorious beaches, Honeymoon and Hawksnest, are currently available for public use.) Others demand a deeper assessment of the cultural and historic artifacts left by the early Taino tribe who settled this land and protection for on-site plantation ruins.

Still, it's hard to argue with Rockefeller's attempts to keep St. John pristine. Thanks to the efforts of Rockefeller and others, today hundreds of the coral gardens that surround St. John (some 12,708 undersea acres) are protected rigorously—any attempt to damage or remove coral is punishable by large and strictly enforced fines. Sustainable tourism programs and eco-friendly practices are part of the island's DNA. More than perhaps any other island in the Caribbean, St. John works hard to ensure the preservation of its natural resources and ecosystems.

impressive. The terrain ranges from arid and dry (in the east) to moist and semitropical (in the northwest), and the variety of wildlife is the envy of naturalists around the world, with some 800 species of plants and 160 species of birds. Miles of hiking trails lead to panoramic views. Many trails wind through the grounds of sugar plantations, past ruined schoolhouses, rum distilleries, molasses factories, and great houses wrapped in lush encroaching vines and trees. At scattered spots along the trails, you can find mysteriously geometric petroglyphs incised on cliffs and boulders beside water pools, believed to be the work of the Taino tribe sometime between A.D. 900 and the 1490s.

At least 20 clearly marked (and well-maintained) walking paths originate from North Shore Road (Rte. 20) or from the island's main east-west artery,

Centerline Road (Rte. 10). Each is marked at its starting point with a pre-planned itinerary; the walks can last anywhere from 10 minutes to 2 hours. Trail maps are available from the **National Park Service Cruz Bay Visitor Center** (www.nps.gov/viis; © **340/776-6201**, ext. 238; daily 8am–4:30pm), right at the ferry docks in Cruz Bay. Be sure to carry a lot of water and wear sunscreen and insect repellent when you hike.

ANNABERG HISTORIC TRAIL ★★   This short but terrific hike (identi-fied by the U.S. National Park Service as trail no. 10) leads pedestrians on a .3-mile ramble around the ruined buildings of the best-preserved plantation on St. John. If you're driving, just park your vehicle in a large parking lot at the start of the trail. The meandering shoreline walk takes about 20 minutes and ends at Leinster Bay—bring snorkel and mask for some excellent snorkeling in the clear shallows from here to Waterlemon Cay. The views are spectacular: From a terrace near the windmill, a map identifies the British Virgin Islands to the north, including Little Thatch, Tortola, Waterlemon Cay, and Jost Van Dyke. Visiting the ruins is free, but contributions are welcome.

CINNAMON BAY TRAIL/CINNAMON BAY LOOP TRAIL   Both of these trails begin at the Cinnamon Bay Campground. The half-mile **Cinnamon Bay Loop Trail** is a marked nature trail, with signs identifying the flora; it's a relatively flat, shady walk through historic Cinnamon Bay Sugar Planta-tion ruins and scented bay rum trees. The 1.1-mile **Cinnamon Bay Trail** starts out steeply but leads into shaded forest along the rutted cobblestones of a former Danish road, past ruins of abandoned plantations, eventually leading to Centerline Road.

LEINSTER BAY TRAIL   If you want to prolong your hiking experience from the Annaberg Historic Trail (above), take the Leinster Bay Trail (trail no. 11), which begins near the point where trail no. 10 ends. It leads past man-grove swamps and coral inlets rich with plant and marine life; markers iden-tify some of the plants and animals. The trail leads up to the Windy Hills Great House ruins above Leinster Point.

RAM HEAD TRAIL   This 2.3-mile out-and-back trek over moderate (and unshaded) terrain rewards with spectacular sea views. The trail leaves from the far end of Salt Pond Bay beach and passes over a pretty, rock-strewn beach to reach rocky cliffs (including Ram Head) with amazing views of St. John's South Shore.

REEF BAY HIKE ★★   One of the most popular hikes on St. John is the 2.5-mile Reef Bay Hike. Many people think it's one of the best hikes in the Caribbean, and it can take anywhere from 2 to 4 hours. It encompasses Danish plantation ruins, the only known petroglyphs on the island (the work of indig-enous Taino from pre-Columbian days), stone walls from St. John's cattle-grazing days, and a waterfall that gushes in the rainy season. Currently the hike is self-guided only; contact the NPS to see if they've resumed guided hikes.

Seeing the Sights

St. John's main village, **Cruz Bay,** is small, easily navigable on foot, and refreshingly relaxing after the hurly-burly of St. Thomas. The ferry drops you off right into the heart of town, with its open market, smoothie stands, and cafes. The town's jumble of waterfront bars, restaurants, boutiques, and pastel-painted cottages may not cry out "historic" like the distinctive colonial Danish architecture of St. Thomas's Charlotte Amalie or St. Croix's Christiansted, but in 2016 the village was granted National Historic District designation. Here new is wrapped into old, in traditional West Indian wooden vernacular cottages holding snappy new restos, jewelry shops in 18th-century walls of native stone and coral, and shopping plazas shaded by 200-year-old trees. A newly restored historic cemetery holds the remains of a free community of people of African descent. **July Fourth** on Cruz Bay is a dual celebration—emancipation of the slaves was proclaimed here on July 4, 1848.

Cruz Bay's historic district is charmingly laid out in the self-guided **Historical Walking Map** ($10), with hand-drawn art by Virgin Islands artist Lisa Etre. Published in 2021 by the St. John Historical Society under the guidance of local historian David W. Knight, Sr., it showcases more than 20 historic sites in a compact six- or seven-block section. Get yours in person at Bajo El Sol Gallery in Mongoose Junction (St. John) or at the Caribbean Genealogy Library (St. Thomas). Or order it from the **St. John Historical Society** (stjohnhistoricalsociety.org) or by calling ℂ **340/344-4303.**

ATTRACTIONS AROUND THE ISLAND

Annaberg Sugar Plantation Ruins ★★ HISTORIC SITE Colonists from St. Thomas settled St. John in the early 18th century to cultivate sugarcane, and by 1733, some 109 working plantations made it a sugar powerhouse. On this site was a thriving plantation and sugar mill worked by slaves brought to the islands by the Danish. It's tough to imagine the hot, brutal, back-breaking business of making sugar in this breathtakingly beautiful site.

CORAL BAY: ST. JOHN'S first settlement

This was the site of the first plantation on St. John, established in 1717 and abandoned long ago. Claimed by the Danes in the 1600s and used to unload Danish ships, the bay still contains a crumbling stone pier. Follow the posted signs to see the remains of **Fort Berg,** which stationed the soldiers that suppressed the 1733 slave revolt. Today, this charming little village shelters a close-knit community of yachting enthusiasts, artists, and expats. Just as folks from St. Thomas come to St. John to "plug out,"

so St. John locals head to rustic Coral Bay to relax and chill out. Ringing the bay's perimeter is a handful of restaurants and bars. You can spend a day in Coral Bay hiking the area's beautiful trails (see "Hiking," p. 223) and swimming and snorkeling in **Salt Pond Bay** (p. 217), where the mud is thought to be rejuvenating for the skin. Have lunch at one of the village's quintessentially laidback cafes and beach shacks, whether **Miss Lucy's** (p. 212) or **Skinny Legs** (p. 213).

The plantation land was granted in 1721 to a Danish gentleman, Christopher William Gottschalk, who named the property after his infant daughter, Anna. Today a National Park Service trail leads from the parking lot to the ruins; NPS plaques throughout the compound identify the plantation buildings, fashioned of native stone known as "blue bitch" set with a mortar of sand, water, lime (fired from seashells and coral), and sugar-juice scum skimmed from big iron kettles known as "coppers." Here and there you'll see bricks brought over as ship ballast used to fashion squares, and sea coral framing doorways. The only 18th-century structures remaining are the Slave House (Marker No. 1) and a wall of the horse mill (Marker No. 6). The handsome windmill, some 38 feet high, dates from the 1840s. There are stupendous views from the plantation grounds of several British Virgin Islands. Look up to the east where the ruins of the Windy Hill Great House

A ruined hilltop windmill at Annaberg Plantation.

are perched on a hillside, lording over everything—you can climb up to the ruins on the Leinster Bay Trail (see "Hiking," p. 223). This is also a great spot to snorkel (see "Snorkeling," p. 222).

Leinster Bay Road, off North Shore Rd., east of Trunk Bay. www.nps.gov/viis. Admission free, donations welcome.

The Battery ★ HISTORIC SITE   The only government building from the Danish Colonial period that remains in Cruz Bay, the Battery building reopened in late 2021 after a $1.13-million restoration. It dates from 1825, the architectural work of a "free-colored" master carpenter born a slave on St. John in the 1700s. Johannes (John) Wright was hired by Danish West Indies Governor Peter Von Scholten (the man who freed the slaves in 1848) to convert Cruz Bay's crumbling battery, known as Christiansfort, into a government office to hold a courtroom and jail, plus a residence for the Danish West Indies government representative. Wright, who had purchased his freedom in 1799, would go on to become a successful building contractor and plantation owner and a vigorous advocate for social justice. The Battery holds government administrative offices and is currently not open for tours.

Cruz Bay, just to the east of the ferry dock.

Fort Berg ★ HISTORIC SITE   St. John was not colonized until more than 4 decades after St. Thomas, and it was at Coral Bay, not Cruz Bay, that the first settlement was built. Danish colonizers, looking for fertile land, landed in 1718 and declared the island the possession of the King of Denmark and the Danish West Indies Company. They built Fort Berg (aka Fortsberg) on a high summit overlooking Coral Bay harbor as a defensive lookout. The fort was the site of the 1733 slave revolt but also served as the base for the French soldiers who brutally crushed the rebellion. The ruins of the citadel fortress, a National Historic Register site, date from 1760 and include a battery with cannons. The fort is an uphill walk from Coral Bay.

SHOPPING

Compared to St. Thomas, St. John's shopping isn't much, but what's here is often much more interesting. Yes, a handful of places sell generic tourist tchotchkes, but most of the boutiques and shops of Cruz Bay are individualized and quite special. **Mongoose Junction** (mongoosejunctionstjohn.com) on North Shore Road, a 5-minute walk from the ferry dock, has the most choices, from clothing shops to jewelry boutiques to a brewery. The area around the renovated **Wharfside Village Hotel** (thewvhotel.com), along the Cruz Bay waterfront just steps from the ferry departure point, is a low-rise complex of courtyards, alleys, and seaside cafes with a handful of stores and gift shops. The **Marketplace of St. John** (stjohnmarketplace.com; ✆ 340/776-6455) has St. John's biggest grocery store (Starfish Market), a pharmacy (Chelsea Drug Store), a hardware store (St. John Hardware), a deli (Sam and Jack's), and a sprinkling of retail shops and cafes.

ARTS & CRAFTS

Bajo El Sol Gallery & Art Bar ★★★   This is *the* place on the island to find a genuine St. John collectible; it's one of the best galleries in the Virgin Islands, period. A cooperative gallery founded by a group of St. John artists

---

The Art of Market Baskets

Basket making is so ingrained in island culture that it was actually taught in the public schools into the 1960s, and the St. John tradition of making market baskets out of cat's claw and hoop vine is particularly strong. Based in St. Croix, the Henry family handcrafts wonderful woven baskets inspired by those traditionally used by slaves on market days on the islands. Marketed as **Crucian Bayside Creations** (www.crucianbay sidecreations.com; ✆ **561/819-2122**), these Crucian market baskets are true works of art, designed in all sorts of remarkable patterns and colors, with handles often made of sanded-down driftwood. Crucian Bayside has no shop of its own, but you can currently find their baskets in **Bajo El Sol Gallery,** in St. John (see above); **Fish Face,** in Charlotte Amalie, St. Thomas (p. 121); and in two shops in Christiansted, St. Croix, **Crucian Gold** (p. 181) and **Eden South** (3 Company St.).

Colorful Caribbean landscapes by local artist Elaine Estern are displayed at Coconut Coast Studios.

in 1993, it carries a splendid collection of local art in a range of mediums, from paintings to glass and metal sculpture to jewelry, market baskets, and wood turning. Local artists include woodworker Avelino Samuel, whose fantastical swirling pieces have been exhibited in the Smithsonian's Renwick Gallery. Bajo El Sol is also a bookstore—and a rum bar! The inhouse cafe (with pastries) does a rum tour of the Caribbean diaspora ($25/person). Down a flute/shot and learn the history of each rum. It's open Monday to Saturday from 10am to 6pm. Mongoose Junction, Cruz Bay. www.facebook.com/bajoelsol gallery. ☏ **340/693-7070.**

Coconut Coast Studios ★

The seaside studio of artist Elaine Estern, who paints colorful Caribbean landscapes, seascapes, and beneath-the-seascapes, is a 5-minute walk past Gallows Bay Resort along the waterfront to Cruz Bay. Her shop sells original watercolors, prints, and giclee prints as well as gifty magnets, souvenirs, and notecards. 265 Tobacco Rd., Frank Bay. coconut coaststudios.com. ☏ **340/776-6944.**

Donald Schnell Studio ★★★

This is the working studio and gallery of Donald Schnell, who fashions stunning hand-crafted ceramics using island shells and seaglass: planters, wall sconces, hanging lamps, even fountains, many of them found in some of the toniest resorts and villas in the Caribbean.

His hand-formed tableware is often trimmed in what he calls "Caribbean magic" blue. Schnell and his wife moved to St. John in their 20s, inspired by the creative environment. The beautiful Amore building is ornamented in Caribbean coral and stone. The studio also sells the works of other artisans, including art glass and stained glass. The Amore Center, Cruz Bay. donaldschnell. com. ✆ **800/253-7107** or 340/776-6420.

FASHION & CLOTHING

Bamboula St. John ★★ Crammed with artisanal flavor, this "Caribbean lifestyle store" has been hawking flirty boho dresses, Haitian art, crafts, and homewares for many years. Look for locally carved and crafted boxes made from the world's hardest hardwood, lignum vitae, as well as colorful steel pan drums. Mongoose Junction, Cruz Bay. www.bamboulastjohn.com. ✆ **340/693-8699.**

Lulee ★★ This chic clothing shop has an airy Martha's Vineyard vibe, crammed with trendy brands like 7 for All Mankind and AG jeans, Cleobella dresses, Super Goop sunscreen, and delicate Gorjana jewelry—offering the kind of upscale beachy-boho looks found in chi-chi resort shops. Its "St. John Collection" includes jute totes and St. John–branded tees, hoodies, onesies . . . Mongoose Junction, Cruz Bay. lulee-st-john.myshopify.com. ✆ **340/693-8444.**

FOOD

St. John Spice ★ Located right next to the ferry dock and up a set of brick stairs, this gift shop has greatly expanded upon what was once a fairly exhaustive collection of Caribbean hot sauces with all manner of gifts, from tween-pleasing braided bracelets to touristy tchotchkes, straw hats, bath soaps and massage oils, books, hats, insect repellent . . . Wharfside Village, Cruz Bay. stjohnspice.com. ✆ **340/693-7046.**

JEWELRY

Bamboo ★★ The stunning custom-made jewelry here is all handcrafted on St. John. You'll not only find the famed Crucian hook bracelet in both sterling silver and gold, but nautical rings and charming Taino, donkey, and turtle charms. Wharfside Village, Cruz Bay. ✆ **340/776-0669.**

Caravan Gallery ★ If you're looking for quality affordable jewelry or a little something to remind you of St. John, check out this upstairs Mongoose Junction shop. It's the only place we found carrying a charm of the iconic St. John woven market basket. It also has tasteful petroglyph pendants and other jewelry with island motifs. Mongoose Junction www.caravangallery.com. ✆ **340/779-4566.**

ST. JOHN AFTER DARK

Bring a good book or two. When it comes to nightlife, St. John is no St. Thomas, and everybody here seems to want to keep it that way. Although you can hear live music most any night of the week at venues around the island, many people are content to have a leisurely dinner and call it a day.

Join the locals at the Tap Room at St. John Brewers, a microbrewery in Cruz Bay.

The **Tap Room ★** is the sunny brewpub of **microbrewery St. John Brewers** (stjohnbrewers.com; ✆ **340/715-7775**), the brainchild of a couple of University of Vermont grads. Located on the second floor of Mongoose Junction in Cruz Bay, the Tap Room already feels rooted, and when you visit you'll sit elbow-to-elbow with locals and visitors sampling from the drinking man's menu (burgers, salads, pizza, tacos) and swigging the brewpub's craft beers and homemade sodas. We very much like their Juicy Booty NEIPA. They also make hard ciders and seltzers. It's open daily 11am to 11pm.

The restaurants and bars at **Wharfside Village** (thewvhotel.com), right on Cruz Bay Beach, reopened in 2022 following a major revamp after the 2017 hurricanes and host lively crowds at four beautifully rebuilt waterfront restaurant/lounges, including **La Tapa** (p. 208). The two most party-hearty are the **Rum Hut** (rumhutstjohn.com; ✆ **340/775-5200**), with tables in the sand and a great little menu that includes tacos, sliders, and big salads; and the **Beach Bar** (beachbarstjohn.com; ✆ **340/777-4220**), a flag-draped open-air St. John landmark with live music, solid pub food, and spine-stiffening drinks. Also in Wharfside Village is the island's only casino, the elegantly compact **Parrot Club** (www.parrotclubvi.com; ✆ **340/715-2582**), which had its grand reopening in 2022 after a shellacking by Hurricane Maria in 2017. It offers slots, roulette, and blackjack along with serious cocktails (and sometimes live jazz). It's open daily 11am to midnight.

Just 150 yards from the ferry dock in Cruz Bay, island institution **Woody's Seafood Saloon** (www.woodysseafood.com; ✆ **340/779-4625**) has a happening happy hour scene from 3 to 6pm when drinks are dirt-cheap ($1 beers) and the crowd spills out onto the street. Adjacent to Woody's, St. John's one and only Irish pub, the **Quiet Mon** (p. 210), is set in a West Indian cottage with walls crammed with photos, memorabilia, and shamrock-themed tchotchkes. **Tap & Still** (www.tapandstill.com; ✆ **340/474-1902**), on Hill Street in Cruz Bay, is a favorite casual hang for watching sports and eating good-value burgers ($6–$8) and Korean-style wings ($5) that are much, much better than they need to be.

A couple of miles east of Cruz Bay along Centerline Road, **Shambles Island Bar & Grill** ★ (shamblesvi.com; ✆ **340/777-4015**) has a festive party atmosphere with live music most nights, cold drinks, and hot smoked brisket, pulled pork sandwiches, and fried-chicken hoagies. It's open Thursday to Tuesday noon to 9pm. Or turn left and head up uphill to the **Windmill Bar** ★★ (windmillbar.com; ✆ **340/244-6002**), on the historic Susannaberg sugar plantation, for sunset drinks and mountaintop vistas that simply don't quit. Named for the site's 1780 windmill, aka Neptune's Lookout, the Windmill Bar hosts a regular schedule of live music and Sunday afternoon bingo games (3–5pm) and also has disc golf on the premises. It serves lunch and dinner (burgers, tacos, a couple of hearty entrees) and is open 11am to 8pm daily (kitchen closes 7:30pm).

THE BRITISH VIRGIN ISLANDS

With its turquoise bays and tucked-away coves, once havens for pirates, the British Virgin Islands are among the world's loveliest cruising grounds. The "Sailing Capital of the Caribbean" attracts sailors and yachties aplenty, but the gorgeous white-sand beaches, soaring emerald peaks, and laidback geniality make this a sublime getaway for anyone and everyone.

The British Virgin Islands embrace 60-odd islands, some no more than spits of rock jutting out of the sea. Only four islands are of any significant size: Virgin Gorda, Tortola, Anegada, and Jost Van Dyke. Smaller islands and cays have quirky and colorful names, such as Fallen Jerusalem. Norman Island is said to have been the prototype for Robert Louis Stevenson's novel *Treasure Island.* On Dead Man's Bay, Blackbeard reputedly marooned 15 pirates and a bottle of rum.

These remote, craggy volcanic islands are just 15 minutes by air or 45 minutes by ferry from St. Thomas. Even though they are part of the same archipelago, the British Virgin Islands and the U.S. Virgin Islands have their differences. It's still a bit sleepy over in the B.V.I. Here the pace is gentle and development less frenetic; in some idyllic spots you can feel as far away from the rat race as you can get, while still enjoying fine food and drink and excellent company.

These islands also have a baked-in conservation and sustainability ethos. This is a place, after all, where an agrarian roots revival inspires local farmers to plant regenerative crops on terraced hillsides, where hurricane wreckage is cleverly repurposed as undersea "art reefs." Where else does a government purposely place tropical guppies in water cisterns to devour mosquito larvae?

Then there's the seclusion. The main island, Tortola, has hundreds of private villas nestled in hillsides, and most of the high-end resorts on Virgin Gorda are so isolated from one another you'll feel your hotel has the island to itself. On the even smaller, more remote islands like Guana Island, you *will* have the island to yourself (and your fellow guests), in rustically private hideaways that are the ultimate in laidback luxury. Barefoot minimalists on a budget can do rustic, too, without spending a fortune, at modest beachside inns

Island-hopping in the British Virgin Islands often means daysailing to a spit of land that's mostly white-sand beach surrounded by clear seas and coral reef.

on Anegada and Jost Van Dyke. You'll get all the seclusion you want, but you'll still probably end up knowing all the locals by week's end.

Forget casinos, splashy entertainment, TVs, and sometimes even air-conditioning: Who needs them when the balmy trade winds blow, the rum is flowing, and sunlight dances like diamonds on the water?

ESSENTIALS

Arriving

BY PLANE

For the first time since 2006, the B.V.I. has direct airlift between the American mainland and Tortola. **American Airlines** (www.aa.com; ✆ **800/433-7300**) began making direct daily flights between Tortola and Miami International Airport in summer 2023. Currently, these flights are limited, so most visitors arrive via the international airports in St. Thomas or San Juan, Puerto Rico, and then fly or ferry to the B.V.I. A handful of regional airlines offer service between Tortola or Virgin Gorda and islands like St. Croix and St. Maarten/ St. Martin. Your gateway to the B.V.I. will most likely be Tortola or Virgin Gorda.

The major airport serving the British Virgins, the **Terrence B. Lettsome Airport** (EIS; www.bviaacloud.com; ✆ **284/394-8000;** informally known as Beef Island Airport), is connected to Tortola by the one-lane Queen Elizabeth Bridge. **Seabourne Airlines/Silver Airways** (www.seaborneairlines.com; ✆ **866/359-8784,** or 340/773-6442 in the U.S.V.I.) offers regularly scheduled flights between Tortola and San Juan, St. Croix, St. Thomas, and St. Maarten. **Cape Air** (www.capeair.com; ✆ **800/227-3247** in the U.S. and U.S.V.I., or

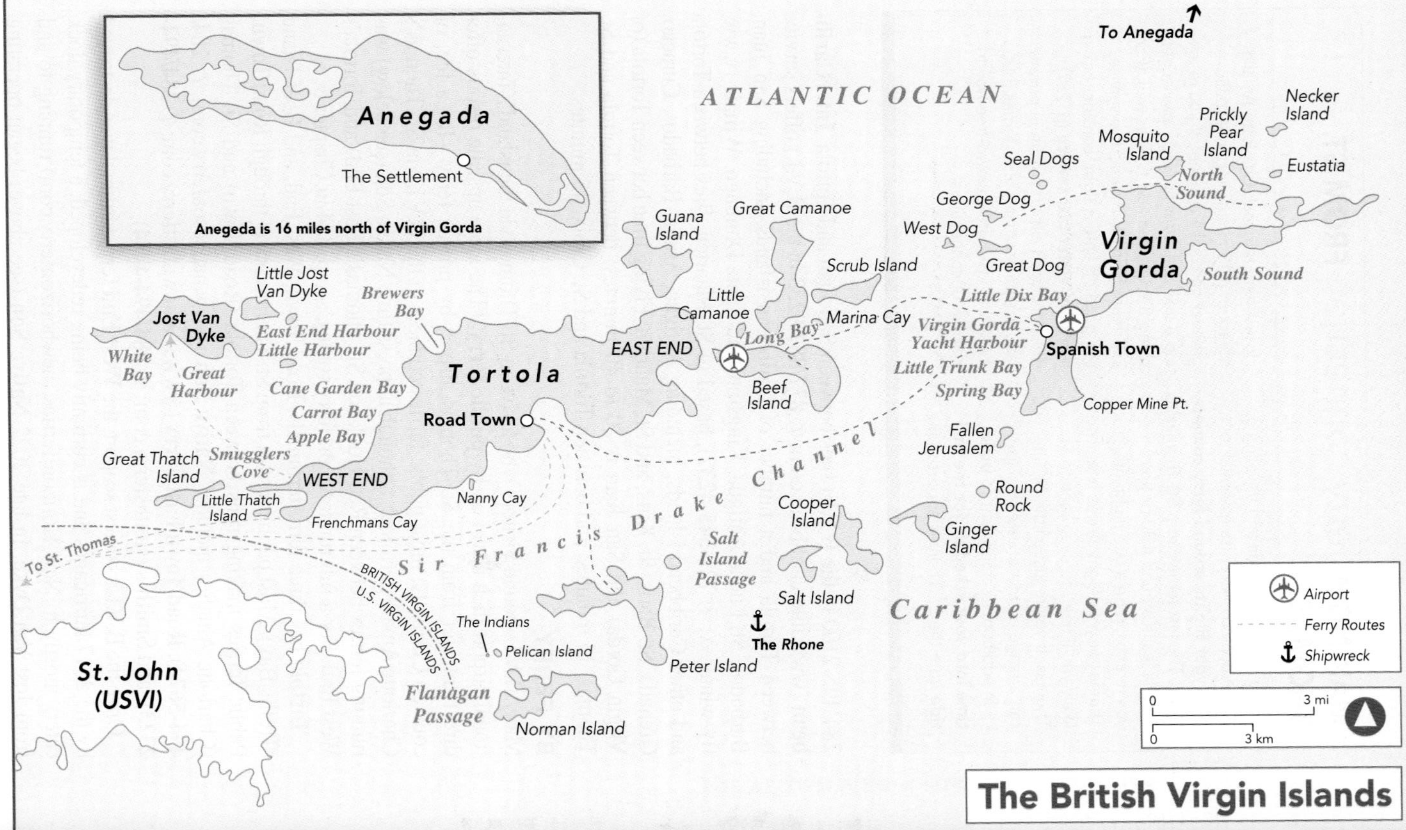
To Anegada
ATLANTIC OCEAN
Anegada
The Settlement
Anegeda is 16 miles north of Virgin Gorda
Necker Island
Prickly Pear Island
Mosquito Island
Eustatia
Seal Dogs
North Sound
George Dog
Virgin Gorda
West Dog
Great Dog
South Sound
Guana Island
Great Camanoe
Scrub Island
Little Camanoe
Little Dix Bay
Marina Cay
Virgin Gorda Yacht Harbour
Spanish Town
Long Bay
EAST END
Beef Island
Little Trunk Bay
Spring Bay
Copper Mine Pt.
Little Jost Van Dyke
Brewers Bay
Jost Van Dyke
East End Harbour
Little Harbour
White Bay
Great Harbour
Cane Garden Bay
Carrot Bay
Apple Bay
Tortola
Road Town
Great Thatch Island
Smugglers Cove
WEST END
Little Thatch Island
Nanny Cay
Frenchmans Cay
Fallen Jerusalem
Round Rock
Sir Francis Drake Channel
Cooper Island
Ginger Island
Salt Island Passage
Salt Island
To St. Thomas
BRITISH VIRGIN ISLANDS
U.S. VIRGIN ISLANDS
The Indians
Pelican Island
The Rhone
Peter Island
Caribbean Sea
St. John (USVI)
Flanagan Passage
Norman Island
Airport
Ferry Routes
Shipwreck
0
3 mi
0
3 km
The British Virgin Islands

MAKING A ferry connection FROM ST. THOMAS

Flying into St. Thomas and traveling on to the B.V.I. by ferry? It's essential to **plan your flights around ferry connections.** The last ferries from St. Thomas to Tortola leave around 4:30 or 5pm. If you're arriving on a late flight into St. Thomas or your flight arrives late, it's likely you'll need to overnight on St. Thomas. If you're just a little bit late, you can arrange a private water taxi (p. 237).

In addition, it's important to **build time into your schedule for the taxi ride** from the St. Thomas airport to the closest ferry terminal, Charlotte Amalie—it's about a 15-minute trip, but traffic gridlock can make it longer. If you're taking a taxi van, stops for other passengers along the way can add time as well. (For information on St. Thomas taxi service, see p. 68.) If time is tight, consider hiring a **private water-taxi service** (p. 237), which includes airport pickup in private taxis; it's pricier than public ferries, but it's also a hassle-free, crowd-free way to make your connections.

284/495-2100 in the B.V.I.) flies between San Juan and Tortola. **InterCaribbean** (www.intercaribbean.com; © 877/887-9233 in the B.V.I.) offers service between Tortola and a number of Caribbean islands, including San Juan, Barbados, St. Lucia, Antigua, Kingston, and Santo Domingo. **Winair** (www. fly-winair.sx; © 721-545-4237), based in St. Maarten, flies between Tortola and other Caribbean islands, including Antigua, Aruba, Barbados, Curacao, Grenada, St. Barts, St. Kitts, and St. Maarten. Flying time between Tortola (or Virgin Gorda) and San Juan is 30 to 40 minutes; between Tortola and St. Thomas, 15 minutes; and between Tortola and St. Croix, 45 minutes.

BY FERRY

Many B.V.I.–bound visitors who arrive in St. Thomas via the island's international airport then travel on by **public ferry.** (The more upscale resorts offer direct transfer from the St. Thomas airport by private ferry—for a fee, of course.) Currently, most public ferries connect to the B.V.I. via St. Thomas's Charlotte Amalie terminal, although at press time Native Son (see below) was running ferries between Red Hook (on St. Thomas's East End) and Tortola's West End. For a full rundown on ferry routes, see p. 314 in Chapter 8.

Tortola has three ferry terminals, Road Town, West End, and Beef Island (Trellis Bay). Most public ferries from St. Thomas travel through **Road Town.** Public ferries making runs between Tortola (Road Town) and St. Thomas (Charlotte Amalie) include: **Native Son** (www.nativesonferry.com; © 284/494-5674), **Road Town Fast Ferry** (www.roadtownfastferry.com; © 284/494-2323), and **Smith's** (smithsferry.com; © 284/494-4454).

Once the B.V.I.'s busiest seaport, the **West End** ferry terminal was destroyed by the 2017 hurricanes and is currently being redeveloped; a temporary dock caters mostly to New Horizon ferries (newhorizonferry.com) running to and from Jost Van Dyke. In late 2022 **Native Son** (see above) began operating between the West End terminal and St. Thomas's Red Hook terminal (one-way $60 adults, $50 children 3–11, $15 children 0–2), which could be convenient for those staying on Tortola's West End. It's a 60-minute trip.

The **Trellis Bay** terminal, which is right by Beef Island Airport on Tortola's East End, is handy for travelers flying into Tortola; it's served by a public ferry, **Speedy's Ferries** (www.bviferries.com; ☎ **284/495-7292**), which operates daily to Virgin Gorda (Spanish Town); round-trip fares are $30 adults ($20 children 5–11). Trellis Bay also handles water launches connecting guests to many Virgin Gorda and private island resorts.

BY WATER TAXI

Sometimes the only way to get to another island without losing a day of vacation is via **private water-taxi service.** It can be much more convenient and not that much more expensive—especially when your private water-taxi ride includes airport pickup. **Dolphin Water Taxi** (www.dolphinshuttle.com; ☎ **340/ 774-2628**) provides "full-service VIP Customs entry to the B.V.I.," which includes private taxi airport pickup from the St. Thomas airport to the Red Hook ferry terminal, with private boat transfers from there to Tortola ($189/person each way, plus international fees) or Spanish Town, Virgin Gorda ($238/person each way, plus international fees). Dolphin also offers water-taxi services throughout the Virgin Islands and day-trip charters to Jost Van Dyke ($199/person round-trip, plus international fees) and the Baths ($219/ person round-trip, plus international fees). A number of charter-boat outfitters also make water-taxi runs, including **SaltShaker Charters** (www.saltshaker bvi.com; ☎ **284/340-1400**) and **Bad Dog Fishing Charters** (baddogcharters. com; ☎ **284-496-9080**), which do one-way transfer trips in the B.V.I. and the U.S.V.I.

> **B.V.I. Public Ferries: Sample Travel Times**
>
> **St. Thomas** (Charlotte Amalie) to **Tortola** (Road Town): 50 min.
> **Tortola** (Road Town) to **Virgin Gorda** (Spanish Town): 25 min.
> **Tortola** (West End) to **Jost Van Dyke:** 20 min.
> **Tortola** (Road Town) to **Anegada:** 60 min.

Visitor Information

On island, the **British Virgin Islands Tourist Board** (www.bvitourism.com; ☎ **800/835-8530**) is located in downtown Road Town, Tortola, in the Akura Building (☎ **284/852-6020**). There's also a guest welcome booth in the airport. Its New York branch is at 1270 Broadway, Suite 705, New York, NY 10001 (☎ **212/6960400-3117**). In the United Kingdom, contact the **B.V.I. Tourist Board,** 15 Upper Grosvenor St., London W1K 7PJ (☎ **207/355-9585**).

Getting Around
BY FERRY

A number of ferry services offer regularly scheduled trips within the British Virgin Islands. Please keep in mind that ferries are slowly getting back up to

island-hopper DAY TRIPPING

If you'd like to island-hop, seeing as many of the different British Virgins as you can on your trip, your best bet is to base yourself in Tortola and take day trips from there. A number of public ferries (and airlines) offer regular trips from Tortola to the larger islands. **Speedy's** (www.bviferries.com) travels between Road Town and Spanish Town, Virgin Gorda. **New Horizon Ferry Service**

(© 284/495-9278) runs the 25-minute trip between Tortola and **Jost Van Dyke.** Spend the day at the beach and lunch at one of the local eateries, such as Foxy's, before returning to Tortola. **Road Town Fast Ferry** (www.roadtownfastferry.com) travels from Road Town to **Anegada** on Monday, Wednesday, and Friday. Once there, of course, you can have a taxi driver deliver you to the beach.

speed after the 2-year pandemic slowdowns and should only expand routes from here on in—and also keep in mind that schedules change, so make advance reservations and confirm times.

TORTOLA & VIRGIN GORDA   **Speedy's Ferries** (www.bviferries.com; © 284/495-7292) operates daily ferry service between Tortola (both Road Town and Trellis Bay) and Virgin Gorda (Spanish Town); round-trip fares are $30 adults ($20 children 5–11); group rates and frequent traveler passes available.

TORTOLA & ANEGADA   The **Anegada Express** (anegadaexpress.com; © 284/343-5343) is a seasonal private ferry (Nov–June/July) operating out of Trellis Bay that runs two round-trips a day every Sunday, Thursday, and Saturday between Tortola and Anegada. Fares are $50 round-trip ($35 one-way) adults, $40 round-trip ($25 one-way) children. **Road Town Fast Ferry** (www. roadtownfastferry.com; © 284/494-2323) also operates seasonal ferries between Road Town and Setting Point, Anegada (via Spanish Town), on Monday, Wednesday, and Friday (round-trip $55 adults, $35 children)

TORTOLA & JOST VAN DYKE   **New Horizon Ferry** (newhorizonferry. com; © 284/499-0952) makes daily runs between West End and Jost Van Dyke; round-trip fares are $30.

TORTOLA & NORMAN ISLAND   A **Norman Island ferry** takes passengers to **Pirate's Bight restaurant** on Norman Island (www.piratesbight. com; © 284/443-1305; daily 11am–9pm) three times daily from Hannah Bay Marina, Tortola (near Nanny Cay). It's no cost if you're eating lunch. Call for schedules.

NORTH SOUND, VIRGIN GORDA   The private resorts around Virgin Gorda's North Sound offer complimentary ferry service from Gun Creek, Virgin Gorda, to the resorts. Book through the resort.

BY CAR, BUS, OR TAXI

There are car-rental agencies on Tortola, Virgin Gorda, Anegada, and Jost Van Dyke. Numerous taxis also operate on these islands, as well as on some of the smaller ones; taxi rates are set by the government and posted on the B.V.I. tourism website and in the free *Welcome Guide* tourist publication distributed everywhere. Bus service is available on Tortola and Virgin Gorda only. See the "Getting Around" section for each island for further details.

TORTOLA

There's no better place to launch your own sailing adventure than in the bareboat capital of the world: Tortola, the biggest (19×5km/12×3 miles) and most populous of the British Virgin Islands. With something like eight marinas, it's the region's hub for a daily procession of bareboat and charter excursions cruising to scores of offshore cays and secluded coves. This is a sea dog's paradise.

Though it's the most populous island in the B.V.I. (24,000 people), Tortola still has a serene, small-town spirit. Seeing the island by water is a great way to appreciate its breathtaking beauty. Sailors and landlubbers alike unwind to the forested emerald peaks that swoop down to sparkling waters, the sunset panoramas, the electric blue bays. This big green island is balm for the soul.

Tortola was devastated by Hurricane Irma in 2017. The monstrous Category 5 storm destroyed coastal roads and the West End ferry terminal, lifted the roofs off schools and churches, and left citizens without power for months. Two years later, the island virtually shut down during the Covid-19 pandemic. Today, however, post-pandemic recovery has beach bars humming, restaurants re-opening, and island celebrations like the BVI Spring Regatta August Emancipation Festival back and bigger than ever, rousing the spirits of Tortolans and visitors alike.

Essentials

ARRIVING

BY PLANE   Tortola's **Terrence B. Lettsome International Airport** (aka **Beef Island Airport**) is the main airport for all of the British Virgin Islands. For information on flights into Tortola, see p. 234. Car-rental agencies **Avis** (www.avis.com; ✆ **284/340-5627**), **National** (www.nationalcar.com; ✆ **284/ 495-2626**), and **Enterprise** (www.enterprise.com; ✆ **284/495-2626**) have locations at the airport. Taxis and multi-passenger safari vans meet every

---

	Christmas Winds

The year-round weather in the British Virgin Islands is generally temperate, with few variations in temperature and winds usually out of the east. In late November and December, however, cold fronts in North America push cold air down from the north, bringing the so-called "Christmas winds" to the islands. While temperatures are minimally affected, Christmas winds can bring 25- to 30-knot blows to the islands for days at a time, making seas choppy and roiling placid bays that are generally calm for snorkeling. Christmas winds generally dissipate by January or early February.

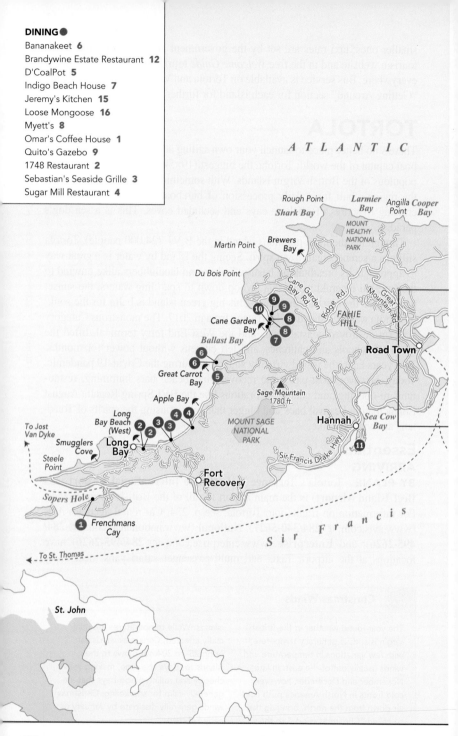

ATLANTIC

Rough Point

Larmier Bay

Angilla Point

Cooper Bay

Shark Bay

Rough Point

MOUNT HEALTHY NATIONAL PARK

Martin Point

Brewers Bay

Du Bois Point

Cane Garden Bay Rd

Ridge Rd.

Great Mountain Rd.

FAHIE HILL

Cane Garden Bay

Ballast Bay

Road Town

Great Carrot Bay

Sage Mountain 1780 ft.

Apple Bay

Long Bay Beach (West)

MOUNT SAGE NATIONAL PARK

Hannah

Sea Cow Bay

To Jost Van Dyke

Smugglers Cove

Long Bay

Steele Point

Sir Francis Drake Hwy.

Sopers Hole

Fort Recovery

To St. Thomas

Frenchmans Cay

S i r   F r a n c i s

St. John

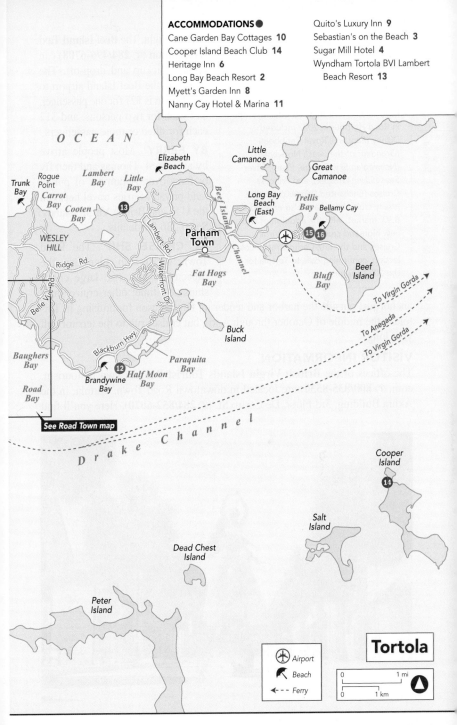

ACCOMMODATIONS ●
Cane Garden Bay Cottages **10**
Cooper Island Beach Club **14**
Heritage Inn **6**
Long Bay Beach Resort **2**
Myett's Garden Inn **8**
Nanny Cay Hotel & Marina **11**

Quito's Luxury Inn **9**
Sebastian's on the Beach **3**
Sugar Mill Hotel **4**
Wyndham Tortola BVI Lambert
   Beach Resort **13**

O C E A N

Trunk
Bay

Rogue
Point

Carrot
Bay

Lambert
Bay

Little
Bay

Elizabeth
Beach

Little
Camanoe

Great
Camanoe

Cooten
Bay

13

WESLEY
HILL

Ridge   Rd.

Lambert Rd.

Long Bay
Beach
(East)

Beef Island Channel

Trellis
Bay

Bellamy Cay

15 **16**

Parham
Town

Belle Vue Rd.

Waterfront Dr.

Fat Hogs
Bay

Bluff
Bay

Beef
Island

To Virgin Gorda

To Anegada

To Virgin Gorda

Baughers
Bay

Blackburn Hwy.

12

Brandywine
Bay

Half Moon
Bay

Paraquita
Bay

Buck
Island

Road
Bay

See Road Town map

D r a k e   C h a n n e l

Cooper
Island

14

Salt
Island

Dead Chest
Island

Peter
Island

⊕ Airport
⌐ Beach
←--- Ferry

Tortola

0   1 mi
0   1 km

Cruise News

The B.V.I. cruise industry expects a return to 100% capacity in the wake of the Covid-19 pandemic, B.V.I. officials have said. Cruise ships scheduling stops in Road Harbour in 2022 included Disney *(Fantasy)*; Royal Caribbean *(Grandeur of the Seas)*; Norwegian *(Norwegian Sky, Escape, Pearl)*; Silver Seas *(Silver Whisper)*; and Princess Cruises *(Enchanted Princess)*. Smaller luxury cruise lines have also entered the B.V.I. market, with the addition of two new high-end cruise brands, Virgin Cruises and the Ritz-Carlton Yacht Collection, confirming calls to Tortola for the 2023 season.

arriving flight. The **Beef Island Taxi Association** (✆ **284/496-6708**) can arrange pickup and drop-off. The fare from the Beef Island airport to Road Town is $27 for one passenger, $14 each for two persons, and $12 each for three or more passengers.

BY FERRY Most people arrive by air into St. Thomas and then fly or ferry over. A number of public (and private) ferries travel between the U.S. and British Virgin Islands. See p 236 for details.

BY CRUISE SHIP The Road Town cruise-ship pier has the capacity to host two large cruise ships at a time; other cruise ships anchor just outside the harbor and tender in. High season for cruising in Tortola is the middle of October through April, but cruises run to the territory all year long.

VISITOR INFORMATION

The offices of the **British Virgin Islands Tourist Board** (www.bvitourism. com; ✆ **800/835-8530**) are located in downtown Road Town, Tortola, in the Akura Building, 3rd Floor, De Castro St. (✆ **284/852-6020**). Here you'll find

Moko Jumbies and other island dancers greet cruise-ship visitors at Tortola Pier Park in Road Town.

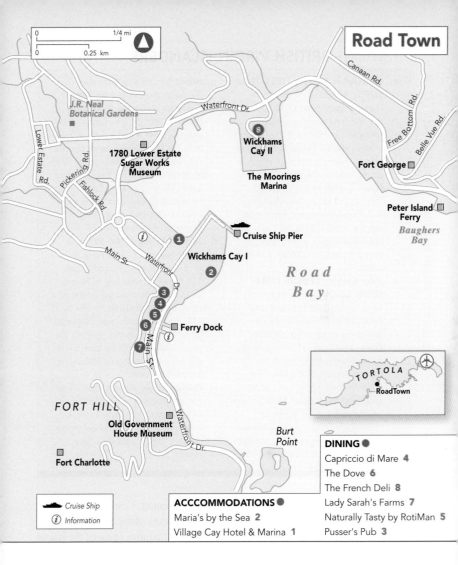

Road Town

0 — 1/4 mi
0 — 0.25 km

J.R. Neal Botanical Gardens

Canaan Rd.

Waterfront Dr.

Lower Estate Rd.

Pickering Rd.

Fishlock Rd.

Free Bottom Rd.

Belle Vue Rd.

1780 Lower Estate Sugar Works Museum

Wickhams Cay II

The Moorings Marina

Fort George

Peter Island Ferry

Baughers Bay

Main St.

Waterfront Dr.

Cruise Ship Pier

1

Wickhams Cay I

2

Road Bay

3
4
5
6

Ferry Dock

7

Main St.

TORTOLA

RoadTown

FORT HILL

Old Government House Museum

Waterfront Dr.

Burt Point

Fort Charlotte

Cruise Ship

Information

ACCCOMMODATIONS ●
Maria's by the Sea **2**
Village Cay Hotel & Marina **1**

DINING ●
Capriccio di Mare **4**
The Dove **6**
The French Deli **8**
Lady Sarah's Farms **7**
Naturally Tasty by RotiMan **5**
Pusser's Pub **3**

---

information about hotels, restaurants, tours, and more. Pick up a copy of the *Welcome Tourist Guide*, which has a useful map of the island.

ISLAND LAYOUT

Tortola is the largest of the British Virgin Islands. Halfway along its south coast, **Road Town** is the capital, a scattered sprawl of low-rise modern buildings wrapped around the harborfront and tucked into green hillsides. Wickham's Cay (sometimes called Wickham's Cay I) and Wickham's Cay II together enclose its Inner Harbour, which contains the cruise-ship pier and the Moorings complex area. Tortola's airport is on **Beef Island,** which is connected by the one-lane Queen Elizabeth II Bridge to the East End of Tortola; at the island's other end is the **West End** ferry terminal and several good

243

famous BRITISH VIRGIN ISLANDERS

o **Christopher Fleming (1851–1935):** Born in the East End of Tortola, Fleming spent most of his life at sea and may even have been a smuggler. In 1890, a B.V.I. Customs officer seized a native boat, and in protest, Fleming led a group of armed men to the commissioner's house. Danish soldiers from St. Thomas put down the rebellion, and Fleming was sentenced to 6 months in jail. Today, islanders look upon Fleming as a hero who protested poverty and unfair economic conditions.

o **John Coakley Lettsom (1744–1815):** Born into a Quaker family on Jost Van Dyke, Lettsom was educated in England and completed his medical education in Edinburgh, Scotland. Rising rapidly and brilliantly, he founded the Royal Human Society of England, the Royal Seabathing Hospital at Margate, and the London Medical Society. Regrettably, he is mainly remembered today for this famous but libelous doggerel: "I John Lettsom . . . Blisters, bleeds, and sweats 'em. If, after that, they please to die . . . I, John Lettsom."

o **Frederick Augustus Pickering (1835–1926):** Born in Tortola, Pickering became a civil service worker who, by 1884, had risen to become the first Black president of the British Virgin Islands. He held the post until 1887 and was the last man to be known as president, as the job title after his presidency was changed to commissioner.

o **John Pickering (1704–68):** Born into a fervent Quaker family in Anguilla, Pickering moved in the 1720s to Fat Hogs Bay in Tortola. In 1736, he became the leader of a congregation of Quakers, and by 1741 he was named first lieutenant governor of the island. Fearing the Virgin Islands would be drawn into war between Spain and Britain, he resigned his post because of his Quaker beliefs. Apparently, he was an "enlightened" plantation owner, as hundreds of enslaved people island-wide mourned his death—or perhaps they feared their new master.

resorts. Tortola's best beaches lie along its **north coast.** Connecting them all is the **Sir Francis Drake Highway,** the coastal route along the south coast; the other main road, **Ridge Road,** follows the mountainous spine of the island along a route that once linked the island's many plantations.

GETTING AROUND

The island is fairly small, so driving distances aren't long. But driving the mountainous Tortola interior is not for the faint of heart, with steep and twisting roads curling up and around blind corners. The key is to drive slow and enjoy the views. Ease-of-traffic-flow projects in Road Town have helped free up rush-hour bottlenecks, but Road Town can get busy during cruise-ship arrival and departure times (around 8am and 4pm), when scores of safari vans pick up or drop off cruise-ship passengers around the pier at Wickham's Cay.

BY TAXI We highly recommend **Hartley "Bozo" Frett** as both taxi driver and entertaining tour guide (*C* **284/543-1366**). He has a big safari van and really knows how to maneuver Tortola's mountain roads. For taxis from the airport at Beef Island, dial the **Beef Island Taxi Association** at ☏ **284/496-6708** (Delvin Green), ☏ **284/547-7352** (Ernest Jacob), or ☏ **284/499-1542** (Alnando Fahie). Taxi fares are standardized throughout the B.V.I. A typical fare from the Tortola airport to Village Cay in the Moorings is $27 for one person ($14 each for two, $12 each for three or more). Individual rates from Nanny Cay to Soper's Hole on the West End are $20.

TAXI TOURS   A 1-hour private tour runs about $55 for one to two people ($70 for groups of three; $85 for groups of four). A 2-hour tour is $110 for one to two people ($130 for three people, $150 for four). Taxi driver Bozo Frett (see above) will take a maximum of 16 passengers on 2-hour tours and requires at least 10 passengers aboard to charge $20 per person. Tours can be customized, but a sample 2-hour tour might take in Bellevue Mountain, Manchester, and the murals at Fahie Hill, with a stop at Long Bay or Stoutt's Lookout Bar and a longer stop at Cane Garden Bay. For taxi tours, contact **Hartley Frett** (☏ **284/543-1366**), the **Virgin Gorda Tours Association** (☏ **284/495-5253** or 284-541-0681), or **Virgin Gorda Transport** (Speedy's; ☏ **284/341-7145,** 284/340-5240, and 284/495-5240).

BY RENTAL CAR   Ask your hotel concierge to recommend a local rental-car agency; many resorts have relationships with rental franchises that will deliver cars right to your hotel. Rentals cost from $43 a day and up for compact and full-size cars to $63 a day and up for SUVs, minivans, and 4x4s.

Local rentals include **Itgo Car Rentals** (www.itgobvi.com; ☏ **284/494-5150**), located at the Mill Mall, Wickham's Cay I, Road Town. **Denzil Clyne Jeep & Car Rentals** (☏ **284/545-4900**) offers rentals on Tortola's West End. **Avis** (www.avis.com; ☏ **284/494-2193**) maintains offices at Wickham's Cay 1 in Road Town and at the airport; **National** (www.nationalcar.com; ☏ **284/494-3197**) and **Enterprise** (www.enterprise.com; ☏ **284/495-2626**) also have airport locations.

Car rental companies will usually offer free hotel pickup. All require a valid driver's license, and renters must be over 25 years of age. Because of the volume of tourism to Tortola, you should always reserve a car in advance, especially in winter.

Remember: Drive on the left! Roads are pretty well paved, but they're often narrow, winding, and poorly lit, and they have few, if any, lines but plenty of speed bumps. Driving at night can be tricky. It's a good idea to take a taxi to that difficult-to-find beach, restaurant, or bar.

[Fast FACTS] TORTOLA

ATMs/Banks   The major B.V.I. banks are **Scotiabank** (www.scotiabank.com), **FirstBank** (www.firstbankvi. com), **First Caribbean** (www.cibcfcib.com), and **Banco Popular** (www.banco popular.com/vi). ATMs are less prevalent in the British Virgin Islands than in the U.S. Virgin Islands; all the aforementioned banks have ATMs at Wickham Cay I in Road Town. There's a First Caribbean ATM at Myett's beach bar in Cane Garden Bay, and Nanny Cay Marina has a FirstBank ATM. Most smaller islands have no ATMs, so if you're planning a visit, visit an ATM on Tortola to cash up first. Each machine charges around $2 to $3 for a transaction fee.

Bookstores The best bookstore is the **National Educational Services Bookstore,** Wickham's Cay I, in Road Town (☏ **284/494-3921**).

Business Hours Most offices are open Monday-Friday 9am-5pm. Government offices are open Monday-Friday 8:30am-4:30pm. Shops are generally open Monday-Friday 9am-5pm and Saturday 9am-1pm.

Dentists For dental emergencies, contact **Crown Dental** (☏ **284/494-2770**) or **Premier Dental** (☏ **284/494-8062**).

Drugstores Medicure Pharmacy is in the Hodge Building, near Road Town Roundabout, Road Town (☏ **284/494-6189**).

Emergencies Call ☏ **999.** If you have a medical emergency, call **Peebles Hospital,** Porter Road, Road Town (☏ **284/494-3497**). Your hotel can also put you in touch with local medical staff.

Hospitals/Clinics Peebles Hospital, Porter Road, Road Town (☏ **284/494-3497**), has X-ray and laboratory facilities. The **B&F Medical Complex,** Mill Mall, Wickham's Cay I, Road Town (www.facebook.com/bandf-medical) is a public day clinic that accepts walk-ins. The **Eureka Medical Centre** (www.eurekamedicalclinic. com), Geneva Place, Road Town, is a privately run urgent-care facility with both in-house doctors and visiting specialists on call; call for an appointment.

Internet Access If you can't connect at your hotel, try **Serendipity Bookshop & Internet Cafe,** Main St., Road Town (☏ **284/494-5865**); the **Pub,** Waterfront Dr., Road Town (☏ **284/494-2608**); or **Trellis Bay Cybercafe,** Trellis Bay (☏ **284/495-2447**).

Newspapers There are two weekly newspapers, the *BVI Beacon* (www.bvibeacon. com), published on Thursday, and *Island Sun* (www. islandsun.com), published every Friday. Both are good sources of information on local entertainment. You can find these in most supermarkets and shops.

Police The main police headquarters is on Waterfront Drive near the ferry dock on Sir Olva Georges Plaza (☏ **284/494-2945**).

Post Office The main post office on Tortola is in Road Town (☏ **284/468-3701,** ext. 5160) and is open Monday-Friday 8:30am-4:30pm. The beautiful collectible B.V.I. stamps are sold here.

Safety The British Virgin Islands in general are quite safe, with a very low crime rate that many attribute to the illegality of owning guns. Minor robberies and muggings occur late at night outside bars in Road Town, especially in poorly lit areas around Wickham's Cay I and along Waterfront Drive. But outside of Road Town, Tortola is a very safe place.

Taxes The British Virgin Islands has no sales tax. It charges a departure tax of $20 per person whether you're leaving by boat or plane. Most hotels add a service charge of around 10%; a 10% hotel accommodation tax is also tacked onto hotel bills. Many restaurants include an automatic 15% service charge.

Telephone All island phone numbers have 7 digits. To call the British Virgins from the U.S., dial 1, the area code 284, and the number; from the U.K. dial 011-44, then the number. To call the U.S. from the B.V.I., just dial 1 plus the area code and the number; to call the U.K. from the B.V.I., dial 011-44, then the number.

Toilets You'll find public toilets in restaurants, beach bars, at the ferry terminals, and at the airport.

Where to Stay on Tortola

Tortola has few hotel-style lodgings. In fact, outside of villas, its accommodation choices are fairly stark. In addition to one or two topnotch boutique resorts, you have a sprinkling of modest marina hotels, informal guesthouses, and basic beach lodgings. None are as high-end luxe as the choices on Virgin Gorda—and many of the island's repeat visitors seem to like that just fine. Remember that most of Tortola's best beaches are on the north/northwestern shore, so guests staying elsewhere (at Road Town, for example) will have to drive or take a taxi to reach them. *Note:* All rates given within this chapter are subject to a 10% government tax and a 10% service charge. Rates are usually discounted significantly in summer.

VILLA RENTALS

Most visitors rent villas for their Tortola stays, often by the week. Here are some recommended villa management companies for Tortola and beyond; you can also rent villas in Tortola through the popular international owner-rental sites, **VRBO.com** and **Airbnb.com**.

BVI Sotheby's (www.bvisothebysrealty.com; ✆ **284/494-5700**), a locally operated branch of international real estate agency Sotheby's, offers vacation villas all over Tortola (as well as Virgin Gorda and Scrub Island), including Long Bay, Beef Island, Little Bay, Belmont Estate, and Smuggler's Bay.

Coldwell Banker/BVI Villa Rental (www.bvivillarental.com; ✆ **284/495-3000**) is another locally operated branch of an international conglomerate, representing properties in Tortola, Virgin Gorda, and Scrub Island. It can arrange provisioning, spa and concierge services, private chefs, and car and boat rentals.

Most visitors rent villas for their stay in Tortola, like this stunner near Trunk Bay, offered by Coldwell Banker/BVI Villa Rental.

Smith's Gore (smithsgore.com; ✆ 284/494-2446), a bespoke B.V.I. real estate agency that has been in business since 1965, has spectacular villas to rent in both Tortola and Virgin Gorda in a balanced range of prices.

Villas of Tortola (villasoftortola.com; ✆ 284/542-7872) has an excellent inventory of Tortola properties in Cane Garden Bay, Apple Bay, Long Bay, the West End, and Brewers Bay in a wide range of prices.

IN & AROUND ROAD TOWN

Tortola has a general paucity of hotels and resorts, but for those business folk, yachties, and others who need to be near the center of Tortola activity, Road Town has a few basic (and basically unexciting) lodging choices.

Moderate

Maria's by the Sea ★ This 38-room family-owned inn in central Road Town is a favorite of folks doing business in Tortola; it's close to the ferry and has little balconies that open right onto the harbor. Rooms are comfortable, if blandly furnished. An exception might be the enormous premium rooms, out-fitted in dark wood furniture, quality bedding, and butter-yellow walls—but at

---

COOPER ISLAND: eco-boutique RETREAT

On the northwest corner of Cooper Island, a 30-minute boat ride from Tortola, the **Cooper Island Beach Club ★★** (cooperislandbeachclub.com; ✆ **800/542-4624** or 284/343-4949) opens onto Manchioneel Bay in a splendid setting of coconut palms. It's popular with divers—many of the Caribbean's most celebrated dive sites, including shipwreck-rich Wreck Alley, are easily accessible—and snorkelers, who come to paddle around in the waters at the south end of Manchioneel Bay. It's a favorite of visiting yachties as well, who stop over to wine and dine in the resort's **beachfront restaurant** and **rum bar,** have a cup of joe in the artisanal coffee shop, or sample Cooper Island's own homemade microbrews. **Sail Caribbean Divers** (www.sailcaribbeandivers.com) is on-site from 8:30am to 4pm to arrange dive and snorkel trips and watersports rentals.

This barefoot retreat has eight good-looking rooms (each with a private balcony) with recycled teak furniture and an emphasis on simple, self-sufficient rusticity. To that end, Cooper Island is a local leader in green initiatives: It has no roads, no TVs, no air-conditioning. Seventy percent of the island's energy comes from solar power. A cistern under each room collects fresh rainwater, which is heated by solar power. All toilets are flushed with seawater. The fryer oil used in the kitchen is recycled as bio-diesel fuel. Bar stools and lounge furniture are made from old fishing boats.

Prices range from $385 ($325 off-season) per night, for a double room with continental breakfast and boat transfers included, to a full-board 3-night package (including boat transfers, all meals, and watersports equipment rentals) for $1,840 (off-season $1,690). An extra person is charged $115–$215 per night, depending on age.

The resort doesn't operate a regular ferry service, but several (free of charge) boat trips are made each week to and from Hodges Creek Marina in Maya Cove on Tortola's East End or from the Joma Marina in Port Purcell in Road Town. Otherwise, you'll have to pay for a private charter to the island. Contact the resort for details.

night you may be too busy inhaling the sea breezes from your balcony and admiring the harbor lights to care. Sample fine Caribbean cuisine at Maria's on-site restaurant, open for breakfast, lunch, and dinner on an alfresco patio overlooking Sir Frances Drake Channel.

Road Town. www.mariasbythesea.com. ✆ **284/852-6600.** 38 units. $130–$230 double; $210–$250 suite. Extra person $40/night. **Amenities:** Restaurant; bar; fitness room; outdoor pool; free Wi-Fi.

Nanny Cay Marina and Hotel ★ The heart and soul of this complex just west of Road Town is the 310-slip marina, headquarters to at least three yacht-chartering companies and permanent home to many fishing and pleasure boats. Rooms in the hotel have all been refreshed. Request one of the spacious rooms in the newer Seaview Wing, which opened in 2021, each with private balconies and marina and sea views. The restaurant, **Peglegs 2.0 on the Beach,** is a reliable choice for standards like steak and grilled fish. **Omar's,** the Soper's Hole coffee shop, has a location here.

Nanny Cay. nannycay.com. ✆ **284/494-2512.** 52 units. $155–$330 double; $450–$900 villa; $300–$420 1-bedroom apt. **Amenities:** Restaurant; bar; coffee shop; babysitting; pool; watersports equipment/rentals; free Wi-Fi.

Village Cay Hotel & Marina ★ This small hotel overlooks the bustling 106-slip Village Cay Marina, and that's often reason enough for many people sailing through to stay here. Another is price: The one- and two-bedroom suites are good value, each outfitted with gleaming wood-plank floors and colorful tropical linens; bathrooms are on the small side (some say cramped). Request a room with a patio overlooking the harbor—that's good value plus. The hotel has a nice big pool as well as an on-site restaurant that serves burgers, steaks, fish, and pizzas. The shops of Wickham's Cay I and ferry service to other islands are a 5-minute walk away.

www.villagecaybvi.com. ✆ **284/494-2771.** 23 units. $185–$350 double. Children 11 and under stay free in parent's room. **Amenities:** Restaurant; bar; outdoor pool; room service; watersports equipment/rentals; free Wi-Fi.

WEST END & NORTH SHORE

The island's most popular beach, **Cane Garden Bay,** has a few simple lodgings, often a modest (and modestly priced) assemblage of rooms above Cane Garden's popular beach bars—which means the music below may well rock you into the night (although in these post-pandemic days, the island's beach bars are closing at more reasonable hours). For a decent if frills-free place to hang your hat on Cane Garden Bay, consider the following. The **Cane Garden Bay Cottages ★** (www.virginislandsholiday.com; ✆ **780/728-5934;** double $235–$260 winter, $160–$190 summer) are hard to beat for excellent value. Set in a coconut grove, each of the four pleasant cottages is full of vibrant tropical color, with tile floors, patios, screened-in dining, and pitched ceilings. Local musician Quito Rymer's various bars and lodgings have come and gone with the hurricanes; the current model, **Quito's Luxury Inn** (quitosbvi.com/quito-inn-hotel; ✆ **284/495-4837**), sits behind his expanded bar and restaurant, **Quito's Gazebo** (p. 258), with 21 units ($290–$345 double, $464–$645 suite, $605–$826 Cool Water Suite). Just west, the completely renovated **Myett's Garden Inn** ★ (www.facebook.com/MyettsBVI; *C* **284/495-9649;** $175–$325 double) has four suites set in the gardens of its centrally located beachfront restaurant and bar. Three suites have two double beds, and one has a king bed.

Expensive

Long Bay Beach Resort ★★   A favorite of travelers since the 1960s, this two-story resort scaled down in late 2013 from 156 units to a boutique-svelte 42 rooms. It has one of the nicest beachfront locales on Tortola, a 1½-mile-long stretch of sandy North Shore beach overlooking Long Bay. Stylish rooms are more beachy minimalist than swanky, each furnished in an off-white palette with sand-colored wood floors; Long Bay beach is spitting distance from your private patio or terrace. All the rooms, suites, and cabanas have ocean views. Twelve suites have full kitchens and big two-person tubs; all other rooms have kitchenettes. Beachfront deluxe rooms have big showers with seats and high wood-beamed ceilings. Spacious and spiffily renovated hillside suites give you a panoramic perspective of Long Bay—and with these views it's easy to see why Tortolans love their mountainside aeries. When the surf is calm (and it can kick up in winter), try snorkeling right off the beach

With its private patios and rustic, beachy decor, the Long Bay Beach Resort makes the most of its North Shore location.

on the reef to the left, but you're also just a stroll from Smuggler's Beach. A brand-new swimming pool, with a swim-up bar, was scheduled for completion in early 2023. The main restaurant, **1748** (p. 257), along with the main lobby and bar, are set in the ruins of an 18th-century sugar mill. Right on the beach, **Johnny's Beach Bar** is thatch-roofed and open-air—where you'll be sitting pretty for a sunset tipple.

Long Bay. www.longbay.com. © **284/345-3773.** 42 units. $389–$489 double; $480–$689 suite. Children 11 and under stay free in parent's room. **Amenities:** Restaurant; 2 bars; babysitting; outdoor pool; spa treatments; 2 tennis courts; limited watersports; free Wi-Fi.

The Sugar Mill Hotel ★★　Historic ruins, fine dining, and intimate accommodations make this small boutique inn, on the site of a 300-year-old sugar mill, a singularly atmospheric place to stay. Built onto a sloping hillside and nestled in flowering tropical foliage and big fruit trees, the Sugar Mill has a natural serenity. It's set across a two-lane road from the beach at Apple Bay, where big-beaked pelicans plunge into the sea hunting for silver bonito. The contemporary accommodations are in a "seaside village" of eight different buildings, and they vary in size and style, from colonial to modern tropical. But all have balconies and good beds and linens. The tight quarters of the pool suites (with one king bed and a sleeper couch) are balanced by nice terraces, big stone outdoor showers, and the evening lullaby of tree frogs. In fact, we turned off the A/C and slept like babies to the music of bird (and frog) song and hillside breezes. For poshing out, try the luxury cottage, the deluxe villa, or the Plantation House suites—the latter have two 1,100-square-foot bedroom suites, a spacious porch, and charming West Indian architectural flourishes, like wood-beamed ceilings and gingerbread trim. Be sure to reserve a night at the acclaimed **Sugar Mill Restaurant** (p. 257), in the old rum distillery. Breakfast, lunch, and brunch are served on the beach at **Tramonti,** a casual Mediterranean spot with a menu of pastas, burgers, and house-made flame-cooked pizza.

Apple Bay. www.sugarmillhotel.com. © **284/344-612.** 24 units. $349–$449 double; $449 and up suites and cottages. Children 11 and over only. Rates include breakfast. All-inclusive rates available. Closed Aug–Sept. **Amenities:** 2 restaurants; 2 bars; babysitting; concierge; outdoor pool; free Wi-Fi.

Moderate

Heritage Inn ★　Locals smartly book a room here to avoid driving the spiraling roads home after dinner at the inn's on-site restaurant, **Bananakeet** (p. 255), one of the best restaurants on the island and reason enough to visit. The frills-free furnishings in this little seven-room inn are clean if motel-basic, but step onto your balcony and a world of panoramic views is laid out before you. Perched on top of Windy Hill, rooms command vistas out over three shimmering bays, including Carrot, Apple, and Long bays, and a dozen islands and cays, like Jost Van Dyke, Great Tobago, and Green Cay. Each of the (very modest) rooms (two 2-bedroom, five 1-bedroom) comes with a full

A good value close to Tortola's airport, the Wyndham Lambert Beach resort has the biggest freshwater pool in the B.V.I.

kitchen—which, if you're smart, you'll only need for breakfast and lunch; otherwise, you'll want to reserve a sunset-viewing spot at Bananakeet. The 2-bedroom units have terraces that stretch the length of your room.

Windy Hill. www.heritageinn.vg. (C) **284/499-1300.** 7 units. $150–$380 double. **Amenities:** Restaurant; bar; outdoor pool; free Wi-Fi.

Sebastian's on the Beach ★

This good-value hotel is a happening spot, with live music in the beach bar, a popular restaurant, and surfers riding Apple Bay waves. It's located on the North Shore, about a 15-minute drive from Road Town. The rooms are housed in three buildings, with only one, a two-story, right on the beach. All are done in a sunny tropical motif with tile floors; the most sought-after are the light and airy beachfront rooms, some mere steps from the surf, others with views from second-floor balconies. The rear accommodations ("tropical yard" rooms) feel like wee country cottages, with butter-yellow wainscotting and beamed ceilings, but lack sea views—but, really, nothing is farther than a short crawl to the beach. **Sebastian's Seaside Grille** (p. 257) overlooks the bay and has a solid menu of island and Continental favorites. Book your stay direct for better deals. The beach is one of the island's best surfing spots, and Sebastian's has surfboard rentals.

Little Apple Bay. sebastiansbvi.com. (C) **284/544-4212.** 39 units. $155–$288 double; $175–$298 suite. Children 12 and under stay free in parent's room. **Amenities:** Restaurant; bar; watersports; free Wi-Fi.

Wyndham Tortola BVI Lambert Beach Resort ★★

This is a real find and a bright spot on an island with fairly abysmal hotel choices. Just 4 miles from the airport and the Trellis Bay ferries, Lambert Beach is a wonderful stopover for late arrivals or early departures and a peaceful spot to use as a base while you're visiting Tortola. It's a 14.4-acre, self-contained property buffered by green hills and approached from a road that coils down to the quarter-mile stretch of glittering Lambert Bay. This good-value resort punches up when it comes to style and layout, drawing people in with the biggest freshwater pool in the B.V.I. and a lovely beachside restaurant and bar, the **Turtle ★**, where you can sip a cold drink with your feet in the sand. The smartly updated rooms are not huge, but all have patios and handsome natural-wood furnishings; some overlook the pool and others face the beachfront (partially obscured by greenery). The resort became a branded Wyndham property in 2018–19 and is deftly managed. Two villas on the hill are also in the rental mix. The half-kilometer beach is serene and utterly beautiful, but a channel running through the bay can make for rough currents. No day passes for now.

East End. www.wyndhamhotels.com. ✆ **284/495-1269.** 50 units. $150–$265 double; $250–$440 suite. **Amenities:** Restaurant; bar; swim-up bar/cafe; clubhouse; fitness room/spa; outdoor pool; free Wi-Fi.

Where to Eat on Tortola

The French Deli ★★ (www.frenchdelibvi.com; ✆ **284/494-2195**), at the Water Edge Building in Wickham Cay 1 (next to the Moorings Marina) in Road Town, is a provisioning gold mine, offering charcuteries, cheeses,

For those stocking up a boat or villa kitchen, the gourmet prepared foods at the French Deli are a godsend.

breads, wine, chocolates, and all sorts of French and European gourmet prepared foods (including plats du jour and hearty soups).

ROAD TOWN
Expensive
The Dove ★★★ CONTEMPORARY INTERNATIONAL   In a vintage West Indian cottage in Road Town, the Dove has its flirty, creative way with haute cuisine, with an eye to seasonality and exceptional ingredients. The small, elegant dining room has a pitched and beamed ceiling and checkerboard wood floors. You might start with the Dove's version of gravlax, cured "BVI gin and tonic" salmon, or the beetroot gnocchi. Entrees include a baked salmon with a furikake crust and an East Indian–style chicken Kiev atop a butternut squash *saag aloo*. The Dove has its own version of casual Fridays with a pub special like bangers and mash or smoked snapper fishcakes ($25). The Dove's gorgeous upstairs bar, the **Dragonfly Lounge,** specializes in herb-infused craft cocktails and serves lunch 3 days a week (poke, rice bowls, fish & chips, steak frites)—sit on the second-floor terrace and watch the harbor action.

67 Main St., across from the Road Town ferry dock. www.thedovebvi.com. © **284/494-0313.** Reservations recommended. Entrees $28–$45 dinner; $12–$32 lunch. Wed–Fri noon–3pm and 5–10pm; Sat 5–10pm.

Moderate
Capriccio di Mare ★★ ITALIAN   Right on Waterfront Drive across from the ferry dock, this casual cafe serves spot-on Italian and terrific pizzas at good prices in a sea of Caribbean eateries. Under new ownership since 2018 (and renovated after Hurricane Irma's ravages in 2017), Capriccio di Mare serves a greatest-hits pasta lineup of Italian standards—carbonara, pesto, amatriciana—but does them just right. Convenience to the ferry docks doesn't hurt. The sunny covered courtyard (with a retractable roof) has an Italian farmhouse feel, with a tiled floor, strung lights, and lots of greenery.

196 Waterfront Dr. capricciobvi.com. © **284/494-5369.** Entrees $25–$30; pastas $12–$25; pizza $10–$20. Mon–Sat 11:30am–9pm.

Lady Sarah's Farms ★★ CARIBBEAN/HEALTHY   What was a little tea shop is now a Caribbean-locavore bistro and farm market. It's a favorite lunch and brunch spot, in a charming garden setting in central Road Town, and dishes come to the table full of color and snap. Lady Sarah's grouper tacos are a case in point: golden fried island fish topped with starfruit salsa and locally grown microgreens. Lunch or brunch soups might be cream of pumpkin soup or a spicy seafood chowder. Pairings are inspired: Curried chickpeas are stuffed into hot fresh roti, and a Bahamian steamed pudding known as guava duff becomes the stuff of pancakes, served with guava butter. Fresh-squeezed juices include lemonade in lavender and beetroot flavors. Finish with Lady Sarah's mango cheesecake.

60 Main St. www.ladysarahsfarms.com. © **284/443-8011.** Entrees $7.95–$22. Mon–Fri 8am–3pm; Sat 10am–3pm.

Naturally Tasty by RotiMan ★★

ROTI/CARIBBEAN   Directly across from the ferry terminal on the Road Town waterfront, this little white-washed building is the place to come for state-of-the-art roti. If you don't know roti, it's an East Indian transplant by way of Trinidad: a soft tortilla-like flatbread folded and filled with curry sauce and vegetables, fish, chicken, or meat. RotiMan makes a truly fantastic shrimp roti—and be sure to sample the lobster roti in season. Have yours with a little hot pepper or mango sauce. RotiMan also makes interesting hand-crafted pizzas—vegan pizzas with a spelt-and-sesame crust and organic nut cheese, or pizzas with fruit- or vegetable-infused crusts—and voluptuous fresh salads. Big bonus: RotiMan squeezes fresh fruit juices every day. Get yours to go for the ferry ride or dine at a scattering of tables outside.

Right by the Road Town ferry, Naturally Tasty by RotiMan puts a delicious Trinidadian spin on East Indian roti.

Waterfront Dr. www.facebook.com/naturallytastybyrotiman. ℂ **284/544-1071.** Roti $10–$25 (seasonal lobster $30). Daily 6:30am–6:30pm.

Pusser's Pub ★ CARIBBEAN/ENGLISH   Yes, this is Tortola's original Pusser's, on the waterfront across from the ferry dock in Road Town. The storied pub still serves a few British standards like shepherd's pie and fish & chips, but Caribbean influences have seeped in and the menu is now awash in conch, jerk chicken and pork, and grilled local fish. The darkly atmospheric pub feels authentically colonial; it's a better spot for dining than the pub's charmless outdoor tables facing Waterfront Drive. In back is a big store selling Pusser's nautically themed clothing and tchotchkes. Fill your Pusser's Navy mug with Pusser's Rum—the classic "single malt of rum" favored by the British Royal Navy since the mid-1600s.

Waterfront Dr. and Main St. pussers.com. ℂ **284/494-3897.** Reservations recommended. Sandwiches $16–$22; bowls $16–$22. Daily 11am–10pm.

WEST END & NORTH SHORE
Expensive

Bananakeet ★★★ CARIBBEAN FUSION   With a warm and friendly staff, a creative menu, and views to kill for, this poolside open-air restaurant is a winner high above the North Shore on Windy Hill. The not-so-good news: It's located in the crook of a steep corkscrew road and the parking lot is small. The good news: Any taxi driver can get you there and back. Sunset on the

groceries, markets & more:
PROVISIONING RESOURCES ON TORTOLA

Tortola is a prime provisioning stop for boaters, but many people who rent houses, villas, condos, and hotel rooms with full kitchens also need to stock their pantries. Even if you're staying in a resort without self-catering facilities, it's always good to know where to buy snacks, drinks, and prepared foods.

o **Gourmet Deli: The French Deli,** at Wickham Cay II in Road Town (p. 253), sells prepared foods, charcuteries, cheeses, breads, liquors, and sweets and delivers to house and boat.

o **Groceries:** Shop in the store or provision online (with delivery) with **RiteWay** (www.rtwbvi.com; *C* **284/437-1188**), the B.V.I.'s biggest grocery store chain, with seven Tortola locations, including its flagship store in Pasea on Wickham's Cay II (with a Cash & Carry next door for bulk purchases). **Bobby's Marketplace** (www.bobbysmarketplace.com; *C* **284/494-2189**), Wickham's Cay I, Road Town, also delivers groceries straight to the ferry docks, marinas, and boat charters. The West End has **Riteway Soper's Hole** (*C* **284/340-2263**) at Soper's Hole Marina.

o **Fresh Seafood:** Buy fresh fish, Caribbean lobster, and conch at the **BVI Fishing Complex** on Baughers Bay (*C* **284/468-5940**). Another source for Caribbean lobster is **Wayne Robinson** (*C* **284/494-4097** or 284/499-2251)—he can hook you up with fishermen who go out daily filling orders for local restaurants.

o **Fresh Produce/Fruit:** A **Saturday farmers market** in Road Town's newly renovated Market Square at Sir Olva Georges Plaza (*C* **284/343-2876;** 7am–3pm) sells fruits

and vegetables from local producers as well as bush teas and jams from Full Belly Farm, homemade juices and kombucha, coconut dumb bread, saltfish, and whelk soup. **Good Moon Farm** (www.goodmoonfarm.com; *C* **284/542-0586**) will deliver fresh organic produce and fruit anywhere in the B.V.I; they also offer full provisioning services from a supply base of local producers and farm boxes of root crops, fresh fruits and veggies, leafy greens, and fresh herbs. **Tidal Roots Farm** (*C* 284/3432876) raises organic fruits and vegetables (heirloom tomatoes, arugula, carrots, herbs) in no-till beds in Belle Vue and offers CSA boxes. In the West End village of Sea Cows Bay, the **Flemming Place market** (*C* **284/496-0969**), at Huntums Ghut, sells starfruit, pineapple, peppers, spinach, and okra, among other fresh produce, from local farms. Call the **BVI Dept. of Agriculture** for more contacts (*C* **284/495-2110**).

o **Meat/Butcher: Steakation,** in Road Town (www.steakationbutchers.com; *C* **284/499-6328**), sells premium beef from Creekstone Farms, Wagyu beef from Bush Brothers Wagyu Beef, Berkshire pork from Berkwood Farms, quality veal and lamb from Catelli Brothers, and chicken from Bell & Evans.

o **Wine, Beer & Liquor: Riteway** (see above), **Tico** (ticobvi.com; *C* **284/494-2211**), and **Caribbean Cellars** (caribbeancellars.com; *C* **284/393-4471**), all with stores in Road Town, have a good selection and will deliver your order to the boat. You can order online.

deck is where you'll find the locals at quitting time. The specialty is seafood (the coconut shrimp is divine), but cooked-from-scratch dishes from the Grenadan-born chef (they call him Chef Spice) include a steak with chimichurri sauce and a pepper tuna. Live music often on tap.

Heritage Inn, Windy Hill (p. 251). www.heritageinn.vg. © **284/494-5842.** Reservations required. Entrees $28–$39. Daily 4:30–10pm.

1748 Restaurant ★ CONTINENTAL   This beachside restaurant has a very cool setting inside an 18th-century rum distillery with original walls of native limestone and shells (you can also sit outside and watch the waves ripple onto Long Bay beach). The menu is a mashup of Continental, Caribbean, and Asian fusion flavors, but ingredients are fresh and local: You might pingpong from Vietnamese fish cases to a Thai coconut green curry or a buttery grilled Caribbean lobster tail.

In the Long Bay Beach Resort (p. 250). www.longbay.com. © **284/340-2281.** Reservations recommended. Entrees $28–$45. Daily 7:30–10am, noon–3pm and 6:30–9pm.

The 1748 Restaurant delivers a fine-dining experience in an old stone distillery.

Sebastian's Seaside Grille ★★ CARIBBEAN/MEDITERRANEAN   On wooden tables scattered indoors and out, you dine just feet from the surf. The Grille (open breakfast, lunch, and dinner) is a lively spot, hosting live music on weekends and bingo and karaoke during the week. Start with a *taco de camarones* with shrimp or a Mediterranean bruschetta. When lobster is in season, be sure to order Sebastian's version, made with a top-secret preparation. Homemade fettuccine comes with fresh seafood, and a chicken cacciatore is all peppery, herb-y goodness. The after-dinner treat: a shot of Sebastian's rum.

Sebastian's on the Beach (p. 252). © **284/495-4212.** Dinner reservations required. Entrees $22–$38. Daily 8am–2:30pm and 6:30–9:30pm.

Sugar Mill Restaurant ★★ CONTINENTAL/CARIBBEAN   Set in the ruins of an 18th-century sugarcane plantation, the Sugar Mill serves food that is immaculately and expertly prepared. It may no longer be the cutting-edge California-fresh food that brought the world to its door years ago, won awards, and spun off cookbooks, but it is still a quietly gracious dining experience serving often excellent food in a truly stupendous setting. (Though it's somewhat unsettling to know that this romantic candlelit space was once the old rum distillery's superheated boiling house, a place of misery in an already tropical climate.) Cobblestones and rock slab in the rubble stone walls were pulled from the streets of Liverpool nearly 400 years ago to use as ballast in trading ships on their way to the Americas. Tables on the Terrace enjoy sea views and briny breezes. Sugar Mill's beachside restaurant, **Tramonti,** sits right on the Apple Bay sands and is open for breakfast (daily 7–9am), lunch (Mon–Fri noon–2:30pm), and Sunday brunch (9am–3pm).

In the Sugar Mill Hotel (p. 251). www.sugarmillhotel.com. *(C)* **284/495-4355.** Reservations required. Entrees $37–$69; 3-course set menu $49. Daily 6:30–9pm.

Moderate

DCoalPot ★★ CARIBBEAN   This popular spot puts a refined spin on Caribbean classics and local seafood, from conch in lemon butter and stewed oxtails to pasta topped with fresh grilled tuna. Glistening stir-fried beef comes with veggies over jasmine rice. Fried grouper is accompanied by a just-right Creole sauce, and the curry vegetables are as colorful as they are delicious.

Shore Rd (Rte 1), Carrot Bay. www.facebook.com/DCoalPotBVIRestaurant. *(C)* **284/545-6510.** Entrees $20–$26. Mon–Fri 4–10:30pm; Sat–Sun 11am–10:30pm.

Inexpensive

If you're looking for a good cappuccino and inspired breakfast and brunch fare, head to Soper's Hole Marina to **Omar's Coffee House** ★ (*(C)* **284/344-0513**), a pretty West Indian–style cottage where you can also get a range of drinks and interesting morning midday eats, like eggs, bagels, crepes, and fruit smoothie bowls. It's open daily from 6:30am to 2:30pm.

CANE GARDEN BAY

Cane Garden Bay is the traditional party central on Tortola, which means it can also be tourist central, especially during high cruising season when it becomes a prime daytime excursion destination for a whole lot of cruise-ship visitors. You can, however, get a dependably decent bite to eat at most of the Cane Garden Bay mainstays, including **Quito's Gazebo** ★ (quitosbvi.com; *(C)* **284/495-4837;** daily 11am–11pm), the domain of reggae musician and artist Quito Rymer, whose mini-empire along the northeastern stretch of Cane Garden Bay also includes **Quito's Luxury Inn** (p. 249). Rymer's open-air beachside restaurant and bar was turned to rubble by the 2017 hurricanes but has been rebuilt bigger and better, now in an airy space with a soaring beamed ceiling. Along with alcoholic libations, Quito's offers tasty, well-prepared food, serving up West Indian dishes (like coconut bread), pasta, and a menu of pizzas plus the occasional lobster mac 'n' cheese and tuna tartare. Quito's other Cane Garden Bay spot, Rhymer's, did not survive the 2017 hurricanes, but nearby **Myett's** ★ (www.facebook.com/MyettsBVI; *(C)* **284/495-9649**) has risen again post-Irma in its prime beachfront location. Look for dependable island food, pub grub, and pizzas. It's open daily noon to 9pm.

Indigo Beach House ★★ SMALL PLATES/INTERNATIONAL A class act tucked away on the southern flank of Cane Garden Bay, Indigo House is so close to the beach you can practically inhale the sea spray. The open terrace overlooking the bay is utterly enchanting, with indigo-blue trim along scalloped wooden edges, wicker chairs, and wood tables. A tree-shaded courtyard has blue shuttered doors, and there's floral stained glass throughout, the work of artist Lin Crook from Island Reflections BVI. A jaunty red tin roof adds to the complete Caribbean vernacular. The food is nothing complicated but delicious, a mix of shareable plates (sticky Asian ribs, chicken mac 'n' cheese, steak kabobs), finger foods like tacos, burgers, and roti, and a couple of fresh salads. It's the vibe, and those views.

Cane Garden Bay. © **284/343-5503.** Shareable plates/tapas $11–$24; tacos, burgers, and roti $14–$20. Daily noon–11pm.

EAST END/TRELLIS BAY
Expensive
Brandywine Estate Restaurant ★★★ MEDITERRANEAN BISTRO Before Hurricane Irma hit in 2017, this restaurant had one of the most beautiful locations on Tortola, sitting pretty on a seafront promontory along

the island's southern coast. But this longtime favorite was no match for the strongest hurricane on record. Roofs were blown away, the gazebo was demolished, and even the landscaping was ripped up. The award-winning renovation, in partnership with Tiger QI Architects, is built to last. Where the loveliness of the old restaurant was finely etched, this new incarnation is handsome and solid—but with those same amazing evening views of inky blue seas and emerald hills. The new garden terrace is covered with a high-pitched roof buttressed by stone-clad columns. A tapas menu features shareable dishes like salmon cigars and lamb meatballs. Mains might include salmon and shrimp puttanesca or a rich truffle gnocchi in a creamy mushroom sauce.

Charcuterie plate at the Brandywine Estate Restaurant.

Brandywine Estate, Sir Francis Drake Hwy. brandywine.vg. © **284/495-2301.** Reservations required. Entrees $32–$44. Wed–Sun noon–11pm.

Moderate
Loose Mongoose ★★ CARIBBEAN/INTERNATIONAL Another casualty of Hurricane Irma has risen from the wreckage and is back bigger

(literally) and better. In size and style, it's made a giant leap from the very modest little 20-seat beach shack restaurant of old. In fact, you might even call it chic, with a long, sturdily constructed stretch of hardwood decking topped by a voluminous shaggy thatched roof. The food is not your standard beach bar fare either. The "casual fine-dining" menu has plenty of verve, with nightly specials like fresh Anegada snapper in a brown stew sauce, shrimp lo mein, lobster quesadilla, and brown-sugar sticky ribs. Have a drink in the open-air loft bar upstairs or hit the boutique. If you're serious about rum, take a seat in the poshed-out **Honor Society Rum Bar** and sample some of the finest *rhum agricole* from around the Caribbean. Sunday is Grill Out day.

Trellis Bay, Beef Island. www.facebook.com/LooseMongoosebeVI. ℂ **284/340-5544.** Entrees $17–$28. Mon–Fri 11am–9pm; Sat-Sun brunch 9am–3pm.

Inexpensive

Jeremy's Kitchen ★★   Long the "unofficial departure lounge" for Beef Island Airport, a 5-minute walk away, Jeremy's bustles with food, drink, and live music from 7:30am to 9pm, and the next morning starts right back up again. The breakfast menu (served until 12:30pm on weekdays) is bigger than the all-day menu, a kitchen-sink assemblage of Indian specialties (Caribbean curry, roti), the Famous Awesome Sandwich (seven-grain bread, grilled cheese, L&T, grilled onions and peppers, and mango kuchela with your choice of veggies, meats, mahi, or lobster), and pasta—of sufficient starch quotient to soak up all that rum. Be here for Jeremy's full-moon parties on the beach.

Trellis Bay. www.jeremyskitchen.com. ℂ **284/345-5177.** Entrees $10–$18.75; sandwiches $12.75–$14.50. Daily 7:30am–9pm.

Exploring Tortola
BEACHES

Tortola's wide, sandy beaches are rarely crowded, unless a cruise ship is in port. The best beaches are on the north/northwestern coast.

Starting at the west coast, **Smugglers Cove ★★**, known for its tranquility and for the beauty of its sands, lies at the extreme western end of Tortola, opposite the offshore island of Great Thatch, and just north of St. John. It's a lovely palm-fringed crescent of white sand with calm turquoise waters. A favorite with locals, Smugglers Cove is also popular with snorkelers, who appreciate the fact that the reef is close to shore. You can see the remains of the old set for the TV-movie remake of *Old Man and the Sea,* filmed here in 1990, but the long-standing honor bar is gone, replaced by a couple of enterprising fellows selling drinks and snacks out of the back of their cars. Reached down a horrible road, riddled with potholes, Smugglers Cove is worth the trouble to get there.

Spectacular sunsets make the 2km-long (1¼-mile) white-sand beach at **Long Bay (West) ★**, reached along Long Bay Road, perfect for romantic strolls. The Long Bay Beach Resort stands on the northeast side of the beach; it's got a lively beach bar for sunset drinks.

Aptly named Long Bay Beach stretches for 2km (1¼ miles) along the north shore of Tortola's West End, with dazzling sand and gentle waves.

Surfers like **Apple Bay** (locally known as Cappoons Bay), just east of Long Bay Beach along North Shore Road. There isn't much beach at Apple Bay, but that doesn't diminish activity when the surf's up—so watch the locals take to the waves after 5pm. This was also the former site of the legendary Bomba Surfside Shack, a classic dive of a beach bar that was demolished by the 2017 hurricanes. Surfing conditions all over the island are best in January and February.

Tortola's finest beach is **Cane Garden Bay ★★★**, on the aptly named Cane Garden Bay Road, directly west of Road Town. You'll have to navigate some roller-coaster hills to get there, but these fine white sands, with sheltering palm trees and gentle surf, are among the most popular in the B.V.I. Calm seas make this a wonderful spot for standup paddleboarding (you can rent paddleboards here, as well). Cane Garden Bay is its own ecosystem, a lively seaside village with beach bars lining the sand (p. 258), and it's a real scene when cruise-ship passengers arrive in big safari vans, bringing vendors and hair braiders out of the woodwork. Still, with green hills rising sharply above the beach, those sparkling sapphire seas, and the shapely contours of Jost Van Dyke on the horizon, it's quite a special place to be. It's easy to rent beach chairs and umbrellas once you're there.

East of Cane Garden Bay, **Brewers Bay ★★**, accessible via the long, steep Brewers Bay Road, has calm, clear, protected waters that are ideal for small children. Snorkeling is fine along the rocky shoreline of the bay's western end. The only gold-sand beach on the island, it's a great place to stroll or just sun and watch the world go by. It even has a sprinkling of plantation ruins. A bare-bones campground is tangled in the tropical foliage along the beach—sometimes operational, sometimes not.

If you'd like to escape from the crowds at Cane Garden Bay and Brewers Bay, head east along Ridge Road until you come to **Josiah's Bay Beach** on the north coast, in the foreground of Buta Mountain. It's a favorite of surfers, but if you visit in winter, beware: On many days there's a strong undertow, and there are no lifeguards. Farther east, **Little Bay ★** is quiet and secluded with good snorkeling when seas are calm.

Moving to the island's East End, near the airport at Trellis Bay, the gorgeous **Long Bay Beach (East) ★★** was for years an under-the-radar, slightly isolated strand known largely to locals. Now with full facilities, it preens for the cruise-ship crowd during the day, and on weekends becomes a favored relaxation spot for islanders with grills and music going. It truly is as pretty as a picture. Unlike the other island beaches, no mountain water runs down to this beach. *Note:* Taxis can provide drop-off and pickup.

On the island's south shore, **Brandywine Bay** is a pretty sweep of crescent beach right next to the highway and is rarely touristed. It was rebuilt with dredged sand.

WATERSPORTS & OUTDOOR ADVENTURES

Most visitors come to Tortola not for historic sights but to explore the island's natural scenery, with its rugged mountain peaks, lush foliage, and wide, sandy beaches.

Watersports

BOAT CHARTERING/BAREBOATING   Tortola boasts the largest fleet of bareboat sailing charters in the world. One of the best places to get outfitted is the **Moorings,** Wickham's Cay II (www.moorings.com; ✆ **888/979-0153** in the U.S. and Canada, or 284/494-2331 in the B.V.I.). Depending on your nautical knowledge and skills, you can arrange a bareboat rental (with no crew) or a fully crewed rental with a skipper, staff, and a cook. Boats come equipped with a portable barbecue, snorkeling gear, dinghy, linens, and galley equipment. If you're going out on your own, expect to get a thorough briefing session on Virgin Island waters and anchorages. The cost for bareboat rentals varies depending on the season and the boat. Powerboats, daysailers, and catamarans can range from $385 to $1,700 per day.

DAYSAILING & BOAT EXCURSIONS   As in many of the other Virgins, some of the most popular daysails in the B.V.I. deliver you to hidden islets and tiny islands only accessible by boat. We highly recommend taking a **customized sailing, snorkeling, or island-hopping excursion** while you're here. The following daysail operators come highly recommended:

Aristocat Daysails ★ (aristocatdaysails.com; ✆ **284/499-1249**) offers shared and private charters aboard luxury 48-foot catamarans for intimate full-day swimming, snorkeling, and paddleboarding excursions. Boats run out of Tortola's West End to destinations like Norman Island and Jost Van Dyke, or

Island-hopping on Kuralu Daysail Charters' catamaran *Day Dream.*

from Road Town to Peter, Salt, and Cooper islands. Cost for a shared catamaran daysail (9:30am–4pm; 25 people max) is $155 per person, $85 children 12 and under, buffet lunch included.

With **Kuralu Daysail Charters ★** (kuralu.com; ✆ **284/495-4381**), you swim, snorkel, and sail on uncrowded daysails aboard *Day Dream,* a 43-foot Leopard sailing catamaran, or *Kurulu II,* a 35-foot Power Cat. Sailing out of Road Town, Kuralu goes to places like Norman Island and the Indians, the Baths, Jost Van Dyke, and Salt, Cooper, and Peter islands. Full-day sails cost $140 adults ($80 children), lunch included.

FISHING   The fishing in the B.V.I. is some of the best in the Caribbean. The deep-water **North Drop,** just north of Anegada, is world-class for sport-fishing and home to big Atlantic blue marlin. Closer in still is the **South Drop,** 2 miles south of Peter and Norman islands, another large drop-off for catching mahi, wahoo, tuna, sailfish, and marlin. Bonefishing the flats of Anegada and Beef Island are also popular fishing trips. Most fishing charters offer convenient pickup and drop-offs. *Note:* You'll need to have a 30-day "pleasure fishing" license ($45/person) to fish in B.V.I. waters; you can apply for a license before you leave home (bvi.gov.vg/services/acquiring-pleasure-fishing-licence) or get one from your charter outfitter when you reserve your fishing trip, which usually takes 1 to 3 days to process.

Locally owned **SaltShaker Charters** (www.saltshakerbvi.com; ✆ **284/340-1400**), based on Tortola's East End, takes private fishing charters out in *Salt-Shaker,* a 33-foot custom L&H walkaround that comfortably seats six passengers (and was previously owned by singer Jimmy Buffett!). The cost for a half-day of inshore fishing is $1,450; a full day is $1,850. A half-day of deep-sea fishing is $1,750; a full day is $2,150. *SaltShaker* also makes island-hopping charters and water-taxi runs for 1 to 12 passengers.

Bad Dog Fishing Charters (baddogcharters.com; ✆ **284-496-9080**), based out of Hodges Creek Marina in Road Town, has a boat that holds eight passengers and offers both deep-sea and inshore fishing expeditions. It costs $1,750 for a half-day, $1,850 for a three-quarter-day, and $2,150 for a full day. For an additional $200, you can be picked up in Jost Van Dyke or Anegada.

KITESURFING   The B.V.I. enjoys some of the region's top kitesurfing conditions. You can "chase the wind" around the territory with **Kitesurf BVI ★**

(kitesurfbvi.com; ℂ **284/541-8622**), which offers kitesurf and wingsurf lessons, board rentals, and kitesurfing trips. Six-hour kitesurf lessons run $270 to $1,100; wingsurf lessons are $230 to $900. Kids' beginner lessons (ages 7–16) are $70.

SCUBA DIVING The region has a number of excellent dive operators, many of which also offer snorkeling excursions and scuba/snorkel rentals. Check with the **BVI Scuba Association** (bviscuba.org; ℂ **731/803-2896**) for a list of outfitters, dive shops, and dive wrecks. But you won't go wrong with the following highly recommended, longtime operators.

Operating since 1975, **Dive BVI ★★** (divebvi.com; ℂ **284/541-9818**) runs lessons and excursions out of Scrub Island, just north of Tortola's Beef Island (there's a second location in the Virgin Gorda Yacht Harbour). It offers a range of dive trips and packages, diving courses, and day excursions, including a snorkeling cruise with an afternoon stop in Jost Van Dyke (excursions $120–$140/person). An Underwater Safari excursion is a guided scuba or snorkel trip with a lunch break at Cooper Island ($120/person for snorkeling, $175/person for scuba). Dive BVI's experienced guides run trips to the wreck of the HMS *Rhone* as well as the *Willy T.* Two-tank dive trips are $130 per person; night dives are $115.

Another longtime presence on the B.V.I. dive scene (since 1980), **Blue Water Divers ★★** (bluewaterdivers bvi.com; ℂ **284/494-2847**) operates out of Nanny Cay and offers guided two-tank dives ($130/person), Discover Scuba courses ($140/person),

Exploring historical shipwrecks around the B.V.I. with We Be Divin'.

and open water and dive master courses. Dive sites include Norman Island, Pelican Island (Rainbow Canyons), and Blonde Rock.

Sail Caribbean Divers ★★ (www.sailcaribbeandivers.com; ℂ **284/541-3483**), in business in the B.V.I. for more than 40 years, has three locations around Tortola: Moorings Marina, Hodges Creek Marina, and Cooper Island. It offers rendezvous diving and daily guided dive trips to sites like Santa Monica Rock, the Indians, Shark Point, Carrot Rock, and the *Willy T.* Two-tank dives are $140 per person and night dives are $97. Dive packages run from $350 to $595.

We Be Divin' ★★ (bviscubadive.com; ℂ **284/494-4320**), on Nibbs Street in Road Town, is led by Chris Juredin, who has been diving the B.V.I. waters for more than 2 decades and works with marine archaeologists on locating

B.V.I. FAVORITE scuba SITES

The British Virgin Islands have a wealth of world-class dive sites, including the area between Salt and Cooper islands known as "Wreck Alley," home to four shipwrecks. The following sites are just a sampling.

o The **wreck of the RMS *Rhone*** ★★ sank in 1867 near the western point of Salt Island. *Skin Diver* magazine called it "the world's most fantastic shipwreck dive." The wreck was featured in the 1977 movie *The Deep*.

o Another excellent dive site off Tortola is the ***Chikuzen,*** a 266-foot steel-hulled refrigerator ship that sank off the island's eastern end in 1981 and is now home to yellowtail, barracuda, black-tip sharks, octopus, and drum fish.

o The inter-island cargo ship ***Island Seal*** went down in 2006 on a reef near Brandywine Bay near Salt Island. It was moved to Wreck Alley in 2013.

o South of Ginger Island, **Alice in Wonderland** is a deep-dive site with a wall that begins at around 3.6m (12 ft.) and slopes gently to 30m (98 ft.). It abounds with rainbow-hued fan coral and mammoth mushroom-shaped coral.

o **Spyglass Wall** is another offshore dive site dropping to a sandy bottom and filled with sea fans and large coral heads. The drop is from 3 to 18m (10–59 ft.). Divers here should keep an eye out for tarpon, eagle rays, and stingrays.

o **Art Reefs:** The beloved floating pirate bar known as **Willy T,** a victim of the 2017 hurricanes, was restored in 2019 as a sunken pirate ship in the "Art Reef" program created by the nonprofit **Beyond the Reef** (https://1beyondthereef.com; ☏ **284/346-1444**) to repurpose hurricane-destroyed vessels in fun and fantastic ways and bring attention to ocean conservation efforts (and raise monies for local learn-to-swim programs through a $5 diving fee). *Willy T,* along with a crew of skeletal "pirates," sits in 65 feet of water in Key Bay, Peter Island. (*Willy T* was named after William Thornton, the Quaker architect born on Jost Van Dyke who designed the U.S. Capitol). Other art reefs include ***Sharkplaneo,*** composed of three wrecked airplanes remade as sharks and sunk in 2019 off Great Dog Island, and the ***Kodiak Queen,*** a decorated WWII Navy fuel barge and former fishing trawler, enveloped in the sculpture of a kraken (sea monster) in a bay just outside Virgin Gorda.

historical wrecks. We Be Divin' offers PADI dive courses, equipment rentals, and customized excursions to places like the Baths, Cooper Island, Norman Island, Jost, and Anegada, from 3-hour one-tank dives to 5-hour two-tank dives to full-day 3-tank trips. Call about rates.

SNORKELING Many who stay on Tortola do snorkeling trips to neighboring islands, but you don't have to leave the island to enjoy a fine snorkel. The coral reef at **Brewers Bay** is probably the best place for snorkeling right off the beach. **Smugglers Cove** is quite good on the left side when seas are calm; nearby **Long Bay** has good snorkeling near the west end of the beach. On the

East End, **Well Beach,** on Beef Island, has calm waters for beginning snorkelers.

Offshore islands offer exceptional snorkeling: including **Norman Island** (p. 270) and its neighboring islands the **Indians,** four fingers of rock jutting out of the sea at depths of between 10 and 50 feet. The Indians have no beach, just moorings to anchor, but if you break bread in the water, reef fish (like yellowtail snappers) will come up to meet you. A number of daysail and scuba operators go to Norman Isle and the Indians. At Soper's Hole marina, **Island Surf and Sail** (bviwatertoys.com; © **284/345-0123**) rents snorkel gear and will deliver to your resort or villa.

STANDUP PADDLEBOARDING (SUP)   Tortola's coves and calm anchorages make great places to paddleboard. Tortola's top SUP spots include the south side of Beef Island, Trellis Bay, Brewer's Bay, Long Bay East, and Long Bay West. You can rent (or buy) from a wide selection of SUP boards at Road Town–based **BVISUPCO** (www.bvisupco.com; © **24/346-1981**), which will deliver them to your villa or charter boat. Most of the basic boards rent for $125 for 1–5 days; more advanced boards rent for $40 to $50 a day. **BVI-SUPCO** also rents inflatable SUPs, kiteboards, foil boards, and freewings. Other SUP rental shops include **Last Stop Sports** (www.laststopsports.com; © **284/494-0564;** $170/week), in Port Purcell; and **Island Surf and Sail**, at Soper's Hole marina (bviwatertoys.com; © **284/345-0123**).

SURFING   Winter is the best time for surfing Tortola, when the swells kick up along the North Shore Atlantic beaches. **Apple Bay** is the island's top surfing spot, but **Josiah Bay** and **Cane Garden Bay** also have whipped-up winter waves. **Island Surf and Sail** (see above) rents shortboards, longboards, body boards, kayaks, and standup paddleboards, among other watersports equipment, and provides free delivery island-wide. So does **Sebastian's on the Beach,** at Little Apple Bay (p. 252).

Outdoor Adventures

HIKING   No visit to Tortola is complete without a trip to **Sage Mountain National Park** ★, rising to an elevation of 523m (1,716 ft.). Here you'll find traces of a primeval rainforest, and you can enjoy a picnic while overlooking neighboring islets and cays. Covering 37 hectares (91 acres), the park protects the remnants of Tortola's original forests, those that were not burned or cleared during the island's plantation era. Go west from Road Town to reach the mountain. Before you head out, pick up the brochure "Sage Mountain National Park" from the tourist office in Road Town; it has a location map, directions to the forest, and an outline of the main trails through the park. From the park's parking lot, a trail leads to the park entrance. The two main trails are the Rainforest Trail and the Mahogany Forest Trail.

Some of the most exciting hikes in the B.V.I. are offered by **Hike BVI** ★★★ (www.hikebvi.com; © **284/441-2315**). Along with Hike BVI's kayaking and snorkel tours, these eco-treks into Tortola's bush forests and mountains weave in island history, culture, nature, and plant medicine and take you to hidden

B.V.I. native Sef Graham's treks with Hike BVI plunge into Tortola's bush forests to learn how the island's ecosystems intertwine with native culture.

gems most visitors never see—a snorkel in a secret lagoon on Tortola's North Shore, say, or a walk along Shark Bay's cliffside beach. The walks are the brainchild of B.V.I. native Sef Graham, who developed the treks and does most of the guiding himself. Graham, who comes from a long line of herbalist "bush doctors," is a fount of wisdom about the myriad ways islanders have long used the astonishing array of flora around them (see "The Bush Doctor Is In," p. 268). A half-mile hike to bamboo meadows leads to a natural spring, the home of big crawfish and little guppies. In the rainy season the government ministry fishes guppies from the spring to place in the island's water cisterns to devour mosquito larvae. The bamboo itself plays an important role in the environment, giving off 30% more pure oxygen than any other plant.

SEEING THE SIGHTS

Post-pandemic **Road Town** has a bright, clean look, with rebuilt docks, brand-new boardwalks, tall palms planted along Waterfront Drive, and freshly painted buildings. Here and there, particularly along the narrow lanes of Main Street, you'll see historic landmarks and examples of the island's West Indian–style vernacular gingerbread architecture. Shops are within easy walking distance of the cruise-ship dock.

A **taxi tour** of the island is a must and a great way to get the lay of the land before you tackle the driving yourself. But the best taxi tours are even more than that, giving you an overview and insight into the island's culture, history, and sociology. Taxi drivers are great resources for insider travel tips as well, like tapping into a network of local fishermen for fresh lobster or finding the beach that's just right for you. We highly recommend **Hartley "Bozo" Frett** (✆ **284/543-1366**) as a warm, reliable, and erudite guide; his van can hold up to 14 passengers. You can also contact the **Virgin Gorda Tours Association** (✆ **284/495-5253** or 284-541-0681) or **Virgin Gorda Transport (Speedy's;** ✆ **284/341-7145,** 284/340-5240, and 284/495-5240). Expect to pay around $55 for two persons for a private 2-hour tour, $215 for four people for a 2-hour tour. A taxi tour might include a visit to Soper's Hole Marina, a marina/dining/shopping complex designed in the colorful Caribbean vernacular on the island's West End; a sweep of the beautiful North Shore beaches (including

THE BUSH DOCTOR IS in

Every native islander, it seems, has an herbalist or bush medicine "doctor" in the family. We've met taxi drivers who gulp down a drink of cayenne pepper, lemon, lemongrass, and cinnamon first thing in the morning (heart health) and a 110-year-old grandmother who makes poultices for rashes with the leaves of the lizard bush. "Bush tea"—recommended for respiratory conditions—is found on many a restaurant menu. Native herbalists and bush doctors use the islands' richly unique indigenous plants and herbs in time-honored ways for therapeutic purposes—passing on from one generation to the next the same plant remedies their ancestors relied on before the advent of modern medicine. On an **eco-trek** into the Tortola bush with **Hike BVI** (p. 266), guide Sef Graham describes a few of the islanders' go-to plants:

o **The Leaf of Life:** Aka the "miracle leaf," the Leaf of Life is used as a respiratory aid; it's said to relieve shortness of breath and remove mucous. It's chewed raw. The Leaf of Life is also used as a paste for cuts. If you put it into a book, it will actually grow roots.

o **Turpentine** (aka the gumbo-limbo or peeling tree): Islanders scrape the bark off the tree and boil it in water to make a gelatinous liquid that's used for cleaning the colon and treating gout. The berries have been used as glue. The tree is often planted as a windbreaker—it sways in the wind and doesn't snap—and island children have long made log boats out of it.

o **Guavaberry:** This reddish fruit ripens in September and October and is used in tonics and wine.

o **Trumpet tree:** This well-used herbal tonic is used for respiratory disorders. Steep the leaf, strain, and drink.

o **Sandbox tree** (aka "Monkey No Climb"): The 3-inch thorns on this tree have been used as arrow tips for hunting, and the fruit is poisonous. Leaves are pressed and mixed with salt and used as a poultice for boils or swellings. The shiny lacquer on the inside of the fruit is used for earrings.

o **Crab bush:** Its leaves are brewed or steeped to treat colds.

o **Morang bush:** Islanders use this bush as a broom. Its pungent smell acts as a natural repellent against bugs coming in the house.

Cane Garden Bay), also on the West End; a drive along historic Main Street in Road Town; and a stop at Sage Mountain National Park (p. 266). If you want to dig deeper into the culture and history of island life, ask your driver to include any of the following gems, all fascinating.

Callwood Rum Distillery ★★ DISTILLERY   With 400 years of history, this, the last distillery still standing on Tortola (once there were 53!), continues to blend and bottle its own rum in an 18th-century stone structure, the very picture of beautiful decay, all tangled in tropical greenery. This is small-scale, old-school distilling. The ramshackle interior has a tobacco patina, and you can sample the rums, of which 50 gallons are produced every day. Buy a bottle or two; they're priced to move and make a great souvenir.

Cane Garden Bay. callwood-cane-rum.myshopify.com. ☎ **284/495-9383.** $5 tour. Tastings $1.

Along the curves of Ridge Road, eye-popping murals by local artists depict various aspects of traditional island culture.

Fahie Hill Murals ★★ PUBLIC ART   A series of colorful murals done by different local artists follows the narrow, sinuous curves of mountainous Ridge Road. Each mural is a vignette of an old way of island life, from "banking" (terracing) crops on the island's steep hills to cutting sugar cane to telling ghost stories by lantern light. Pull over to give these wonderful murals a good look.

Fahie Hill, Ridge Rd., btw. Great Mountain Rd. and Johnson's Ghut Rd. Free admission.

J.R. O'Neal Botanic Gardens ★ GARDEN   Created by the B.V.I. National Parks Trust, this little 1.6-hectare (4-acre) park in the middle of Road Town is an increasingly important repository of endangered and threatened island species. It has an orchid house, a small rainforest, and a palm grove. In summer the aptly named flamboyant trees blaze with brilliant scarlet blooms.

Botanic Rd. www.bvinpt.org. ✆ **284/494-2069.** Admission $3 adults, $2 children.

North Shore Shell Museum ★ MUSEUM   This strange and wonderful "museum" is as local as it gets, overseen by Egberth Donovan, proprietor and folk artist. There may be no one in sight when you visit, but you're welcome to explore on your own. Donovan has created this splendidly cluttered, open-air ode to shells. Shells comprise its floors and walls and are fashioned into shell boats and mobiles and wind chimes that tinkle in the breezes. The collection includes lots of wise words scribbled on boards and surfaces. At press time, the former second-floor restaurant had still not been renovated following the 2017 hurricanes.

North Coast Rd. Free admission.

Exploring "Treasure Island"

Across Drake Channel from Tortola lies the former pirate den known as **Norman Island.** Legend has it that Norman Isle was the inspiration for Robert Louis Stevenson's *Treasure Island,* first published in 1883. You can row a dinghy into the southernmost cave of the island—with bats overhead and phosphorescent patches—where Stevenson's Mr. Fleming supposedly stowed his precious treasure. A series of other Norman Isle caves are some of the best-known snorkeling spots in the B.V.I., teeming with spectacular fish, octopuses, squid, and colorful coral. Intrepid hikers climb through scrubland to the island's central ridge, Spy Glass Hill. Many cruisers make Norman Isle a favorite stop, and a number of daysail operators (p. 262) and scuba outfitters (p. 264) offer excursions here. You can dine at Norman Island's lively beach bar and restaurant, **Pirate's Bight** (www.piratesbight.com; ✆ **284/443-1305;** daily 11am–9pm), by taking a **Norman Island ferry,** which runs three times daily from Hannah Bay Marina, Tortola (near Nanny Cay).

Old Government House Museum (OGH) ★ MUSEUM   The handsome former residence of the British governor of the B.V.I. sits on Government Hill, a rise above Road Harbour. With a freighted history as the seat of the old colonial government and the official home for visiting royals (Princess Margaret stayed here, Queen Elizabeth II visited twice, and a famed garden party was held here yearly to celebrate the queen's birthday), the house was nicknamed "Olympus" by locals. The original wooden structure was destroyed by a 1924 hurricane—so vicious a storm that a two-masted schooner carrying contraband whiskey was reportedly grounded on the area that now holds the tennis court—and replaced by this white-stone manor in 1926. In 2002, a new governor's residence was built next door and the Old Government House was converted into a museum; in the process, the walls of an 18th-century barracks were excavated and are now preserved in the new house. Severely damaged by the 2017 hurricanes, OGH reopened in 2020 following a 3-year renovation. Although the role of the governor has greatly diminished, OGH is still the site of state functions and ceremonial events. The museum is an interesting assemblage of artifacts from the house's past. A celebrated Stamp Room holds a collection of vintage B.V.I. stamps dating back to 1866. The beautiful **English gardens** ★★ were planted in the painterly, densely stacked style of famed horticulturist Gertrude Jekyll.

Drakes Hwy., Road Town. www.oghm.org. $5 adults, free for children 11 and under. Mon–Fri 9am–3pm; Sat–Sun prearranged tours only.

1780 Lower Estate SugarWorks Museum ★ MUSEUM   At press time the SugarWorks Museum remained closed for repairs following the 2017 hurricanes, but a reopening was in the works; call for updates. Built by 18th-century enslaved people, this original 1780 sugar factory structure was once part of a thriving harborside sugar plantation. Inside the simple structure is a treasure trove of island artifacts: old muskets, coal irons, bedding stuffed with banana leaves, woven baskets; a maritime display; a native folk medicine exhibit; and a rotating art gallery.

Station Ave., Road Town. www.facebook.com/LowerEstateSugarWorks. © **284/494-9206.** Free admission. Mon–Fri 9am–3pm.

Tortola Shopping

Unlike the U.S. Virgin Islands, the British Virgins have no duty-free shopping. British goods are imported without duty, though, and you can find some good buys among these imported items, especially in English china. In general, store hours are Monday to Saturday from 9am to 4pm.

ROAD TOWN

You'll find the densest concentration of shops and restaurants at **Wickham's Cay** in Road Town. Along Road Town Harbour, **Crafts Alive Village** (© **284/ 342-8595**) is a collection of colorful West Indian–style cottages designed to tout B.V.I.–made arts and crafts. (Some visitors grouse that's it's more tourist grist than original art.) Look for **Asante Studio,** where B.V.I. artist (and a founding member of the BVI Art Foundation) Joseph Hodge paints watercolors and acrylics (often genre scenes of local farming and fishing). Also look for embroidered children's dresses and homemade "lollies," made with the juice of local fruits like guava and Caribbean cherry. Another collection of shops in the West Indian vernacular, **Tortola Pier Park** (www.tortolapier. com) was built to attract the cruise-ship crowds with jewelry shops, a Rolex Boutique, a Crocs shop, and a cigar bar.

Bamboushay Pottery ★★ HOUSEWARES   Bamboushay makes handsome kiln-fired stoneware—tableware, wall sconces, animal mugs—in its boutique shop in Road Town, close to the ferry terminal. Look for pieces with "marine impressions" made from shells and coral as well as flora, like palm fronds. Many of Bamboushay's works come in its signature blue-green sea grape hue. Waterfront Dr., inside Bamboushay Restaurant & Lounge. bamboushaypottery.com. © **284/494-7752.**

Nutmeg & Co. ★★ GIFTS   As far as gift shops go, this is a big cut above, a customized gift shop making a real effort to curate locally made, eco-conscious products—and they do a fine job. Look for Bella's Sparks' darling teacups-turned-soy-candles, cool retro B.V.I. travel posters, gorgeous hand-blown glass demi-johns,

Locally painted "art bowls" of B.V.I. landmarks, sold at Nutmeg & Co.

and original "art bowls" with B.V.I. landmarks. Add to that jewelry, B.V.I. books, organic sunscreen, and gifts of whimsy and cheek, including mermaid bottle openers. Top it all off with the much-loved spices and condiments of Sunny Caribbee Spice Co., whose (now closed) eponymous shops in Tortola were popular stops for cruisers. 164 Waterfront Dr. nutmeg-and-co.shoplightspeed. com. *(C)* **284/494-1426.**

Pusser's Company Store ★ FOOD/WINE   The little empire that is Pusser's sells clothing, nautical tchotchkes, and gourmet food items including Pusser's famous Rum Cake, meats, spices, fish, and a nice selection of wines. Pusser's Rum is one of the best-selling items here. It's in back of Pusser's **Road Town Pub.** Main St. and Waterfront Rd. pussers.com. *(C)* **284/494-3897.**

WEST END

You'll find shops at **Soper's Hole Marina,** including **Zenaida** ★ (*(C)* **284/495-4867**), an atmospheric little store selling handblock fabrics and scarves, sarongs, and Moroccan lamps; outposts of both **Sunny Caribbee** and **Pusser's** (see above); the **Arawak Surf Shop** (*(C)* **284/494-5240**), selling island clothing, crafts, and gifts; and the **Harbour Market grocery** (*(C)* **284/347-1250**).

EAST END

Aragorn's Local Arts and Crafts Center ★★ ART/GIFTS   Any search for wonderful local art should start at Aragorn's Studio, a showcase for the most talented artisans in the islands. Tortola-born Aragorn is a printmaker, potter, and sculptor; his giant "fireballs"—silhouetted metal sculptures—are set ablaze during the monthly Fireball Full Moon Parties on Trellis Bay. Look for miniature fireballs (candle holders), beautiful original prints, pottery, jewelry, and gifts, the work of Aragorn, inhouse artisans, and regional artists. It also sells gourmet delicacies: organic produce and herbs from Aragorn's Good Moon Farm; salt raked from the old salt ponds on Salt Island; and traditional coconut bread and banana bread baked in the nearby Mangrove Bakery. Trellis Bay. www.aragornsstudio.com. *(C)* **284/495-1849.**

Tortola After Dark

Ask around to find out which hotel might have entertainment on any given evening. Steel bands and fungi or scratch bands (musicians who improvise on locally available instruments) appear regularly. Pick up a copy of *Limin' Times*, an entertainment magazine that lists what's happening locally; it's usually available at hotels.

Alas, **Bomba Surfside Shack,** on Cappoons Bay, the oldest and most famous hangout on the island, was destroyed by Hurricane Irma in 2017. Of course, a beachside shack cobbled together with scrap driftwood, corrugated metal, rubber tires, and other flotsam and jetsam was never guaranteed to withstand a Category 5 hurricane, but Bomba Callwood's celebrated shack had actually survived big ones before (including Hurricane Earl). It was quite the enterprise, famed for its full-moon bashes and "herbal" mushroom tea simmering in a cauldron in the bushes. Long live Bomba's.

Cane Garden Bay beach is the place to go for rollicking barefoot seaside restaurant/bars pumping with live music and live entertainment. The folks at **Paradise Club Lounge Bar & Restaurant** ★ (www.facebook.com/paradise clubvi; ✆ **284/494-2541**) really know how to throw a party. You can dance to live bands with your feet in the sand or join in on Sunday pig roasts and full-moon howls; it's open 10am to 10pm. Quito Rymer's open-air beachside restaurant and bar, **Quito's Gazebo** ★ (p. 258), is back with drinks, food, and live music—expect to see Rymer playing solo or with his band, the Edge, on Friday nights. Quito's other Cane Garden Bay bar/restaurant, **Rhymer's,** did not survive the 2017 hurricanes. Another Cane Garden Bay old-timer, **Myett's** ★ (www.facebook.com/MyettsBVI; ✆ **284/495-9649**) was flattened by Hurricane Irma but has been reborn in its prime location right on the beach. It serves good island food and hosts sunset happy hours, Sunday Beach Jams, and karaoke; Myett's is open daily noon to 9pm.

To sip a cold drink as you gaze down on Cane Garden Bay from the top of Windy Hill, **Stoutt's Lookout Bar** ★ (✆ **284/442-0432**) is an experience that's hard to beat. This colorful and welcoming open-air spot serves up alcoholic libations and what many believe are the best smoothies on the island. Prince Stoutt is the friendly owner, and the Banana Baileys Coconut the bar's signature drink. Also on the West End, at nearby Little Apple Bay, check out **Seaside Grille** at **Sebastian's on the Beach** (sebastiansbvi.com; ✆ **284/495-4212;** p. 252). Expect live music or Bingo Karaoke every Thursday, Friday, and Saturday night and Sunday brunch.

Another island hotspot is **Trellis Bay,** on the island's East End, where restaurant/bars like the **Loose Mongoose** (p. 259), **Jeremy's** (p. 260), and the **Trellis Bay Market & Grill** (trellisbaymarket.com; ✆ **284/540-1421;** Sat and Sun 6am–11pm) all have lively bar scenes and even livelier full-moon parties.

VIRGIN GORDA ★★★

The third-largest island in the British cluster, Virgin Gorda has a population of nearly 4,000 people and a fleet of some 1,500 boats. Christopher Columbus, on his second voyage to the New World in 1493, thought the island resembled a "fat virgin" in recline—and so it was named. It's located 19km (12 miles) east of Tortola and 41km (25 miles) east of St. Thomas.

Virgin Gorda was a fairly desolate agricultural community until Laurance Rockefeller established the resort of Little Dix here in the early 1960s, following his success with Caneel Bay on St. John in the 1950s. He envisioned a "wilderness beach" where moneyed seclusion and solitude reigned. Other hotels followed in the wake of Little Dix, but privacy is still a highly prized commodity on the island. Why else do some of the world's richest men make this their personal playground? Many visitors think Virgin Gorda is home to some of the most beautiful natural attractions in the world, including the boulder-strewn beach known as the Baths; the island's highest point, Gorda

Peak; and the luminous seas of the Valley and North Sound. It's a hard point to argue.

But Virgin Gorda is also a small-town, church-going kind of place with strong neighborly bonds, the kind of place where prominent local families like the Flaxes and the Vanterpools remain fully present, engaged boosters. Crime is rare—the police don't carry guns—even in a population that's a multicultural melting pot. The threads of community are not easily unwound here. Consider the example of Czech billionaire Peter Kellner, an avid kitesurfer who fell in love with Virgin Gorda and became a crucial benefactor to the battered island after the hurricanes hit in 2017. When Kellner died in a heli-skiing accident before the reopening of his newly rebuilt Saba Rock resort, the islanders gave him a passionate sendoff with a procession that traveled from the Valley to Savannah Bay.

Essentials

ARRIVING

BY PLANE   The **Virgin Gorda Airport** (VIJ; Taddy Bay International Airport; www.bviaacloud.com; ✆ 284/394-8000) is located in the Valley. **Air Sunshine** (www.airsunshine.com; ✆ 954/434-8900) has regularly scheduled service between Virgin Gorda and San Juan, St. Thomas, and St. Kitts.

BY BOAT   **Speedy's** (www.bviferries.com; ✆ 284/495-5235) operates daily ferry service six times a day between Beef Island/Trellis Bay, Tortola, and Spanish Town, Virgin Gorda, as well as ferry service five times a day Monday through Saturday between Road Town, Tortola, and Virgin Gorda's Spanish Town; round-trip fares are $30 adults, $20 children 5–11. Most of the

---

CHRISTMAS IN JULY: pond bay

The celebration known as Christmas in July was back in force in 2022. The *BVI Beacon* reported that a record-breaking 4,000 attendees and more than 400 boats descended on Virgin Gorda for the annual party in Pond Bay after 2 years of dormancy during the Covid-19 pandemic. The party started 15 years ago when a group of boaters calling themselves the "Puerto Rican Navy" traveled to the island in the summer, typically low season for tourism. It's been a big shot in the arm for businesses in the B.V.I. ever since. The Puerto Rican owner of the fabulous Glass House overlooking Pond Bay/Savannah Bay hosted the first Saturday event on the beach at Pond Bay. Since then, the nautical gathering has grown into a week-long party, with boaters hitting hot spots all over the B.V.I., to places like the Baths, the North Sound, Leverick Bay, Jost, and Norman Island.

Many participants are the same people who arrived in a large flotilla of boats from Puerto Rico carrying essential supplies and evacuation support in the immediate wake of the 2017 hurricanes. It's been a mutual love affair between Virgin Islanders and Puerto Ricans ever since.

Events are open to the public, including live music, food stalls, and full-moon parties. The main event is held the Saturday closest to July 25 from 9am to 7pm. Check with the **B.V.I. Tourism Board** (www.bvitourism.com) for details.

Virgin Gorda

Airport ✈
Beach 🏖
Ferry ▼- - -

0 1/2 mi
0 0.5 km

Pajaros Point

Oil Nut Bay ⑮

Prickly Pear Island

Deep Bay

Berchers Bay

John O Point ⑬ ⑬ ⑭

Birns Creek

Berchers Bluff

North Sound

Robin Bay

Joe Bay

Gun Creek ○

South Sound

Mosquito Island

Blunder Bay ⑫ ⑫

⑪

No Sound Rd.

Little Bay

South Sound Bluff

Mountain Point

Long Bay

Nail Bay ⑩ Point Gorda Peak 1,500 ft.

Plum Tree Bay

⑨

GORDA PEAK NATIONAL PARK

Soldier Bay ○

Caribbean Sea

Mahoe Bay ⑧

Pond Bay

Savannah Bay ➤

Handsome Bay

Taylors Bay

Sir Francis Drake Channel

Little Dix Bay ⑦ ⑦ ⑥ ⑤

St Thomas Bay

The Valley (Spanish Town) ○

Ferry to Tortola ▼

④

Trunk Bay ➤

Spring Bay ➤

The Baths ② ①

③

Princess Quarters ○ ✈

DEVILS BAY NATIONAL PARK

Copper Mine Point

Crooks Bay

Copper Mine

DINING ●

Bath & Turtle/Chez Bamboo **5**
Coco Maya **3**
Dixie's **6**
Hog Heaven **10**
North Sound Bistro **11**
The Restaurant at Leverick Bay **12**
Restaurants at Little Dix Bay **7**
Saba Rock **13**
Sugarcane **9**
Top of the Baths **1**

ACCOMMODATIONS ●

Bitter End Yacht Club **14**
Fischer's Cove Beach Hotel **4**
Guavaberry Spring Bay Vacation Homes **2**
Leverick Bay Resort & Marina **12**
Mango Bay Resort **8**
Oil Nut Bay **15**
Rosewood Little Dix Bay **7**
Saba Rock Resort **13**

A jumble of mighty boulders surrounds the Baths, Virgin Gorda's most memorable sight.

high-end resorts have their own boats to transfer guests from Beef Island/Trellis Bay to Virgin Gorda.

There is no direct ferry service from St. Thomas to Virgin Gorda at this time; you will need to ferry to Tortola first (likely Road Town, although recently service was launched connecting St. Thomas's Red Hook and Tortola's West End). The last ferry from Road Town to Spanish Town, Virgin Gorda, leaves at 4:30pm; if you arrive in Road Town later, you'll need to taxi to Beef Island/Trellis Bay to catch a ferry to Spanish Town (the last ferry from Trellis Bay leaves at 9pm).

VISITOR INFORMATION

The island's tourist office is in the Virgin Gorda Yacht Harbour, Spanish Town (© **284/495-5181**).

ISLAND LAYOUT

The northern side of Virgin Gorda is mountainous, with **Gorda Peak** reaching 417m (1,368 ft.), the highest spot on the island. In contrast, the southern half of the island is flat, with large boulders at every turn. As an aerial view of Virgin Gorda will show you, the southwest and northeast sections are connected to the mountainous middle by two very narrow isthmuses; the **North Sound** resorts are not even accessible by road, requiring ferry transfers from

Gun Creek. North Sound Road will take you from the **Baths** (in the extreme southeast) through **Spanish Town,** across a narrow neck, then around the mountainous edges of Gorda Peak to the northwesterly tip of the island's road system, ending at **Gun Creek.** Here, a mini-armada of scheduled ferryboats runs between Gun Creek and North Sound resorts such as Bitter End, Saba Rock, and Oil Nut Bay.

GETTING AROUND

BY TAXI Taxis are widely available, and, like everywhere else in the islands, drivers double as solid tour guides. Contact the good folks at **Andy's Taxi & Jeep Rental** (✆ **284/495-5511**), **Speedy's** (✆ **284/341-7145**), or **Potters' Taxi Service** (✆ **284/495-5329**) for excellent taxi service and island tours. The **Valley Taxi Association** can be reached at ✆ **284/495-5539.** The standard fee for traveling between Spanish Town and Gun Creek is $30 ($17 each for two passengers, $13 each for three or more passengers; kids aged 4–10 pay half-fare). Many drivers operate open-sided **safari buses** that can hold up to 26 passengers. These buses charge upwards of $4 to $6 per person to transport passengers from the Valley to the Baths, say, depending on the number of people traveling. **Taxi tours** of the island are highly recommended. A 1-hour tour runs about $55 for one to two people ($70 total for groups of three, $25 per passenger after that).

BY CAR If you'd like to rent a car, try one of the local firms, such as **Virgin Gorda Car Rental** (www.virgingordacar.com; ✆ **284/540-2222**) or **Mahogany Rentals** (www.mahoganycarrentalsbvi.com; ✆ **284/495-5469**), both in the Valley close to the yacht harbor. Both companies also offer taxi tours and transfers. *Remember:* Drive on the left. Road conditions on Virgin Gorda range from good to extremely poor, but traffic is never really an issue.

[FastFACTS] VIRGIN GORDA

Banks/ATMs **Scotiabank** (www.scotiabank.com) has a full-service bank in Spanish Town near the Yacht Harbour Shopping Centre. Both Scotiabank and **First Caribbean** (www.cibcfcib.com) have ATMs at the Yacht Harbour Shopping Centre.

Dentists & Doctors Contact **Apex Medical Center,** Millionaire Rd., the Valley (✆ **284/495-6557**).

Drugstore Go to **Island Drug Centre** in Spanish Town (✆ **284/495-5449**).

Emergencies Call ✆ **999** or 911.

Internet Access The **Bath & Turtle** restaurant, in Yacht Harbour Marina (✆ **284/495-5239**), has free Wi-Fi.

Police There is a station in the Valley in Spanish Town (✆ **284/495-7584**).

Where to Stay on Virgin Gorda

At press time, the long-dormant **Biras Creek Resort,** on the North Sound, was said to be finally under redevelopment. The resort's wonderful Hilltop restaurant, a dreamy site overlooking the sea, survived the 2017 hurricanes, and it's hoped will be back in business by the time you read this.

VILLAS, CONDOS & ESTATES

Villa rentals are a great way to go in Virgin Gorda—from some of the world's most luxurious private houses to more modest hillside retreats. Virgin Gorda has a very healthy rental market, with bountiful choices in **Mahoe Bay, Spring Bay, Leverick Bay,** and the centrally located **Nail Bay Estates,** a sprawling 148-acre development of villas up on the mountainside. A 5- or 7-night minimum stay is often required. Most accommodations have pools (and private pools); some even provide access to dining facilities, a spa, tennis

One of the "treehouse" cottages offered for rent by Guavaberry Spring Bay Vacation Homes.

courts, and extensive watersports. Rental rates are all over the map, but this is a pricey destination with some seriously luxe weekly digs. Here are some recommended villa rental and management companies in Virgin Gorda (see also p. 247 for companies that rent in both Tortola and Virgin Gorda). **White Oleander Destinations** (whiteoleanderdestinations.com; ✆ **284/346-0781**), a full-service local company based in Virgin Gorda, offers villa rentals throughout Virgin Gorda and Anegada, as well as itinerary planning, concierge services, and event management (including weddings). **Virgin Gorda Villa Rentals** (www.vgvirgingordavillarentals.com; ✆ **284/542-4014**) is another locally owned rental and management company that handles properties around the island, including many in the Mahoe Bay area. **Guavaberry Spring Bay Vacation Homes** (www.guavaberryspringbay.com; ✆ **284/495-5227** or 284/544-7186) rents excellent-value one- to three-bedroom vacation cottages in the Guavaberry Spring property, a short walk from Spring Bay beach. Cottages are fully outfitted redwood "treehouses" on stilts with kitchens and sundecks overlooking Sir Francis Drake Passage. A one-bedroom (two people) cottage rents for $185 to $225 a day. Virgin Gorda rentals are also available through the international online homestay services **VRBO** and **Airbnb.**

HOTELS & RESORTS

Expensive

Bitter End Yacht Club ★★★ This legendary resort and recreational marina, which opens onto the North Sound's gorgeous deep-water harbor, was flattened by Hurricane Irma in 2017. What began in the 1950s as a primitive sailors' stop had become a full-service 64-acre resort complex, beloved by generations of families and seafaring souls. Irma turned it all to matchsticks. The wooden hillside chalets, the beachfront cottages, the happy Clubhouse hung in a thousand nautical flags, the mosaic-tiled pool: gone. Today, 5 years later, the BEYC, built up again from the foundations, is back in a much smaller footprint and with downsized ambitions. But the spirit of the place is there in full. As one BEYC staff member said, "We're just copying our roots." When we visited, boats big and small packed the new 25-slip **marina.** In the "nautical village," two restaurants were serving up farm-to-table food as good as any on the island: the **Clubhouse,** with wooden shutters that open up to views of the North Sound; and the high-ceilinged **Buoy Room,** with a ship-wheel chandelier hung with salvaged red buoys. A kids' room has a baby climbing wall. The shops are back in full, from the **Reeftique Boutique,** selling Bitter End's classic line of nautical-themed clothing, to the **Market,** with a head-spinning provisioning collection of fresh produce, meats, booze, body scrubs, local jams (from Tortola's Full Belly Farm), and candles made here in Virgin Gorda. The **Watersports Center** can set you up for sailing, kiteboarding, wingsurfing, standup paddleboarding—you name it. Longtime outfitter **Sunchaser Scuba** (p. 290) is on-site for dive trips, and the kiteboarding outfit **Up 'n' Under** (p. 290) offers lessons. The only lodgings are a couple of fantastic overwater marina lofts, duplexes of polished wood with a bedroom upstairs, a daybed down, and cool touches like nautical cleats as towel holders and Dark and Stormy drink set-ups (with instructions). The ultimate plan is a resort with no more than 20 lodgings, where the pre-Irma BEYC had 85. Like any good shipwrecked sailor, Bitter End recycled its hurricane salvage. The "Line Wall" at the Watersports Center is a pretty tangle of rope culled from the North Sound, and the old resort ferry, *Irma,* was pulled from the sea bottom to become the **Reef Sampler Bar,** the B.V.I.'s only boat bar. An old dock has been resurrected as a swim platform. Hand-drawn signs throughout the resort are crafted from driftwood, and salvaged room signs have become part of the decor. Hammocks dotting the grounds are *not* recycled, however; they were bought with post-hurricane donations from long-time guests and families.

North Sound. beyc.com. © **284/393-2745.** 2 units. $655-$885 double. **Amenities:** 2 restaurants; 2 bars; marina; market and shops; watersports equipment/rentals; free Wi-Fi.

Oil Nut Bay ★★ This 400-acre North Sound high-luxe hotel, marina, and villa community is tucked into the far northeastern tip of Virgin Gorda, unreachable by anything but boat or helicopter. The resort now has a heliport that has been ASSI-approved for international flights, which means guests and villa owners can fly in and out between here and Puerto Rico, St. Maarten, St. Bart's, or most anywhere else in the Caribbean (with on-site Customs and Immigration clearance). If you arrive in more pedestrian fashion, by boat, know that Oil Nut Bay has its own full-service 93-berth marina, with boutique shops and boat slips available for nightly reservations—just right for a pop-in lunch or dinner at the beautiful overwater restaurant, **Nova** (open Sat, Mon, and Tues 11:30am–8:30pm, Sun 10:30am–8:30pm). No boat? You can take

The high-luxe Oil Nut Bay resort hugs the coast of the North Sound.

the Oil Nut Bay ferry ($20/person) from Gun Creek. The beach is grand, as it should be—the pearly-pink sand was trucked in from Barbuda. You can rent one-bedroom suites along the bay or up in the cliffs, or book a vacation villa as compact or grand as you need, with all the accoutrements (private chefs, full provisioning, concierge itinerary planning). A watersports center on-site can set you up with sailing, SUP, kayaking, and kiteboard and -winging lessons (the North Sound is a kiteboarding paradise) for an extra cost, and a rescue barn is home to horses, an emu, and red-footed tortoises. The hard-working staff greases the wheels in every way, making this breezily exclusive, chillingly expensive spot feel welcoming.

North Sound. www.oilnutbay.com. © **866/920-0451.** Bay Suites $650 and up; Cliff Suites $850 and up; 1- and 2-bedroom villas $2,205 and up, 3- and 4-bedroom villas $3,050 and up. **Amenities:** 2 restaurants; 2 bars; coffee shop; children's programs; hiking trails; fitness center; marina; playground; outdoor pool; 2 grass tennis courts; 2 pickleball courts; spa; watersports (extensive); free Wi-Fi.

Rosewood Little Dix Bay ★★★   This carefully coiffed monument to casual elegance is back in full after near-annihilation from Hurricane Irma in 2017, to the relief of many long-standing guests. A new walkway winds between the road and villas, and a little farm has been added, growing fruits, sweet potatoes, greens, and peppers; easy-riding white bikes are provided for guests to get around the 500-acre grounds. This former RockResort holds a special place in the hearts of many. Laurance Rockefeller set the tone for casual luxury when he built his "wilderness resort" on Little Dix Bay back in 1964, and it remains comfortingly familiar, although a newfangled butler system is still working out a few kinks. Endearingly, rooms have not had keys since the resort opened 60 years ago—Virgin Gorda is notable for its lack of crime—although you are free to lock yourself in securely at night. All rooms face that fabulous crescent beach, many with private terraces with sea views. Marbled bathrooms are big enough to hold a small quintet. Just steps away is the beach, where you can slip into radiant seas with snorkel and mask and watch hawksbill turtles dive for seagrass and rays skim the sandy bottom, all in the serenity of a sun-dappled morning. Families generally stay at the Ocean Cottages, four buildings on the south end of the resort, close to the complimentary **Rosewood Explorers** kids' club. The **Sense Spa ★★★** is set in a tropical glade on the resort's western flank; the spa infinity pool looks onto the Dog islands in the distance (non-guests can book spa treatments here as well). The soaring **Pavilion** (p. 285) survived the hurricanes, and it's still one

The Sugar Mill restaurant, one of several romantic restaurants at Virgin Gorda's longtime classic resort, Rosewood Little Dix Bay.

of the most romantic dining rooms imaginable, but we particularly love the smaller, cinematically lit **Sugar Mill.** Of course, the eateries of Spanish Town are less than a mile away. Be sure to reserve one of the resort's rentable jeeps or mini-mokes to tootle around the island in—they get booked up fast.

Little Dix Bay Rd. www.littledixbay.com. ℂ **888/767-3966** in the U.S., or 284/495-5555. 100 units. Winter $725–$950 double, from $1,200 suite; off-season $380–$775 double, from $875 suite. Extra person $75. Private ferry from Tortola airport $115/person round-trip (children 5–11 $58); charter aircraft transfers from St. Thomas also available. **Amenities:** 3 restaurants; 2 bars; babysitting; children's programs; exercise room; pool; room service; spa; 7 tennis courts; watersports equipment; free Wi-Fi.

Saba Rock Resort ★★★ This charismatic retreat is perched on a rock in its own little 1-acre cay in the dead center of North Sound. In the late 1960s, legendary diver and shipwreck hunter Bert Kilbride put Saba Rock on the map with his revelrous Pirates' Pub. The "last pirate of the Caribbean," Kilbride discovered some 90 shipwrecks in and around the B.V.I., and his scuba-diving resort course is taught around the world. Even as it evolved into a hotel, restaurant, and bar, Saba Rock remained an effervescent North Sound fixture. Then Hurricane Irma hit in 2017, virtually wiping it clean, with one wall left and debris from St. Martin washed up on its shores. Czech billionaire and avid windsurfer Peter Kellner came to its rescue, hiring Czech architectural firm ADR to rebuild it to withstand any Category 5 storm, with new concrete walls, floors, and ceilings; practically indestructible hardwoods like Ipe flooring and a pressed-wood roof; and structural stainless-steel cables that are now a key element in the striking island-industrial decor. The rebuild became a passion project for its new owner, who also donated generators and building supplies to islanders in the storm's brutal aftermath. When he died in a heli-skiing accident right before the new resort opened, islanders gave him a mournful sendoff.

Today, Bert's private rock is swinging once more, with a new upstairs bar, the **Sunset Bar,** a spa treatment room (**Spa & Sparkle**), and a gorgeous tiered open-air **restaurant** (p. 286). The resort has seven boat slips and 18 mooring balls and is the launching pad for numerous watersports activities. Beachside hammocks and shelters make for quiet spaces to contemplate sea and sky. The wonderful seven oceanfront rooms and suites have a playful nautical-meets-midcentury decor with pops of blue and red; two absolutely massive suites (sleeping four) have outdoor terraces, and two rooms adjoin for family stays. And families do come, as do raucous sailors from Necker Island, diners from the "mainland," and just about any and everyone who likes a jolly good time on an old rock. Luckily, room soundproofing is state of the art. Saba Rock even has a little **Nautical Museum** with shipwreck artifacts accumulated by Bert, who first saw the potential in this magical rock. The surrounding waters are still littered with artifacts; as Saba Rock manager Alain Prion notes, "If you ride in a glass-bottom boat, you can still see cannons under the water."

North Sound. sabarock.com. ✆ **284/393-9220.** 7 units. $550–$750 ($1,150 Aug-Sept) double. Rates include breakfast and boat transfers from Gun Creek and Leverick Bay. **Amenities:** Restaurant; bar; marina; spa; watersports equipment/rental; free Wi-Fi.

Moderate/Expensive

Mango Bay Resort ★★   Nestled around a cinematically beautiful bay amid lushly landscaped grounds, this fetching collection of resort suites and villas is its own private village complex. It's not a resort per se—there are no real amenities like restaurants, shops, or pools. But it has all the comforts and conveniences of home. In fact, all units but studios have full kitchens, and the property has two outdoor grills. (If you don't want to cook, Spanish Town is just around the corner.) The lodgings are extremely adaptable, with a number of rooms that can be connected for larger groups. Villa duplexes have high-ceilinged great rooms with furnishings in warm earth tones and tile patios with dining tables and rattan chairs. Big picture windows and doors open to the trade winds and the clear, sheltered waters of Mahoe Bay. The powdery beach is a half-mile long, and a snorkeling reef lies about 50 feet offshore. With a western exposure, flaming sunsets provide evening fireworks. Kayaks, snorkel equipment, and floating mattresses are included, and you're also just around the corner from reef snorkeling at Savannah Bay. *One minor issue:* Suites and villas tend to be closer together than private rental houses, in case utter privacy is a top consideration.

Mahoe Bay. www.mangobayresort.com. ✆ **284/495-5672.** 26 units. Winter $295 studio, $435/$495 1-bedroom suite/villa, $585/$755 2-bedroom suite/villa, $985 3-bedroom villa; off-season $220 studio, $300/$360 1-bedroom suite/villa, $440/$580 2-bedroom suite/villa, $695 3-bedroom villa. **Amenities:** Restaurant; bar; pool (private villas only); limited watersports; free Wi-Fi.

Moderate

Fischer's Cove Beach Hotel ★   Set on white-sand Paradise Beach, this locally owned beach hotel has four beachfront stone cottages, each with one or two bedrooms and a living/dining space, as well as two garden studios and 12 smallish hotel rooms with balconies to soak up the sea views. Rooms have tile floors, gauzy curtains, and an oyster-shell palette. A food store near the grounds is a great place to stock up. The open-air **Reef Restaurant** serves up island comfort food (fried pot fish, seafood boil) and live music (Brandon on sax) on Saturdays.

The Valley. www.fischerscove.com. ✆ **284/495-5253.** 18 units. $180–$375. Children 12 and under stay free in parent's room. **Amenities:** Restaurant; bar; gift shop; children's playground; spa; watersports equipment/rentals; free Wi-Fi.

Leverick Bay Resort & Marina ★   There's a lot going on at this multi-hyphenate marina complex set along the southern edge of North Sound. The main action swirls around the **Restaurant at Leverick Bay** (p. 284), serving juicy steaks and serious cocktails; **Jumbies Beach Bar,** with a kid-friendly menu and a lively Friday-night buffet with Moko Jumbie entertainment; and the on-site **Blue Rush Water Sports** (www.bluerushwatersports.com), offering sailboat, kayak, and SUP rentals as well as jet-ski tours (restricted zone only). But you can also stay here in good-value accommodations, including 14 hillside rooms outfitted in tropical hues, with tile floors and rattan furnishings and private seafront verandas—each room can sleep four people. Four one- to two-bedroom suites come with full kitchens, grills, and big terraces. The complex offers a marina, food market, and two small beaches, and the crystalline shallows of Savannah Bay are only a 10-minute drive away.

North Sound. www.leverickbayvg.com. ✆ **284/542-4011.** 18 units. $160–$195 double; $171–$214 suite **Amenities:** Restaurant; bar; marina; outdoor pool; tennis court; watersports equipment/rentals/shop; free Wi-Fi.

Where to Eat on Virgin Gorda
EXPENSIVE

Coco Maya ★★ ASIAN FUSION/LATIN   This saucy, sprawling spot is on everyone's radar, as well it should be. It's the sexiest beach hut you'll ever see, where you can sit around a firepit with your feet in the sand and admire sunset views over the Sir Francis Drake Channel. Coco Maya was designed to blend into its quintessentially Virgin Gorda environment of volcanic boulders and swaying palms; "rustically refined" elements include a thatched roof, oversized straw pendant lights, and sun-dappled sailcloth overhead. A menu of sharable large and small plates—gyoza, pad Thai noodles, Thai "money bags" (pork and ginger deep-fried wontons), shrimp lettuce wraps—makes it ideal for groups. Throw in a few of the creative sushi rolls and you've jetted around the Asia Pacific, flavorfully. Is this the best rum punch in the Caribbean, as one pundit claimed? Dunno—but it's mighty good. And yes, Harry Styles and Taylor Swift were here. Of course.

Spanish Town. www.cocomayavg.com. ✆ **284/495-6344.** Small plates $9–$24; large plates $21–$49; sushi rolls $16–$54. Tues–Sat 3–10pm

North Sound Bistro ★★ INTERNATIONAL/ISLAND   Opened in early 2022 in the North Sound's newest marina, **Blunder Bay** (✆ **284/542-5400**), the North Sound Bistro is already a destination spot with a menu that combines standard bistro fare (burgers, Caesar salad, grilled chicken) with some tantalizing island dishes, like barbecue ribs with a tamarind glaze, conch fritters, and grilled local mahi. It's a good-looking place, with stupendous North Sound views and craft cocktails. You'll need to reserve dinner in advance by 4pm. Complimentary weekend ferry services leave from Gun Creek at 6:30pm.

North Sound, west of Leverick Bay. www.blunderbaymarina.com. ✆ **284/499-2400.** VHF Channel 16. Reservations required. Entrees $22–$38. Tues–Sun 6–closing (in season, weekend lunches open at noon).

The Restaurant at Leverick Bay ★★★ STEAKHOUSE   Old school and reveling in it, the house restaurant at Leverick Bay Resort is a favorite of cigar-chomping Boomers and kitesurfing Gen Zers alike. If you crave sleek style updates, head elsewhere. If you want a proper steak and a two-fisted cocktail, this is your place. Ask for a seat on the second-floor terrace, with panoramic sea views and velvety Caribbean breezes. Start with a classic Caesar salad or the eggplant Napoleon and move on to the grilled T-bone, served

groceries, markets & more:
PROVISIONING RESOURCES ON VIRGIN GORDA

Most villa management companies and resorts have full provisioning services and will stock your pantries in advance, but it's always good to know where to stock up when you're here.

○ **Groceries: RiteWay** (www.rtwbvi. com; ✆ **284/347-1205**) has a full-service supermarket in Spanish Town, open daily 7am-9pm. At Leverick Bay Marina (www.leverick bayvg.com), **Chef's Pantry** (✆ **284/ 541-2881**) is a gourmet grocery and deli that's open daily 7am-7pm. In South Valley, **Rosy's Supermaket** (www.rosysbvi.com/rosy-s-super market; ✆ **284/495-5245**) is a one-stop shop for groceries, booze, and cleaning supplies; it's open daily 8:30am-8pm (closes 8:30pm Sat and 6pm Sun). **Buck's Market** (www. bucksmarkets.com; ✆ **284/495-5423**) is a fully stocked grocery in South Valley, open daily 7am-8pm (till 7pm Sun).

○ **Fresh Produce/Fruit:** Look for the fresh **greenhouse lettuces and microgreens** grown in the North Sound by **Agri-Paradise VG** (✆ **284/543-0379**) in Riteway, Chef's Pantry, and Rosy's Supermarket (and elsewhere around the Virgin Islands). **Rasta Livity Farm** (✆ **284/ 342-8204**) in the Valley on Coppermine Road has a farm market near the basketball courts (Mon–Thurs 4:30–6pm, Fri–Sat 7:30–11:30pm) selling herbs (basil, lemongrass, thyme), veggies, fruit, and honey. In shops like Nutmeg & Co. (p. 271), look for the **fruit jams and bush teas** produced at **Full Belly Farm** (www.fullbellyfarmbvi. com) atop Sage Mountain.

○ **Wine, Beer & Liquor: Riteway** (see above) has all the basics: liquor, wine, and beer. **Chef's Pantry** (see above) at Leverick Bay Marina sells fine wines.

The seaview second-floor terrace at Leverick Bay Resort's restaurant, a proud holdout for old-school steakhouse favorites.

with a red-wine demi-glace and steakhouse fixins', here meaning pureed potatoes and a buttery veggie medley. Or try the tender veal chop in a creamy portobella mushroom sauce. The grilled Anegada lobsters are as celebrated as the steaks, and the rum-tinged Chef Stanley's Coconut Curry Shrimp is a stone-cold winner. All of it is executed without a hitch, and the wine list is excellent. All in all, expect a memorable evening spent with like-minded folk of all ages. A more casual menu is served in the beachside **Cove** restaurant, open 11am to 9pm.

North Sound. www.leverickbay.com. ℂ **284/495-7154.** Entrees $26–$50. Daily 6–9pm.

The Restaurants at Little Dix Bay ★★ INTERNATIONAL The three open-air restaurants at Little Dix are all magical in their own ways, with knockout sea views and ultra-chic midcentury-meets-South Seas stylings, each trying to outdo the other in witchy candlelit ambience. Expect fresh and flavorful food and a warm staff attentive to the point of overzealousness (we don't mind). But these prices—yeesh. The iconic **Pavilion** will forever be enchantment incarnate, a soaring vaulted space hung with (on-trend) basket pendant lighting. The breakfast buffet here is a buzzy and bright scene, with omelets and eggs made to order and a raft of fresh juices and smoothies. The **Sugar Mill,** next door, is smaller and more intimate, with walls of rubble stone; it has a raw bar and menu of small plates for sharing. The handsome new **Reef House,** with seating right over the beach, has perhaps the most innovative menu of them all, serving dishes like stout-barbecued Kurobata pork chops or a Southeast Asian-inspired Cornish hen pot with hints of ginger and lemongrass. Every meal is special here—and the resort's little farm provides a lot of the lettuces and herbs. As good as the Little Dix restaurants are, know that you are just minutes away by vehicle or taxi from Spanish Town

and its array of sexy, fun, and more reasonably priced restos. You're also just 20 minutes from town on foot.

Rosewood Little Dix Bay Resort (p. 280), 1km (⅔ mile) N of Spanish Town. www.rosewoodhotels.com/en/little-dix-bay-virgin-gorda. ℂ **284/495-5555.** Reservations required. Pavilion entrees $29–$64; Sugar Mill small plates $20–$44; Reef House entrees $30–$82. All restaurants daily noon–3pm and 6–9:30pm; Pavilion also daily 7:30–10:30am.

Saba Rock ★★★ INTERNATIONAL   The restaurant traces the contours of the rock on which it stands, like a record on a turntable, giving you a front-row seat for glittering North Sound nights. In high season, the bay becomes a liquid highway where boats skitter back and forth from one dock to another for dinner drop-offs. It's a happy, colorful sight, and at Saba you're at the center of it all. Serving lunch and dinner, the open-air restaurant is not only great-looking, but the food is fresh and exemplary. Look for sprightly, creative appetizers like a beetroot salad with passionfruit in a Key-lime-and-honey dressing or the steak tartare in a jerk dressing. The fresh fish of the day is served with a bouillabaisse sauce, and (if it's on the menu) grilled Caribbean lobster is cooked to perfection. Saba Rock's happy hour is often enlivened by boats arriving from surrounding islands in time to see the daily tarpon feedings at 5pm.

North Sound. sabarock.com. ℂ **284/393-9220.** Reservations required. Entrees $55–$100. Daily 11:30am–9:30pm.

Saba Rock's restaurant gives diners a front-row seat for the North Sound's aquatic comings and goings.

Sugarcane ★★★ INTERNATIONAL/ISLAND   This gorgeous Nail Bay spot is back after the entire compound was leveled by Hurricane Irma in 2017. What began as a burger joint is now something else entirely, sleek and chic and very, very sturdy—this place has been built to last (like its sister restaurant, Saba Rock, above). Reopened in 2019, the poolside sea-facing restaurant has got to be one of the prettiest places to dine on Virgin Gorda. The food is straightforward but good as it gets. Starters range from a grouper ceviche to gazpacho to a Sugarcane Caesar. The dinner menu leans Italian, weighted with pasta dishes like seafood linguine, lasagna, and a hearty penne pasta with sausage, broccoli, and olives; for lunch you might opt for a (very good) pizza, burger, mahi wrap, or pork taco. It's just a 10-minute drive from the ferry docks in Spanish Town.

Nail Bay. www.sugarcane.vg. ℂ **284/495-5455.** Entrees $30–$60; pasta/risotto $20–$32; pizza $16–$26. Wed–Sun 11:30am–10:30pm (kitchen closes 9pm).

MODERATE

If you're hanging around at the Virgin Gorda ferry dock in Spanish Town and feeling peckish, walk outside the terminal parking lot and across the street to **Dixie's** (℗ **284/495-5640**). Its daily buffet is packed with island dishes like oxtail stew, rice/peas, and plantains. It has a full bar, and refreshing fruit juices are $5.

Bath & Turtle/Chez Bamboo ★ CARIBBEAN/ASIAN   Bath & Turtle, a longtime harborfront institution in Spanish Town, moved next door to its sister restaurant after Hurricane Irma hit in 2017. In a colorful shaded courtyard of bamboo and bougainvillea, Bath & Turtle serves breakfast entrees like omelets, johnnycakes, and saltfish for breakfast and burgers, salads, sushi, and Asian specialties (pork shu mai and sesame-crusted tuna) for lunch and dinner ($18–$25). Next door, **Chez Bamboo** is the red-hued night spot, serving pizza along with Asian/Caribbean specials. The restaurants share the same longtime owner and the **Rendezvous Bar,** known for its impressive cocktails.

Across from ferry docks, Spanish Town. www.bathturtle.com. ℗ **284/545-1861.** Breakfast $7–$18.50; burgers and wraps $18–$25; sushi $17–$24. Daily 7:30am–9pm.

Top of the Baths ★ CARIBBEAN   This breakfast and lunch restaurant has a great location, overlooking the famous Baths beach. It's built over a few

---

SIR FRANCIS DRAKE WAS A pirate

His name is known everywhere in the Virgin Islands, most notably by boaters cruising the **Sir Francis Drake Channel,** which snakes through the archipelago from the western tip of Virgin Gorda to the eastern tip of St Thomas. But don't let his title bedazzle you: Drake was a real pirate of the Caribbean.

Arriving in the West Indies as the young captain of the *Judith*, the 16th-century English navigator and explorer (1543–96) found fame (and knighthood) in 1588 as the leader of his country's defense against the Spanish Armada. But his relentless attacks on Spanish ships and plunder of Spanish treasures in the New World made him a pirate enemy to the Spaniards. During his 30 years of circumnavigating the high seas, he proved a cunning, daring sailor, reputedly using the protected cove at Gun Creek, Virgin Gorda, as a hideout.

Drake discovered his eponymous channel in 1595, on his final voyage to the New World. A longtime favorite of

Queen Elizabeth I, the naval hero was brought out of retirement at the ripe old age of 52 for one last West Indies expedition with his fellow adventurer John Hawkins. Their mission: to attack the Spanish fleet in San Juan.

After their plans were discovered, they retreated to Virgin Gorda to wait out the Spaniards. On the night of November 4, their ships slipped out of Virgin Gorda and sailed an unpatrolled, protected route—the new channel—for a surprise attack. Upon arrival, however, they found the San Juan harbor completely blockaded. Drake promptly turned the expedition around to attack Panama.

In the end, the mission wasn't just a bust, it was a tragedy. An already ill Hawkins died before they even reached San Juan, and Drake himself would succumb to dysentery months later aboard ship off the coast of Honduras. Drake and Hawkins were buried together at sea in a lead coffin. But a new sea route had been chartered.

Baths boulders and even has a nice pool to cool off in while you wait for your food. The setting is cool, and the food—a mix of standard Americanized bar food and Caribbean homestyle cooking—is satisfying. We're talking burgers, tuna salads, pastas, and wraps, or local cuisine like conch fritters, curried shrimp, and conch in butter sauce.

The Baths. topofthebaths.com. ✆ **284/495-5497.** Entrees $16–$25; sandwiches & salads $12–$18. Daily 8am–4pm.

INEXPENSIVE

Hog Heaven ★ BARBECUE   It's barbecue with a view at this lunch and dinner hilltop joint, where a sensational panorama of the North Sound is the main draw. Spread out before you, Moskito Island, Necker Island, Eustatia, Saba Rock, Prickly Pear, and Leverick Bay dot the blue seas— on a clear day you can even see the island of Anegada in the distance. The hearty menu includes mains like barbecue ribs, pork, and chicken, conch in butter sauce, and fried chicken (with sides like potato salad, coleslaw, plantains), pulled pork sandwiches, and burgers. Hog Heaven is a prime viewing point to watch powerboats zipping by during the **One Virgin Islands Poker Run** festival, held in mid-July.

North Sound New Rd. ✆ **284/547-5964.** Entrees $18–$25; sandwiches & burgers $9–$11. Daily 10am–10pm.

Exploring Virgin Gorda

The best way to see the island is on an **island tour**—see p. 277 for information on taxi tours. Cost is from $55 (1 hr.) to $220 (4 hr.) for one or two persons, adding $15 to $30 per person more depending on the group size. You can be picked up at the ferry dock if you give 24 hours' notice.

BEACHES

Don't miss the beauty of the **Baths ★★★**, one of the top sights in all the Virgin Islands, where giant boulders exposed by ancient volcanic activity form a series of tranquil pools and grottoes. Located at Virgin Gorda's far southwest tip, the Baths and immediate area are part of the **Baths National Park** (www.bvinpt.org/the-baths; daily 9am–4pm; admission $3 adults, $2 children). A 15-minute trail leads from the Baths beach through the boulders to a secluded coral-sand beach at the adjoining 58-acre **Devil's Bay National Park ★★**. Nearby snorkeling and swimming are excellent, but winter swells can create strong currents.

Moving north up the coast from the Baths you'll find **Spring Bay ★★★**,

The tempting white sands of Spring Bay.

one of the best of the island's beaches, with white sand, clear water, and good snorkeling, and **Trunk Bay,** with its wide sandy beach reachable by boat or along a rough path from Spring Bay. North of Spanish Town, **Savannah Bay ★★★** is a long sandy beach with shallow seas, and **Mahoe Bay ★★★,** fronting the Mango Bay Resort, has a gently curving beach with neon-blue water.

In the North Sound, where most beaches are attached to resorts, the lovely white-sand beach at uninhabited **Prickly Pear Island ★★★** makes an idyllic stopover for a dip in crystal-clear seas and lunch at the **Sand Box Bar & Grill** at Vixen Point. The 180-acre island is a protected national parkland and bird sanctuary. Another sweet white-sand beach lies on the island's north shore facing Eustatia Island, and in between are salt ponds that attract pink flamingos; a hiking trail links both. You'll need your own skiff (or water taxi pickup and drop-off) to get here. The island has an anchorage at Vixen Point and another on the northwest side of Cactus Reef.

WATERSPORTS & OUTDOOR ADVENTURES

Virgin Gorda is a world-class destination for watersports, from diving to snorkeling to kiteboarding to sailing. The North Sound area, protected by Eustatia Reef, has near perfect conditions for kitesurfing and windboarding sports.

DAY CHARTERS & BOAT EXCURSIONS   Offering private island-hopping charters for small groups as well as boat rentals (in boats custom-built here in Virgin Gorda), **Bradley Powerboats BVI ★★** (www.virgingorda powerboatrentals.com; ☏ **284/345-3941**) is a highly recommended local outfitter. Bradley offers day charters out of the Leverick Bay Marina and "join-in" six-person boating and snorkeling excursions to places like Norman Island, the Dogs, and Cooper Island. The rates for full-day charters (including boat, qualified captain services, fuel, cruising permits, snorkel equipment, and a cooler filled with iced beverages of your choice) are $1,250 to $2,950 per day, depending on the boat and number of passengers.

Having a local take you on customized tours of hidden coves and bays in a small boat is pure pleasure. If the boat has a clear bottom, even better. Virgin Gorda native Allington Creque, aka Gumption, is the owner and proprietor of **Sea It Clear Tours ★★** (www.seaitcleartours.com), and his reef and nature tours in glass-bottomed boats are pretty wonderful. **Reef tours** skim the clear jade seas of the Eustatia Reef, just beyond the North Sound, where the marine life is amazing—you may even spot an old cannon on the sea floor. Gumption's 1- and 2-hour tours are $40 an hour ($30 children 12 and under); the 3- and 5-hour tours cost $500 for up to six people ($25/extra person after that, maximum 10 passengers), and full-day adventures are $740 for up to six people ($25/extra person, up to 10 people). Night reef tours are also available. Gumption, who started his business with a $50,000 loan from Sir Richard Branson's Centre for Entrepreneurs Caribbean (in 6 months, Gumption paid it back in full), also offers an exclusive educational **nature tour** of Branson's Necker Island. It's a fun way to get a peek at this private island resort (p. 309) with its menagerie of endangered animals from lemurs to tortoises. Group nature tours cost $115 per adult ($90 seniors, $75 children 5–12) and run daily from 9–11:45am or 1–3:45pm.

HIKING   Virgin Gorda has some of the most breathtaking panoramic vistas in the Caribbean. A good way to see the sights from the heights is on a trek along the stairs and hiking paths that crisscross Virgin Gorda's largest stretch of undeveloped land, the **Gorda Peak National Park.** To reach the best departure point, drive north of the Valley on North Sound Road for about 15 minutes (it'll be very hilly—a four-wheel-drive vehicle is a good idea). Stop at the base of the stairway leading steeply uphill. There's a sign pointing to the Gorda Peak National Park. It should take between 25 and 40 minutes to reach the summit of Gorda Peak, the highest point on the island, where views out over the scattered islets of the Virgin Islands archipelago await you. There's a tower at the summit, which you can climb for even better views.

KAYAKING   You can also do your own Virgin Gorda exploring in **kayaks.** You can rent clear-bottom kayaks or regular tandem kayaks at **Blue Rush Water Sports** (www.bluerushwatersports.com; ✆ **284/343-2002**), at the Leverick Bay Marina on the North Sound, just north of Gun Creek.

KITESURFING/WINDSURFING/KITE SPORTS   Steady trade winds and protected seas make the North Sound one of the top spots in the world for kite sports like windsurfing, kitesurfing (aka kiteboarding), wingsailing, and wingfoiling—it was here, after all, where local island owner Sir Richard Branson gave former U.S. president Barack Obama a kitesurfing lesson. The conditions are ideal: consistent east-northeast trade winds and crystal-clear, relatively shallow, flat waters thanks to protection from the Eustatia Reef. Wingsailing is kiteboarding using an unattached handheld inflatable sail; "foiling" uses a hydrofoil or foilboard that lifts out of the water as you kitesurf. Led by lead instructor Nick Hall, the longtime watersports manager for Richard Branson's nearby Necker and Moskito islands, **Up 'n' Under** (www.upnunderwatersports.com; ✆ **284/340-7340**), at the Saba Rock resort, offers beginner, intermediate, and advanced lessons in kiteboarding and wingfoiling. A full-intro half-day kiteboarding course costs $350 to $440. The Watersports Shack at the **Bitter End Yacht Club** (p. 278) also offers basic kiteboarding and wingsailing lessons and rents equipment.

SAILING   Steady winds and protected waters make the North Sound a great place for sailing. You can rent single-sail, 14-foot Hobie Cats or four-seater 17-foot Hobie Getaways at the Leverick Bay Marina from **Blue Rush Water Sports** (www.bluerushwatersports.com; ✆ **284/343-2002**).

SCUBA DIVING   Founded in 1975 by Bert Kilbrides, the legendary diver and undersea treasure hunter, **Sunchaser Scuba ★** is back at the Bitter End Yacht Club at North Sound (sunchaserscuba.com; ✆ **284/344-2766**), back in business after the 2017 hurricanes. Sunchaser offers full PADI dive instruction, daily boat dives, and dive packages. Dive sites include the Dog Islands, Ginger Island, Cooper Island, Salt Island (home of the RMS *Rhone*), and "art reef" wrecks like *Sharkplaneo* and *Kodiak Queen*. A two-tank dive costs

$135; a one-tank dive in the afternoon is $100. With nearly 50 years of experience in the British Virgin Islands, **Dive BVI** ★ (divebvi.com; ℂ **284/541-9818**) offers full PADI certification courses, single and boat dives, and multi-day dive packages, out of its location at the Virgin Gorda Yacht Harbour. Two-tank dives are $130; night dives are $115.

SNORKELING   Virgin Gorda has some of the region's best and most pristine **snorkeling sites** ★★★, including the world-famous Baths, Spring Bay, Mahoe Bay, and Savannah Bay, in the Valley. In the North Sound, the best snorkeling is inside Eustatia Reef and around Oil Nut Bay. The beach at Little Dix Bay has amazing snorkeling right off the beach, where you'll see lots of sea turtles, rays, tangs, and more. Most hotels and resorts offer complimentary full snorkel gear.

Bradley Powerboats BVI (p. 289) offers six-passenger "join-in" snorkel excursions ($165/person) out of Leverick Bay Marina to places like Anegada, Jost Van Dyke, and Norman and Cooper islands in custom-built powerboats. Its popular "Millionaire Playground" day trip sticks to all things Virgin Gorda: taking passengers first to the Baths, then for a snorkel around the *Kodiak Queen* wreck, to lunch at Oil Nut Bay, and on to snorkel Eustatia Reef, past Google founder Larry Page's Eustatia Island. The trip ends with a visit to Honeymoon Beach on Sir Richard Branson's Moskito Island. **Dive BVI** (see above) offers snorkel excursions around the islands, including the Island Hopper Cruise, a morning of snorkeling followed by lunch and an afternoon at Jost Van Dyke ($140/person), and a full-day Underwater Safari excursion to diving or snorkeling sites around the B.V.I., plus lunch at Cooper Island ($175 diver, $120 snorkeler).

STANDUP PADDLEBOARDING (SUP)   Virgin Gorda's protected bays and covers are ideal for standup paddleboarding. You can rent SUP boards at **Blue Rush Water Sports** (www.bluerushwatersports.com; ℂ **284/343-2002**), at the Leverick Bay Marina.

The watersports center at Oil Nut Bay Resort offers sailing, kayaking, kiteboarding, and many other aquatic activities.

Virgin Gorda Shopping

Shops are sparse here; most of the best shopping is found in the boutiques in the island's upscale resorts. The **Pavilion Shop** (www.rosewoodhotels.com) in the Little Dix Bay resort has a nicely curated selection of beachwear, casual wear, and high-end sunscreens. Look for pretty sweaters and shirts from B.V.I. brand HIHO. Shops at the **Bitter End Yacht Club** (✆ 284/393-2745) include **Reeftique,** with a good selection of kurtas, cotton T's, Henleys, Bitter End beach bags, and the Dritek collection of lightweight quick-dry clothing, and **The Market,** which takes provisioning to a whole other level, with prime steaks, local micro-greens, and jams from Tortola's Full Belly Farm. **Pusser's Company Store,** Leverick Bay Marina (✆ 284/495-7369), sells the usual lineup of Pusser rum products, sportswear, and gift items.

Virgin Gorda After Dark

Evening sees the dance of lights reflected in inky black seas as boats criss-cross the North Sound for **romantic, starlit dinners** in restaurants at Saba Rock, Oil Nut Bay, Leverick Bay, and Blunder Bay Marina, most only accessible via water. The Restaurant at Leverick Bay hosts a seasonal Friday night beach barbecue at its **Cove Restaurant & Jumbies Beach Bar,** featuring Moko Jumbies and fire dancers and dancing to DJ tunes. It's a fun affair, with a full buffet, so book early. Go to www.leverickbayvg.com or call ✆ 284/541-8879 ($40 adults, $20 children 11 and under).

In Spanish Town, the **Bath & Turtle** pub (p. 287; ✆ 284/495-5239), near the ferry terminal, brings in local entertainment on Wednesday nights and Sunday afternoons. Check out the weekly *Welcome Guide to the British Virgin Islands* to see what's happening at the time of your visit.

JOST VAN DYKE ★★★

Home to a few hundred souls, Jost (pronounced "yost") has a rustic, free-spirited character. This rugged 10-sq.-km (4-sq.-mile) island is located right in the middle of the Virgin Islands action, just 3 miles from Tortola, 5 miles from St. John, and 9 miles from St. Thomas. It's named for Captain Jost Van Dyke, a 17th-century Dutch settler and privateer. In the 1700s, a Quaker colony settled here to develop sugar-cane plantations. (One of the colonists, William Thornton, won a worldwide competition to design the U.S. Capitol building in Washington, D.C.).

Along Jost's south shore are two of the British Virgin Islands' prettiest

White Bay on Jost Van Dyke is a top day-trip spot, with its sugary sands and famed beach bars.

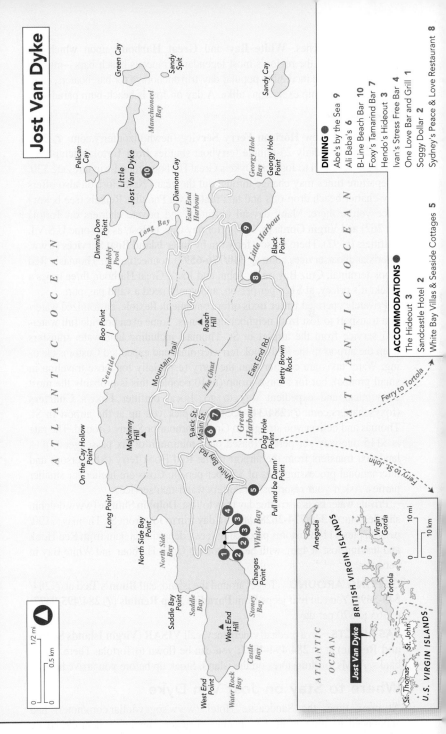

Jost Van Dyke

DINING ●
Abe's by the Sea **9**
Ali Baba's **6**
B-Line Beach Bar **10**
Foxy's Tamarind Bar **7**
Hendo's Hideout **3**
Ivan's Stress Free Bar **4**
One Love Bar and Grill **1**
Soggy Dollar **2**
Sydney's Peace & Love Restaurant **8**

ACCOMMODATIONS ●
The Hideout **3**
Sandcastle Hotel **2**
White Bay Villas & Seaside Cottages **5**

sugary-sand beaches, **White Bay** and **Great Harbour,** upon which are plopped some of the region's most legendarily raucous beach bars—making this little island an incredibly popular day-trip anchorage for bareboaters, charters, and cruise-ship excursions alike. A day on Jost is beach-bum paradise.

Essentials

ARRIVING   **New Horizon Ferry Service** (newhorizonferry.com; $\textcircled{c}$ **284/ 495-9278**) runs daily 25-minute ferryboat shuttles from Tortola's temporary West End terminal to Jost Van Dyke's Great Harbour; round-trip fares are $30. (Departure times may change throughout the year.) New Horizon also offers day-charter beach drop-offs and taxi rentals via Paradise Rentals (see below) once you're there. Many daysail outfitters and private charters on Tortola (p. 262) and Virgin Gorda (p. 289) offer day trips to Jost, as do some U.S.V.I. outfitters (p. 97). There's also a ferry run by **Inter Island Boat Services** (www. interislandboatservices.com; $\textcircled{c}$ **340/776-6597**) connecting St. Thomas's Red Hook terminal, Cruz Bay on St. John, and Jost's Great Harbour, three times a week; it's pricey, at $120 per person, and you'll need a valid passport.

Privately operated **water taxis** offer convenient, flexible, customized water-taxi transport to Jost from neighboring islands. Some even provide full water-taxi service from the airport in St. Thomas, including land/water transfers from the airport to the Red Hook ferry terminal and expedited Customs clearing. Water taxis are costlier than the ferry (especially for those traveling in small groups), but for a large group (8–10 people), this is probably the most economical and expedient way to go. Local outfitter **Foxy's Charters** (foxyscharters.com; $\textcircled{c}$ **284/346-0356**) can pick you up at the airport in St. Thomas and deliver you straight to Great Harbour or Sandy Ground. The rate is $115 one-way per person (based on a minimum of six passengers), plus land-taxi transfers from the airport to the Red Hook ferry ($19/person) and international processing fees of $50 per person. Costs are higher for smaller parties. Ask if your resort or villa offers water-taxi service.

Private water taxis also offer day trips to Jost. **Dolphin Shuttle** (www.dolphin shuttle.com; $\textcircled{c}$ **340/774-2628**) offers a day trip to Jost from St. Thomas ($190/ person, plus $110 Customs processing fees), departing at 9am from Red Hook and leaving Jost at 4pm, with beach stops at Great Harbour and White Bay in between.

GETTING AROUND   To get around the island, call **Bunn's Taxi** at $\textcircled{c}$ **284/ 543-3695.** You can rent jeeps from **Paradise Jeep Rentals** ($\textcircled{c}$ **284/495-9477**) at $65 to $70 per day.

FAST FACTS   In a medical emergency, call **VISAR (Virgin Islands Search and Rescue)** at $\textcircled{c}$ **284/494-4357;** you can be flown to Tortola. There are no banks, ATMs, or drugstores on the island. Stock up before you arrive here.

Where to Stay on Jost Van Dyke

At press time, the Sandcastle Hotel (www.soggydollar.com/hotel) had announced its long-awaited reopening, 5 years after being demolished by

Hurricane Irma. Long joined at the hip to the legendary beach bar **Soggy Dollar** (p. 296), this barefoot hotel first opened in 1970.

The Hideout ★★   Which came first, the beach bar or the hotel? In this case, the beautiful restaurant/bar **Hendo's Hideout** made its splashy debut on White Bay in 2016 (and reopened again in 2018 and 2021; see p. 297). Making an equally splashy entrance, the adjacent seven-villa luxury retreat opened for business in 2022. Fully formed from the get-go, the Hideout brings design-mag boutique fancy to laidback Jost: private plunge pools for each villa, tasteful design stylings, and private ground-level beach lounges. Five villas are on the ocean, two on a hillside with garden views. Two two-bedroom villas sleep four guests and have full kitchens and 1,326 square feet of indoor/outdoor living space.

White Bay. thehideoutbvi.com. ✆ **284/393-9200.** 7 units. $595–$650 1-bedroom villa; $795–$915 2-bedroom villa. **Amenities:** Restaurant/bar; watersports equipment; free Wi-Fi.

White Bay Villas & Seaside Cottages ★★   With its eye-candy sea views and easy access to a white-sand beach, this is a tranquil, secluded retreat on raucous Jost. Perched above the sea, all the handsome cottages were built by owner John Klein and comprise a range of fully equipped accommodations, from one-, two-, and three-bedroom houses to a five-bedroom villa for up to 10 guests—the Plantation Villa, which has a great room and kitchen decorated with murals depicting the island's culture. New is the private beach-level **White Bay Beach Club,** with lockers and beach loungers and towels and a menu of drinks and snacks (like pizza). The staff throughout is warm and welcoming. For an additional fee, White Bay Villas will arrange provisioning services for your villa, so your kitchen is fully stocked when you arrive. They can also arrange water taxi land/water transfers from the St. Thomas airport.

White Bay. www.jostvandyke.com. ✆ **800/778-8066** or 284/541-1900. 20 villas. $329–$489 double; $1,299 Plantation Villa; call about rates for other villas. **Amenities:** Beach club/bar; watersports equipment; free Wi-Fi.

An offshoot of Hendo's Hideout restaurant, the Hideout brings a note of luxury to the beach shack aesthetic.

Soggy Dollar Bar & the Infamous Painkiller

Even the lowliest beach shack on Jost has some version of the two-fisted rum drink known as the Painkiller—served with a dainty jar of powdered nutmeg to sprinkle on top. A blend of island rum, orange juice, pineapple juice, and cream of coconut, the Painkiller got its start at the **Soggy Dollar Bar** (www.soggydollar. com; ✆ 284/495-9888), the quintessential Jost beach bar ("a sunny place for shady people"), on the sugary sands of White Bay. An Englishwoman, Daphne Henderson, is said to have invented the drink in the 1980s. Today the Painkiller is probably the most popular drink among sailors (and landlubbers) in the B.V.I., and many people believe the Soggy Dollar makes the definitive version. A visit to the Soggy Dollar is a rite of passage for visitors to Jost.

Where to Eat & Drink on Jost Van Dyke

Abe's by the Sea ★ WEST INDIAN   This all-purpose sailors' stop serves lunch and dinner and specializes in seasonal local seafood like lobster and conch. "Casual" doesn't begin to describe the low-key nature of this modest dockside spot, cobbled together with plywood and serving what fans say is the coldest beer on island.

Little Harbour. www.facebook.com/abesrestuarantbvi. ✆ **284/544-9981** or 284/496-8429. Reservations recommended for groups of 5 or more. Dinner $20–$45. Daily 11:30am–11pm.

Ali Baba's ★ CARIBBEAN   Fashioned from unvarnished beams and planks, this restaurant near the edge of the harbor has a breezy veranda right next to the Customs House. Lots of people swear by the delicious seafood preparations and well-executed versions of island staples, such as fresh mahi topped with peppers and onions, spiny lobster, conch chowder, conch fritters, and savory pumpkin

A stop at the Soggy Dollar bar is practically a ritual for visitors to Jost Van Dyke.

soup. They'll even cook up your just-caught fish for you. If you're on the island in time for breakfast, drop in to join the locals for a tasty wake-up meal.

Great Harbour. www.alibabasrestaurantandbarbvi.com. ✆ **284/495-9280.** Breakfast from $10; entrees lunch $9–$12, dinner $18–$22. Daily 9am–11pm.

B-Line Beach Bar ★ CARIBBEAN Opened on the south side of Little Jost Van Dyke in 2019, the B-Line is in fact pretty much the *only* establishment on this 163-acre island off Jost's east end—and, like the best of the seadog beach shacks, it's only accessible by boat. The B-Line is basically a wooden roof, some chairs, a bar, some more chairs (lounge) on the white-sand beach, and a cornhole game. The booze includes a rum infused with honey. Food is now on the menu, and very good food, too, as you might expect from the owner of one of Tortola's best restaurants, Bananakeet (p. 255). Think barbecued shrimp, ribs, and chicken, curry chicken, and grilled fish, with sides of coleslaw or pasta salad. Bring snorkel gear—you won't want to miss the undersea extravaganza here.

Little Jost Van Dyke. www.facebook.com/blinebeachbar.vi. ✆ **284/343-3311.** Entrees $25–$28. Daily 9am–6pm.

Foxy's Tamarind Bar ★ WEST INDIAN On an island known for its legendary beach bars, this may be the most famous. Opened in the 1960s by sixth-generation Jost Van Dyke native Philicianno "Foxy" Callwood, Foxy's gets rambunctious most nights, with music ranging from rock 'n' roll to reggae to soca. The food is good and plentiful—order up a Foxy's Painkiller punch along with lobster, conch fritters, and pan-seared mahi mahi with Creole sauce. On Friday and Saturday nights, the beach barbecue buffet ($35/person), starring grilled barbeque ribs, chicken, and mahi, is definitely the place to be. But the biggest party of all is Foxy's Old Year's Night celebration around New Year's.

Great Harbour. foxysbar.com. ✆ **284/442-3074.** Reservations recommended. Lunch $10–$15; dinner $18–$35. Daily 9am–11pm.

Foxy Callwood, longtime proprietor of Foxy's Tamarind Bar, poses for selfies with partiers.

Hendo's Hideout ★★ CARIBBEAN A winner from the get-go, this locally owned beachfront restaurant is a great-looking spot bringing foodie-friendly fine dining to the sands of White Bay. The vibe is casual, but the fresh, creative food is notches above standard beach-bar fare. Consider the seafood sandwich, wherein a house-made crab cake is topped with jerked

PROVISIONING jost

Many villas can arrange provisioning services. In Tortola, both **Riteway** (www.rtwbvi.com; ℂ **284/437-1188**) and **Bobby's Marketplace** (www.bobbysmarketplace.com; ℂ **284/494-2189**) have direct provisioning services via ferry to Jost Van Dyke, for a fee. Jost has loads of restaurants and beach bars, but only a handful of small grocery stores, selling a range of

fresh foods, snacks, dry provisions, beer, wine, sodas, and liquor. In Great Harbour, **Rudy's Marketplace** (rudysjvd.wixsite.com/rudys; ℂ **284/441-5771**), has the largest selection and free delivery, open Monday-Friday 7am-7pm, Saturday 8am-7pm, Sunday 9am-6pm; there's also **JVD Grocery** (jvdgrocery.com; ℂ **284/343-6443**), open daily 8am-8pm.

shrimp and "crabslaw"—hellooo! Or the rum-and-Coke pulled pork sandwich. Or the lobster ravioli in a winey tomato cream sauce. Fresh-rolled sushi (including a Pink Pirate Roll—salmon on the outside, shrimp tempura on the inside) is served on Sushi Thursdays (5–8pm). So do your Soggy Dollar thing next door and then settle in for a serious dinner here.

White Bay. hendoshideout.com. ℂ **284/340-0074.** Entrees $28–$58. Mon–Tues 10am–4pm; Wed–Sat 10am–8pm; Sun brunch 10am–6pm.

Ivan's Stress Free Bar ★ BURGERS/PUB GRUB   Seventh-generation Jost Van Dyke native Ivan Chinnery oversees Ivan's Stress Free Bar sundowners with sailors and locals at your elbows, while also playing guitar in the White Bay International Ever-Changing All Star Band (the house band). Lunch fare is simple, from grilled fish to burgers to tasty island-centric wraps (jerk chicken mango, creamy coconut shrimp, veggie curry). Visiting musicians often drop in, and the Wednesday night beach barbecue buffet—a groaning board of barbeque chicken and ribs, grilled steak, garlic butter conch, jerk pork, and grilled fish—is a must (6:30–9:30pm; $35/person). Happy hour (5–7pm) offers two-for-one cocktails and $5 wings. Ivan also runs **Ivan's Stress Free Guesthouse,** two island cottages with four suites for rent on the hillside above the bar ($175–$275/night, 3- to 4-night minimum stays, or $1,000–$1,900/week).

White Bay. www.ivanswhitebay.net or www.facebook.com/ivansstressfreebarjvd. ℂ **284/547-3375.** Entrees $11–$21; wraps $13–$21. Daily 10am–sunset.

One Love Bar and Grill ★★ CARIBBEAN   Seddy Callwood, Foxy's oldest son (p. 297), operates one of the liveliest spots on the island. The house policy of "No Shoes, No Shirt, No Problem" is said to have inspired Kenny Chesney's hit song. The menu (daily 10am–5pm) includes lobster quesadillas, seafood pastas, grouper sandwiches—washed down with a knee-knocking Bushwhacker. One Love features live reggae music in the afternoons; as soon as the sun sets, Seddy locks up and goes home.

White Bay. seddysonelovebarandgrill.com. ℂ **282/495-9829.** Entrees $15–$28. Daily 10am–sunset.

Sydney's Peace & Love Restaurant ★★ LOBSTER/ISLAND This good-value, casual-dining family-run spot has some of the best local food on island, including Caribbean lobster and barbecued chicken. Preparations are simple and no-frills. Many people have been coming to Sydney's for years.

Little Harbour. ⓒ **284/495-9271.** Reservations required for dinner by 4pm. Entrees $22–$33. Daily 10am–9pm.

Watersports & Outdoor Adventures

Most of the activities on Jost are water-based, although the island has botanical trails and nature preserves for your hiking and nature-watching pleasure. A one-stop shop is the island's top outfitter and only dive center, Jost Van Dyke Scuba (**JVD Scuba;** jostvandykescuba.com; ⓒ **284/443-2222**), in Great Harbour. JVD Scuba is an affiliate of B.V.I. Eco-Tours and as such offers a wide range of services and excursions. Its exclusive daily **scuba diving trips** visit newly opened diving sites in the Northwest Territory out-islands. A two-tank dive is $135, and a night dive is $140. A 3-day Out-Island Scuba Dive package (six dives, six sites) is $355 per person; a 5-day package (10 dives, 10 sites) is $550; and a 10-day package (20 dives, 20 sites) costs $925. JVD also offers a full range of PADI dive courses and certifications.

JVD Scuba can also set you up with **snorkeling trips** and **eco-tours** to places like Norman Island and Virgin Gorda. One popular Jost-centric trip combines snorkeling, hiking, sightseeing, and bird-watching: Jost Van Dyke by Sea travels to places like Sandy Spit and Green Cay and includes a little hike to Jost's **"bubbly pools"**: a natural jacuzzi and tidal pool on the island's north shore. This full-day excursion is $99 per person (minimum four people).

The B.V.I. has some of the region's best **sportfishing,** both deep-sea and inshore, and Jost is just 11 miles away from the world-famous North Drop, where giant blue marlin and other pelagic big boys congregate. Inshore fishing trips include tarpon hunts and flyfishing for bonefish. JVD Scuba runs custom charters for both. Half-day rates for deep-sea fishing trips for four

---

Sandy Spit: The Corona Beach

Across a narrow channel from Jost Van Dyke's northeast corner, Little Jost Van Dyke is home to the **B-Line Bar** (p. 297) and not much else. Just southeast of Little Jost, Sandy Spit is exactly what it sounds: a small, uninhabited spit of an isle that is the castaway beach of your dreams. It's known as the "Corona beach" for its fame in a beer commercial. Hurricane Irma whittled down the island acreage somewhat, but this little half-acre cay has retained its pristine good looks, a fringe of green ringed in powdery white sand and aqua seas. Bring everything you need (there's nothing on Sandy Spit) and get here early so you won't have to share the sand. A number of day charters (including JVD Scuba, see above) can deliver you there, anchoring off the island and letting you dinghy or swim ashore.

people are $895; full-day deep-sea trips are $1,495. Half-day inshore sport-fishing charters for four people are $695; 2-hour inshore trips are $495.

JVD also offers **watersports rentals:** snorkel gear ($15/day); standup paddleboards (SUP; $60/day, $295/week); kayaks ($50–$75/day); and complete scuba gear ($50/day; tank rental or filling $10).

ANEGADA ★★★

The most remote of the British Virgins, 15-square-mile Anegada is the second-largest island in the B.V.I. chain, yet its permanent population is only around 315 people, most of whom live in or around the main village, known as the **Settlement.** Located 30 miles east of Tortola and 15 miles north of Virgin Gorda, Anegada is an outlier from the other British Virgins in other ways as well. In contrast to their voluptuous volcanic topography, Anegada is a flat atoll of coral and limestone (its name is Spanish for "drowned island"). The highest point on the island only reaches 8m (26 ft.); when you're sailing to Anegada, it's barely a blip on the horizon.

Horseshoe Reef ★★★, the bony necklace of coral that encircles and protects the island, is the fourth-largest coral reef on the planet and a notorious scourge of mariners. More than 300 wrecks litter the reef; many a B.V.I. bareboating fantasy has run aground here. It's also the closest island in the B.V.I. to the legendary North Drop (20 min. by boat), where the sloping sea wall plunges into undersea canyons and game fish thrive. Snorkeling, sport-fishing, and kitesurfing are major draws.

Any trip to Anegada has to include a visit to the idyllic **beaches ★★** on its northern and western shores, including **Loblolly Bay,** a breathtaking stretch of blinding white sand; **Cow Wreck Beach,** where kiteboarders skim flat lagoon-like seas; and the fringing reefs of **Flash of Beauty,** which draw snorkelers. Nature lovers will find much to love here: The B.V.I. National Parks Trust has established a flamingo colony here (they flock to the old salt ponds), and it's also the protected home of several varieties of heron, ospreys, and terns. Much of the island's interior is a preserved habitat for Anegada's animal population of some 2,000 wild goats, donkeys, and cattle.

Many of the young staff at Virgin Gorda's top resorts come to Anegada to chill, hang out, and do a little kitesurfing. In fact, when we last visited, a group of community-minded twentysomethings rushed to the island on their day off when they heard a pod of about 40 pilot whales had mysteriously beached on the white sands. They spent hours shepherding the handful of whales that were still alive over the sharp-edged reef back into open sea.

Anegada is a low-key, friendly, unspoiled place to relax to the retro rhythms of the Caribbean. Don't expect a single frill, and be prepared to put up with a few minor hardships, such as roads made of concrete and sand. Come to Anegada for the community, the wild beauty, and the tranquility, not so much for posh pampering. But come soon: Ever so slowly, the modern world is coming to Anegada.

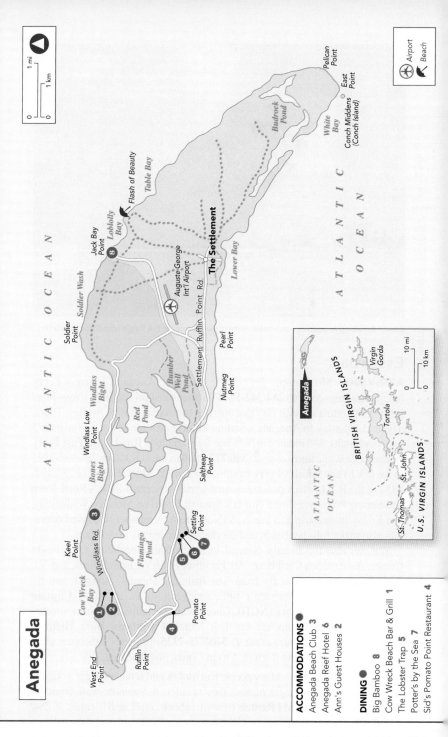

Anegada

ATLANTIC OCEAN

West End Point

Cow Wreck Bay

Keel Point

Windlass Rd.

Ruffin Point

Pomato Point

Setting Point

Saltheap Point

Flamingo Pond

Red Pond

Bones Bight

Windlass Low Point

Windlass Bight

Soldier Wash

Soldier Point

Jack Bay Point

Flash of Beauty

Table Bay

Loblolly Bay

Bumber Well Pond

Nutmeg Point

Pearl Point

Auguste George Int'l Airport

Settlement Ruffin Point Rd.

The Settlement

Lower Bay

Budrock Pond

White Bay

Conch Middens (Conch Island)

East Point

Pelican Point

ATLANTIC OCEAN

ACCOMMODATIONS ●
Anegada Beach Club **3**
Anegada Reef Hotel **6**
Ann's Guest Houses **2**

DINING ●
Big Bamboo **8**
Cow Wreck Beach Bar & Grill **1**
The Lobster Trap **5**
Potter's by the Sea **7**
Sid's Pomato Point Restaurant **4**

0 — 1 mi
0 — 1 km

Airport
Beach

BRITISH VIRGIN ISLANDS

ATLANTIC OCEAN

Anegada

Virgin Gorda

Tortola

St. Thomas

St. John

U.S. VIRGIN ISLANDS

0 — 10 mi
0 — 10 km

301

Conditions along Anegada's north coast make it the top spot in the Virgin Islands for kitesurfing.

Essentials

ARRIVING   Most people get here by boat. The **Anegada Express Ferry** (anegadaexpress.com; ✆ 284/343-5343) is a seasonal private ferry (Nov–June/ July) from Tortola's Trellis Bay that operates two round-trips on Sunday, Thursday, and Saturday to Anegada's Setting Point. Fares are $50 round-trip ($35 one-way) adults, $40 round-trip ($25 one-way) children. **Road Town Fast Ferry** (www.roadtownfastferry.com; ✆ **340/777-2800** in the U.S.V.I. or 284/494-2323 in the B.V.I.) and **Smith's Ferry** (smithsferry.com; ✆ **340/775-7292** or 284/494-4454 in the B.V.I.) also operate seasonal ferries between Tortola's Road Town and Setting Point (via Virgin Gorda's Spanish Town) on Monday, Wednesday, and Friday (round-trip $55 adults, $35 children). A number of daysail operators also make full-day beach and snorkeling excursions to Anegada.

You can also fly directly. Several local air charter operators (Ace Flight Center, Air America Caribbean, Air Paradise, Fly BVI, Island Birds, and V.I. Airlink, to name a few) fly from San Juan, St. Thomas, Antigua, and St. Maarten directly to Anegada's little smidgeon of an air strip, **Captain Auguste George Airport (NGD).** Check with the individual airlines to see which of these locations are on their routes. **Caribbean Buzz Helicopters** (www.caribbean-buzz.com; ✆ **340/775-7335**) provides helicopter charters between St. Thomas, Tortola, Virgin Gorda, and Anegada.

GETTING AROUND   Many people rent **mokes and scooters** to get around— go with the four-passenger mokes; they're safer. A 5-minute walk from the Anegada ferry dock, **L&H Rentals** (www.facebook.com/LandHRentals; ✆ **284/ 441-0799**) specializes in moke sightseeing cars ($80/day) and free delivery anywhere on the island. **Anegada Amazing Rentals** (www.facebook.com/

anegadascooters; ✆ **284/346-5658**), in Setting Point, rents scooters ($45/day), mini-mokes ($80/day), and SUVs ($85/day). They even sell lobsters.

Taxi drivers offer both transfers and island tours. Recommended drivers include **L&M's Taxi** (✆ **284/441-0563**). One-way trips are $20 for one to two people, and $10 per person for three or more. Taxi rates are standardized by the government. L&M also rents cars ($75 and up per day), scooters ($50/day), and dirt bikes ($60/day).

FAST FACTS   Anegada has a small fire department and a little library, but it has no banks, ATMs, or drugstores. Make adequate arrangements for supplies before coming here.

Where to Stay on Anegada

Anegada Beach Club ★★★   Named the 2022 Small Hotel of the Year by *Caribbean Journal,* this glamping resort brings boutique style to Anegada. While a stay in the hotel's beachside tents was pretty awesome pre-Irma, the stunning (and sturdy) ocean view Palapa Retreats rebuilt after the hurricane are simply amazing. The palapas all have king canopy beds, rain-shower bathrooms, and swinging deck hammocks; one beachside palapa even has an extra deck with two side-by-side soaking tubs. The restored pool is beautiful; the excellent **poolside restaurant ★** serves breakfast, lunch, and dinner (the house specialty is Anegada BLLT, with lobster, of course). The resort has a complete watersports center in the on-site **Tommy Gaunt Kitesurfing** (www.tommygauntkitesurfing.com; ✆ 284/344-9903), a full-service kitesurfing school that also offers kite, paddleboard, and kayak rentals, sailing lessons and sailboat rentals, and kayak eco-trips into the island mangroves. *One thing to remember:* ABC is fairly remote, with no real stores or other restaurants

Thatch roofs and hammocks bring a castaway vibe to the glamping resort Anegada Beach Club.

The Conch Islands

If there's one thing Anegadans have a surplus of, it's **conch,** which thrive in the island's reef-protected beds of seagrass. On the eastern shores of the island tall mounds of conch shells are piled high in shallow seas. Scientists believe these shell middens are thousands of years old, begun by the Arawak people who lived on Anegada in pre-Columbian times. Carbon data done on one of the mounds in 2013 revealed radiocarbon dates going back to A.D. 1245. Of course, fishermen have been piling on ever since; the largest mounds have reached heights of 10 to 12 feet, even weathering hurricanes of Category 5 strength. You can visit the conch islands and even take a swim around them on **boat tours** (p. 306).

nearby, but the resort also owns the **Lobster Trap** (p. 305) at Setting Point and offers free shuttles there and back.

Keel Point. anegadabeachclub.com. (C) **284/346-4005.** 25 units. $235 hotel room; $435 family suite; $390–$460 1-bedroom palapa; $775 2-bedroom palapa. Ages 6 and older only in palapas. **Amenities:** Restaurant; bar; gift shop; guest laundry; kitesurfing school; outdoor pool; watersports equipment; free Wi-Fi.

Anegada Reef Hotel ★★ For more than 45 years, this has been the island's main lodging, opened in 1976 by Lowell and Vivian Wheatley. Still owned and operated by the Wheatley family, the Anegada Reef sits right on a white-sand beach, about a 5-minute drive west of the airport. It's a friendly, casual place with newly refreshed rooms, all with private porches and ocean views. Have a sunset cocktail in the **Sunset Bar** and then dinner at the alfresco **hotel restaurant ★**, serving breakfast, lunch, and dinner daily; its evening specialty is Anegada spiny lobster. If you're visiting the island for the day, you can use the hotel as a base and arrange to go deep-sea fishing or bonefishing. You can also rent a **mini-moke** here through **L&H Rentals** (p. 302).

Setting Point. www.anegadareef.com. (C) **284/495-8002.** 20 units. $175–$275 double. **Amenities:** Restaurant; bar; babysitting; free Wi-Fi.

Ann's Guest Houses ★ In a neat lineup in the sands on Cow Wreck Beach, these eight new guest cottages come in an array of bright tropical hues. Four are 650-square-foot one-bedroom cottages with front porches and full kitchens; two are two-bedroom cottages with 1,100 square feet of space and kitchens; and two are 500-square-foot studios with kitchenettes. All come with personal barbeque grills, but you may find yourself too busy dining in the complex "clubhouse"—**Tipsy Bar**—to even get the grill going.

Cow Wreck Beach. www.cowwreckbeachbvi.com. (C) **284/440-4149** or 954/516-8957. $175–$200 studio or 1-bedroom cottage; $375 2-bedroom cottage. **Amenities:** Restaurant/bar; free Wi-Fi.

Where to Eat on Anegada

Anegada is famous for its **lobster,** which can grow up to 18 pounds here. The Anegada lobster is celebrated yearly at the **Anegada Lobster Festival ★★** on Black Friday weekend in November.

For a sparsely populated island, Anegada seems to have an awful lot of buzzing beachside restaurants and bars. Priorities, people! The most important thing is to **reserve your dinner table in advance.** Most places ask that you call in by phone or VHF channel and make a reservation by 4 or 5pm and place your lobster order in advance. Also keep in mind that most businesses shut down somewhere between mid-August and late October.

Big Bamboo ★★ CARIBBEAN   Big Bamboo's cocktails, as one patron put it, get you where you want to go, but we can't imagine being anywhere but here on beautiful Loblolly Beach. This popular local bar/restaurant has a large, open-air dining pavilion set away from the beach. Fancy it is not, but locals and day-tripping sailors alike rave about the fresh Anegada lobster. You can also order baby back ribs and conch fritters. Rest your weary alimentary canal after a big meal in a nearby hammock beneath a coconut palm, as waves roll up on the beach and cows stroll by.

Loblolly Bay. bigbambooanegada.com. ☎ **284/346-5850.** Reservations recommended for large groups. Entrees $16–$40 lunch; $22–$45 dinner. Daily 10am–6pm.

Cow Wreck Beach Bar & Grill ★★ CARIBBEAN/SEAFOOD   Don't miss a sunset sundowner at this family-run old-timer, a favorite among yachties anchoring at Anegada. Diners relax on a terrace where tables and plastic chairs feature views of the water just steps away. If you go during lunch, you can snorkel in the sparkling seas until your food is ready. Fans claim the Cow Wreck serves the best lobster in the B.V.I., but it also offers tasty grilled steaks, ribs, chicken, and local grilled fish.

Lower Cow Wreck Beach. www.facebook.com/cowwreck.beach. ☎ **284/495-8047.** Reservations required for dinner. Entrees $18–$53. Daily 7am–6pm; dinner at 6pm but later reservations can be accommodated. Bar open "until the last customer departs."

The Lobster Trap ★★ CARIBBEAN/SEAFOOD   If you like your fresh grilled Anegada lobster in a beachfront sunset setting, this smartly renovated palapa-topped restaurant is a fine place for it. A spacious deck has its feet literally planted in the calm blue seas. Tables beneath big teal roofs overlook a harbor filled with boats; twinkly fairy lights greet you as you tie up your dinghy to the pier. The Caribbean spiny lobster here comes in many iterations, from blackened to grilled to thermidor to lobster cakes, and is cooked the Anegada way, in oil-drum barbecues over open-air flames. For those taking a lobster break, the kitchen does deft preparations of seafood pastas, steaks, burgers, and more. Full-moon parties come with bonfires, DJs, and s'mores. The Lobster Trap is in the Anegada Beach Club family (p. 303), and the resort offers a free shuttle ride over for meals.

Setting Point. www.facebook.com/thelobstertrapbvi. ☎ **284/495-5055.** Reservations required for dinner. Entrees $10–$50. Daily 11am–10pm.

Sid's Pomato Point Restaurant ★★ LOBSTER/CARIBBEAN/TACOS Set back from the sea, fans whirring, breezes blowing, this large, open-air restaurant opened in 2019 but only had its first full season in 2021. It's already a must-do on the Anegada dining circuit. The owner is celebrated local bartender Sidney Wheatley, who has created a rustically stylish spot with whitewashed beamed ceilings, a hand-crafted bar, wooden decking, and comfy lounge seating. Inside Sid's serves lobster, of course, conch in several iterations (stew, fritters, ceviche), fish dinners, ribs, and steaks. It also has a taco menu, including a smashing lobster taco.

Pomato Point. ✆ **284/441-5565.** Reservations required for dinner. Entrees $18–$55. Daily 11am–11pm.

Potter's by the Sea ★★ LOBSTER/CARIBBEAN   The open charcoal barbecue grills at Potter's are the real workhorses at this seafront restaurant. Lobster, fresh local fish (mahi, grouper), ribs, and chicken are all cooked on the grills, flavored by torchwood collected right here on Anegada. Potter's also serves several excellent shrimp dishes, including a buttery shrimp scampi, curry shrimp, and shrimp fettucine. Tie your dingy up to the large dock and dine in a colorful deck stretching out over the water. Then dance to DJ'd tunes under the stars. Dinner reservations and orders required by 4pm.

Setting Point. pottersanegada.com. ✆ **284/341-9769.** VHF Channel 16. Reservations required for dinner; book by 4pm. Entrees $25–$50. Daily 8am-1am.

Watersports & Outdoor Adventures

Anegada is all about laidback beach days and full-tilt water adventures. Snorkeling Horseshoe Reef can be one of the highlights of any trip to Anegada. The best way to take it all in is on a **charter boat tour.** Two outfitters are highly recommended. Sherwin Walcott's **Sea Adventures** with **TeamWork Charters** ★★ (www.facebook.com/teamworkfishing; ✆ **284/440-3243**) runs half- and full-day powerboat excursions that might include snorkeling Horseshoe Reef, a visit to Cow Wreck Beach, and seeing the conch islands. On **Kelly's Land & Sea Tours** ★★ (www.facebook.com/AnegadaTours; ✆ **284/496-0961**), Captain Kelly leads snorkeling, sightseeing, lobster hunting, and conch harvesting. Some of these tours include a "float snorkel" over part of

An excursion to the conch islands with Sea Adventures with TeamWork Charters.

Horseshoe Reef. It is illegal to anchor on the reef, and there are no moorings, so float snorkels let you float with the current over the reef as the boat maneuvers around to pick you up.

KITESURFING/KAYAKING/STANDUP PADDLEBOARDING With miles of flatwater lagoons and steady winds, Anegada has probably the best conditions in the B.V.I. for kite and board sports. Led by kitesurfer Tommy Gaunt, **Tommy Gaunt Kitesurfing** (www.tommygauntkitesurfing.com; ☎ **284/344-9903**) is a full-service kitesurfing school at the Anegada Beach Club, offering all levels of kiting and standup paddleboarding (SUP) lessons and guided trips from November through June. It also offers kite and paddleboard rentals, guided mangrove paddle/kayak trips, and sailing lessons and sailboat rentals.

FISHING This sportfishing paradise also has some of the best and most pristine **bonefishing flats ★★★** in the world. Take a flyfishing expedition for bonefish with **Danny's Bonefishing ★** (dannysbonefishing.com; ☎ **284/441-6334**), guided trips to the southern and eastern flats of Anegada. Half-day trips for one to two people are $400; three-quarter-day trips $600; extra person $75.

THE PRIVATE ISLAND RESORTS

Among the smaller islands and cays of the B.V.I. are a number of exclusive private island resorts, many of them owned by some of the world's wealthiest people, which offer uniquely bespoke island experiences in uncrowded, luxurious surrounds.

Five years after being pummeled by hurricanes Irma and Maria, the **Peter Island Resort and Spa** was still in rebuilding mode at press time and remained silent on when (and if) the 720-hectare (1,779-acre) resort would open. The B.V.I.'s largest private island had 52 hotel rooms and three villas, a spa, and a marina. Check for updates at www.peterisland.com.

Guana Island ★★★

This 340-hectare (840-acre) island resort is one of the most private hideaways in the Caribbean. Don't come here looking for action; do come if you seek serenity and rustic old-school luxury. Just off the north coast of Tortola, Guana has virgin beaches, nature trails, and rare and unusual species of plant and animal life, including iguana, red-legged tortoise, and the Caribbean roseate flamingo. Arawak relics have even been discovered here. You can climb 242m (794-ft.) Sugarloaf Mountain for a panoramic view. Guana Island sends a boat to meet arriving guests at the Beef Island airport on Tortola (trip time is 10 min.).

Guana Island was purchased in 1974 by dedicated conservationists Henry and Gloria Jarecki, and it's both a nature preserve and wildlife sanctuary. This is one stunning, 840-acre landscape: Upon your arrival by boat, you're met at the docks and transported up one of the most scenic hills in the region. From above you'll see an old salt pond dotted with pink flamingos and the lacy fringes of beautiful White Bay, the island's main beach. Guana even has the

Guana Island is part luxury resort, part nature sanctuary.

ruins of an old sugar-cane plantation. The island has seven beaches in all, five of which are only accessible by boat. All have sand as soft as talcum powder, lapped by clear sapphire seas.

Accommodations are in a cluster of white-stone cottages built as a private club in the 1930s, on the foundations of a Quaker homestead. Each cottage has its own unique decor, but the theme throughout is rustic elegance: wood-beam ceilings and New England–style wainscotting. Because the 18 dwellings are staggered along a flower-dotted ridge overlooking the Caribbean and Atlantic seas, the sense of privacy is almost absolute. You stay in seaside cottage rooms or one of five villas, each with its own infinity pool and four with a private golf cart. The North Beach villa has its own pool *and* beach. Most cottages have air-conditioning, but guests find the hillside breezes plenty cooling. Hors d'ouevres are served nightly (6:30pm) in the stone Clubhouse, followed by 7:30pm candlelight dinner on the veranda. The farm-to-table food includes fruit and microgreens from the island's 5-acre organic orchard. Kids 8 and under stay free at Guana during "Kids' Weeks" in July and August. The entire island can be rented by groups of up to 35.

www.guana.com. ℂ **800/544-8262** in the U.S., or 284/494-2354. 18 units. $975–$1,776 seaview rooms; $2,175–$6,600 villas. Rates include all meals, drinks (excludes reserve), and snacks. Closed Sept–Oct. Children welcome certain times of year. **Amenities:** Restaurant; bar; babysitting; croquet; hiking trails; spa; 2 tennis courts; watersports equipment/rentals; free Wi-Fi.

Scrub Island Resort, Spa & Marina ★★

Just 1½ miles off the coast of Tortola, this fully developed island resort is packed with amenities. Some of the territory's top outfitters have locations on-site, including the scuba outfitter **Dive BVI** (divebvi.com) for dive trips, dive certifications, and island excursions; and the prestigious **Scrub Island Offshore Sailing School** (www.offshoresailing.com), led by a former America's Cup sailor. The 55-slip deep-water Scrub Island Marina is the base for **Dream Yacht Charter** (www.dreamyachtcharter.com), where you can charter a boat with all the trimmings or your own personal bareboating needs. For those who just want to stay put, Scrub Island has a big lagoon pool with waterfalls and swim-up bars, and white-sand beaches where you can kayak, standup paddleboard, and snorkel. Accommodations are in spacious, comfortably outfitted rooms, suites, and villas, done up in tropical woods and colonial West Indies furnishings, many with four-poster beds and all with private balconies. All suites and villas have full gourmet kitchens, and the resort offers provisioning services. Some rooms have sea views; others overlook the marina. Scrub Island is actually two islands—Big Scrub and Little Scrub—connected by an isthmus and totaling 93 hectares (230 acres), but just about every parcel of land is developed.

www.scrubisland.com. ✆ **877/890-7444.** 52 hotel units; 11 villas. $590–$860 double; $1,505–$1,790 2-bedroom suite; $2,390–$2,500 4-bedroom villa. Rates include airport and boat transfers and sunset cruise. **Amenities:** 2 restaurants; 2 bars; market/deli; babysitting; concierge; fitness room; two pools; spa; watersports equipment; free Wi-Fi.

Necker Island ★★★

Necker is one of two North Sound islands (the other, Moskito, is an active real-estate development) owned by Sir Richard Branson, founder of the Virgin Group and avid kitesurfer. (Branson reportedly braved out the 2017 hurricanes huddled here in his wine cellar.) The 30-hectare (74-acre) Necker Island is as exclusive as they come, generally only available as a total island buyout for 48 adults and 6 children, except at certain times of year during what is called Celebration Weeks, when booking opens for individual rooms. You'll be paying through your nose either way, but by every imaginable measure, this place is a dream. There *is* a way to see some of Necker Island for less, however, and that's on a nature tour with local entrepreneur Gumption and his **Sea It Clear Tours** (www.seaitcleartours.com; see p. 289) to see Necker's menagerie of exotic animals; you may be able to snatch a peek of the luxe surrounds while you're there. Necker lies in open ocean just north of North Sound but is protected by its own fringing reefs.

www.virginlimitededition.com. ✆ **212/994-3070.** 24 units. Exclusive-use rates $113,000–$134,500/night for entire island; Celebration Week room rates $3,700–$8,400 double. Children $1,850/night 12 and older, $850/night 6–11 years. Rates include all meals, drinks, and return boat transfers. **Amenities:** Restaurant; bar; concierge; fitness room; 5 infinity pools; spa; 2 tennis courts; watersports equipment; free Wi-Fi.

Eustatia Island ★★★

If you're a windsurfer, kitesurfer, or wakeboarder, or if you're itching to learn some new kite/board sports, Eustatia Sound is ground zero. Steady trade winds and calm, protected waters make for some of the region's best conditions for kiteboarding sports. In fact, that's reportedly what drew its secretive zillionaire owner (Google's Larry Page would be an excellent guess) to buy Eustatia Island in the first place. A stay on this glorious 14-hectare (35-acre) island gives you and 13 friends full island access. You sleep quite comfortably in one of four guest homes, enjoy chef-prepared meals, daily drinks, and well-stocked kitchens, and have full use of all watersports equipment (and two on-site watersports instructors)—plus you get to take a B.V.I. boat cruise. The island is a model of sustainability, off the grid and 100% powered by solar, with cisterns for capturing rainwater and its own reverse-osmosis desalination fresh-water maker. Incredible views, sweet white-sand beaches, excellent snorkeling, and you're just around the corner from the resorts in neighboring North Sound.

North Sound. eustatia.com. 4 units. Call for exclusive-use rates. Rates include all meals, drinks, and return boat transfers. **Amenities:** Concierge; bikes; watersports equipment; free Wi-Fi.

PLANNING YOUR TRIP TO THE VIRGIN ISLANDS

A little preparation is essential before you start your journey to the Virgin Islands, especially if you plan on traveling to more than one island. This chapter tackles the basic how-tos of a trip to the Virgin Islands, from finding the best airfare to deciding when to go. It also drills down on tours and excursions. For on-the-ground resources, head straight to "Fast Facts," beginning on p. 323.

GETTING THERE

For American citizens, visiting the U.S. Virgin Islands is relatively easy and hassle-free. Because it's part of the U.S. territory, you won't even need a passport to enter the country on arrival. American citizens do need a passport to enter the British Virgin Islands, however. For complete information on passports and visas, go to "Fast Facts," later in this chapter.

By Plane

A number of major airlines have regularly scheduled nonstop air service from cities all over North America into St. Thomas, the major international gateway to the Virgins; others include stopovers in Miami or San Juan.

Beginning in summer 2023, the B.V.I. will once again have a direct air link to the American mainland, with **American Airlines** (www.aa.com; *℄* **800/433-7300**) making direct daily flights between Tortola and Miami International Airport. Currently, there are no other direct flights from North America or Europe to any of the British Virgin Islands—most people planning to visit the B.V.I. will likely have to fly into St. Thomas, San Juan (Puerto Rico), or Miami, then make a connection by ferry or air (there are also connections through St. Kitts and Antigua). Those traveling from overseas will also most likely make a connection in St. Thomas, St. Croix, or San Juan after first connecting in the mainland U.S.

COVID-19 protocols

The handling of Covid-19 in the Virgin Islands during the height of the pandemic was a tale of two approaches—with the U.S.V.I. allowing entry with proof of vaccination or negative test results and the B.V.I. practically shut down to outsiders. These days, like the rest of the world, the islands are grudgingly accepting the fact that living with Covid is the new reality. That said, both the U.S.V.I. and the B.V.I. maintain basic Covid-19 protocols for visitors to follow.

Americans entering St. Croix, St. John, and St. Thomas from other parts of the U.S. no longer have to submit proof of vaccination or negative test results. Non-U.S. citizens arriving by sea or air, including from the British Virgin Islands, must be fully vaccinated but are no longer required to show negative test results. You can find out more on U.S.V.I. travel at **www.usvitravelportal.com**.

Strict protocols for entry into the British Virgin Islands (such as a negative test within 2 days of arrival) were lifted in July 2022, and travelers to the B.V.I. are no longer screened for Covid upon arrival. Persons who are ill or suspect that they may have Covid-19 or have been exposed to the virus must be tested and should self-isolate for a period of 7 days. For updates, go to **bvi.gov.vg/travel-protocols**.

The wearing of face masks/coverings is no longer mandated by law throughout the Virgins. It is now a matter of choice in public spaces or can be requested as a policy of a business or other establishment.

The biggest and busiest airport in the U.S. Virgin Islands (and all the Virgin Islands) is **Cyril E. King Airport** (STT; www.viport.com/cekastt; ⓒ **340/774-5100**) on St. Thomas. On St. Croix, **Henry E. Rohlsen Airport (STX),** Estate Mannings Bay (www.viport.com/herastx; ⓒ **340/778-1012**), is a small international airport about 6 miles southwest of the town of Christiansted. The main airport in the British Virgin Islands, the **Terrance B. Lettsome International Airport** (EIS; formerly Beef Island Airport; bviaacloud.com/arrivals), on Tortola's East End, serves largely as a hub for inter-Caribbean airlines. Both Virgin Gorda and Anegada have small airports suitable for charters and private planes.

For more information on getting to each island, see the "Getting There" sections in the individual island chapters.

By Cruise Ship

The Virgin Islands are a popular stop for cruise ships traveling the Caribbean, in particular Charlotte Amalie in St. Thomas, one of the world's busiest cruise ports. Historic Frederiksted in St. Croix also welcomes cruise ships on a weekly basis in high season. Tortola is another popular stop on the cruise-ship circuit, one that is becoming increasingly inviting for luxury high-end cruise ships. The high season for cruising the Virgin Islands is the **middle of October through April,** although cruise ships come to call all year long.

THE CRUISE PORTS
St. Thomas
Most major cruise lines include regular stops in St. Thomas in their Caribbean itineraries, including the biggest cruise ships in the world, such as Royal

Caribbean's mega ships *Allure of the Sea* and *Oasis of the Sea,* each with a maximum passenger capacity of more than 6,000 people; Norwegian Cruise Line's *Epic;* and Princess Cruise Line's *Royal Princess.* Cruise ships dock at one of two major terminals: **Havensight** (West Indian Company Ltd.; wico-ltd. com; ☎ 340/774-1780) and **Crown Bay** (Austin "Babe" Monsanto Marine Terminal; www.viport.com/austin-babe-monsanto-marine-termina; ☎ 340/774-2132). Havensight is closer to the shops and attractions in Charlotte Amalie and has room for three mega-ships at a time; Crown Bay has room for two. In high season, it's not unusual for an additional one or two ships to anchor in the harbor, delivering cruise-ship passengers to shore in tenders. A number of smaller cruise ships visit the waters of the Virgin Islands without docking, including Star Clipper and Windstar Cruises.

In the U.S.V.I, a gambling ordinance keeps cruise ships from overnighting — the last ship needs to be out to sea by 10pm.

St. Croix
The island's only cruise-ship pier, the **Anne E. Abramson Marine Facility** (www.viport.com/ann-e-abramson-marine-facility) in downtown Frederiksted, can handle one mega-ship at a time. Cruise lines that made stops in St. Croix in 2022 included Celebrity *(Silhouette);* Royal Caribbean *(Enchantment of the Seas);* and Virgin Voyages *(Valiant Lady).*

Tortola
The **Cruise Pier** in Road Town, Tortola (BVI Ports Authority: ☎ 284/494-3435), can handle two big ships at a time. The facility includes the **Cyril B. Romney Tortola Pier Park** (www.tortolapier.com), an outdoor commercial complex of colorful West Indian–style cottages with some 70 shops and cafes. Cruise ships that docked in Tortola in 2022 included Disney *(Fantasy);* Norwegian *(Sky, Escape);* Silver Seas *(Whisper);* and Celebrity (Apex, *Infinity).*

GETTING AROUND
By Plane & Seaplane
Regular flights are scheduled between St. Thomas and St. Croix, and between St. Thomas and Tortola. **Seaborne Airlines** (www.seaborneairlines.com; ☎ 866/359-8784) flies between St. Thomas and St. Croix on several runs daily; Seaborne also flies between St. Thomas and Beef Island, Tortola. **Cape Air** (www.capeair.com; ☎ 866/227-3247 in the U.S. and U.S.V.I.) offers regularly scheduled flights between St. Thomas and both St. Croix and Tortola. Note that St. John has no airport; passengers usually land first at St. Thomas, then take the 20-minute ferry ride to St. John.

By Boat
Ferry service is a vital link on the Virgin Islands and a fabulous way to see these beautiful islands by water. On the U.S. Virgin Islands, public ferries between St. Thomas and St. John run at regular intervals all day long (private

ferry COMPANIES: WHERE THEY GO

Ferry service is an essential transportation link in the Virgins, and most of the ferries get you where you want to go with speed and efficiency. Boats vary from high-speed catamarans to older, no-frills models. Some ferries are more reliably on time than others; also check to see if your ferry is "nonstop"—some ferries, like Inter Island, may make pit shops on the way to your final destination. Fares are not necessarily economical; in addition, non-residents traveling by sea now have to pay a $20 passenger tax per person ($10 B.V.I. residents) anytime they depart the B.V.I. Still, we love the ferries—they're scenic bliss and instant meditative balm.

Here is a breakdown of the various public ferry companies and where they go; keep in mind that itineraries are **subject to change and may be cut back during slow periods.** The ferry to Anegada, for instance, stops running altogether during hurricane season, from August through October. Note that children and seniors pay discounted fares,

and that some ferries charge an extra $2 per piece of luggage. And note that you'll save (a little) by buying round-trip tickets.

Anegada Express (anegadaexpress. com; 𝄃 **284/343-5343**): Seasonal private ferry (Nov–June/July) leaving from Trellis Bay operates two round-trips on Sunday, Thursday, and Saturday between Tortola and Anegada. Fares are $50 round-trip ($35 one-way) adults, $40 round-trip ($25 one-way) children.

Inter Island Boat Services (www.inter islandboatservices.com; 𝄃 **340/776-6597**): Makes runs between Cruz Bay (St. John) and Crown Bay (St. Thomas). They also travel between Red Hook (St. Thomas), Cruz Bay, and Jost Van Dyke three days a week. Rates between St. Thomas and St. John are $20 one-way ($10 children).

Native Son (www.nativesonferry.com; 𝄃 **340/774-8685**): Makes daily runs between St. Thomas (Charlotte Amalie) and Tortola (Road Town); one-way rates are $60 ($50 kids 3–11). Three days a

water taxis also operate on this route). Launch services link St. Thomas's two ferry terminals (Red Hook, on the East End of St. Thomas, and Charlotte Amalie) to Cruz Bay in St. John. A high-speed ferry makes the 90-minute sea trip between St. Thomas and St. Croix a few days a week.

Inter-island public ferries are a vital link between the U.S. Virgins and the B.V.I. Ferries run from both ferry terminals on St. Thomas (Charlotte Amalie and Red Hook) to either West End or Road Town on Tortola, a 45- to 55-minute voyage. There's also service to and from Virgin Gorda and some of the smaller islands, such as Anegada and Jost Van Dyke—but ferries are still recovering from pandemic shutdowns (the B.V.I. was in a near-complete lockdown), and schedules can be fluid. On some of the really remote islands, boat service may run only once a week and may even shut down in slower times. Many of the private island resorts, such as Little Dix Bay, provide launches from Tortola or from the airport in St. Thomas.

For more details on specific ferry connections, including sample fares, see the "Getting Around" sections of the individual island chapters.

week, it also runs a 90-minute ferry between St. Thomas (Charlotte Amalie) and St. Croix (Gallows Bay); it's $120 adults, $90 children.

New Horizons Ferry (newhorizonferry. com; © **284/499-0952**): Makes daily runs between West End, Tortola, and Great Harbour, Jost Van Dyke; round-trip fares are $30.

QE IV Ferry (www.qe4ferry.com; © **340/ 473-1322**): Offers service between St. Croix and St. Thomas daily except Tuesday, leaving the Gallows Bay terminal at 8am and returning from the Blyden Terminal (Charlotte Amalie) at 3pm. Fares are $70 one-way ($120 round-trip).

Road Town Fast Ferry (www.roadtown fastferry.com; © **340/777-2800** in the U.S.V.I or 284/494-2323 in the B.V.I.): Offers regular runs between Charlotte Amalie (St. Thomas) and Road Town (Tortola), on sleek air-conditioned high-speed catamarans. Fares are $103 round-trip; group rates available. Road Town also operates seasonal ferries

between Road Town and Setting Point, Anegada (via Spanish Town), on Monday, Wednesday, and Friday (round-trip $55 adults, $35 children).

Smith's Ferry Service (smithsferry.com; © **340/775-7292** or 284/494-4454 in the B.V.I.): Aka the "Tortola Fast Ferry," operates daily between Tortola (Road Town) and St. Thomas (Charlotte Amalie), for $100 adults ($90 children 3–11; $30 infants) round-trip. Smith's also operates seasonal ferries between Road Town and Setting Point, Anegada (via Spanish Town), on Monday, Wednesday, and Friday (round-trip $55 adults, $35 children).

Speedy's (www.bviferries.com; © **284/ 495-7292**): The unofficial Virgin Gorda ferry operates regular routes between Virgin Gorda and Tortola (Road Town and Trellis Bay). Round-trip fares are $30 adults ($20 children 5–11); group rates and frequent traveler passes available. Suspended at press time were Speedy's ferries from Virgin Gorda to Charlotte Amalie, St. Thomas.

By Car

A rental car is a great way to get around each of the Virgin Islands. Just remember the most important rule: In both the U.S. and the British Virgin Islands, *you must drive on the left.*

U.S. VIRGINS All the major car-rental companies are represented in the U.S. Virgin Islands; many local agencies also compete in the car-rental market (for detailed information, see "Getting Around" sections in individual island chapters). On St. Thomas and St. Croix, you can pick up most rental cars at the airport. On St. John, the car rental stands are generally within walking distance of the ferry dock. Note that cars are often *in short supply* during high season, so reserve as far in advance as possible.

Parking lots in the U.S. Virgin Islands can be found in Charlotte Amalie, on St. Thomas, and in Christiansted, on St. Croix (in Frederiksted, you can generally park on the street). Most hotels, except those in the congested center of Charlotte Amalie, have free parking.

BRITISH VIRGINS   Even though taxi service in the British Virgin Islands is readily available, we highly recommend renting a car, particularly in Tortola. (If you plan to stay in the B.V.I. longer than 30 days, you must purchase a temporary local driver's license for $10 from police headquarters or a car-rental desk in town.) You must be at least 25 years old to rent a car in the B.V.I. Most major U.S. car-rental companies are represented on these islands, but you'll find a number of reliable local companies as well, many conveniently located near the ferry docks and in the main towns. Vehicles come in a wide range of styles and prices, including Jeeps, Land Rovers, mini-mokes, and six- to eight-passenger Suzukis. Weekly rates are usually slightly cheaper. *Note:* There are no car-rental agencies at the airport on Virgin Gorda.

DRIVING SAFETY   Driving on the left is the rule of the road in both the British and the U.S. Virgin Islands. Often you'll be driving along two-lane roads that can feel like roller-coaster rides. **Four-wheel-drive vehicles are highly recommended.** Steep, curvy roads are often poorly lit at night; many are potholed or have been eroded by rain runoff. St. Croix's road network is composed of rocky roads through the interior; Mahogany Road in particular can be rough going. As a result, car-rental insurance is higher on this island than the others. On St. John there's a reason most (if not all) rental cars are 4WD Jeeps—the national park roads are excellent along the northern beaches but elsewhere roads trace corkscrew hills and switchbacks up and around mountains—take exceptional care driving at night and in the rain. Ditto for Tortola. The island's West and East Ends are relatively flat, but driving the interior, especially in mountainous rural neighborhoods like Windy Hill, can be wild and woolly. For those travelers unaccustomed to driving on the left, we suggest forgoing night driving altogether and taking taxis.

Also remember that **wearing seatbelts** is the law.

All the major islands, including St. Thomas, St. John, St. Croix, Tortola, and Virgin Gorda, have garages that will tow vehicles in the event of **breakdowns.** Always call the rental company first if you have a breakdown. If your car requires extensive repairs because of a mechanical failure, a new one will be sent to replace it.

GASOLINE/PETROL   St. Thomas has plenty of service stations, especially on the outskirts of Charlotte Amalie and at strategic points in the north and in the more congested East End. On St. Croix, most gas stations are in Christiansted, but there are also some along the major roads and at Frederiksted. St. John has two gas stations, one in Cruz Bay and the other on Centerline Road.

Gas stations are not as plentiful on the British Virgin Islands. Road Town, the capital of Tortola, has the most gas stations; fill up here before touring the island. Virgin Gorda has a limited but sufficient number of gas stations. Chances are you won't be using a car on the other, smaller British Virgin Islands.

Taxes are included in the printed price at the pump. One U.S. gallon equals 3.8 liters or .85 imperial gallons.

By Taxi

Taxis are the main mode of transport on all the Virgin Islands. On **St. Thomas,** taxi vans carry up to a dozen passengers to multiple destinations; smaller private taxis are also available. You'll find plenty of taxis on arrival at the airport. On **St. John,** both private taxis and vans for three or more passengers are available. On **St. Croix,** taxis congregate at the airport, in Christiansted, and in Frederiksted, where the cruise ships arrive. On all the islands, taxi drivers rely on **open-air safari "buses"** (more like retrofitted flat-bed trucks) to transport groups (in particular, cruise-ship passengers) on island tours and excursions. These safari vans are capable of handling up to 30 passengers but are increasingly used as pickup and drop-off taxis.

Throughout the U.S.V.I., standard per-person taxi rates are set by the local government (look for a complete rate listing at the St. Thomas airport or in free local magazines like *This Week*)—but it's always good to confirm the rate before the ride begins. The standard taxi tour on St. Thomas, for example, is $55 for one passenger; for two or more it's $25 per extra passenger.

On the **British Virgin Islands,** taxis are readily available and, on some of the smaller islands, often the best way to get around. Service is available on Tortola, Virgin Gorda, and Anegada; rates are fixed by the local government.

Tip: If you find a good taxi driver on the islands, get his or her card—not only will you have a reliable driver to drop you off and pick you up places, but most drivers are smart and entertaining island guides. Rates for sightseeing taxi tours are also regulated by the government.

By Bus

The only islands with recommendable bus service are **St. Thomas** and **St. Croix.** On St. Thomas, buses leave from Charlotte Amalie and circle the island; on St. Croix, air-conditioned buses run from Christiansted to Frederiksted. Bus service elsewhere is highly erratic; it's mostly used by locals going to and from work.

TIPS ON ACCOMMODATIONS

Throughout this book, we provide detailed descriptions of recommended properties so that you can get an idea of what to expect. Keep in mind that many of the more high-end island resorts also charge a **daily resort fee** of between $35 and $50.

Resorts and hotels in the Virgin Islands offer money-saving package deals galore. You can find land-air (and land-air-rental-car) packages on almost all the online travel agencies (Expedia.com, Orbitz.com, Priceline.com, Cheap-Caribbean.com), and be sure to check the hotel's own websites, which often offer some of the best rates plus multi-stay or theme deals (especially in the off-season).

Like most Caribbean islands, the Virgins have traditional high and low seasons, and hotel properties are often priced accordingly—although it's our experience that the line between high and low season is increasingly blurred (summer, traditionally a slow time, has become much more popular—just try snagging a villa rental or even a rental car on St. John at the last minute in June). Still, if you have flexible travel dates, know that there are often deals to be had on hotel stays in the off-season (mid-April to mid-December). The most exorbitant rates are charged during the Christmas and New Year's holidays.

Renting Your Own Villa or Vacation Home

A popular lodging alternative, and a smart option if you're traveling with a large party of family or friends, is renting a villa, condo, apartment, or cottage for your Virgin Islands vacation. Having your own self-catering facilities can be a big money-saver—dining out is chillingly pricey in the Virgin Islands. *Note:* If you're planning your trip for the high season, reservations should be made *at least* 5 to 6 months in advance.

Dozens of agencies throughout the United States and Canada offer rentals in the Virgin Islands (for those that specifically target certain destinations, see the island chapters). **Villas of Distinction** (www.villasofdistinction.com; *©* **800/289-0900**) offers "complete vacations," including car rental and domestic help. Its private luxury villas have one to seven-plus bedrooms, and many have swimming pools. Rates run from $500 a night and up. **At Home Abroad** (www.athomeabroadinc.com; *©* **212/421-9165**) has a roster of private luxury homes, villas, and condos for rent in St. Thomas, St. John, Tortola, and Virgin Gorda; maid service is included in the price.

You can also find excellent deals on popular owner-rented vacation lodging websites, including **Airbnb** (www.airbnb.com) and **VRBO** (www.vrbo.com), which list numerous attractive villas, condos, and more throughout the Virgins. What you will *not* get with these rentals is service (unless advertised). Before you book, be sure to check the guest reviews and owner rankings for guarantees that the rental is all that it appears to be.

SPECIAL-INTEREST TRIPS & TOURS

You will have endless opportunities to sit by the surf sipping tropical drinks, but remember that these islands offer more than just ribbons of fetching white-sand beach. Coral reefs and deep-water channels provide backdrops for a variety of watersports, from snorkeling to sea kayaking to sailing, and the lush island interiors make ideal playgrounds for scenic hikes. This section presents an overview of tours, special-interest trips, and outdoor excursions on the Virgin Islands. See individual chapters for more specific information on locations and outfitters. *Note:* During the low summer season, tours and excursions may not run regularly unless enough people book, so always call in advance to confirm.

Air Tours

See the Virgin Islands as the birds do: by air. Helicopter sightseeing tours, island-hopping day trips, and heli-adventures (heli-fishing in Anegada, for example) are available through **Caribbean Buzz Helicopters,** in St. Thomas (www.caribbean-buzz.com; ✆ **340/775-7335**). Helicopters seating eight passengers are flown by two pilots and are also available to rent for island and airport transfers. A 17-minute **aerial sightseeing tour** in a full helicopter with eight passengers is $1,500 ($187.50/person); a 30-minute tour is $2,500; and a 1-hour tour is $5,000. A smaller, three-passenger helicopter will also be onboard for tours in 2023.

Adventure Trips

Dive in: The Virgin Islands is one big outdoor playground, with aquatic pleasures, rainforest peaks, and breathtakingly scenic sightseeing.

BIKING   Biking the roads of the Virgin Islands has its challenges; not only do you have mountainous, switchback terrain to maneuver, but the default road throughout the islands is usually two-lane, curving, and narrow. St. Croix and Tortola in particular offer biking activities; see those chapters for more information. **The Virgin Islands Cycling Federation** (vicycling.org), based in Christiansted, St. Croix, actively promotes cycling throughout the U.S. Virgins.

FISHING   The Virgin Islands are home to some of the best fishing grounds in the world. More than 20 sportfishing world records have been set in the Virgin Islands in the last few decades, mostly for the big kahuna of the sea, blue marlin. Other abundant fish in these waters are bonito, tuna, wahoo, sailfish, and skipjack. Sportfishing charters, led by experienced local captains,

---

Sea Turtle Etiquette

These are some of the most highly endangered species in the oceans. Catching even a passing glimpse of a sea turtle is a magical experience, but you'll blow the chance unless you heed some basic guidelines. When you first spot a sea turtle, resist the urge to move in and get a closer look; you will only scare it off and ruin the opportunity for others to see it. Instead, stay still and watch at a respectful distance as it goes about its business, searching for food or gliding along gracefully. Keep an eye out for identification tags on their flippers or shells—a sure sign these fellas are being closely studied and well protected. You should never approach a turtle or its nest, and never touch or try to touch one—for your safety and theirs. Although it seems harmless to humans, it is in fact quite stressful for the turtles (how'd you like to be chased around the grocery store by strangers all day?). **Warning:** Do not swim above the turtles; it will prevent them from surfacing to breathe and subject them to undue respiratory stress. And, of course, if someone offers you sea turtle shell, egg, or meat products, just say no.—Christina P. Colón.

abound in the islands; both half-day and full-day trips are available. But you needn't go out to sea to fish. On St. Thomas, St. John, and St. Croix, the U.S. government publishes lists of legal shoreline fishing spots (contact local tourist offices for more information). Closer inshore, you'll find kingfish, mackerel, bonefish, tarpon, amberjack, grouper, and snapper. On **St. Thomas,** many people line-fish from the rocky shore along Mandahl Beach, which is also a popular spot for family picnics. The shore here is not the best place for swimming, because the seafloor drops off dramatically and the surf tends to be rough. On **St. John,** the waters in Virgin Islands National Park are open to fishermen with hand-held rods. No fishing license is required for shoreline fishing, and government pamphlets available at tourist offices list some 100 good spots. Call the **Virgin Islands National Park Service** at ✆ **340/776-6201** for more information.

HIKING TOURS The best islands for hiking are **Tortola** and **St. John.** In Tortola, the best hiking is through **Sage Mountain National Park,** spread across 37 hectares (91 acres) of luxuriant flora and fauna. On St. John, the Virgin Islands National Park has dozens of trails for hiking, including the **Reef Bay Trail,** which passes not only sugar plantation ruins but pre-Columbian Taino tribe petroglyphs. **St. Croix** also has good hiking opportunities, including a popular walk down the mountainside to the crystalline tidal pools and saltwater baths of Annaly Bay. Off the coast of St. Croix, **Buck Island** (www. nps.gov/buis), beloved by snorkelers and scuba divers, is also fascinating to hike. You can easily explore the island in a day—it's just a half-mile wide and a mile long.

The **Virgin Islands Trail Alliance** (vitrails.org) works to develop nature trails, public parks, and pedestrian pathways throughout the U.S. Virgins. Its most recent completed works includes bypass bike lanes around Christiansted, St. Croix, and the opening of 12 miles of public walking and biking trails in Windsor Farm, St. Croix.

While hiking in the Virgin Islands, you'll encounter many birds and flowers—but no poisonous snakes. Be sure to look for the trumpet-shaped Ginger Thomas, the U.S. Virgin Islands' official flower.

SAILING & YACHTING The Virgin Islands are a sailor's paradise, offering crystal-clear turquoise waters, secluded coves and inlets, and protected harbors for anchoring. The weather is perfect with tropical conditions between 80°F and 85°F (27°C–29°C); winds blow at approximately 15 to 20 knots out of the east year-round. The inviting crystal-clear Caribbean turquoise waters are about 82°F (28°C) year-round.

The most popular cruising area around the Virgin Islands is the deep and lushly scenic **Sir Francis Drake Channel,** which runs from St. John to Virgin Gorda's North Sound. The channel is rimmed by mountainous islands and boasts steady trade winds year-round. In heavy weather, the network of tiny islands shelters yachties from the brute force of the open sea. The waters surrounding St. Croix to the south are also appealing, especially near Buck Island. Outside the channel, the Virgin Islands archipelago contains reefy areas that separate many of the islands from their neighbors.

For details on arranging a multi-day boat charter—**bareboat** (on your own) or **fully crewed**—see "Chartering Your Own Boat," below. Most visitors, however, are content with **day sail excursions ★★★**, the most popular activity in the islands. You really shouldn't leave the islands without spending at least one day on the water, even if you have to load up on Dramamine or snap on some acupressure wristbands before you go. For sailing outfitters and boat excursions on each island, go to the individual chapters.

If you don't know how to sail but want to learn, there's no better place than the Virgin Islands. On Tortola, the **Tortola Sailing School** (✆ **800/390-7594**) is an accredited American Sailing Association sailing school, with courses in both sailing and bareboating running out of Soper's Hole Marina on the island's West End. It offers a full-day "Learn the Ropes" basics course on a 36-foot monohull for $175 per person. It also offers multi-day liveaboard sailing and bareboating courses. The year-round **Offshore Sailing School** (www. offshoresailing.com; ✆ **888/454-7015** or 239/454-1700) is the official sailing school for The Moorings, one of the world's biggest bareboat, power, and crewed yacht charter companies and a longtime presence in Tortola. Most of The Moorings' sailing cruising courses operate from Scrub Island Resort, but the Moorings' 1-week Fast Track® to Power Cruising Course—where you can earn a U.S. powerboat certification on a big power cat—is taught from The Moorings' base in Tortola. On St. Thomas, **Go Sail Virgin Islands** (www. gosailvi.com), operating out of Compass Point Marina, offers 7-day on-board cruising catamaran courses for bareboat certification led by Captain Genevieve Evan ("Captain G").

Heritage & Cultural Tours

St. Thomas Historical Trust (www.stthomashistoricaltrust.org; ✆ **340/774-5541**) leads fascinating and informative historical walking tours on the island

CHARTERING YOUR OWN boat

There may be no better way to experience the "Sailing Capital of the World" than on the deck of your own yacht. Impossible? Not really. No one said you had to *own* the yacht. Experienced sailors and navigators with a sea-wise crew might want to rent a **bareboat charter**—a fully equipped boat with no captain or crew, where you are the master of the seas, charting your own course, and do your own cooking and cleaning. If you're not an expert sailor but yearn to hit the high seas, consider a **fully crewed charter,** which includes a captain and chef. The cost of a crewed boat is obviously more than that of a bareboat and varies according to crew size and experience.

Most boats, bareboat or crewed, are rented on a weekly basis and come equipped with a GPS system. Full-service crewed boats come in all shapes and sizes, from traditional sailboats to roomy multihulls to elegant motor yachts. Crewed charters generally come with a fully stocked kitchen (or a barbecue) and bar, fishing gear, and watersports equipment. For details on crewed yachts, go to **www.crewedyachtsbvi.com**. Private boats are given up to 30 days to cruise

the B.V.I. and are required to pay a 30-day cruising fee based on tonnage (maximum fee $55). Contact **His Majesty's Customs Department** (✆ 284/468-6852) for current cruising permit requirements.

Among the many outfitters in the Virgin Islands, **The Moorings** in Tortola (www.moorings.com; ✆ 800/334-2435) offers both bareboat and fully crewed charters equipped with such extras as a barbecue, snorkeling gear, a dinghy, and linens. The company even supplies windsurfing equipment for free with crewed boats (and for an extra cost with bareboats). The experienced staff of mechanics, electricians, riggers, and cleaners is extremely helpful, especially if you're going out on your own. They'll give you a thorough briefing about Virgin Islands waters and anchorages. If you're looking for bareboat and full-crew charter companies in St. Thomas, you'll find the craft you're looking for through the **American Yacht Harbor** (www.igymarinas.com/marinas/american-yacht-harbor; ✆ 340/775-6454), a full-service marina located in Red Hook and home to numerous charter companies.

of St. Thomas with expert guides, including a downtown walking tour of historic Charlotte Amalie and another of Hassel Island.

On St. Croix, the island's cultural riches are explored on tours run by **Crucian Heritage & Nature Tourism** (CHANT; chantvi.org; ✆ 340/772-4079). In addition to historic walking tours of the colonial towns of Christiansted and Frederiksted, CHANT offers a nature-rich "Bushman" hiking tour along the Annaly Ridge to the Annaly tidepools, as well as underwater photography classes and oral-history workshops.

In the B.V.I, **Hike BVI** (www.hikebvi.com; ✆ 284/441-2315) offers some of the Caribbean's most profound cultural and historical eco-hikes and kayak and snorkeling tours, where you'll go places most visitors never see: a bamboo forest, fields of pineapple, and hidden lagoons, all the while learning how the islanders long used the unique natural flora around them for food, shelter, and bush medicine.

[FastFACTS] THE VIRGIN ISLANDS

Accessibility   Hotels and restaurants in the U.S.V.I. are required to comply with the regulations imposed by the Americans with Disabilities Act (ADA). Both the **Buccaneer,** St. Croix (p. 138), and the **Ritz-Carlton,** St. Thomas (p. 78), maintain "accessible" rooms (rooms that can be reached without navigating stairs) and can arrange beach wheelchairs. Keep in mind that many guesthouses and villas in the hills of **Charlotte Amalie,** St. Thomas, have built-in challenges to those with mobility issues, including steep steps and no elevators. On St. John, **Trunk Bay** beach has beach wheelchairs, wheelchair-accessible parking and restrooms, and accessible paths to the water, and you'll find wheelchair-accessible boardwalks on the **Cinnamon Bay Self-Guided Trail** and at **Francis Bay.** The **Cinnamon Bay Campground** has accessible units in eco-tents and cottages as well as ADA-accessible bathrooms and parking. Throughout the U.S.V.I., persons with disabilities ride on **VITRAN public buses** (www.vitranvi.com) for free.

Accessible Island Tours (www.accessvi.com; ☏ **340/344-8302**), a tour operator in St. Thomas, offers a land-based tour of St. Thomas in

a custom wheelchair-accessible vehicle. Originating from Wico Dock at Havensight or Crown Bay at the Subbase, tours stop at Magens Bay, Drake's Seat, and the Skyline Drive and cost $37 per person (minimum six passengers). It also offers equipment rentals.

In the B.V.I. where many accommodations and restaurants lie in challenging, hilly, or remote terrain, wheelchair-accessible facilities are less standardized, but you'll find that hotel and restaurant staff go out of their way to help persons with disabilities wherever they are.

Area Codes   The area code for the U.S.V.I. is **340;** in the B.V.I., it's **284.** You can dial direct from North America; from outside North America, dial 001, plus the number for the U.S.V.I., and 011-44 plus the number for the B.V.I.

Crime   See "Safety," later in this section.

Customs   Every visitor to the U.S.V.I. 21 years of age or older may bring in, free of duty, the following: (1) 1 liter of wine or hard liquor; (2) 200 cigarettes, 100 cigars (but not from Cuba), or 3 pounds of smoking tobacco; and (3) $100 worth of gifts. These exemptions are offered to travelers who spend at least 72 hours in

the United States and who have not claimed them within the preceding 6 months. It is altogether forbidden to bring into the islands foodstuffs (particularly fruit, cooked meats, and canned goods) and plants (vegetables, seeds, tropical plants, and the like). Foreign tourists may carry in or out up to $10,000 in U.S. or foreign currency with no formalities; larger sums must be declared to U.S. Customs on entering or leaving, which includes filing form CM 4790. For details regarding U.S. Customs and Border Protection, consult your nearest U.S. embassy or consulate, or **U.S. Customs** (www.cbp.gov; ☏ **800/232-5378**).

Visitors to the B.V.I. can bring in food, with the exception of meat products that are not USDA-approved. Visitors can bring up to $10,000 in currency and 1 liter of alcohol per person.

Australian Citizens: A helpful brochure available from Australian consulates or Customs offices is "Know Before You Go." For more information, contact the **Australian Customs Service,** Customs House, 5 Constitution Ave., Canberra City, ACT 2601 (www.homeaffairs.gov.au; ☏ **1300/363-263** or 61-2-9313-3010 from outside Australia).

Canadian Citizens: For a clear summary of Canadian rules, write for the booklet "I Declare," issued by the **Canada Border Services Agency,** Ottawa, Ontario, K1A 0L8 (www.cbsa-asfc.gc.ca; ☏ **800/461-9999** in Canada or 204/983-3500).

New Zealand Citizens: Most questions are answered in a free pamphlet available at New Zealand consulates and Customs offices: "New Zealand Customs Guide for Travellers, Notice no. 4." For more information, contact **New Zealand Customs Service,** the Customhouse, 1 Hinemoa St., Harbour Quays, Wellington 6140 (www.customs.govt.nz; ☏ **04/901-4500**).

U.K. Citizens: From the B.V.I., U.K. citizens can bring back (duty-free) 200 cigarettes (250g of tobacco), 2 liters wine, 1 liter strong liquor, 60cc perfume, and £145 of goods and souvenirs. Larger amounts are subject to tax. For further information, contact **HM Revenue & Customs,** Crownhill Court, Tailyour Road, Plymouth, PL6 5BZ (www.gov.uk/government/organisations/hm-revenue-customs; ☏ **0300/200-3700**).

U.S. Citizens & Residents: From the U.S.V.I., the duty-free allowance is $1,600 per person (including children). U.S. citizens can bring back 5 liters of liquor duty-free, plus an extra liter of rum (including Cruzan rum) if one of the bottles is produced in the Virgin Islands.

Goods made on the island are also duty-free, including perfume, jewelry, clothing, and original paintings; however, if the price of an item exceeds $25, you must be able to show a certificate of origin.

Be sure to collect receipts for all purchases in the Virgin Islands, and beware of merchants offering to give you a false receipt—he or she might be an informer to U.S. Customs. Also, keep in mind that any gifts received during your stay must be declared. For the most up-to-date specifics on what you can bring back **from the B.V.I.** and the corresponding fees, contact the **U.S. Customs & Border Protection (CBP),** 1300 Pennsylvania Ave. NW, Washington, DC 20229 (www.cbp.gov; ☏ **877/227-5511**).

Doctors You should have no trouble finding a good doctor in the Virgin Islands. See "Fast Facts" in individual island chapters for information on doctors.

Drinking Laws In both the U.S. Virgins and the B.V.I., the legal age for purchase and consumption of alcoholic beverages is 18. Proof of age is required and often requested at bars, nightclubs, and restaurants, so it's a good idea to bring ID when you go out. Do not carry open containers of alcohol in your car or any public area that isn't zoned for alcohol consumption; the police can fine you on the spot. In the B.V.I., you

can have an open container on the beach, but be you can be fined if you litter. Don't even think about driving while intoxicated.

Although 18-year-olds can purchase, drink, and order alcohol, they cannot transport bottles back to the United States with them. If an attempt is made, the alcohol will be confiscated at the Customs check point. The same holds true for the B.V.I.

Driving Rules In both the U.S.V.I. and the B.V.I., you must **drive on the left.** See "Getting Around," earlier in this chapter.

Electricity The electrical current in the Virgin Islands is the same as on the U.S. mainland and Canada: 110 to 120 volts AC (60 cycles), compared to 220 to 240 volts AC (50 cycles) in most of Europe, Australia, and New Zealand. Downward converters that change 220-240 volts to 110-120 volts are difficult to find in the United States and even on the islands, so plan to bring one with you.

Embassies & Consulates There are no embassies or consulates in the Virgin Islands. If you have a passport issue, go to the local police station, which in all islands is located at the center of government agencies. Relay your problem to whomever is at reception, and you'll be given advice about which agencies can help you.

Emergencies Call 🕻 **911** in the U.S.V.I. or 🕻 **999** in the B.V.I.

Gasoline Please see "Getting Around," earlier in this chapter, for information.

Health For "Hospitals," see below. Also see "Medical Requirements," p. 326.

It is not difficult to get a prescription filled or find a doctor on St. Thomas, St. Croix, and Tortola. Pharmacies are few and far between on the smaller islands, so you should get any prescriptions refilled before you venture into more remote territory. Often it requires a phone call from the U.S.V.I. to a stateside pharmacy or to the doctor who prescribed the medicine in the first place. CVS and Wal-Mart are the best for contacting a stateside branch of those chains, if your prescription is on a computer file. To avoid possible hassles and delays, it is best to arrive with enough medication for your entire vacation.

○ **Bugs & Bites Mosquitoes** are a nuisance in the Virgin Islands, but they aren't the malaria-carrying mosquitoes you might find elsewhere in the Caribbean. **Sand flies,** which appear mainly in the evening, are a bigger annoyance. Screens can't keep these critters out, so use bug repellent.

○ **Dietary Red Flags** If you experience **diarrhea,** moderate your eating habits and drink only bottled water until you recover. If symptoms persist, consult a doctor. Much of the fresh water on the Virgin Islands is stored in cisterns and filtered before it's served. Delicate stomachs might opt for bottled water. Some say a nightly drink of **ginger ale and bitters** helps soothe tummies.

○ **Seasickness** The best way to prevent **seasickness** is with the scopolamine patch by Transderm Scop, a prescription medication. Bonine and Dramamine are good over-the-counter medications, although each causes drowsiness. Smooth Sailing is a ginger drink that works quite well to settle your stomach. You might also opt for an acupressure wristband available at drugstores (www.sea-band. com). Some say a ginger pill taken with a meal and followed by Dramamine an hour before boating also does the job.

○ **Sun Exposure** The Virgin Islands' sun can be brutal. To protect yourself, consider wearing sunglasses and a hat, and use **sunscreen** (SPF 15 and higher) liberally—but remember only to purchase reef-safe sunscreen; it's the law. Limit your time on the beach for the first few days. If you overexpose yourself, stay out of the sun until you recover. If your sunburn is followed by fever, chills, a headache, nausea, or dizziness, see a doctor.

Note that there is no hyperbaric chamber in the B.V.I.; divers requiring treatment for decompression illness are transferred to St. Thomas.

Hospitals The largest hospital in St. Thomas is the **Schneider Regional Medical Center** (p. 69), with 24-hour emergency-room service. Islanders from St. John also use this hospital, which is about a 5-minute drive from Charlotte Amalie. The other major hospital is the **Governor Juan F. Luis Hospital & Medical Center** on St. Croix (p. 137); it has a Level IV trauma center offering 24-hour emergency-room service. Both offer air and ground-level support to hospitals with more extensive facilities. The payment of Medicare and Medicaid operates as it does in the United States. If you walk into a hospital without any coverage or insurance, you are expected to pay.

On Tortola, in the British Virgin Islands, the main hospital in the little country is **Peebles Hospital** (p. 246), with surgical, X-ray, and laboratory facilities. The **Eureka Medical Centre** (www.eurekamedicalclinic. com), Geneva Place, Road Town, Tortola, is a private-run urgent-care facility. If you are on one of the out islands, you are generally taken to Tortola for treatment. Please note that U.S. Medicare and Medicaid programs do *not* apply in the British Virgin Islands; doctors and hospitals expect immediate cash payment for health services. Make sure your medical plan provides overseas coverage or purchase supplemental travel health insurance.

In very serious cases, patients in the U.S. Virgins and the B.V.I. are transported to Puerto Rico.

Internet & Wi-Fi Internet access is available all around the Virgin Islands, but it can be spotty on some more remote islands. Most hotels and resorts and many bars and cafes throughout the Virgin Islands have free Wi-Fi access. See the "Fast Facts" section of each island chapter for recommendations on public hot spots.

Language English is the official language of both the U.S. and British Virgin Islands.

Legal Aid While driving, if you are pulled over for a minor infraction (such as speeding), never attempt to pay the fine directly to a police officer; this could be construed as attempted bribery, a much more serious crime. Pay fines by mail, or directly into the hands of the clerk of the court. If accused of a more serious offense, say and do nothing before consulting a lawyer. In the U.S.V.I., the burden is on the state to prove a

person's guilt beyond a reasonable doubt, and everyone has the right to remain silent, whether he or she is suspected of a crime or actually arrested. Once arrested, a person can make one telephone call to a party of his or her choice.

LGBT Travelers Both the British and the U.S. Virgin Islands are some of the most gay-friendly destinations in the Caribbean, but discretion is still advised. The Virgins have a long history of tolerance and acceptance of others, but islanders tend to be religious and conservative, and displays of same-sex affection, such as holding hands, are frowned upon. Gay marriage is legal in the U.S. Virgins (as is gay adoption).

While St. Thomas is the most cosmopolitan of the Virgin Islands, it is no longer the gay mecca it was in the 1960s and '70s, and gay nightlife is still somewhat in the closet. St. Croix hotels are particularly welcoming to the gay market, including the **Fred** (p. 145) and the gay-owned **Sand Castle on the Beach** (p. 146).

Mail At press time, domestic postage rates in the U.S.V.I. were 44¢ for a postcard and 60¢ for a letter up to 1 ounce. For international mail, a first-class postcard or letter stamp costs $1.40. For more information, go to **www.usps.com**. Always include zip codes when mailing items in the U.S. If you don't know your zip code, visit **www.usps.com/zip4**.

If you aren't sure what your address will be in the U.S. Virgin Islands, mail can be sent to you, in your name, c/o General Delivery at the main post office of the city or region where you expect to be. (Call ✆ **800/275-8777** for information on the nearest post office.) The addressee must pick up mail in person and must produce proof of identity (driver's license, passport, and so on). Most post offices will hold your mail for up to 1 month, and are open Monday to Friday 8am-6pm, Saturday 9am-3pm.

Postal rates in the British Virgin Islands to the United States or Canada are 35¢ for a postcard (airmail), and 50¢ for a first-class airmail letter (½ oz.). Mailing a postcard to the U.K. costs 50¢ and a first-class letter via airmail costs 75¢ (½ oz.). **B.V.I. postage stamps** are beautiful and highly coveted; contact the **BVI Philatelic Bureau** (✆ **284/494-7789**) for information about exhibitions.

Medical Requirements Unless you're arriving from an area known to be suffering from an epidemic (particularly cholera or yellow fever), inoculations or vaccinations are not required for entry into the U.S. Virgin Islands or the British Virgin Islands. See the box on Covid requirements, p. 312.

If you have a medical condition that requires **syringe-administered medications,** carry a valid signed prescription from your physician; syringes in carry-on baggage will be inspected. Insulin in any form should have the proper pharmaceutical documentation. If you have a disease that requires treatment with **narcotics,** you should also carry documented proof with you—smuggling narcotics aboard a plane carries severe penalties in the U.S.

Mobile Phones In the U.S. Virgin Islands: The two largest cellphone operators in the U.S.V.I. are Sprint PCS (www.sprint.com) and AT&T Wireless (www.att.com/wireless). Phones operating in the mainland U.S. under those plans will usually operate seamlessly in the U.S.V.I. without any excess roaming charges. If your phone operates through some other carrier, it's wise to call them before your departure to sign up (at least temporarily) for an international plan, which will save you money on roaming charges during your trip. If your cellphone is not equipped for reception and transmission in the U.S.V.I., consider renting (or buying) a cheap cellphone for temporary use, or, less conveniently, head for a Sprint PCS or AT&T sales outlet (each maintains offices on all three of the U.S.V.I.'s major islands) for a substitute SIM card, which can be inserted into your existing phone.

In the British Virgin Islands: The three largest cellphone operators in the B.V.I. are CCT Global

Communications (www.cctwireless.com), LIME (www.lime.com), and Digicell BVI (www.digicelbvi.com), all with offices in Road Town and on Virgin Gorda. Other than that, the cellphone situation is roughly equivalent to what's described above for the U.S.V.I. The electrical system in the B.V.I. is the same as that within the U.S.V.I. and the mainland U.S. (115 volts), so British and European visitors may want to bring adaptors and transformers for their phone chargers. Hotels in the B.V.I. often have the appropriate adaptors, and in some cases, those adaptors are physically built directly into the wall sockets.

Money & Costs The U.S. Virgin Islands and the British Virgin Islands both use the **U.S. dollar** as the form of currency. Before departing, consult a currency exchange website such as **www.xe.com** to check up-to-the-minute exchange rates. Banks on the islands are your only option if you need to **exchange currency.** These rates can be expensive, and additional charges are often tacked on; it is best to change money before you arrive.

ATMs throughout the Virgin Islands dispense U.S. dollars. ATMs are most prevalent on St. Thomas in Charlotte Amalie (on the downtown streets, near the cruise-ship terminals, within the large resorts, and in shopping malls) and in

Christiansted on St. Croix. You will also find several ATMs in Cruz Bay on St. John. ATMs are less prevalent in the British Virgin Islands; you will find a cluster of banks in Wickham Cay I, Road Town, Tortola, and a couple in the harbor in Spanish Town, Virgin Gorda. The other islands do not have ATMs, so if you're planning a visit, visit an ATM to get some cash beforehand (or have your resort front you some petty cash). Each machine charges around $2 to $3 for a transaction fee. Nearly all the machines are operated by three banks: **Oriental** (formerly **Scotiabank;** orientalbank.com/en/vi), **First-Bank Virgin Islands** (www.1firstbank.com/vi/en), and **Banco Popular** (www.popular.com/vi).

Most establishments in the Virgin Islands accept **credit cards;** we note in our reviews a few places that accept cash only. Master-Card and Visa are widely accepted on all the islands that cater to visitors; in the past few years, more merchants have dropped American Express because of its high transaction rates. However, visitors should not rely solely on credit cards. Many taxi drivers and safari vans only deal in cash. You'll need cash for farm markets and fruit stands and for tipping on excursions.

Before traveling, check with your credit card issuer to see what fees, if any, will be charged for overseas transactions. Recent

Money & Costs

legislation in the U.S. has curbed some exploitative lending practices, but many banks have responded by increasing fees in other areas, including fees for customers using credit and debit cards while out of the country—even if those charges were made in U.S. dollars. Fees can amount to 3% or more of the purchase price. Check with your bank before departing to avoid any surprise charges on your statement.

Passports & Visas If you're a U.S. citizen and you travel directly to the U.S.V.I. and do not visit the British Virgin Islands, you do not need a passport—but you are highly encouraged to carry one. If you return to the mainland U.S. from the U.S.V.I. through another country (Mexico or Bermuda, for example), you will need a passport to get back home.

For **non–U.S. citizens,** visiting the U.S. Virgin Islands is just like visiting the mainland United States: You need a passport and visa, and may also be asked to produce an onward ticket. See "Visa Offices," below.

A passport is necessary for *all* visitors to the British Virgin Islands (including citizens of the U.K.). Visitors who stay for less than 6 months don't need a visa if they possess a return or onward ticket.

For information on how to get a passport, contact your passport office (see below). Allow plenty of time before your trip to apply for a passport; processing normally takes 7 to 10 weeks but can take longer during busy periods. And keep in mind that if you need a passport in a hurry, you'll pay a higher processing fee. When traveling, safeguard your passport in an inconspicuous, inaccessible place like a money belt, and keep a copy of the critical pages with your passport number in a separate place. There are no foreign consulates in the Virgin Islands, so if you lose your passport, go to the local police station.

Passport Offices
Australia Australian Passport Information Service (www.passports.gov.au; ☎ **131-232**).

Canada Passport Office, Passport Canada Program, Gatineau QC K1A 0G3 (www.canada.ca).

Ireland Passport Office, Frederick Buildings, Molesworth Street, Dublin 2 (www.dfa.ie).

New Zealand Passports Office, Department of Internal Affairs, 109 Featherston St., Wellington, 6140 (www.passports.govt.nz).

United Kingdom Visit your nearest passport office, major post office, or travel agency, or contact the **HM Passport Office,** 4th Floor, Peel Building, 2 Marsham St., London, SW1P 4DF (www.gov.uk/government/organisations/hm-passport-office).

United States To find your regional passport office, check the U.S. State Department website (travel.state.gov) or call the **National Passport Center** (☎ **877/487-2778**) for automated information.

Visa Offices
For information about U.S. visas, go to **travel.state.gov** and click on "U.S. Visas." Or contact one of the following offices: For **Australian** citizens, the U.S. Embassy Canberra, Moonah Place, Yarralumla, ACT 2600 (au.usembassy.gov/embassy-consulates/canberra/; ☎ **02/6214-5600**); for **British** subjects, the U.S. Embassy Visa Appointment Line (ais.usvisa-info.com/en-gb/niv; ☎ **020/3608-6998** from within the U.K., or ☎ **703/439-2367** from within the U.S.); for **Irish** citizens, the **U.S. Embassy Dublin,** 42 Elgin Rd., Ballsbridge, Dublin 4 (ie.usembassy.gov; ☎ **01 903-6255** from within the Republic of Ireland); for **New Zealand** citizens, the **U.S. Embassy New Zealand,** 29 Fitzherbert Terrace, Thorndon, Wellington (nz.usembassy.gov; ☎ **04 462 6000** from within New Zealand).

Petrol Please see "Getting Around," earlier in this chapter for information.

Pets To bring your pet to the U.S.V.I., you must have a health certificate from a mainland veterinarian and show proof of vaccination against rabies. Very few hotels allow animals, but a number of villas do, so check in advance. If you're strolling with your dog through the national park on St. John, you must keep it on a leash. Pets are not allowed at campgrounds, in picnic areas, or on public beaches. Both St. Croix and St. Thomas have veterinarians listed in the Yellow Pages.

Your dog or cat is permitted entry into the B.V.I. without quarantine, if accompanied by an Animal Health Certificate issued by the Veterinary Authority in your country of origin. This certificate has a number of requirements, including a guarantee of vaccination against rabies.

Police   Dial © **911** for emergencies in the U.S.V.I. The Crime Line phone number is © **340/777-8700.** The main police headquarters is located in the Alexander Farrelly Criminal Justice Center in Charlotte Amalie (© **340/774-2211**). In the B.V.I., the main police headquarters is on Waterfront Drive near the ferry docks on Sir Olva George's Plaza (© **284/494-2945**) in Tortola. There are also police stations on Virgin Gorda (© **284/495-5222**) and on Jost Van Dyke (© **284/495-9345**). See individual island chapters for more detailed information.

Safety   The Virgin Islands are a relatively safe destination. The small permanent populations are generally friendly and welcoming. That being said, wandering the back streets of Charlotte Amalie in **St. Thomas** at night (particularly on Back St.) is not recommended. Guard your valuables or

store them in hotel safes if possible.

The same holds true for the back streets of Christiansted and Frederiksted in **St. Croix.** While most crime on both these islands is petty theft aimed at unguarded possessions on the beach, unlocked parked cars, or muggings at night, St. Croix was experiencing an uptick in gun violence among residents as this book was going to press. Exercise the same amount of caution you would if you were traveling to an unfamiliar town on the mainland. Whether on St. Thomas or St. Croix, take a taxi home after a night out.

Muggings and petty theft do happen on sparsely inhabited **St. John,** but such occurrences are rarely violent and crime is rare in general.

The **British Virgin Islands** are very safe, and you can count the number of firearms deaths yearly on two hands (sometimes one). It is illegal to own a firearm in the B.V.I.—even police officers in the Royal Virgin Islands Police Force generally leave their weapons in the office as they go about their business. Minor drug-related robberies and muggings do occur late at night outside bars in Road Town, especially in poorly lit areas around Wickham's Cay I and along Waterfront Drive. On Virgin Gorda, most resorts don't even have room keys (although you can lock yourself in at night), and some people report dropping off rental cars at the airport

with the keys still in the lock.

For information on **driving safety,** see "Getting Around" earlier in this chapter.

Smoking   In the U.S.V.I, smoking is prohibited in restaurants and public buildings; bars may allow smoking outdoors as long as it's 20 feet from entrance and service areas. On the B.V.I., smoking is banned in public places (bars, restaurants, nightclubs, airports, offices, and sports facilities) and within 50 feet of any public space.

Student Travel   St. Thomas has perhaps the most youth-oriented scene of any of the Virgin Islands, British or American. Many young people who visit St. Thomas stay in the guesthouses in and around Charlotte Amalie. Beyond St. Thomas, the island of St. Croix attracts a large array of young, single travelers, mainly in and around Christiansted and Frederiksted.

Taxes   For the U.S. Virgin Islands, the United States has no value-added tax (VAT) or other indirect tax at the national level. The U.S.V.I. may levy their own local taxes on all purchases, including hotel and restaurant checks and airline tickets. These taxes will not appear on price tags. A 12.5% room tax is added to hotel bills.

The British Virgin Islands has no sales tax. It charges a departure tax of $20 per person for those leaving by boat or airplane. Most hotels add a service charge of around 10%; there's also a 10% government room tax. Most restaurants tack on an automatic 15%–20% service charge.

Telephones   In the Virgin Islands, hotel surcharges on long-distance and local calls are usually astronomical, so you're better off using your **cellphone** or a **public pay telephone.** Many convenience stores, groceries, and packaging services sell **prepaid calling cards** in denominations up to $50; for international visitors these can be the least expensive way to call home. Many public pay phones at airports now accept American Express, MasterCard, and Visa credit cards. **Local calls** made from pay phones in most locales cost either 25¢ or 35¢ (no pennies, please). Many of the most rural or expressly private resorts and hotels have no in-room phones, only phones in their lobbies or common areas.

To make calls within the United States, including the U.S. Virgins, and to Canada, dial 1 followed by the area code and the seven-digit number. **For other international calls,** dial **011** followed by the country code, city code, and the number you are calling.

You can **call the British Virgins** from the United States by just dialing **1,** the area code **284,** and the number; from the U.K. dial **011-44,** then the number. **To call the U.S. from the**

B.V.I., just dial **1** plus the area code and the number; **to call the U.K. from the B.V.I.,** dial **011-44,** then the number.

Calls to area codes **800, 888, 877,** and **866** are toll-free. However, calls to area codes **700** and **900** (chat lines, bulletin boards, "dating" services, and so on) can be very expensive—usually a charge of 95¢ to $3 or more per minute, and they sometimes have minimum charges that can run as high as $15 or more.

For **reversed-charge or collect calls,** and for person-to-person calls, dial the number **0,** then the area code and number; an operator will come on the line, and you should specify whether you are calling collect, person-to-person, or both. If your operator-assisted call is international, ask for the overseas operator.

For **local directory assistance** ("information"), dial ✆ **411;** for long-distance information, dial **1,** then the appropriate area code and ✆ **555-1212.**

Time   The Virgin Islands are on Atlantic Standard Time, which is 1 hour ahead of Eastern Standard Time. However, the islands do not observe daylight saving time, so in the summer, the Virgin Islands and the East Coast of the U.S. are on the same time. In winter, when it's 6am in Charlotte Amalie, it's 5am in Miami; during daylight saving time it's 6am in both places.

Tipping   In hotels, tip **bellhops** at least $1 per bag ($2–$3 if you have a lot of luggage) and tip the **chamber staff** $1 to $2 per day (more if you've left a disaster area for him or her to clean up). Tip the **concierge** only if he or she has provided you with some specific service (obtaining difficult-to-get dinner reservations, for example). Tip the **valet-parking attendant** $1 every time you get your car.

Note that **many local restaurants tack on a service charge to the total bill,** often between 10% and 15%; you may want to add extra if the service was good. Otherwise, tip waitstaff 15%-20% of the check. In bars and nightclubs, tip **bartenders** 15%-20% of the check, tip **checkroom attendants** $1 per garment, and tip **valet-parking attendants** $1 per vehicle.

As for other service personnel, tip **taxi drivers** 15% of the fare; tip **skycaps** at airports at least $1 per bag ($2–$3 if you have a lot of luggage); and tip **hairdressers** and barbers 15%-20%. It's always a good idea to tip **tour guides** or **charter captains** at the end of an excursion, generally 15%-20% of the cost.

Toilets   You won't find public toilets or restrooms on the streets, but they can be found in hotel lobbies, bars, restaurants, museums, department stores, bus stations, and service stations. Large hotels are often the best bet for clean facilities.

Visitor Information

Go to the **U.S.V.I. Division of Tourism**'s website at www.visitusvi.com. The **British Virgin Islands Tourist Board** can be found at www.bvitourism.com.

Water   Many visitors to both the U.S. and British Virgins drink the local tap water with no harmful effects. To be prudent, especially if you have a delicate stomach, stick to bottled water. Many hotels and resorts have their own desalination plant, making delicious and highly potable water out of seawater.

Women Travelers   St. John and the British Virgin Islands have a low crime rate, while St. Thomas and St. Croix have the highest crime rate against women in the archipelago. To put that into context, however, you are far safer in the Virgin Islands than you would be walking the streets of any major U.S. city. Follow the usual precautions that you'd follow in any major U.S. city.

Index

Restaurants

Photo Credits

CONTENTS

LIST OF MAPS

ABOUT THE AUTHOR

Alexis Lipsitz Flippin is a writer and editor based in New York City and the author of *Frommer's Turks & Caicos* and *Frommer's St. Maarten/St. Martin, Anguilla & St. Barts*. She is the coauthor of *Cabin Tripping* and *How to Sleep*. She has written for numerous consumer webzines, including CNN.com, MSNBC.com, Zagat.com, and AARP.com and is a former senior editor for Frommer's Travel Guides.

ACKNOWLEDGMENTS

I'd like to acknowledge the tremendous assistance, advice, and goodwill afforded me by both the U.S.V.I. Department of Tourism and the B.V.I. Tourism Board and in particular Desiree Wilkes, Alani Henneman-Todman, and Sharon Rosario (U.S.V.I.) and Keith Dawson (B.V.I.). I'd also like to thank Felipe Ayala and Valerie Peters for their time and wisdom.

ABOUT THE FROMMER TRAVEL GUIDES

For most of the past 50 years, Frommer's has been the leading series of travel guides in North America, accounting for as many as 24% of all guidebooks sold. I think I know why.

Though we hope our books are entertaining, we nevertheless deal with travel in a serious fashion. Our guidebooks have never looked on such journeys as a mere recreation, but as a far more important human function, a time of learning and introspection, an essential part of a civilized life. We stress the culture, lifestyle, history, and beliefs of the destinations we cover, and urge our readers to seek out people and new ideas as the chief rewards of travel.

We have never shied from controversy. We have, from the beginning, encouraged our authors to be intensely judgmental, critical—both pro and con—in their comments, and wholly independent. Our only clients are our readers, and we have triggered the ire of countless prominent sorts, from a tourist newspaper we called "practically worthless" (it unsuccessfully sued us) to the many rip-offs we've condemned.

And because we believe that travel should be available to everyone regardless of their incomes, we have always been cost-conscious at every level of expenditure. Though we have broadened our recommendations beyond the budget category, we insist that every lodging we include be sensibly priced. We use every form of media to assist our readers, and are particularly proud of our feisty daily website, the award-winning Frommers.com.

I have high hopes for the future of Frommer's. May these guidebooks, in all the years ahead, continue to reflect the joy of travel and the freedom that travel represents. May they always pursue a cost-conscious path, so that people of all incomes can enjoy the rewards of travel. And may they create, for both the traveler and the persons among whom we travel, a community of friends, where all human beings live in harmony and peace.